Working Memory in Perspective

The Baddeley and Hitch (1974) Working Memory model holds a central place in experimental psychology and continues to be extremely successful in guiding and stimulating research in applied and theoretical domains. Yet the model now faces challenges from conflicting data and competing theories. In this book, experienced researchers in the field address the question: Will the model survive these challenges? They explain why it is so successful, evaluate its weaknesses with respect to opposing data and theories, and present their vision of the future of the model in their particular area of research. The book includes a discussion of the 'Episodic Buffer' component which has recently been added to the working memory model.

The result is a comprehensive and critical assessment of the working memory model and its contribution to current research in human cognition, cognitive development, neuroscience and computational modelling. This collection serves as a case study to illustrate the range of factors that determine the success or failure of a theory and as a forum for discussing what researchers want from scientific theories. The book begins with an accessible introduction to the model for those new to the field and explains the empirical methods used in working memory research. It concludes by highlighting areas of consensus and suggesting a programme of research to address issues of continuing controversy. *Working Memory in Perspective* will be a valuable resource to students and researchers alike in the fields of human memory, language, thought and cognitive development.

Jackie Andrade is a lecturer in psychology at the University of Sheffield.

Working Memory in Perspective

With a foreword by Alan Baddeley and Graham Hitch

Edited by

Jackie Andrade

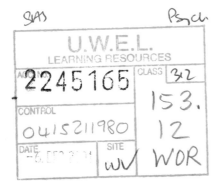

PSYCHOLOGY PRESS
ALERE FLAMMAM
Taylor & Francis Group

First published 2001 by Psychology Press Ltd
27 Church Road, Hove, East Sussex, BN3 2FA

Simultaneously published in the USA and Canada
by Taylor & Francis Inc,
29 West 35th Street, New York, NY 10001

Psychology Press is part of the Taylor & Francis Group

© 2001 Jackie Andrade

Typeset in Times by Mayhew Typesetting, Rhayader, Powys
Printed and bound in the UK by Biddles Ltd, Guildford and
King's Lynn
Cover design by Jim Wilkie

British Library Cataloguing in Publication Data
A catalogue record for this book is available from the British Library

Library of Congress Cataloging-in-Publication Data
Working memory in perspective / edited by Jackie Andrade ; with a
foreword by Alan Baddeley and Graham Hitch.
    p. cm.
Includes bibliographical references and index.
ISBN 0-415-21198-0
1. Short-term memory. I. Andrade, Jackie, 1964–

BF378.S54 W67 2001
—dc21

                                                        2001031843

ISBN: 0-415-21198-0

To my family

Contents

Figures

Tables

Contributors

Anne-Marie Adams Centre for Applied Psychology, School of Human Sciences, Henry Cotton Campus, Liverpool John Moores University, 15–21 Webster Street, Liverpool L3 2ET. Email: a.adams@livjm.ac.uk

Jackie Andrade Department of Psychology, University of Sheffield, Western Bank, Sheffield S10 2TP. Email: j.andrade@sheffield.ac.uk

Steve Avons Department of Psychology, University of Essex, Colchester CO4 3SQ. Email: savons@essex.ac.uk

Alan Baddeley Centre for the Study of Memory and Learning, Department of Experimental Psychology, University of Bristol, 8 Woodland Road, Bristol BS8 1TN. Email: alan.baddeley@bristol.ac.uk

Colin Hamilton Division of Psychology, University of Northumbria at Newcastle, Newcastle Upon Tyne NE1 8ST. Email: colin.hamilton@unn.ac.uk

Richard Henson Institute of Cognitive Neuroscience & Wellcome Department of Cognitive Neurology, University College London, Alexandra House, 17 Queen Square, London WC1N 3AR. Email: r.henson@ucl.ac.uk

Graham J. Hitch Department of Psychology, University of York, Heslington, York YO10 5DD. Email: G.Hitch@psych.york.ac.uk

Carmel M. T. Houston-Price Department of Experimental Psychology, University of Oxford, South Parks Road, Oxford OX1 3UD. Email: carmel.houston-price@psy.ox.ac.uk

Chris Jarrold Centre for the Study of Memory and Learning, Department of Experimental Psychology, University of Bristol, 8 Woodland Road, Bristol BS8 1TN. Email: C.Jarrold@bristol.ac.uk

Peter Lovatt Research Centre for English and Applied Linguistics, University of Cambridge, Keynes House, Trumpington Street, Cambridge CB2 1QA.

Jon May Department of Psychology, University of Sheffield, Western Bank, Sheffield S10 2TP. Email: jon.may@sheffield.ac.uk

Mike Page Department of Psychology, University of Hertfordshire, College Lane, Hatfield AL10 9AB. Email: psyqmp@herts.ac.uk

David G. Pearson Department of Psychology, University of Aberdeen, Aberdeen AB24 2UB. Email: d.g.pearson@abdn.ac.uk

Louise H. Phillips Department of Psychology, University of Aberdeen, Aberdeen AB24 2UB. Email: louise.phillips@abdn.ac.uk

John N. Towse Department of Psychology, Lancaster University, Lancaster LA1 4YF. Email: j.towse@lancaster.ac.uk

Geoff Ward Department of Psychology, University of Essex, Colchester CO4 3SQ. Email: gdward@essex.ac.uk

Catherine Willis Centre for Applied Psychology, School of Human Sciences, Henry Cotton Campus, Liverpool John Moores University, 15–21 Webster Street, Liverpool L3 2ET. Email: c.willis@livjm.ac.uk

Preface

The model of working memory proposed by Alan Baddeley and Graham Hitch in 1974 is one of the longest lived and most widely used models in cognitive psychology. This book was inspired by my suspicion that many of the researchers who used the model did so despite unease about its imperfections. It seeks to evaluate the working memory model more critically and comprehensively than is possible in journal papers. Achieving this aim involved a huge amount of hard work and commitment from the contributors. The process began with each contributor submitting a draft chapter which evaluated the strengths and weaknesses of the working memory model, compared it with competing models in their field, and commented on their vision of the future of the model. Each contributor reviewed the chapters of several other contributors. We then met for three days to discuss our chapters and try to reach a consensus in our evaluation of the working memory model. This meeting was funded by the US Army, European Research Office under contract number N68171-99-M-6084. I am very grateful for their support, and particularly for the encouragement I received from Dr Michael Strub, then at the European Research Office. I would like to thank Victor Buchanan and his staff at The White Swan hotel, Pickering, North Yorkshire, for keeping us so comfortable and well fed that the long hours of heated discussion flew past.

After the Pickering meeting, contributors revised their chapters, often extensively, re-read other people's revisions, and commented on my Introduction and Conclusion chapters. I then asked them to revise their chapters again, to ensure consistency of style and coherence of arguments across the book as a whole. I am indebted to all the contributors for the exceptional effort they have devoted to this project. In particular, I would like to thank Jon May for helping with every aspect of the book, inside and outside of working hours, and John Towse for his unflagging efforts at perfecting my own chapters.

Three editors helped to bring this project to fruition. I am grateful to Vivien Ward for her enthusiasm and encouragement, and to Caroline Osborne, Kristin Susser and staff at Psychology Press for guidance during preparation of the manuscript.

JACKIE ANDRADE
Sheffield, March 2001

Foreword

Alan D. Baddeley and Graham J. Hitch

Towards the end of our first joint grant, we received an invitation from Gordon Bower to write a piece in the forthcoming volume of *The Psychology of Learning and Motivation*. We were delighted, but also had misgivings; we had really not properly sorted out our model, but on the other hand it seemed too good an opportunity to miss, so we accepted. The present volume indicates that we were right on both counts, it was indeed a good opportunity, and if we had waited until everything was sorted out, we would still be waiting. We are therefore very pleased to welcome a book that indicates that the concept of working memory continues to present a stimulating challenge to colleagues at the same stage of career as we were when we first proposed our model. They indicate that the model continues to generate new findings, and to stimulate theoretical controversy, and hence that it continues to earn its living. We particularly like the attempt to link the various chapters by requiring the authors each to answer a series of questions. Indeed, we were sufficiently intrigued by this device to be encouraged to try to answer them ourselves. Below (briefly!) are our answers.

What did we get right?

We think we were right to propose a fractionation of the older concept of short-term memory, and to emphasise the functional significance of our proposed multi-component system. In doing so, we produced a model that had more obvious links with areas outside the traditional concern of memory. The range of topics and approaches within the present volume indicates that that has indeed been a useful feature of the model. Our division into separable phonological, visuo-spatial and executive components also seems to have been productive, in particular combined with the series of methods based on similarity effects and dual task methodology that make the approach readily applicable to new areas of investigation. The suggestion that these subsystems are themselves complex and fractionable has allowed the model to serve as a broad framework within which much more detailed and sophisticated investigation and modelling could proceed, again as illustrated by the chapters that follow.

What did we get wrong?

This can be divided into two sections: general limitations of the model, and specific studies that we wish we had done differently.

General limitations: The lack of specificity that is a strength in allowing new developments within a broad framework is of course also a limitation. Our model of the phonological loop for example did not even have a mechanism for explaining how serial order was retained. Nevertheless, the model provided a framework incorporating a rich array of empirical constraints that has led to considerable and successful activity in the modelling area, as reflected in the chapter by **Page and Henson** (chapter 8).

A particular problem with the model is the underspecification of the central executive. In the initial stages of development, the neglect of the executive was intentional since we suspected, correctly, that its investigation presented a particularly difficult problem. It is, however, essential that progress is made on tackling the central executive, and in recent years we have been making consistent attempts to tackle this area (Baddeley, 1996), resulting as mentioned below in the proposal for a fourth component of the model.

Specific problems: We now suspect that the relatively simple story of the role of subvocal rehearsal in the phonological loop is in fact over simple, and may also be atypical of rehearsal elsewhere within working memory. Attempts to find an equivalent rehearsal mechanism to subvocal articulation in the visuo-spatial sketchpad, for example, have proved fruitless, while it seems likely that, in young children at least, rehearsal probably involves a more basic and automatic process (Gathercole & Hitch, 1993). We also probably over-emphasised the importance of rehearsal during maintenance within the loop and neglected the equally important issue of forgetting during recall, as very clearly demonstrated by Cowan et al. (1992). It seems likely that the word-length effect, for example, operates through both rehearsal and output delay, a state of affairs that is implied by the initial model but not explicitly discussed.

A related issue is our assumption of trace decay within the phonological store, justified principally in terms of the study indicating that word duration rather than complexity is the principal determinant of forgetting (Baddeley, Thomson & Buchanan, 1975). However, as the chapter by **Lovatt and Avons** points out, although our findings are replicable using our set of words, they do not generalise to other sets of words. We had clearly committed the 'language-as-fixed-effect fallacy' (Clark, 1973) in not attempting to replicate and extend our findings using new sets of material. Even without this result, however, we might well have opted for a trace decay mechanism on the grounds of simplicity, and of the great difficulty, then as now, of deciding between a whole range of potential mechanisms underpinning short-term forgetting (see Cowan, Nugent, Elliot & Gear, 2000) for a useful discussion of this point). Fortunately, the model is not greatly affected by changing from a simple decay to a rather general interference model, although we would not wish to opt for the specific stimulus-response associative interference theory (Melton, 1963) that was still active at the time we developed the model.

Relationship to other models?

Miyake and Shah (1999) recently published a book based on a workshop in which about 10 different theorists discussed the way in which their models of working memory would handle a series of standard questions. Despite what appeared to be enormous differences in theoretical style, the meeting ended with a remarkable degree of unanimity as to the broad characteristics of working memory, the issues we understood and those to be tackled. The most obvious distinction was between our own model, with much of the work focusing on the subsidiary systems, and the approach more characteristic of North America in which the emphasis is on executive processing, often based on studies employing individual difference measures. There was however a general acceptance of the need to assume both a general executive system and specific verbal and visual subsystems. Very recently, one of us (ADB) has proposed a new component, the episodic buffer, specifically to give an account of the interface between the slave systems, the central executive and long-term memory (Baddeley, 2000). The aim is to provide a theoretical mechanism for considering a whole range of important phenomena involving the role of chunking in complex cognition that were comparatively neglected by the existing framework. The buffer is assumed to have a limited capacity and to be responsible for optimising this capacity by integrating information from slave systems and long-term memory into coherent episodes. As such it is not dissimilar to Cowan's concept of short-term memory (Cowan, 1995, 2001). Cowan is, however, relatively non-committal about the number and nature of lower level or slave systems feeding into the store, an important aspect of our own model. He also regards short-term memory as simply reflecting activated portions of long-term memory. We prefer to regard working memory as a separate system albeit one that utilises much of the apparatus that evolved for perception and action. We make this assumption, not on any a priori grounds, but simply because the neuropsychological evidence appears to point to clearly separable systems (Jonides et al., 1996). In general, however, we believe, with Miyake and Shah, that various models of working memory are gradually becoming increasingly similar, although there will continue to be important differences resulting from the concern to emphasise different empirical problems, and to use different theoretical tools.

Where next?

In the case of one of us (ADB), having proposed a new component to working memory, the episodic buffer, I intend to attempt to develop techniques based on both normal subjects and neuropsychological patients that will allow the concept to be specified more precisely and manipulated systematically. This immediately raises the challenging question of whether it is possible to disrupt storage within the episodic buffer without simultaneously disrupting the two slave systems and/or the attention control processes of the central executive. In the case of the other (GJH), I intend to follow up a theoretical proposal arising from modelling the phonological loop, namely that an internal timing signal is responsible for encoding and retrieving serial order information (Burgess & Hitch, 1999). Such a proposal raises the general question of whether there is a single system for serial ordering or whether there are a number of different ordering systems, and suggests it will be interesting to study serial order in visuo-spatial working memory. Ideas about serial ordering also have implications for item learning and chunk formation in long-term memory, and it will be interesting to explore these too.

So much then for our own view of how the model has fared over the last 25 years. How it will fare in the future depends ultimately on our younger colleagues, so read on!

REFERENCES

Baddeley, A. D. (1996). Exploring the central executive. *Quarterly Journal of Experimental Psychology, 49A*, 5–28.

Baddeley, A. D. (2000). The episodic buffer: a new component of working memory? *Trends in Cognitive Sciences, 4*(11), 417–423.

Baddeley, A. D., Thomson, N. & Buchanan, M. (1975). Word length and the structure of short-term memory. *Journal of Verbal Learning and Verbal Behaviour, 14*, 575–589.

Burgess, N. & Hitch, G. J. (1999). Memory for serial order: a network model of the phonological loop and its timing. *Psychological Review, 106*, 551–581.

Clark, H. H. (1973). The language-as-fixed-effect fallacy: a critique of language statistics in psychological research. *Journal of Verbal Learning and Verbal Behavior, 12*, 335–359.

Cowan, N. (1995). *Attention and Memory: An Integrated Framework.* Oxford Psychology Series, No. 26. New York: Oxford University Press.

Cowan, N. (2001). The Magical Number 4 in short-term memory: A reconsideration of mental storage capacity. *Behavioral and Brain Sciences, 24*(1), 87–185.

Cowan, N., Day, L., Saults, J. S., Keller, T. A., Johnson, T. & Flores, L. (1992). The role of verbal output time in the effects of word length on immediate memory. *Journal of Memory and Language, 31*, 1–17.

Cowan, N., Nugent, L. D., Elliot, E. M. & Geer, T. (2000). Is there a temporal basis of the word length effect? A response to Service (1988). *Quarterly Journal of Experimental Psychology*, *53A*, 647–660.

Gathercole, S. E. & Hitch, G. J. (1993). Developmental changes in short-term memory: a revised working memory perspective. In A. F. Collins, S. E. Gathercole, M. A. Conway & P. E. Morris (Eds.), *Theories of Memory* (pp. 189–209). Hove, UK: Lawrence Erlbaum Associates Inc.

Jonides, J., Reuter-Lorentz, P. A., Smith, E. E., Awh, E., Barnes, L. L., Drain, M., Glass, J., Lauber, E., Patalano, A. L. & Schumacher, E. (1996). Verbal and spatial working memory in humans. In D. Medin (Ed.), *The Psychology of Learning and Motivation* (pp. 43–88). London: Academic Press.

Melton, A. W. (1963). Implications of short-term memory for a general theory of memory. *Journal of Verbal Learning and Verbal Behavior*, *2*, 1–21.

Miyake, A. & Shah, P. (1999). Toward unified theories of working memory: emerging general consensus, unresolved theoretical issues, and future research directions. In A. Miyake & P. Shah (Eds.), *Models of Working Memory: Mechanisms of active maintenance and executive control* (pp. 442–481). Cambridge, UK: Cambridge University Press.

Acknowledgements

My thanks to Alan Baddeley for the use of his Working Memory model as part of the cover illustration. Thank you also to Geoff Ward and Jon May for the use of their figures on the cover, and also to Jon May for his work on the cover design.

Part I
Introduction

1   An introduction to working memory

Jackie Andrade

Ulric Neisser defined cognition as 'all the processes by which the sensory input is transformed, reduced, elaborated, stored, recovered, and used' (Neisser, 1967, p. 4). The concept of 'working memory' refers to a set of processes or structures that are intimately associated with many of these processes, making it a cornerstone of cognitive psychology. Understanding how we temporarily store and process information is fundamental to understanding almost all other aspects of cognition. In 1974, Baddeley and Hitch proposed a model of working memory that comprised separate, limited-capacity storage and processing components. Many different models have been put forward since, but Baddeley and Hitch's model remains extremely influential not only in cognitive psychology but also in neuroscience and developmental psychology. It has been particularly successful as a tool for exploring cognition outside the laboratory, helping explain data and generate new hypotheses in fields as diverse as mental imagery, language acquisition, and learning disability.

This book offers a case study of research driven by the working memory model proposed by Baddeley and Hitch (1974) and updated by Baddeley in 1986 (hereafter referred to as the WM model). It focuses on a single theory because I was impressed by the variety of research for which the WM model is used, and by the fact that researchers are using this model despite dissatisfaction with some aspects of it. With the exception of Jon May and Geoff Ward, who provide contrasting theoretical perspectives, the contributing authors were selected because they use the WM model in their day-to-day research, but are not the original authors of the model. I felt that they were thus the best people to give an objective critique of the model, a sense of what it is like to use the model to guide psychological research, and an evaluation of the likely future of the model. In the hands of a new generation of researchers, will the WM model gradually run out of steam and be superseded by competing theories or will it continue to go from strength to strength?

I asked contributors to assess their satisfaction with the WM model by considering the extent to which its success in generating new data or explanations outweighed the challenge posed by contradictory data or competing theories. Each author answered four questions:

1   What are the strengths of the WM model for your research?
2   What are its weaknesses?
3   How does it compare with competing models in your field?
4   What is the future of the model in your line of research?

Research using the WM model has been so productive that it is becoming increasingly difficult for a single researcher to keep track of all the new findings in the field and thereby to assess the balance between the usefulness of the model and the contradictory evidence. Collectively, the answers to questions 1 and 2 provide an up-to-date assessment of the weight of evidence for and against the model. Question 3 sets the WM model in a broader theoretical context. Some of its competitors are other models of working memory, some are models with quite a different focus, for example Kosslyn's (1994) model of imagery, or a different level of explanation, for example Barnard's (1999) Interacting Cognitive Subsystems. Question 4, about the future of the WM model, asks authors to assess the relative importance of the strengths, weaknesses, and competing models for future WM research. Overall, the questions provide a coherent thread through the book and their answers constitute an in-depth analysis of the role of the WM model in current psychological research.

The book is organised in four parts. This introductory chapter in the first part explains the historical context of the WM model and summarises the current evidence supporting it. It also describes the various methodologies employed in working memory research, and which form the basis for the research discussed in subsequent chapters. For readers new to the working memory field, this introduction sets the scene for the subsequent chapters; the background reading sections at the ends of the chapters suggest starting points for additional reading. The main body of the book is broadly divided into applied and theoretical approaches. Part II on Applied Perspectives illustrates the use of the WM model as a conceptual tool for guiding research into other aspects of cognition. Chapters in the Applied Perspectives part evaluate the model's contribution to research in mental imagery, consciousness, neuroimaging, language acquisition, and individual differences in cognition across typical and atypical lifespan development. The third part, Theoretical Perspectives, assesses some new data and alternative theoretical approaches which challenge the WM model and the assumptions on which it was built. Chapters in this part evaluate explanations of verbal short-term memory phenomena in terms of working memory, and provide a commentary on the concept of the central executive. The division into applied and theoretical research is somewhat arbitrary because the two are mutually informative. Applied research has contributed to the evolution of WM theory and theoretical developments have influenced applied research. The concluding part uses the authors' answers to the four questions to conclude that the WM model remains a viable framework for applied and theoretical research, but that several weaknesses in the model must be addressed if it is to remain useful in the future. A programme is outlined for future research to address these weaknesses while retaining the strengths of the WM model. The book concludes with a discussion of the implications of the newly proposed 'episodic buffer' component of the WM model.

THE HISTORY OF WORKING MEMORY

Working memory refers to a system that enables temporary storage of the intermediate products of cognition and supports transformations of those products. Reviewing competing contemporary theories of working memory, Richardson concludes that they share the assumption that 'there is some mechanism responsible for the temporary storage and processing of information and that the resources available to this mechanism are limited' (1996, p. 23). Miyake and Shah suggest there is consensus among working memory researchers that 'Working memory is those mechanisms or processes that are involved in the control, regulation, and active maintenance of task-relevant information in the service of complex cognition' (1999, p. 450).

The roots of working memory are in theories of short-term memory that focused on the temporary storage of information, rather than on the role that temporary storage or transformation played in general cognition. They aimed to explain phenomena such as the particularly good recall for the last items in a list (the recency effect) and the difficulty of verbatim immediate recall of more than a few items (the limited capacity of short-term memory). Nonetheless, some early authors discussed short-term memory as a system for holding information that was currently in use by other cognitive processes. For example, Atkinson and Shiffrin (1968) argued that 'The short-term store is the subject's working memory' (p. 90) and that transfer of information from long-term storage into the short-term store occurred 'in problem solving, hypothesis testing, and "thinking" in general' (p. 94). This section explains the development of the Baddeley and Hitch WM model from earlier theories of short-term memory.

Short-term memory

William James (1918) distinguished between primary memory, i.e., our continued awareness of what has just happened or the 'feeling of the specious present' (1918, p. 647), and secondary memory, i.e., 'knowledge of a former state of mind after it has already once dropped from consciousness' (p. 648). Hebb (1949) suggested a neural mechanism for this binary memory system, primary memory being the result of temporarily reverberating electrical circuits in the brain and secondary memory reflecting permanent synaptic changes. Burgeoning interest in computers influenced memory research in two ways, by providing a new language for describing memory structures and functions ('hardware' versus 'software' or 'processing') and by raising new questions. In particular, interest in information theory (Shannon & Weaver, 1949) encouraged people to think about how incoming sensory information is processed, what limits how much information can be processed at any time, and what determines the chance of information being retained in long-term memory. For example, Broadbent (1958) explained the difficulty of attending to more than one stream of information at once by proposing a tripartite information-processing system. The S system temporarily stored parallel streams of sensory information, feeding them via a selective filter into the limited-capacity P system where they were stored briefly or transferred again to output mechanisms or a much larger capacity long-term store. Information could be maintained in immediate memory by a rehearsal loop which repeatedly transferred information between the P and S systems. The new computer models made explicit the need to buffer information being used in current computations, and the likelihood that the capacity to do this was limited. The computer analogy thus reinforced James' assumption of separate primary and secondary memory systems.

Broadbent's model stimulated research into the structure of memory, with subsequent models typically including a limited capacity short-term memory system as the route into permanent memory (Murdock, 1974). Two of the most influential accounts will be mentioned briefly here. Waugh and Norman (1965) developed a quantitative model of the function of James' primary memory, in which recall probability was a function of the number of intervening items. A recently perceived stimulus could be represented in the primary and secondary stores simultaneously, could be transferred into secondary memory by rehearsal, and would be displaced from primary memory by subsequent stimuli if not rehearsed. Whereas James described primary memory in terms of temporal duration, Waugh and Norman described it in terms of the limited number of events it could store. Atkinson and Shiffrin (1968) included a similar short-term store in their model of memory. Incoming sensory information entered the short-term store, a limited-capacity, temporary storage system, via sensory registers. Rehearsal processes copied, or 'transferred', information from the short-term store into a long-term store which was relatively permanent and unlimited in capacity. Atkinson and Shiffrin explicitly assumed that the short-term store functioned as a working memory, a buffer for information being used in complex cognitive activities, but their paper did not address this aspect of memory.

Atkinson and Shiffrin cited two reasons for distinguishing between short-term and long-term storage structures. First, Milner (1966) reported amnesic patients with intact short-term memory function despite having impaired long-term memory, suggesting that the two types of memory depended on different anatomical structures. Second, they argued that it was more parsimonious to explain the recency effect in terms of two memory stores than one. The recency effect refers to the preferential recall of the last items in free recall of a supra-span list (e.g., Murdock, 1962). Atkinson and Shiffrin attributed it to the persistence of the last list items in short-term storage, from which they could be rapidly and accurately retrieved. An interpolated task, such as mental arithmetic, abolished the recency effect (Glanzer & Cunitz, 1966; Postman & Phillips, 1965) because it used representations that displaced the recency items from their slots in the short-term store.

Atkinson and Shiffrin's model was consistent with contemporary neuropsychological and experimental data, and also with the introspection data, eloquently described by James, that our sense of 'the specious present' (1918, p. 647) or 'just past' (1918, pp. 646–647) is different from our long-term store of knowledge and memories. However, although the two-store view of memory was popular and offered a relatively parsimonious explanation of the data, there were also strong arguments against the view. Melton (1963) argued that the apparent dissociation between short-term and long-term storage systems could be explained in terms of interference within a single memory system. Norman (1968) argued that short-term and long-term memory phenomena could arise from a single storage system, and indeed that they must arise from a single system because perceptual identification of familiar stimuli could not be so rapid if sensory information only gained access to representations in long-term storage after being processed in a short-term store. In Norman's scheme, short-term memory results from temporary excitation of stored representations, which can be accessed or triggered by incoming sensory information, whereas long-term memory results from permanent excitation of stored information.

Problems with the short-term store → long-term store model of memory

Empirical problems for Atkinson and Shiffrin's model came from two of the sources that originally supported their distinction between short-term and long-term storage. In neuropsychology, Warrington and Shallice (1969; Shallice & Warrington, 1970) reported a patient, KF, with the converse pattern of memory impairment to that shown by Milner's amnesic patients. KF's ability to learn word lists and remember stories was normal, but his digit span was only two or three items, well below the norm of seven plus or minus two items (Miller, 1956). This neat dissociation supports the hypothesis of separate memory systems underlying short-term and long-term memory, but is completely inconsistent with Atkinson and Shiffrin's claim that a unitary short-term store is the route into long-term storage. Free recall also proved problematic when Tzeng (1973; see also Bjork & Whitten, 1974) demonstrated that, although the recency effect was abolished by a period of counting backwards between the end of the list and the start of recall, it could be reinstated by interpolating backward counting between every list item. Tzeng's finding was not compatible with an account that assumed recency items were well recalled because they had not yet been displaced from a limited-capacity short-term store.

Craik and Watkins (1973) challenged the assumption that each rehearsal of an item increased its probability of transfer into long-term storage. They asked participants to listen to a list of words and remember the last word beginning with a specified letter. They manipulated the length of time for which a word must be remembered before being superseded by another word starting with the same letter. For example, if subjects are asked to remember words beginning with 'g', they should rehearse grain for longer than garden in the following list: daughter, oil, garden, grain, table, football, anchor, giraffe, pillow, thunder. On a surprise recall test, participants remembered the most rehearsed words no better than they remembered the least rehearsed words, suggesting that mere maintenance rehearsal does little to promote long-term retention of information.

There was little empirical support for Atkinson and Shiffrin's assumption that the short-term store functioned as a working memory. Atkinson and Shiffrin did not address this issue experimentally and those who did found evidence that learning and recall tasks require general processing resources (e.g., Murdock, 1965) but no evidence that they loaded short-term memory. For example, Patterson (1971) found no disruption of recall when participants counted backwards between each item recalled, a task that should have disrupted any retrieval plans held in the short-term store.

Working memory

Baddeley and Hitch (1974) directly tested the assumption that the limited-capacity short-term store functioned as a working memory, i.e., that it supported general cognition by processing as well as storing information. They noted that short-term memory research typically used two tasks, immediate serial recall and free recall, with the recency portion of the free recall curve being assumed to reflect retrieval from short-term storage. Although there were discrepancies in the data from these two tasks, they consistently pointed to the short-term store having limited capacity. Baddeley and Hitch therefore took limited capacity to be the defining characteristic of short-term memory, and tested its role in cognition by asking participants to maintain a digit load while performing comprehension, reasoning and long-term memory tasks. If these tasks compete with digit span for 'slots' in the short-term store, then each increase in digit load sʰ ᵘld cause a decrease in performance on the concurrent task. Contrary to ʰᵖothesis, Baddeley and Hitch found no effect of a three-digit load ʾ almost half the normal capacity of short-term memory) on ᵐprehension, and only a small effect on retrieval from long-ʾ one- or two-digit load had no effect on logical reasoning ᵃad impaired performance on all three tasks, but did not suggesting that the reasoning, comprehension, and component of working memory that was separate store used for digit span.

Conrad (1962) observed acoustic confusion errors (e.g., recalling P instead of V) in immediate recall of visually presented letters. Subsequent research showed that immediate serial recall was poorer for similar sounding stimuli (Baddeley, 1966a; Conrad & Hull, 1964; Wickelgren, 1965). Baddeley and Hitch (1974) therefore tested the role of the short-term store in reasoning and comprehension by looking for signature phonemic similarity effects. They found that both reasoning and comprehension were poorer when the stimuli sounded alike, for example, participants were slower to comprehend sentences like 'Red headed Ned said Ted fed in bed' than 'Dark skinned Ian thought Harry ate in bed'. As with concurrent digit loads, the effects of phonemic similarity were smaller than might be expected if performance depended solely on the short-term store. Concurrent articulation of a simple syllable ('the the the') was also known to impair short-term memory (Murray, 1967) but Baddeley and Hitch reported only slight impairments in reasoning and free recall with concurrent articulation (see Richardson & Baddeley, 1975).

Baddeley and Hitch concluded that the tasks assumed to load working memory, i.e., reasoning, comprehension, and recall from long-term storage, loaded the same short-term store as digit span. Because the effects of memory load, concurrent articulation, and phonemic similarity were quite small, they argued that the verbal short-term store is only one component of working memory, and that tasks like reasoning loaded another component as well. They proposed that working memory is a 'workspace', the capacity of which can be divided between processing and storage. The lack of effect of sub-span digit loads suggested that there is a dedicated storage component, and that memory span tasks only compete for general processes when they exceed its capacity. Baddeley and Hitch referred to the storage component as the 'phonemic buffer' or 'phonemic loop' and to the flexible general processing system as the 'central executive'. They characterised the phonemic loop as a limited-capacity system for storing serially ordered speech-based information. Evidence that memory span was lower for longer words (later published by Baddeley, Thomson & Buchanan, 1975) suggested that individuals had fixed storage capacity. The phonemic loop was assumed to be the locus of the phonemic similarity and concurrent articulation effects in short-term memory performance, and possibly also to play a role in speech errors. The functions of setting up rehearsal routines, extracting information from the phonemic buffer, recoding and chunking incoming information, and strategically applying retrieval rules were attributed to the central executive.

Most short-term memory research had focused on verbal recall, and contemporary theories of memory followed suit. For example, Atkinson and Shiffrin specified only the 'auditory-verbal-linguistic' component of their short-term store. However, Brooks (1967, 1968) had shown visual interference with visual but not verbal memory, while Kroll and colleagues had shown that concurrent articulation (a verbal shadowing task) had less effect on memory for visually presented letters than aurally presented letters (Kroll, Parks, Parkinson, Bieber & Johnson, 1970), suggesting that different storage systems may underlie auditory and visual short-term memory. Baddeley and Hitch used findings like these to argue for a dedicated visual storage system in working memory. They speculated that the strategic components of both visual and verbal memory tasks were the function of a common central executive.

Baddeley and Hitch's WM model provided an explanation of the finding that was most awkward for Atkinson and Shiffrin's model, that is, KF's preserved long-term memory and general intellectual function despite impaired digit span. They suggested that KF had a selective impairment of the phonemic loop but normal central executive function, allowing material to enter long-term storage even though it could not be stored temporarily for immediate serial recall.

The recency effect

Baddeley and Hitch (1974) found no effect of concurrent digit load, phonemic similarity, or concurrent articulation on the recency effect. Together with observations of recency in conditions which should have removed recency items from short-term storage (Bjork & Whitten, 1974; Glanzer, 1972; Tzeng, 1973), these data suggested that the recency effect could not be attributed to buffering of information in a short-term store or working memory prior to entry into long-term storage. Baddeley and Hitch favoured Tulving's (1968) explanation that people use ordinal cues, for example, differential trace strengths of recent and distant items, to help retrieve item information from memory. Later theories also explained verbal recency in terms of retrieving memory traces differing in strength or discriminability from long-term storage, without invoking short-term storage (e.g., Baddeley, 1986, chapter 7; Baddeley & Hitch, 1993; Glenberg et al., 1980). Note, however, that visual recency effects (e.g., Phillips & Christie, 1977) are still often interpreted in terms of retrieval from a limited-capacity visual short-term memory store (Baddeley, 1986, chapter 6; Baddeley & Logie, 1999; Phillips, 1983; see Logie, 1995, chapter 1 for further discussion).

CURRENT EVIDENCE FOR THE WM MODEL

Baddeley's (1986) monograph on working memory integrated the empirical data which had accumulated since 1974 and consolidated the position of the WM model in cognitive psychology. Some changes in terminology have occurred since then, for example, the 'phonemic buffer' (Baddeley & Hitch, 1974) became the 'articulatory loop' (Baddeley, 1986), which then became the 'phonological loop' (Baddeley, 1990, p. 71), but the essence of the model has been retained. This section summarises the current evidence supporting

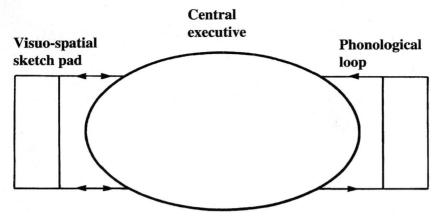

Figure 1.1 A simplified representation of the working memory model. Reprinted from Baddeley (1990, 1997) with permission from the author.

Baddeley and Hitch's tripartite working memory system containing modality-specific, limited-capacity storage components, or 'slave systems', subserving a limited-capacity general processor. Figure 1.1 shows what has become the standard representation of the WM model.

The phonological loop

The following findings support the hypothesis that verbal short-term memory comprises a temporary storage system, the phonological store, and an active rehearsal system, the articulatory control process.

The phonological similarity effect: Poorer short-term memory for similar-sounding stimuli (Baddeley, 1966a; Conrad & Hull, 1964) supports the notion of a temporary storage system specifically for speech-based or 'phonological' material. The memory traces for similar-sounding items are assumed to be harder to discriminate at recall (Baddeley, 1990, p. 72). Long-term memory by contrast shows effects of semantic similarity but not phonological similarity (Baddeley, 1966b).

The word length effect: Better short-term memory for shorter words (Baddeley, Thomson & Buchanan, 1975) suggests that short-term memory is limited by the rate at which we can rehearse information to prevent it decaying.

Articulatory suppression: Preventing articulation of to-be-remembered words, by requiring subjects to repeat a simple syllable aloud, impairs short-term memory for verbal material (Murray, 1967) but not visual material (Smyth, Pearson & Pendleton, 1988), suggesting that it does not merely distract general resources away from the memory task but rather that it prevents maintenance of information in a speech-based store. The finding that articulatory suppression obliterates the phonological similarity effect if and only if verbal stimuli are presented visually (Estes, 1973; Levy, 1971; Murray, 1968; Peterson & Johnson, 1971), suggests that it prevents recoding of visual information into the phonological code needed for storage in the phonological store (Baddeley, 1986, p. 85). The finding that articulatory suppression removes the word length effect with both visual and auditory presentation suggests that it also acts by preventing subvocal rehearsal (Baddeley, 1986, p. 84; Baddeley, Lewis & Vallar, 1984).

Irrelevant speech: Colle and Welsh (1976) showed that background German speech reduced English-speaking subjects' immediate serial recall of visually presented numbers. Salamé and Baddeley (1982) found that spoken digits (one, two) and other words comprising the same phonemes (tun, woo) interfered equally with digit span. Words that were phonologically dissimilar (happy, tipple) from the items to be remembered interfered somewhat less. Pulsed noise had no effect on immediate recall (Salamé & Baddeley, 1987). These data support the claim that speech has obligatory access to the phonological store, and suggest that information in the phonological store is encoded at a phonological (sub-lexical) level rather than semantically. Articulatory suppression removes the effect of irrelevant speech when to-be-remembered stimuli are presented visually (Salamé & Baddeley, 1982), supporting the claim that articulatory suppression prevents recoding of visual to verbal information, leaving no representations in the phonological store for irrelevant speech to disrupt.

Four chapters in this volume focus on the phonological loop. **Page** and **Henson** (this volume, chapter 8) explore recent quantitative models of the phonological loop that have helped specify the detailed mechanisms of verbal working memory. **Lovatt** and **Avons** (chapter 9) discuss recent failures to replicate the word length effect and their implications for the assumption that verbal working memory depends on subvocal rehearsal processes offsetting decay. **Ward** (chapter 10) criticises the assumption that recency and memory span reflect the operation of separate memory systems, and proposes that a General Episodic Memory system can explain both phenomena. **Adams** and **Willis** (chapter 4) evaluate the success of the working memory model as a framework for guiding research into language acquisition and explaining the evidence that verbal working memory correlates with vocabulary knowledge.

The visuo-spatial sketchpad

Baddeley (1986) hypothesised that the visuo-spatial sketchpad (VSSP) served imagery as well as short-term memory functions, arguing that there 'appears to be good evidence for the occurrence of a temporary visuo-spatial store . . . that is capable of retaining and manipulating images' (p. 143). Logie, Zucco and Baddeley (1990) found empirical support for this hypothesis, showing mutual and selective interference between visual imagery and visual short-term memory. Much of the subsequent research into VSSP function has used imagery rather than memory tasks.

Brooks (1967) showed that visual interference disrupted performance on an imagery task. His task required participants to memorise a series of sentences of the form 'in the starting square put a 1, in the next square to the *left* put a 2, in the next square *up* put a 3 . . .' by visualising the locations of the numbers in an imaginary matrix. The imagery component was controlled for by asking participants in another condition to remember nonsense sentences, 'in the starting square put a 1, in the next square to the *good* put a 2, in the next square to the *slow* put a 3 . . .' by rote rehearsal. Requiring participants to read the sentences as well as listen to them selectively impaired performance in the imagery condition. Baddeley and Lieberman (1980) used Brooks' task to test whether the VSSP was essentially visual or spatial. They observed a disruptive effect on imagery of concurrent spatial activity (blindfolded tracking of a pendulum using auditory feedback) but not of concurrent visual activity (judging the brightness of slides) and concluded that the VSSP is spatial. Tracking had no effect on recall of the nonsense sentences. However, subsequent studies did reveal effects of brightness judgements (Beech, 1984; Quinn, 1988), suggesting that both visual and spatial processes contribute to imagery of the matrices.

Paivio (1969) argued that concrete words tend to be recalled better than abstract words because they are represented in two forms, as propositions and as visual images. Baddeley, Grant, Wight and Thomson (1975) hypothesised that the recall advantage for concrete nouns depended on the imagery function of the VSSP, but then found that concurrent spatial tracking did not remove the advantage of concreteness and concluded that the VSSP could not be involved. Matthews (1983) later found that a concurrent visual task (shape-matching) did remove the advantage for concrete words, suggesting that visual but not spatial working memory processes support learning of imageable words. The use of imagery mnemonics for learning concrete words is disrupted by concurrent spatial tracking (Baddeley & Lieberman, 1980) as well as by irrelevant visual stimuli (Logie, 1986; Quinn & McConnell, 1996, 1999).

Smyth and colleagues used short-term memory tasks to test VSSP function, showing that concurrent spatial tasks impair memory for movements or for sequences of spatial locations in the Corsi blocks task (Smyth et al., 1988; Smyth & Pendleton, 1989). Concurrent articulation did not impair memory for locations (Smyth et al., 1988), supporting the claim of separate visuo-spatial and verbal temporary storage systems.

The VSSP is susceptible to visual similarity effects, akin to the phonological similarity effects observed in verbal short-term memory. Young children are poorer at remembering visually similar stimuli than dissimilar stimuli (Hitch, Halliday, Schaafstal & Schraagen, 1988), and so are older children and adults if they are prevented from verbally recoding the stimuli (Hitch, Woodin & Baker, 1991) or if they are required to remember novel stimuli such as Chinese characters (Hue & Ericsson, 1988). Kemps (1999) reported complexity effects in recall of spatial locations, suggesting that the VSSP is susceptible to rehearsal constraints analogous to the word length effect in verbal short-term memory.

To summarise, research into visuo-spatial short-term memory and imagery supports the hypothesis that visuo-spatial information is temporarily stored in a separate system from verbal information by showing selective visuo-spatial interference with imagery mnemonics but not rote rehearsal, and visuo-spatial but not verbal interference with visuo-spatial short-term memory. Visual similarity effects suggest that information is represented in the VSSP in a visual code. The disruptive effects of irrelevant visual information suggest that it has direct access to the VSSP (Quinn & McConnell, 1999). Thus visuo-spatial short-term memory appears to show effects of active interference (e.g., arm movements), passive interference (e.g., irrelevant pictures), complexity, and similarity that are analogous to the effects of articulatory suppression, irrelevant speech, word length and phonological similarity in verbal short-term memory.

In chapter 2 of this book, **Pearson** argues that theoretical development may have been hindered by assuming that visual imagery and short-term memory tap identical processes. He discusses how the WM model guided his research into creative design and mental imagery, leading to a revised model of visuo-spatial working memory. **Andrade** (chapter 3) also discusses the use of the WM model to guide research into visual imagery, using studies of image vividness and traumatic imagery as a springboard for assessing the more general role of working memory in consciousness.

The central executive

Baddeley and Hitch (1974) explained their finding that comprehension was impaired by a 6-item digit load but not a 3-item load by suggesting that, when the capacity of the phonemic buffer is exceeded, central executive resources must be devoted to storage. This hypothetical dual-purpose, processing and storage, role led to the central executive becoming what Baddeley (1986, p. 224) described as a 'conceptual ragbag', comprising all the functions attributed to working memory but not performed by the phonological loop or visuo-spatial sketchpad. As a first attempt at characterising the central executive as a processing module, he borrowed a model of attentional control already developed by Norman and Shallice (1980, 1986).

Norman and Shallice proposed three levels of action selection. When a stimulus triggers a single action programme or schema, that action is carried out in an automatic, reflex fashion. When several, conflicting action schemata are triggered, the most appropriate or urgent schema gains priority by inhibiting competing schemata more strongly than they inhibit it. They called this relatively automatic system of action selection contention scheduling. Reliance on contention scheduling alone would make it very difficult to break habits or learn new tasks. We are able to change our habitual behaviour, learn new tasks, and monitor our behaviour for errors because of a third level of action selection known as the supervisory attentional (or activating) system. When a task demands a novel response or interruption of an action that is already in progress, the supervisory attentional system overrides contention scheduling by activating weaker action schemata so they gain priority over the stronger, habitual schema. Norman and Shallice's model achieved two purposes. It helped Norman explain everyday action slips, for example intending to make a cup of black coffee for a friend and habitually adding milk (see Norman, 1988), and it helped Shallice explain the pattern of behaviour typically shown by patients with frontal lobe damage (see Shallice, 1982), including their tendency to perseverate with an initial course of action even when the task requires a new response. Action slips and perseveration suggest a failure of the supervisory attentional system to override habitual responses selected by the lower-level process of contention scheduling.

Baddeley's decision to adopt the supervisory attentional system as the central executive in his WM model was influenced partly by its ability to explain data from his earlier studies of random generation (Baddeley, 1966c). People's ability to generate random letters can be measured as the proportion of stereotyped sequences in their output, for example, ABC, MTV, HIV. Baddeley found that stereotypy increased (randomness decreased) if less time was allowed for each response. He suggested that random generation required the supervisory attentional system to monitor output and override the contention scheduling process which favoured familiar, stereotyped sequences over more random sequences. The lawful decrease in randomness with increased speed suggested that the task placed constant demands on the limited-capacity supervisory attentional system.

Thus the central executive evolved, as a theoretical concept, from being a flexible system which could employ resources for storage or processing, to being purely a processing system (see Baddeley & Logie, 1999, for further discussion) performing functions such as strategy switching, selective attention, retrieval from long-term memory and dual task co-ordination (Baddeley, 1996). Two chapters in this volume specifically evaluate this concept. **Towse** and **Houston-Price** (chapter 11) argue that there is little evidence that the different processes of task co-ordination, attention, etc. are the function of a single processing module. **May** (chapter 12) proposes that Barnard's (1985, 1999) concept of a 'central engine', comprising subsystems dealing with propositional and implicational levels of meaning, offers a more appropriate level of explanation of the complex cognitive phenomena traditionally ascribed to the central executive.

Cultural variations in the concepts of central executive and working memory

The concept of executive function shows important cultural variations. Until fairly recently, European research into working memory focused primarily on characterising the storage components of working memory, i.e., the phonological loop and visuo-spatial sketchpad. Baddeley explicitly advocated this strategy of addressing the more tractable questions of short-term storage before tackling the more difficult problem of processing (see Baddeley, 1996, p. 6). North American research has taken a different direction, exploring the role of working memory in complex cognitive tasks such as reading and language comprehension. Daneman and Carpenter (1980) devised a task to capture the essence of working memory as a system with temporary storage and processing functions. Their working memory span or complex span task measured subjects' capacity to process a series of sentences (e.g., to decide whether each sentence made sense) and, at the same time, to remember the last word of each sentence for subsequent serial recall. Working memory span correlated strongly with reading comprehension, whereas simple memory span measures such as immediate serial recall of words did not (Daneman & Carpenter, 1980; Masson & Miller, 1983; Turner & Engle, 1989). Superficially, the general North American concept of working memory maps onto the general European concept of the central executive (see Richardson, 1996, for discussion) and there is increasing mutual agreement and reciprocal influence between researchers on either side of the Atlantic (see Miyake & Shah, 1999). There are also important differences between the two traditions. Implicit and often explicit in the choice of the complex span task is the notion that storage and processing resources are interchangeable (e.g., Daneman & Green, 1986). Thus more efficient processing (faster sentence comprehension) leaves more capacity available for storage (hence better recall of the last words). This contrasts with Baddeley's (1986) WM model in which the processing function of the central executive is supported by the independent storage functions of the phonological loop and visuo-spatial sketchpad.

Three chapters in the Applied Perspectives part compare Baddeley's (1986) fractionated WM model with the integrated models of the North American tradition, which assume a trade-off between processing and storage in a single system, and with alternative explanations of cognitive phenomena which attribute no causal role to working memory. **Adams** and **Willis** (chapter 4) and **Phillips** and **Hamilton** (chapter 5) respectively evaluate the WM model as a tool for investigating children's language acquisition and cognitive changes during adult aging. **Jarrold** (chapter 6) explores whether working memory deficits can explain the patterns of atypical cognitive development seen in Down and Williams syndromes.

TOOLS AND METHODS FOR RESEARCHING WORKING MEMORY

Experimental, laboratory studies of human cognition have probably influenced the European conception of working memory more than any other studies and were therefore the focus of the preceding discussion. However, data from other sources have supported, extended and challenged the WM model. This section summarises the different tools available for investigating working memory because subsequent chapters describe research using a range of techniques.

Experimental manipulations

As described above, Baddeley and Hitch (1974) built the WM model on the basis of *dual task studies* which investigated the effect of concurrent digit span on other cognitive tasks. The rationale for such studies is that, if two tasks require the same cognitive processes or compete for the same limited-capacity storage systems, then it will be impossible to perform both tasks together as well as one could perform them individually. If researchers know that one task taps a certain process, they can combine that task with a second, less well understood task to find out whether the second task also involves that process. In the case of Baddeley and Hitch's dual task studies, there was only a small effect when digit span and reasoning were combined, leading them to conclude that reasoning was not heavily dependent on the short-term store needed for good digit span. The finding that concurrent articulation impaired digit span (Murray, 1967) but not spatial span (Smyth et al., 1988) supported the hypothesis of separate verbal and visuo-spatial short-term stores.

Dual task techniques have been used as a way of mimicking the effects of brain lesions. In their study of a patient known as PV, Baddeley, Papagno and Vallar (1988) observed that verbal short-term memory deficits were accompanied by difficulty learning new words but no problem with remembering familiar words, suggesting that the phonological loop is needed for vocabulary learning. Papagno, Valentine and Baddeley (1991) found support for this hypothesis by testing a healthy population's ability to remember new and old words with articulatory suppression. As predicted from the study of PV, articulatory suppression impaired learning of the new words but not of the already familiar words. Both the dual task and lesion studies are open to Richard Gregory's criticism that what happens when you remove a particular component of the cognitive system does not necessarily tell you about the normal function of that component, thus 'The removal of any of several widely spaced resistors may cause a radio set to emit howls, but it does not follow that howls are immediately associated with these resistors, or indeed that the causal relation is anything but the most indirect. In particular, we should not say that the function of the resistors in the normal circuit is to inhibit howling' (Gregory, 1961, p. 323).

Interference studies are a type of dual task study where the second task is simply to hear or see irrelevant stimuli. The fact that irrelevant, supposedly unattended stimuli disrupt short-term memory suggests direct, obligatory access of those stimuli to the appropriate short-term store. Irrelevant stimuli are assumed to disrupt memory by interfering with the contents of the short-term store, therefore the effects of different types of irrelevant stimuli reveal something of the nature of stored representations. For example, Salamé and Baddeley's (1982) finding, that irrelevant speech disrupted immediate verbal recall most when it shared phonemic features with the stimulus words, suggested that words were stored phonologically rather than semantically in working memory.

Stimulus manipulations have told us about storage and rehearsal in short-term memory. Comparisons of memory span for similar- and dissimilar-sounding words suggest that words are represented phonologically rather than semantically in short-term memory (e.g., Baddeley, 1966a). Comparisons of span for long and short words support the hypothesis that subvocal rehearsal processes maintain information in working memory, from which that information would otherwise be lost within a couple of seconds because of trace decay (Baddeley, Thomson & Buchanan, 1975; but see **Lovatt** and **Avons**, chapter 9, for further discussion).

Experimental manipulations like these are often used as a marker or signature of working memory involvement in cognitive tasks. For example, Ellis and Sinclair (1996) explored the effects of articulatory suppression on language learning, observing that Welsh vocabulary and grammar were learned more poorly if English-speaking subjects were prevented from rehearsing the stimulus phrases during the study phase. They concluded that verbal working memory contributes to long-term learning of foreign languages. Baddeley and Andrade (2000) tested the effects of concurrent verbal or visuo-spatial tasks on subjects' ratings of vividness of imagery. They observed a cross-over interaction between the modality of the concurrent task (articulation or spatial tapping) and the modality of the image (auditory or visual), concluding that processing of sensory information in working memory contributes to vivid imagery (see **Andrade**, chapter 3).

Correlational studies

Studies of individual differences in working memory function have been a prominent feature of North American working memory research and of developmental studies of working memory in Europe. There are two ways of conducting and analysing a correlational study. One is simply to measure the performance of a large and varied population on tasks requiring working memory and the other cognitive function of interest. Daneman and Carpenter (1980) used this method to show that people with better working memory span are better at reading. The other method is to select two sub-sets of a population on the basis of their working memory span and then compare their performance on the other cognitive task of interest. Cantor and Engle (1993) used this method to show that people with high working memory span were better at retrieving information from long-term memory than people with low working memory span.

Correlational methods have been used to research working memory development in children and to draw conclusions about working memory constraints on other aspects of cognitive development. For example, Hulme, Thomson, Muir and Lawrence (1984) found a strong correlation between memory span and speech rate, supporting the hypothesis that speech-based rehearsal processes prevent decay of verbal representations in the phonological store. Faster speech means that more words can be prevented from decaying, hence higher memory span. Several studies have shown correlations between verbal working memory and language learning (Gathercole & Baddeley, 1989; Service, 1992), contributing to Baddeley, Gathercole and Papagno's (1998) hypothesis that language acquisition is the essential function of the phonological loop.

Correlational analyses can reveal that two abilities are related, but not that one ability causes the other. Thus memory span may correlate with vocabulary knowledge because working memory is a prerequisite of vocabulary learning, or because better vocabulary knowledge makes it easier to remember words in short-term memory tasks, or because a third, unidentified factor is required for good working memory and good vocabulary knowledge. The chapters by **Adams** and **Willis**, **Phillips** and **Hamilton**, and **Jarrold** (chapters 4, 5 and 6, respectively) discuss these issues. Statistical techniques such as cross-lagged correlations (Gathercole & Baddeley, 1989) and partial correlations (e.g., Turner & Engle, 1989) can help interpret relationships between variables. For example, Gathercole and Baddeley (1989) tested working memory capacity and vocabulary knowledge in a group of 4-year-olds and then repeated the tests a year later when the children were 5 years old. Working memory capacity correlated strongly with vocabulary knowledge on both occasions but, more interestingly, memory capacity at age 4 correlated significantly with vocabulary knowledge at age 5 even when the effect of age 4 vocabulary knowledge had been accounted for. These findings suggest that working memory development precedes and predicts language learning. Nonetheless, correlational data must be treated with caution when making claims about causality.

Neuropsychology

Studies of memory function following brain lesions have strongly influenced theorising about working memory. As explained above, the difficulty of explaining KF's preserved intellectual function and long-term memory despite very poor digit span provided a stimulus for Baddeley and Hitch's early research. Baddeley et al.'s (1988) later studies of PV suggested that verbal short-term memory contributes to long-term learning of novel words. This hypothesis helped to explain the pattern of impairment reported in a subsequent case study. ELD showed a similar combination of preserved long-term memory for sets of familiar stimuli and impaired memory for novel stimuli but, in her case, it was learning of novel visual information that was impaired (Hanley, Pearson & Young, 1990). Subsequent testing revealed a selective impairment of visual, but not verbal, working memory (Hanley, Young & Pearson, 1991).

Finding someone with a deficit in one aspect of working memory can help test predictions about the function of that part of working memory and about its role in general cognition. This would be particularly beneficial in the case of the central executive, which is currently less well specified than the slave systems of working memory. Baddeley and his colleagues suggested that people with Alzheimer's disease have central executive deficits (Baddeley, Logie, Bressi, Della Sala & Spinnler, 1986), and that these deficits can explain their typically poor verbal and visuo-spatial memory span. Morris (1984) had already shown that the poor verbal memory span of mildly demented elderly subjects was not due to impairment of, or failure to use, the phonological loop because they showed normal phonological similarity and word length effects, and normal interactions between those effects and articulatory suppression. Co-ordination of the phonological loop and visuo-spatial sketchpad is a defining feature of the central executive. Baddeley et al. therefore tested the ability of participants in the early stages of Alzheimer's disease to perform a verbal and visuo-spatial task concurrently. They matched the performance of young, elderly and demented subjects on digit span and spatial tracking tasks, then asked them to perform both tasks at once. The people with Alzheimer's disease were considerably more impaired by the dual task requirement than the normal young or elderly subjects (Baddeley et al., 1986), and the degree of impairment caused by the secondary task increased as the disease progressed (Baddeley, Bressi, Della Sala, Logie & Spinnler, 1991). These studies pave the way for future research into the relationship between dual task impairments in dementia and deficits in other putative functions of the central executive.

Quantitative modelling

To create a mathematical model or computer simulation of human short-term memory performance, researchers must specify many details which are rather vague in the original WM model. For instance, how is order information encoded in working memory? How is this information used to ensure retrieval of items in correct serial order? How are the starts and ends of lists marked in memory? Which, and how many, items are rehearsed on a given trial? The chapters by **Page** and **Henson** and **Lovatt** and **Avons** (chapters 8 and 9, respectively) illustrate how different researchers have suggested different answers to these questions, resulting in different models of short-term memory. The fact that a computer model provides a convincing simulation of human performance does not prove that the computer and human are 'programmed' in the same way. Nonetheless, computational modelling has many benefits as a research tool. It allows one to rule out incorrect hypotheses about human memory function by showing that computational models built on those hypotheses do not simulate human memory well. Perhaps more importantly, computational modelling is an excellent tool for generating detailed hypotheses about how human memory works. 'Black box' models like the WM model are qualitative descriptions of cognition, whereas mathematical and computational models make quantitative predictions about memory performance.

For example, Henson (1998) argued that different computational models of short-term memory make different predictions about the proportions of different types of errors in serial recall. Because previous studies of human short-term memory typically used memory span procedures to measure memory capacity, requiring subjects to recall increasingly long lists until they made errors, error data were unavailable for testing Henson's predictions. Therefore Henson generated a new pool of data by testing human participants repeatedly on span-length lists and observing the numbers and types of errors they made. Thus computational modelling helps generate new data on which to build theories of human memory. Hopefully the current success of the modelling enterprise will encourage researchers interested in the visuo-spatial sketchpad or central executive to specify their hypotheses in sufficient detail to provide the basis for future modelling work.

Brain imaging

Techniques such as positron emission tomography (PET) and functional magnetic resonance imaging (fMRI) reveal the brain areas that are most metabolically active during different cognitive tasks. Research using these techniques typically employs 'subtraction' methods. For example, to discover the brain areas underlying immediate serial recall, one could compare brain activation during performance of a digit span task with activation during recall of a known list, e.g., 1 2 3 4 5 6 7. The choice of control task depends heavily on the theoretical perspective of the investigators. However, imaging research has the potential to influence future theoretical development in working memory research. Understanding memory anatomy can help constrain and test hypotheses about memory function. For instance, if we know the site of the phonological loop, we can test Baddeley et al.'s (1998) hypothesis that the phonological loop is important for vocabulary learning by testing whether that site is activated during

ing of novel but not familiar words. A drawback of brain imaging techniques is that their temporal resolution is relatively poor, too poor for example to compare responses to items in different list positions of a conventional serial recall task. However, recent methodological advances have substantially improved temporal resolution, for example by combining fMRI with recording of event related potentials (which have poorer spatial resolution but much better temporal resolution), so this may cease to be a problem in the future.

The chapter by **Henson** (chapter 7) illustrates how the WM model has guided brain imaging research and how imaging data have complemented neuropsychological evidence in helping define the anatomical localisation of the different components of working memory.

SOME CHALLENGES FOR THE WORKING MEMORY MODEL

The techniques described above have produced converging evidence for the WM model, but they have also produced data that are problematic for the model. For example, recent studies of the word length effect have failed to replicate Baddeley, Thomson, and Buchanan's (1975) finding that span for long words is lower than span for short words (e.g., Lovatt, Avons & Masterson, 2000). Hanley (1997) and Macken and Jones (1995) demonstrated irrelevant speech effects in recall of visually presented letter and digit lists, despite articulatory suppression which should have prevented recoding of the stimuli into speech-based representations. These studies challenge the empirical basis of the phonological loop. Jones, Farrand, Stuart and Morris (1995) reported that irrelevant speech and articulatory suppression impaired serial recall of spatial locations as much as they impaired verbal recall, contradicting the hypothesis of modality-specific storage systems in working memory. Jones (e.g., 1993) hypothesises that changing auditory information disrupts serial recall by interfering with coding of order information rather than item information. In proposing a unitary memory system, Jones argues that the apparent separation between visual and verbal short-term memory is an illusion caused by the use of tasks requiring retention of serial order for testing verbal memory but not visuo-spatial working memory. Jones' model has yet to be applied to the extensive neuropsychological data that support the WM model, but it is potentially a serious competitor. **Lovatt** and **Avons** (chapter 9) and **Andrade** (chapter 13) discuss the implications for the WM model of one of these problematic findings, the failure to replicate the word length effect.

Studies of visuo-spatial working memory show that a range of visual and spatial secondary tasks interfere with a range of visual and spatial short-term memory and imagery tasks. Closer inspection of the data reveals double dissociations between spatial and visual processing, with several studies showing that spatial interference impairs spatial working memory more than visual working memory, and vice versa (Logie & Marchetti, 1991; Tresch, Sinnamon & Seamon, 1993; Vuontela, Rama, Raninen, Aronen & Carlson, 1999). Neuropsychological evidence also shows selective damage to visual and spatial systems (Levine, Warach & Farah, 1985; Owen, Sahakian, Semple, Polkey & Robbins, 1995). Logie interprets this pattern of data as evidence for a visuo-spatial working memory system which retains pictorial and location information by a combination of spatial and visual processes (Baddeley & Logie, 1999; Logie, 1995; see **Pearson**, chapter 2, this volume, for discussion). He argues that spatio-motor processes (the 'inner scribe') help maintain or 'rehearse' representations in a passive visual store (the 'visual cache'). This view of visuo-spatial working memory parallels Baddeley's (1986) account of articulatory rehearsal processes and phonological storage in verbal working memory. However, the data are also consistent with there being separate visual and spatial working memory systems, each having a passive store and active rehearsal mechanism. This alternative hypothesis has not been directly and fully tested.

Researchers have tended to identify the central executive with frontal lobe function, probably in part because Shallice (1982) was using the concept of supervisory attentional system to explain behaviour following frontal damage when Baddeley adopted it as a model of the central executive. However, scores on different neuropsychological tests of frontal function tend to correlate quite weakly with each other and with measures of working memory function (Lehto, 1996). Impairment on one aspect of putative central executive function does not necessarily mean impairment on another (Baddeley, Della Sala, Papagno & Spinnler, 1997). Therefore the central executive may not be a unitary module in working memory serving several functions, but rather there may be multiple, separate control processes (an 'executive committee', Baddeley, 1986, p. 26). Although this conclusion is not, in itself, a problem for the WM model, excessive fractionation of executive function would threaten the parsimony and usefulness of the model.

CONCLUSION

The WM model offers a parsimonious account of a large body of data. It has been widely used as a framework for guiding applied research into diverse topics and for steering theoretical research into the nature of cognition. It continues to be used despite conflicting data and alternative explanations of the phenomena. This book evaluates the current success and future potential of the WM model in the face of these empirical challenges and competing theories.

ACKNOWLEDGEMENTS

I would like to thank the other book contributors, particularly John Towse, Steve Avons, Rik Henson, Peter Lovatt, Jon May and Louise Phillips, for their constructive suggestions for this chapter, and also the undergraduates who commented anonymously on an earlier draft.

BACKGROUND READING

Baddeley, A. D. (1986). *Working Memory*. Oxford: Oxford University Press.

This monograph discusses the general concept of working memory and then describes and updates the specific working memory model proposed by Baddeley and Hitch (1974), showing how well the model explains a large and diverse body of empirical data.

Miyake, A. & Shah, P. (Eds., 1999). *Models of Working Memory: Mechanisms of active maintenance and executive control*. Cambridge, MA: MIT Press.

Richardson, J. T. E., Engle, R. W., Hasher, L., Logie, R. H., Stoltzfus, E. R. & Zacks, R. T. (1996). *Working Memory and Human Cognition*. New York: Oxford University Press.

These two excellent books compare different conceptualisations of working memory, with commentaries that should encourage more cross-talk between what are still rather separate European and American traditions of working memory research. Richardson et al. discuss three versions of working memory, the 'European view' of Baddeley and Hitch with subsequent modifications, and two accounts of the 'American view' which focus on the executive functions of inhibition and retrieval from long-term memory. Miyake and Shah present a thorough analysis of the strengths and weaknesses of many different theories of working memory according to a formal set of criteria.

REFERENCES

Atkinson, R. C. & Shiffrin, R. M. (1968). Human memory: A proposed system and control processes. In K. W. Spence & J. D. Spence (Eds.), *The Psychology of Learning and Motivation, Vol. 2* (pp. 89–195). New York: Academic Press.

Baddeley, A. D. (1966a). Short-term memory for word sequences as a function of acoustic, semantic, and formal similarity. *Quarterly Journal of Experimental Psychology, 18*, 362–365.

Baddeley, A. D. (1966b). The influence of acoustic and semantic similarity on long-term memory for word sequences. *Quarterly Journal of Experimental Psychology, 18*, 302–309.

Baddeley, A. D. (1966c). The capacity for generating information by randomization. *Quarterly Journal of Experimental Psychology, 18*, 119–129.

Baddeley, A. D. (1986). *Working Memory*. Oxford: Oxford University Press.

Baddeley, A. D. (1990). *Human Memory: Theory and practice*. Hove, UK: Psychology Press.

Baddeley, A. D. (1996). Exploring the central executive. *Quarterly Journal of Experimental Psychology, 49A*, 5–28.

Baddeley, A. D. (1997). *Human Memory: Theory and practice* (revised edition). Hove, UK: Psychology Press.

Baddeley, A. D. & Andrade, J. (2000). Working memory and the vividness of imagery. *Journal of Experimental Psychology: General, 129*(1), 126–145.

Baddeley, A. D., Bressi, S., Della Sala, S., Logie, R. & Spinnler, H. (1991). The decline of working memory in Alzheimer's disease. *Brain, 114*, 2521–2542.

Baddeley, A., Della Sala, S., Papagno, C. & Spinnler, H. (1997). Dual-task performance in dysexecutive and nondysexecutive patients with a frontal lesion. *Neuropsychology, 11*(2), 187–194.

Baddeley, A., Gathercole, S. & Papagno, C. (1998). The phonological loop as a language learning device. *Psychological Review, 105*, 158–173.

Baddeley, A. D., Grant, W., Wight, E. & Thomson, N. (1975). Imagery and visual working memory. In P. M. A. Rabbit & S. Dornic (Eds.), *Attention and Performance V* (pp. 205–217). London: Academic Press.

Baddeley, A. D. & Hitch, G. J. (1974). Working memory. In G. Bower (Ed.), *The Psychology of Learning and Motivation*, pp. 47–89. New York: Academic Press.

Baddeley, A. D. & Hitch, G. (1993). The recency effect — implicit learning with explicit retrieval. *Memory & Cognition, 21*(2), 146–155.

Baddeley, A. D., Lewis, V. J. & Vallar, G. (1984). Exploring the articulatory loop. *Quarterly Journal of Experimental Psychology, 36A*, 233–252.

Baddeley, A. D. & Lieberman, K. (1980). Spatial working memory. In R. S. Nickerson (Ed.), *Attention and Performance VIII* (pp. 521–539). Hillsdale, NJ: Lawrence Erlbaum Associates Inc.

Baddeley, A. D. & Logie, R. H. (1999). Working memory: The multiple-component model. In A. Miyake & P. Shah (Eds.), *Models of Working Memory: Mechanisms of active maintenance and executive control*, pp. 28–61. Cambridge, UK: Cambridge University Press.

Baddeley, A., Logie, R., Bressi, S., Della Sala, S. & Spinnler, H. (1986). Dementia and working memory. *Quarterly Journal of Experimental Psychology, 38A*(4), 603–618.

Baddeley, A. D., Papagno, C. & Vallar, G. (1988). When long-term learning depends on short-term storage. *Journal of Memory and Language, 27*, 586–595.

Baddeley, A. D., Thomson, N. & Buchanan, M. (1975). Word length and the structure of short-term memory. *Journal of Verbal Learning and Verbal Behavior, 14*, 575–589.

Barnard, P. J. (1985). Interacting cognitive subsystems: A psycholinguistic approach to short-term memory. In A. Ellis (Ed.), *Progress in the Psychology of Language, Vol. 2* (pp. 197–258). London: Lawrence Erlbaum Associates Inc.

Barnard, P. (1999). Interacting cognitive subsystems: Modeling working memory phenomena within a multiprocessor architecture. In A. Miyake & P. Shah (Eds.), *Models of Working Memory: Mechanisms of active maintenance and executive control* (pp. 298–339). Cambridge, UK: Cambridge University Press.

Beech, J. R. (1984). The effects of visual and spatial interference on spatial working memory. *Journal of General Psychology*, *110*, 141–149.

Bjork, R. A. & Whitten, W. B. (1974). Recency-sensitive retrieval processes in long-term free recall. *Cognitive Psychology*, *6*, 173–189.

Broadbent, D. E. (1958). *Perception and Communication*. Oxford: Pergamon Press.

Brooks, L. R. (1967). The suppression of visualisation by reading. *Quarterly Journal of Experimental Psychology*, *19*, 289–299.

Brooks, L. R. (1968). Spatial and verbal components in the act of recall. *Canadian Journal of Psychology*, *22*, 349–368.

Cantor, J. & Engle, R. W. (1993). Working memory capacity as long-term memory activation: an individual differences approach. *Journal of Experimental Psychology: Learning, Memory, and Cognition*, *19*, 1101–1114.

Colle, H. A. & Welsh, A. (1976). Acoustic masking in primary memory. *Journal of Verbal Learning and Verbal Behavior*, *15*, 17–32.

Conrad, R. (1962). An association between memory errors and errors due to acoustic masking of speech. *Nature*, *193*, 1314–1315.

Conrad, R. & Hull, A. J. (1964). Information, acoustic confusion and memory span. *British Journal of Psychology*, *55*, 429–432.

Craik, F. I. M. & Watkins, M. J. (1973). The role of rehearsal in short-term memory. *Journal of Verbal Learning and Verbal Behavior*, *12*, 599–607.

Daneman, M. & Carpenter, P. A. (1980). Individual differences in working memory and reading. *Journal of Verbal Learning and Verbal Behavior*, *19*, 450–466.

Daneman, M. & Green, I. (1986) Individual differences in comprehending and producing words in context. *Journal of Memory and Language*, *25*, 1–18.

Ellis, N. C. & Sinclair, S. G. (1996). Working memory in the acquisition of vocabulary and syntax: putting language in good order. *Quarterly Journal of Experimental Psychology*, *49A*(1), 234–250.

Estes, W. K. (1973). Phonemic coding and rehearsal in short-term memory for letter strings. *Journal of Verbal Learning and Verbal Behavior*, *12*, 360–372.

Gathercole, S. E. & Baddeley, A. D. (1989). Evaluation of the role of phonological STM in the development of vocabulary in children: a longitudinal study. *Journal of Memory and Language*, *28*, 200–215.

Glanzer, M. (1972). Storage mechanisms in recall. In G. H. Bower (Ed.), *The Psychology of Learning and Motivation: Advances in research and theory Vol. V* (pp. 129–193). New York: Academic Press.

Glanzer, M. & Cunitz, A. R. (1966). Two storage mechanisms in free recall. *Journal of Verbal Learning and Verbal Behavior*, *5*, 351–360.

Glenberg, A. M., Bradley, M. M., Stevenson, J. A., Kraus, T. A., Tkachuk, M. J., Gretz, A. L., Fish, J. H. & Turpin, B. A. M. (1980). A two-process account of long-term serial position effects. *Journal of Experimental Psychology: Human Learning and Memory*, *6*, 355–369.

Gregory, R. L. (1961) The brain as an engineering problem. In O. L. Zangwill & W. H. Thorpe (Eds.), *Current Problems in Animal Behaviour* (pp. 307–330). Cambridge, UK: Cambridge University Press.

Hanley, J. R. (1997). Does articulatory suppression remove the irrelevant speech effect? *Memory*, *5*(3), 423–431.

Hanley, J. R., Pearson, N. A. & Young, A. W. (1990). Impaired memory for new visual forms. *Brain*, *113*, 1131–1148.

Hanley, J. R., Young, A. W. & Pearson, N. A. (1991). Impairment of the visuo-spatial sketch pad. *Quarterly Journal of Experimental Psychology, 43A*, 101–125.

Hebb, D. O. (1949). *Organization of Behavior*. New York: Wiley.

Henson, R. N. A. (1998). Short-term memory for serial order: the start-end model. *Cognitive Psychology, 36*, 73–137.

Hitch, G. J., Halliday, S., Schaafstal, A. M. & Schraagen, J. M. C. (1988). Visual working memory in young children. *Memory & Cognition, 16*(2), 120–132.

Hitch, G. J., Woodin, M. E. & Baker, S. (1991). Visual and phonological components of working memory in children. *Memory & Cognition, 17*, 175–185.

Hue, C. & Ericsson, J. R. (1988). Short-term memory for Chinese characters and radicals. *Memory & Cognition, 16*, 196–205.

Hulme, C., Thomson, N., Muir, C. & Lawrence, A. (1984). Speech rate and the development of short-term memory span. *Journal of Experimental Child Psychology, 38*, 241–253.

James, W. (1918). *The Principles of Psychology, Vol. I*. London: Macmillan & Co. Ltd. (Original work published 1890.)

Jones, D. M. (1993). Objects, streams and threads of auditory attention. In A. D. Baddeley & L. Weiskrantz (Eds.), *Attention, Selection, Awareness and Control* (pp. 87–104). Oxford: Oxford University Press.

Jones, D., Farrand, P., Stuart, G. & Morris, N. (1995). Functional equivalence of verbal and spatial information in serial short-term-memory. *Journal of Experimental Psychology: Learning, Memory and Cognition, 21*, 1008–1018.

Kemps, E. (1999). Effects of complexity on visuo-spatial working memory. *European Journal of Cognitive Psychology, 11*(3), 335–356.

Kosslyn, S. M. (1994). *Image and Brain: The resolution of the imagery debate*. Cambridge, MA: MIT Press.

Kroll, N. E. A., Parks, T., Parkinson, S. R., Bieber, S. L. & Johnson, A. L. (1970). Short-term memory while shadowing: recall of visually and of aurally presented letters. *Journal of Experimental Psychology, 85*(2), 220–224.

Lehto, J. H. (1996). Are executive function tests dependent on working memory capacity? *Quarterly Journal of Experimental Psychology, 49A*, 29–50.

Levine, D. N., Warach, J. & Farah, M. (1985). Two visual systems in mental imagery: dissociation of "what" and "where" in imagery disorders due to bilateral posterior cerebral lesions. *Neurology, 35*, 1010–1018.

Levy, B. A. (1971). Role of articulation in auditory and visual short-term memory. *Journal of Verbal Learning and Verbal Behavior, 10*, 123–132.

Logie, R. H. (1986). Visuo-spatial processing in working memory. *Quarterly Journal of Experimental Psychology, 38A*, 229–247.

Logie, R. H. (1995). *Visuo-spatial Working Memory*. Hove, UK: Lawrence Erlbaum Associates Inc.

Logie, R. H. & Marchetti, C. (1991). Visuo-spatial working memory: Visual, spatial or central executive? In R. H. Logie & M. Denis (Eds.), *Mental Images in Human Cognition* (pp. 105–115). Amsterdam: Elsevier.

Logie, R. H., Zucco, G. M. & Baddeley, A. D. (1990). Interference with visual short-term memory. *Acta Psychologica, 75*, 55–74.

Lovatt, P. J., Avons, S. E. & Masterson, J. (2000). The word-length effect and disyllabic words. *Quarterly Journal of Experimental Psychology, 53A*, 1–22.

Macken, W. J. & Jones, D. M. (1995). Functional characteristics of the inner voice and the inner ear — single or double agency? *Journal of Experimental Psychology: Learning, Memory, & Cognition, 21*(2), 436–448.

Masson, M. E. J. & Miller, J. A. (1983). Working memory and individual differences in comprehension and memory of text. *Journal of Educational Psychology, 75,* 314–318.

Matthews, W. A. (1983). The effects of concurrent secondary tasks on the use of imagery in a free recall task. *Acta Psychologica, 53,* 231–241.

Melton, A. W. (1963). Implications of short-term memory for a general theory of memory. *Journal of Verbal Learning and Verbal Behavior, 2,* 1–21.

Miller, G. A. (1956). The magical number seven, plus or minus two: some limits on our capacity for processing information. *Psychological Review, 63,* 81–97.

Milner, B. (1966). Amnesia following operation on the temporal lobes. In C. W. M. Whitty & O. L. Zangwill (Eds.), *Amnesia* (pp. 109–133). London: Butterworths.

Miyake, A. & Shah, P. (1999). Toward unified theories of working memory: Emerging consensus, unresolved theoretical issues, and future research directions. In A. Miyake & P. Shah (Eds.), *Models of Working Memory: Mechanisms of active maintenance and executive control* (pp. 442–481). Cambridge, UK: Cambridge University Press.

Morris, R. G. (1984). Dementia and the functioning of the articulatory loop system. *Cognitive Neuropsychology, 1,* 143–158.

Murdock, B. B. (1962). The serial position effect in free recall. *Journal of Experimental Psychology, 64,* 482–488.

Murdock, B. B. (1965). Effects of a subsidiary task on short-term memory. *British Journal of Psychology, 56,* 413–419.

Murdock, B. B. (1974). *Human Memory: Theory and data.* Hillsdale, NJ: Lawrence Erlbaum Associates Inc.

Murray, D. J. (1967). The role of speech responses in short-term memory. *Canadian Journal of Psychology, 21,* 263–276.

Murray, D. J. (1968). Articulation and acoustic confusability in short-term memory. *Journal of Experimental Psychology, 78,* 679–684.

Neisser, U. (1967). *Cognitive Psychology.* New York: Appleton-Century-Crofts.

Norman, D. A. (1968). Toward a theory of memory and attention. *Psychological Review, 75*(6), 522–536.

Norman, D. A. (1988). *The Psychology of Everyday Things.* New York: Basic Books.

Norman, D. A. & Shallice, T. (1980). Attention to action: Willed and automatic control of behavior. *University of California San Diego CHIP Technical Report no. 99.*

Norman, D. A. & Shallice, T. (1986). Attention to action: Willed and automatic control of behavior. In R. J. Davidson, G. E. Schwartz & D. Shapiro (Eds.), *Consciousness and Self-regulation* (pp. 1–18). New York: Plenum.

Owen, A. M., Sahakian, B. J., Semple, J., Polkey, C. E. & Robbins, T. W. (1995). Visuo-spatial short-term recognition memory and learning after temporal lobe excisions, frontal lobe excisions or amygdalo-hippocampectomy in man. *Neuropsychologia, 33*(1), 1–24.

Paivio, A. (1969). Mental imagery in associative learning and memory. *Psychological Review, 76,* 241–263.

Papagno, C., Valentine, T. & Baddeley, A. D. (1991). Phonological short-term memory and foreign-language vocabulary learning. *Journal of Memory and Language, 30,* 331–347.

Patterson, K. A. (1971). *Limitations on retrieval from long-term memory.* Unpublished doctoral dissertation. University of California, San Diego.

Peterson, L. R. & Johnson, S. T. (1971). Some effects of minimizing articulation on short-term retention. *Journal of Verbal Learning and Verbal Behavior, 10,* 346–354.

Phillips, W. A. (1983). Short-term visual memory. *Philosophical Transactions of the Royal Society of London, series B, 302*(1110), 295–309.

Phillips, W. A. & Christie, D. F. M. (1977). Components of visual memory. *Quarterly Journal of Experimental Psychology, 29,* 117–133.

Postman, L. & Phillips, L. W. (1965). Short-term temporal changes in free recall. *Quarterly Journal of Experimental Psychology, 17,* 132–138.

Quinn, J. G. (1988). Interference effects in the visuo-spatial sketchpad. In M. Denis, J. Engelkamp, & J. T. E. Richardson (Eds.), *Cognitive and Neuropsychological Approaches to Mental Imagery* (pp. 181–189). Dordrecht: Martinus Nijhoff.

Quinn, J. G. & McConnell, J. (1996). Irrelevant pictures in visual working memory. *Quarterly Journal of Experimental Psychology, 49A*(1), 200–215.

Quinn, J. G. & McConnell, J. (1999). Manipulation of interference in the passive visual store. *European Journal of Cognitive Psychology, 11*(3), 373–389.

Richardson, J. T. E. (1996). Evolving concepts of working memory. In J. T. E. Richardson, R. W. Engle, L. Hasher, R. H. Logie, E. R. Stoltzfus & R. T. Zacks (1996). *Working Memory and Human Cognition* (pp. 3–30). New York: Oxford University Press.

Richardson, J. T. E. & Baddeley, A. D. (1975). The effect of articulatory suppression in free recall. *Journal of Verbal Learning and Verbal Behavior, 14,* 623–629.

Salamé, P. & Baddeley, A. D. (1982). Disruption of short-term memory by unattended speech: implications for the structure of working memory. *Journal of Verbal Learning and Verbal Behaviour, 21,* 150–164.

Salamé, P. & Baddeley, A. D. (1987). Noise, unattended speech and short-term memory. *Ergonomics, 30,* 1185–1193.

Service, L. (1992). Phonology, working memory and foreign-language learning. *Quarterly Journal of Experimental Psychology, 45A,* 21–50.

Shallice, T. (1982). Specific impairments of planning. *Philosophical Transactions of the Royal Society of London, 298,* 199–209.

Shallice, T. & Warrington, E. K. (1970). Independent functioning of verbal memory stores: a neuropsychological study. *Quarterly Journal of Experimental Psychology, 22,* 261–273.

Shannon, C. & Weaver, W. (1949). *The Mathematical Theory of Communication.* Urbana, IL: University of Illinois Press.

Smyth, M. M., Pearson, N. A. & Pendleton, L. R. (1988). Movement and working memory: patterns and positions in space. *Quarterly Journal of Experimental Psychology, 40A,* 497–514.

Smyth, M. M. & Pendleton, L. R. (1989). Working memory for movements. *Quarterly Journal of Experimental Psychology, 41A,* 235–250.

Tresch, M. C., Sinnamon, H. M. & Seamon, J. G. (1993). Double dissociation of spatial and object visual memory: evidence from selective interference in intact human subjects. *Neuropsychologia, 31,* 211–219.

Tulving, E. (1968). Theoretical issues in free recall. In T. R. Dixon & D. L. Horton (Eds.), *Verbal Behavior and General Behavior Theory*. Englewood Cliffs, NJ: Prentice-Hall.

Turner, M. L. & Engle, R. W. (1989). Is working memory capacity task dependent? *Journal of Memory and Language, 28*, 127–154.

Tzeng, O. J. L. (1973). Positive recency effect in a delayed free recall. *Journal of Verbal Learning and Verbal Behavior, 12*, 436–439.

Vuontela, V., Rama, P., Raninen, A., Aronen, H. J. & Carlson, S. (1999). Selective interference reveals dissociation between memory for location and colour. *Neuroreport, 10*(11), 2235–2240.

Warrington, E. K. & Shallice, T. (1969). The selective impairment of auditory verbal short-term memory. *Brain, 92*, 885–896.

Waugh, N. C. & Norman, D. A. (1965). Primary memory. *Psychological Review, 72*, 89–104.

Wickelgren, W. A. (1965). Short-term memory for phonemically similar lists. *American Journal of Psychology, 78*, 567–574.

Part II
Applied perspectives

2 Imagery and the visuo-spatial sketchpad

David G. Pearson

Try to imagine the tripartite model of working memory as a family and until recently the visuo-spatial component would have been its under-developed youngest child, over-shadowed by both the more popular verbal sibling and the ambitious parental executive. One of the most widespread criticisms levelled at the Baddeley and Hitch working memory model has been the lack of specification associated with the central executive component. Until recently, however, an equally valid criticism would have been that the model was only able to offer a comprehensive account of verbal working memory, as the experimental evidence and associated theoretical modelling of the visuo-spatial sketchpad appeared minuscule in comparison to the corresponding literature on the operation of the phonological loop. This position has changed radically over recent years, prompted both by an increase in the amount of experimental research specifically into visuo-spatial working memory, and also by recent methodological and theoretical advances in the study of the sketchpad and insights into its possible cognitive architecture. This chapter will review some of these advances in visuo-spatial working memory (VSWM) in comparison to its main theoretical alternative, the computational model of mental imagery proposed by Stephen Kosslyn (1980, 1994). The chapter will also examine how the working memory model can be applied to the experimental investigation of mental synthesis, and how such research can help understand the cognitive processes underpinning activities such as creative design.

THE VISUO-SPATIAL SKETCHPAD

The concept of a separate visual short-term store, functionally distinct from its verbal equivalent, has long formed part of attempts to cognitively model human working memory. Although Atkinson and Shiffrin's seminal 1968 paper 'Human memory: A proposed system and its control processes' is most widely known for its description of an auditory-verbal-linguistic buffer, the authors also acknowledged the probable existence of an additional visual buffer, but avoided any attempt to specify its nature due to a lack of relevant experimental evidence. In the early development of the multi-component model of working memory, Baddeley and Hitch also proposed that a separate visual memory system most probably existed in conjunction with a functionally distinct verbal rehearsal buffer, with both systems relying in part on the presence of a single common central processor (Baddeley & Hitch, 1974). Again, however, there was insufficient empirical evidence to allow any detailed specification of the operation of this visual short-term memory.

This immediately highlights one of the major differences between the theoretical development of the phonological loop and the subsequent development of the visuo-spatial sketchpad. During the 1970s the theoretical development of verbal working memory was based not only on a reaction to pre-existing models (such as Atkinson and Shiffrin's a-v-l buffer), but also on an attempt to account for the huge range of experimental findings that had been collected on the characteristics of short-term memory for auditory and verbal information, some of which had been demonstrated as far as back as the end of the 19th century. In contrast to this, most researchers postulated the existence of a distinct visual short-term store because of theoretical necessity rather than because there was sufficient empirical evidence to warrant the existence of such a mechanism. One consequence of this is that while modelling of the phonological loop has tended to be in response to experimental findings, modelling of the visuo-spatial sketchpad has instead *driven* the direction of research rather than responded to it. This is particularly evident in recent attempts to demonstrate similarities between the workings of the verbal and visuo-spatial slave systems, such as mutual vulnerability to irrelevant modality-specific input (speech in the case of the phonological loop, and pictures in the case of the sketchpad), and the assertion that both systems rely on a passive storage system in which material is maintained by an active rehearsal mechanism. One concern is that there may be insufficient empirical evidence to support this symmetry, and that if it is accepted prematurely researchers may seek confirmatory evidence for it at the expense of evidence that might argue against such structural similarities.

Because theoretical development of the sketchpad has lagged behind that of verbal working memory, there is less consensus in the literature concerning its purpose or function than exists for the phonological loop. Most researchers, however, accept some form of separation between visual and spatial storage and processing within the working memory system.

This possibility was first suggested by Baddeley and Lieberman (1980), who found that a concurrent non-visual tracking task produced a larger decrement in performance on the Brooks matrix task than a purely visual concurrent task. They also found that spatial tracking disrupted the use of the Method of Loci mnemonic (which is based on memory for landmarks in specific locations) much more than the pegword mnemonic system (which involves the generation of images related to specified pegwords rather than specific locations). Baddeley and Lieberman concluded from these results that the operation of the sketchpad component was predominantly spatial in nature rather than visual. However, they also considered the existence of a possible passive visual store that was separate from the mechanism responsible for the short-term retention of spatial information. This store would underlie performance on imagery tasks such as pegword mnemonics, and also temporally retain non-spatial information such as colour, brightness, or shape.

Some evidence for a passive visual store comes from visual similarity effects in visual short-term memory (i.e., Hue & Ericsson, 1988; Wolford & Hollingsworth, 1974; see also Logie, Della Sala, Wynn & Baddeley, 2000), which were reminiscent of the phonological similarity effect in verbal working memory (Baddeley, 1966). In addition, Logie (1986) had shown that the presentation of irrelevant pictures selectively disrupted retention using the pegword mnemonic strategy, while irrelevant speech selectively disrupted retention using rote rehearsal. This demonstration of the apparent vulnerability of VSWM to irrelevant visual input showed strong similarities to the irrelevant speech effect found in verbal working memory (Salamé & Baddeley, 1982).

In his book *Working Memory* (1986, pp. 115–121) Baddeley proposed that the visuo-spatial sketchpad might comprise a passive perceptual input store linked to an active rehearsal mechanism based on a response system such as eye movement. This proposal was partly based on an unpublished study by Idzikowski et al. (reported in Baddeley, 1986) which had shown disruption of the Brooks matrix task by concurrent eye movements. Baddeley also acknowledged, however, that the rehearsal mechanism could be based upon a visual attentional control system rather than eye movements *per se*, and that while the analogy between this system and the phonological loop was certainly attractive, the actual empirical evidence for rehearsal of a visual trace via implicit motor activity was relatively weak.

Paradoxically, while most recent research has focused on similarities between the verbal and visuo-spatial slave systems, their initial conception was substantially different. First, while the phonological loop was assigned the storage of material in only the auditory domain, the sketchpad was implicated in the rehearsal of both visual *and* spatial material, despite the fact that spatial material can clearly be represented in non-visual modalities (see Barcelo, MartinLoeches & Rubia, 1997; Kerr, 1983). Second, the sketchpad has been mainly characterised as responsible for the generation and manipulation of visuo-spatial images rather than visual and spatial material in general (Baddeley, 1986, 1988). This is in marked contrast to the development of the phonological loop, which has been characterised as responsible for the short-term storage of verbal material in the form of phonological traces, rather than for the generation and manipulation of auditory images. When the issue of auditory imagery has been considered in relation to working memory in the literature (i.e., Baddeley & Logie, 1992;

Smith, Reisberg & Wilson, 1992) the emphasis has been on the role played by the phonological loop during some aspects of auditory imagery, thereby recognising that the conscious experience of auditory imagery can be distinguished from the short-term rehearsal of phonological traces.

A distinction between imagery and short-term memory has not been prevalent in the literature on visuo-spatial working memory. Therefore evidence for the visuo-spatial sketchpad has been gathered from a much wider range of experimental paradigms than the evidence for the phonological loop. Broadly, the evidence that has fed the development of VSWM comes from two distinct sources. One source is studies that have focused on purely the short-term retention of visual and spatial material in the absence of explicit imagery instructions, using methodology based largely on tasks such as Corsi blocks (i.e., Smyth & Pendleton, 1989; Smyth & Scholey, 1994) and matrix span (i.e., Logie & Pearson, 1997; Phillips & Christie, 1977). The other source involves studies that have explicitly required participants to generate, maintain and inspect conscious visual images using paradigms such as the Brooks matrix task (Baddeley, Grant, Wight & Thomson, 1975; Quinn & Ralston, 1986) or imagery mnemonics (Logie, 1986; Quinn & McConnell, 1996). The underlying assumption in the literature has been that both types of evidence reflect the operation of the visuo-spatial sketchpad component. I will argue that this fusion of conscious visual imagery with visuo-spatial short-term memory may be inappropriate, and that greater explanatory power may be achieved by considering the processes which underlie the conscious experience of imagery as being functionally distinct from the processes that underlie the short-term retention of visual material in a more general (non-image based) form.

KOSSLYN'S COMPUTATIONAL MODEL OF VISUAL IMAGERY

To assess how useful the visuo-spatial sketchpad may be in accounting for performance of mental imagery, it is important to consider other theoretical alternatives to the working memory approach. By coincidence, the year in which Baddeley and Hitch first proposed their multi-component model of working memory also saw the publication of a PhD dissertation entitled 'Constructing visual images: An exercise in neo-mentalism' by Stephen M. Kosslyn (1974). Kosslyn has since become a pivotal figure not only in re-establishing mental imagery as a legitimate area for scientific concern, but also in applying neuropsychological and brain imaging techniques to the further understanding of human cognition.

Kosslyn began his research career during a period sometimes referred to as 'neomentalism' (Paivio, 1975), in which researchers were attempting to establish more objective means of investigating mental imagery by focusing on behavioural data such as response times and accuracy scores. However, despite the use of more rigorous experimental procedures to investigate imagery, many critics of the approach argued that the theories that developed from this research were still far too vague in their explanations for the nature of the representations underlying imagery, and in particular how these images were generated, inspected, and transformed (i.e., Pylyshyn, 1973, 1981).

Kosslyn's response to this was to develop a computational model of both mental imagery and high-level visual perception. The inspiration for this was the computational approach to perception pioneered by David Marr, in which cognition is understood in terms of processing subsystems that carry out a series of data-transforming computations. The benefit of this approach is that, in contrast to the 'black box' style adopted by some cognitive models, it supplies detailed arguments as to why a specific computation or group of computations should be performed by a specified system.

In Kosslyn's computational model of imagery the most important component is the visual buffer, which is the medium in which conscious mental images are represented. In his original version of the model (Kosslyn, 1980) the buffer was basically analogous to a computer array which functioned as if it were a coordinate space, representing objects or parts of objects by selectively 'filling in' cells of the matrix. In 1994 Kosslyn published a substantially revised version of his model in which the buffer was more closely aligned to research findings from the neurophysiological domain, in that it corresponded to a set of topographically mapped visual areas situated within the occipital cortex, which are anisotropic and non-homogeneous in nature. Kosslyn's research suggests that the buffer has an area of 'high resolution' in the centre which decreases towards the periphery, and that it has limited spatial capacity, making it possible for large images to 'overflow' the medium (Kosslyn, 1978). These properties are very similar to the resolution and spatial extent of the retina, and some critics have argued that Kosslyn's experimental findings result from participants simulating perceptual experience, rather than from the structural properties of the buffer itself (Baddeley, 1986; Pylyshyn, 1984). Kosslyn has responded to this by stating that the buffer is utilised both during visual perception and during mental imagery, therefore it is inevitable that its properties are determined by the limitations of perception (Kosslyn, 1980, 1994).

Kosslyn's assertion that the visual buffer occupies primary visual cortex within the brain has proved to be highly contentious, particularly as some neuropsychological studies have described patients with impaired imagery ability but no corresponding perceptual deficit (Guariglia, Padovani, Pantano & Pizzamiglio, 1993). Imaging studies carried out using positron emission tomography (PET) have also yielded conflicting data. Mellet, Tzourio, Denis, and Mazoyer (1995) reported no activation of primary occipital cortex during mental exploration of a map in comparison to visual exploration of the same map. In contrast, Kosslyn et al. (1999) carried out a PET study which shows activation of primary occipital cortex (specifically Area 17) during both the perception and visualisation of patterns of stripes. This is clearly an issue that will continue to provoke controversy.

SKETCHPAD OR BUFFER?: WORKING MEMORY VERSUS THE COMPUTATIONAL MODEL

Weaknesses of the WM model

How does the multi-component working memory approach compare with Kosslyn's model in terms of explanatory power? The computational approach to imagery has several advantages over the visuo-spatial sketchpad. First, the computational model specifies in detail many concepts that are ambiguous in visuo-spatial working memory, particularly the nature of the processes and representations that underlie the storage and processing of visuo-spatial material. Second, Kosslyn has been able to implement aspects of his theory as a working computer simulation (Kosslyn & Shwartz, 1977, 1978), thereby demonstrating that depictive representations can have computational utility, and can be used as a basis for image processing (see also Baron, 1985; Glasgow & Papadias, 1992). In contrast, while considerable advances have been made in formal modelling of the phonological loop (e.g., Burgess & Hitch, 1992), no similar attempts have yet been made to formally model the visuo-spatial sketchpad.

In addition, as discussed previously, the primary function of the visuo-spatial sketchpad was initially believed to be the generation and manipulation of visual images. While this original model of the sketchpad allows for a separation between visual and spatial short-term storage, all visual information is considered to be maintained within a single passive visual store component. This is true for tasks that require participants to consciously maintain and inspect a mental image (such as the Brooks matrix task) and also for tasks such as matrix span that do not explicitly require participants to generate and maintain mental images. If this model is an accurate reflection of the structure of VSWM then the passive visual store component of the sketchpad should be synonymous with the visual buffer component of the computational model, as both have been specified as being the medium in which conscious mental images are represented. However, an attempt to directly equate the two models raises a number of serious theoretical difficulties.

First, although Kosslyn has been quite circumspect regarding the conscious nature of imagery within his model, he nevertheless assumes that there is a direct correspondence between activation within the buffer and the conscious experience of quasi-perceptual images by the subject (Kosslyn, 1987). If this were also the case for the visual store, then it would mean that the only way in which an individual could temporarily maintain visual and spatial material was in the form of a consciously experienced mental image. Even on a purely phenomenological basis, this is clearly not the case. A good example of this is the phenomenology associated with the use of the pegword mnemonic strategy, which has been widely used as an experimental measure of visual working memory (Logie, 1986; McConnell & Quinn, 2000; Quinn & McConnell, 1996, 1999). The strategy initially requires participants to learn a list of 'pegwords'; i.e., 'one is a bun, two is a shoe, three is a tree' etc. (Bower, 1973). Participants are then required to retain a sequence of novel words by generating a distinctive mental image for each word–pegword pairing. For example, if the first word to be retained was 'car' then a participant might generate a mental image of a car shaped like a bun. If the second word was 'fish', they might imagine a fish wearing a pair of shoes, and so on. If each of these images could only be maintained in the form of a conscious visual image, then after presenting ten words to be retained each participant should subjectively have a mental image that represents all ten word–pegword images simultaneously. Instead of this, however, most participants report experiencing each image as a separate entity rather than a single composite representation; i.e., if consciously experiencing an image of a fish wearing shoes, the participant would not consciously experience the other images at the same time. However, this information must be readily available somewhere in their cognitive system, as participants can easily generate conscious images of their word–pegword combinations when required.

This point leads on to a second problem for the 'visual store equals visual buffer' theory, which is that the visual buffer as described by Kosslyn is ill-suited to the range of cognitive tasks that have been attributed to the visual store. When an image is generated within the buffer the topographically mapped areas work together to produce a multi-scaled structure, in which an image is represented at different spatial scales. However, although parts can be added and deleted from an image being maintained within the buffer, these manipulations are always carried out on a single unitary represen-tation. The visual buffer is therefore not capable of representing a *sequence* of different visual representations, which is an essential component of working memory tasks such as serial pattern recall (Avons & Mason, 1999; Walker, Hitch & Duroe, 1993) or pegword mnemonics (Quinn & McConnell, 1996). Kosslyn's computational model accounts for perfor-mance on tasks such as these by assigning the storage of sequentially pre-sented visual material to something termed a 'pattern activation subsystem' which is both functionally and structurally distinct from the visual buffer (Kosslyn, 1994, pp. 117–145). However, the original model of the sketchpad allows for no such distinction, and instead attempts to assign the storage of conscious mental images and sequential visual patterns to a single representational medium, the passive visual store.

A third problem for the working memory approach is that if the operation of the sketchpad really does encompass both visual imagery and more general visuo-spatial temporary storage, then damage to the sketch-pad via brain injury should result in both imagery and visuo-spatial working memory becoming impaired. Instead, the neuropsychological literature indicates apparent dissociations between imagery processes and visuo-spatial short-term memory in head-injured patients (e.g., Farah, Hammond, Levine & Calvanio, 1988; Hanley, Young & Pearson, 1991; Morris & Morton, 1995; Morton & Morris, 1995; Riddoch, 1990). This suggests that the two-component visual store/spatial rehearsal model of the sketchpad may be an over-simplification of the underlying cognitive architecture involved in visuo-spatial working memory.

Strengths of the WM model

Despite the greater level of specification offered by the computational model there remain aspects of imagery that it has difficulty accounting for. These include the finding that concurrent articulatory suppression sig-nificantly improves participants' performance on image subtraction and reinterpretation tasks, but only for those items which can be easily verbally encoded (Brandimonte & Gerbino, 1993; Brandimonte, Hitch & Bishop, 1992). In addition, Intons-Peterson (1996) has shown that performance of image subtraction declines when linguistic processing is encouraged, and increases when the visual aspects of the task are emphasised. Kosslyn (1994) has attempted to account for these findings by arguing that con-current suppression can prevent the verbal recoding of visual stimuli, and the subsequent storage of descriptions of specific parts and properties within semantic memory (pp. 338–339). This can then benefit novel dis-coveries from imagery by allowing the initial perceptual organisation of an image to be changed. However the mechanism by which such verbal recoding occurs is not specified within the computational model, and the suggestion that concurrent suppression can block verbal labelling has been also strongly criticised as being empirically unsubstantiated (Logie, 1995; Reisberg, 1996).

Additionally, while the computational model does allow for mental images to be generated on the basis of verbal descriptions, it does not assume that any verbal storage or processing is necessary during the mani-pulation and inspection of representations within the visual buffer. The computational model therefore has difficulty accounting for the finding that concurrent articulatory suppression significantly disrupts performance of mental synthesis, but only when there is a task requirement for participants to mentally retain the identity of the symbols which are to be combined (Pearson, Logie & Gilhooly, 1999a). The working memory approach can account for these findings if it is accepted that the processing of visual representations can be supported by temporary storage of material in a visually based form via the sketchpad and by additional verbally based storage within the phonological loop, depending on the nature of the cognitive task being performed. Concurrent articulatory suppression therefore does not prevent verbal recoding during imagery, but instead impairs the storage of these verbal representations within the phonological loop. This issue is discussed further in the section on mental synthesis.

LOGIE'S REVISED MODEL OF VSWM

The previous section has argued that there are considerable difficulties in attempting to equate the original model of the visuo-spatial sketchpad with the computational model of imagery proposed by Kosslyn, despite the fact that both theories purport to offer an account of the generation and manipulation of visuo-spatial images. The computational model has difficulty in explaining the influence of verbal processing on visual imagery, whereas the working memory model has difficulty in explaining phenomenological and neuropsychological dissociations between short-term memory and imagery. A potential solution to this is a revised model of visuo-spatial working memory proposed by Logie (1995). Logie's model fractionates the sketchpad into two inter-dependent visual and spatial components. One component is a passive visual storage system (the 'visual cache'), while the other is an active spatial rehearsal mechanism (the 'inner scribe'). Information held within the visual cache is subject to decay, and also to interference from new visual input entering the cache (hence the presence of an irrelevant pictures effect). The contents of the visual cache are refreshed via the operation of the active inner scribe mechanism, which is also implemented during the planning and execution of movement. A direct consequence of this is that the production of physical movement, or even just the planned production of movement, should interfere with any concurrent task that also requires the operation of the inner scribe. Although the cache can represent spatial locations in the form of static visual patterns (see Smyth & Pendleton, 1989), the retention of sequential locations or movements (such as those that occur during Corsi blocks) requires the operation of the inner scribe. The scribe is also implicated in the extraction of information from the visual cache to allow for targeted movement.

Logie's revision of the sketchpad differs from the original version in two major respects. The first is that input into VSWM occurs via activated long-term memory representations, rather than directly from perceptual input. Thus disruption of material within the visual cache by irrelevant visual material is considered to result from activation of representations within long-term memory, rather than from input arriving directly from the perceptual system. Logie therefore considers working memory as a cognitive 'workspace' for activated long-term memory rather than as a gateway through which all input must pass before gaining access to the long-term store. This view can be seen as a synthesis of opposing theories on the nature of working memory, which conceptualise it either as a functionally distinct memory system (i.e., Atkinson & Shiffrin, 1968; Baddeley & Hitch, 1974) or else as activated representations within the long-term store (i.e., Cowan, 1993).

The second major departure from the previous model of VSWM, and the one that is most relevant to the present discussion, is that Logie clearly distinguishes the operation of the visual cache from the operation of a 'visual buffer' in which conscious visual images are represented. Instead, the visual cache and inner scribe are conceived as acting as temporary stores for visual and spatial material held in a form separate from conscious imagery. Information held in these stores can be extracted via the operation of the central executive and then utilised during the completion of a given cognitive task, as can semantic information held in long-term memory and phonological/articulatory information held in the phonological loop. During performance of mental imagery the visual cache temporarily stores information which can then be transferred into the visual buffer when it needs to be consciously manipulated or inspected in some way. Hence, while the passive visual cache may play an important role during the operation of visual imagery, it is not the medium in which the conscious visual images are represented.

WORKING MEMORY AND MENTAL SYNTHESIS: A WINDOW INTO CONCEPTUAL DESIGN?

Logie's revised model proposes a visual cache as a functionally separate system from the visual buffer in which conscious mental images are represented. Not only does this model avoid some of the difficulties experienced by the original version of the sketchpad, but it also allows a greater degree of specification when accounting for the processes which may operate during both image based and non-image based cognitive tasks. However, there are a number of aspects of the model which require greater clarification. These include a more detailed explanation of what role the central executive plays during the execution of mental imagery operations, as well as a greater elaboration on the nature and function of the spatial 'inner scribe' component. These issues can be considered in greater detail by examining the role played by VSWM during a form of visuo-spatial reasoning known as mental synthesis. Mental synthesis refers to the manipulation and transformation of visual images to produce new configurations or discover novel emergent properties. There are many anecdotal reports of such synthesis providing the basis for important scientific and artistic discoveries, including Einstein's use of 'combinatory play' during the development of his general theory of relativity (Ghiselin, 1952) or Watson's insights into the double-helix structure of DNA (Watson, 1968). Mental synthesis is also believed to play a fundamental role during the concept phase of design in disciplines such as architecture and engineering (Purcell & Gero, 1998; Verstijnen, van Leeuwen, Goldschimdt, Haeml & Hennessey, 1998a, b).

Much of the research literature on design is based upon analyses of design protocols (i.e., Goldschimdt, 1989; Suwa & Tversky, 1996). In a review of this literature Purcell and Gero (1998) have argued that, although such research has produced undeniably interesting results, it is essentially descriptive in nature, and therefore does not provide a good basis for the building of models or theories of conceptual design. They propose an alternative way forward in which design problem solving is interpreted using theoretical frameworks taken from cognitive psychology, such as the Geneplore model of creativity (Finke, Ward & Smith, 1992) or the tripartite model of working memory (Baddeley & Hitch, 1974).

Much of the research on mental synthesis has used a creative synthesis task developed by Finke and Slayton in 1988. The basic procedure for this task consists of verbally presenting participants with a series of labels describing alphanumeric or geometric symbols (e.g., an example trial could be 'triangle, square, rectangle, rectangle, capital T'). Participants are then given up to two minutes to mentally combine the given symbols into a recognisable pattern. They are allowed to alter the orientation and size of the symbols in any way they wish, provided that this does not distort the basic shape (i.e., a rectangle could not be changed into a square). At the end of the designated construction period participants record a verbal description of their synthesised pattern on a response sheet prior to actually drawing the pattern, to ensure that the discovery of the pattern results from imagery alone rather than from drawing support (see Pearson, Logie & Green, 1996). Some examples of synthesised patterns produced using the creative synthesis procedure are given in Figure 2.1.

Most previous research on the creative synthesis task has focused on participants' ability to produce a legitimate pattern from the presented symbols and the creativity and originality of these productions as rated by independent judges (i.e., Anderson & Helstrup, 1993; Helstrup & Anderson, 1996). However, it is also possible to examine the storage requirements of the task independently from the mental synthesis process itself. This is important because during the task an individual must not only attempt to combine the presented symbols into a recognisable pattern, but must also accurately retain the identity of the component symbols during the construction period. Failure on the synthesis task can therefore result from at least two sources: an inability to synthesise the presented symbols into a pattern, or an inability to retain some or all of the presented symbols during the construction period.

We investigated this issue by modifying the basic Finke and Slayton procedure (Pearson, Logie & Gilhooly, 1997). If a participant was unable to think of a legitimate pattern by the end of the two-minute construction period, they were instructed to write down the symbols that they could

PRESENTED SYMBOLS

" rectangle, triangle, rectangle, letter V, number 8 "

EXAMPLES OF LEGITIMATE PATTERNS

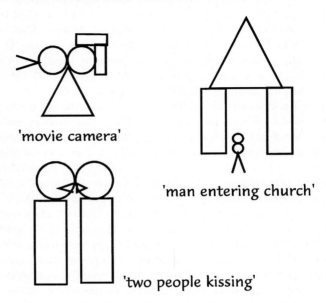

'movie camera'

'man entering church'

'two people kissing'

Figure 2.1   Example of legitimate patterns produced using the creative synthesis procedure.

remember being presented initially. This provided a measure of participants' memory for the symbols as well as their ability to combine them into a legitimate pattern. We varied the number of presented symbols from four to six, thereby varying the storage load of the task. Both the number of legitimate patterns produced by participants, and the number of trials on which they could correctly recall all of the presented symbols, significantly decreased as the number of presented symbols grew larger (Figure 2.2). This demonstrated that performance on the task was constrained by the resource limitations of whatever cognitive systems were involved. However, participants' ability to recall the symbols was always significantly better than their ability to mentally combine the symbols into a legitimate pattern. Hence, failure on the synthesis task could not be attributed to errors in memory alone.

This study raised two empirical questions. First, what cognitive mechanism were participants using to retain the identity of the presented

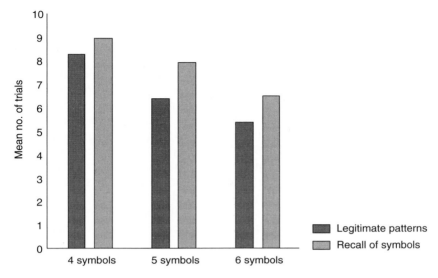

Figure 2.2 Mean number of trials on which a legitimate pattern was produced and on which all presented symbols were correctly recalled for four, five and six symbol trials.

symbols? Second, was this retention mechanism the same as that which they used to transform and manipulate the symbols? To answer these questions we examined performance of the creative synthesis task in conjunction with performance of concurrent spatial and verbal secondary tasks (Pearson et al., 1999a). One candidate for the manipulation process was the inner scribe component of the visuo-spatial sketchpad, which Logie has suggested is involved during the execution of dynamic image transformations (Logie, 1995). If this were the case then a concurrent spatial task (pressing keys in a continuous 'figure-of-eight' pattern) should interfere with individuals' ability to assemble the component parts into a legitimate pattern within the visual buffer. We found that concurrent tapping reduced the number of legitimate patterns produced in comparison to a control condition, which supported a role for the inner scribe in manipulating images represented within the visual buffer.

However, concurrent tapping did not affect participants' ability to recall correctly all of the presented symbols, which suggested that the inner scribe was not the mechanism being used to retain the identity of symbols during the construction interval. Previous research has shown that some image-based discovery tasks appear to involve the rehearsal of verbal material within the phonological loop (i.e., Brandimonte & Gerbino, 1993; Brandimonte et al., 1992; Intons-Peterson, 1996). Because stimuli in the creative synthesis task are orally presented to participants in the form of verbal labels, it is possible that the maintenance of these labels occurs within the phonological loop rather than within the visual buffer. If this were the case, then concurrent articulatory suppression should interfere not only with the number of legitimate patterns produced, but also with participants' memory for the symbols themselves.

However, Helstrup and Anderson (1991) suggested an alternative possibility. They argued that articulatory suppression could disrupt performance by interfering with the verbal interpretation phase of the task rather than with the retention of the symbols themselves. An experiment carried out by Pearson et al. (1999a) found little evidence to support this, as there was no effect of concurrent articulatory suppression on judges' correspondence ratings between verbal descriptions and synthesised patterns (concurrent tapping was also found not to affect correspondence ratings). In contrast, articulatory suppression did significantly reduce the number of trials on which participants correctly recalled all of the presented symbols, which was consistent with the hypothesis that symbol identities were maintained as phonological traces rather than purely in a visuo-spatial form.

An additional test of the hypothesis that the phonological loop is used to retain the identity of the presented symbols would be to examine mental synthesis under conditions in which it is not necessary to remember the symbols. Without a verbal memory load there should be no effect of a concurrent verbal secondary task on mental synthesis. We tested this hypothesis by examining the effect of a demanding verbal secondary task (oral random generation) on performance of synthesis under imagery-alone and stimulus-supported conditions (Pearson, Logie & Gilhooly, 1999b). Oral random generation severely disrupted mental synthesis in the imagery-alone condition but had no effect when synthesis was performed using a computer-based graphics package that continuously represented the symbols on the screen. Removing the requirement on participants to maintain symbol identity in working memory thus substantially reduced the interference caused by the concurrent verbal task.

On the basis of these empirical findings we formulated a cognitive model that describes how the visual buffer and the various components of working memory are involved in mental synthesis (Figure 2.3). The operation of this model is best illustrated with reference to a hypothetical experimental trial, in which a participant is presented with the symbols 'triangle, circle, D, square, line'. As the symbols are orally presented to participants via verbal labels, they should initially gain direct access to the phonological store component of working memory and then be maintained there via the operation of the articulatory loop. Participants generate conscious images of the symbols using these verbal representations as cues, but continue to maintain the representations within the loop to provide a memory back-up for the symbols that is separate from their use of visual imagery.

This model elaborates on the issue of the function performed by the central executive during mental imagery tasks by assigning the executive the specific role of image maintenance. For example, during an experimental

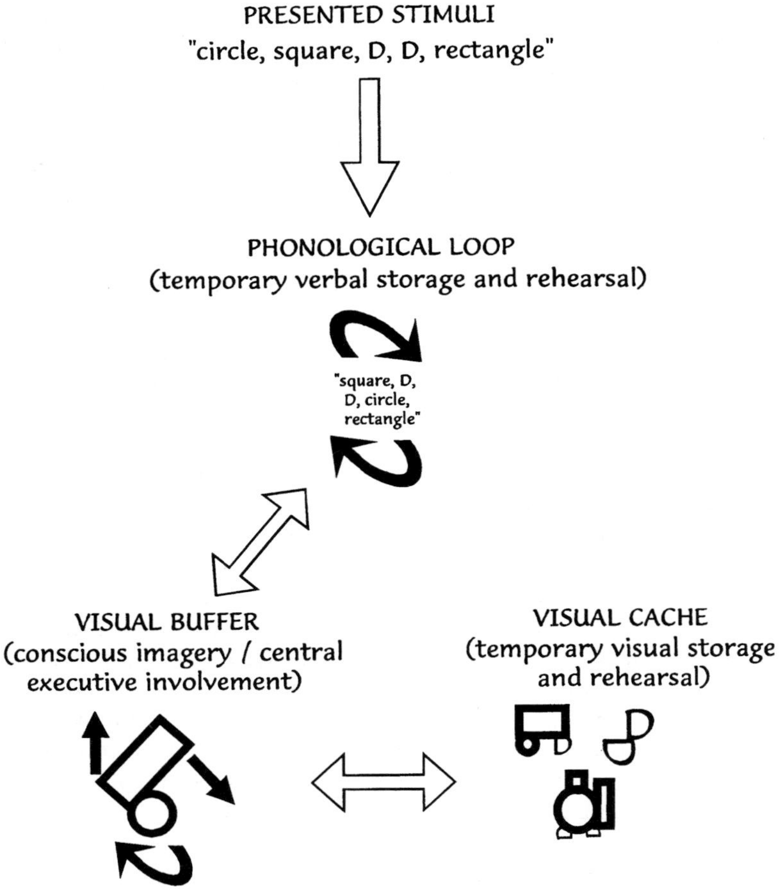

PRESENTED STIMULI
"circle, square, D, D, rectangle"

PHONOLOGICAL LOOP
(temporary verbal storage and rehearsal)

"square, D,
D, circle,
rectangle"

VISUAL BUFFER   VISUAL CACHE
(conscious imagery / central   (temporary visual storage
executive involvement)   and rehearsal)

Figure 2.3   Diagram depicting the involvement of working memory components
during mental synthesis. Adapted from Pearson et al. (1999a).

trial a participant may generate a visual image of a triangle and a square
within the buffer and then begin to manipulate them using the inner scribe.
According to Kosslyn's computational model an image begins to decay
rapidly once generated, to avoid interfering with the operation of normal
perception (Kosslyn, 1983). Images can be maintained either by continuous
reactivation of representations in long-term visual memory, or by the
continued fixation of an 'attention window' which selects portions of the
image in the visual buffer for additional processing. Both processes adapt
very quickly, making it increasingly difficult to maintain a visual image over
longer retention intervals.

Empirical evidence suggests that the maintenance of conscious images
depends on general attentional resources (i.e., Bexton, Heron & Scott, 1954;

Cocude, 1988). In terms of the working memory model, this can be interpreted as suggesting that the maintenance of material within the visual buffer is largely dependent on the resources of the central executive component. This interpretation would predict that an executively demanding secondary task should severely disrupt an individual's ability to maintain conscious visual images. Some support for this hypothesis has been provided by the demonstration that concurrent random generation can have a substantial effect on participants' subjective experience of image duration during the performance of creative synthesis (Pearson & Logie, 2000).

Hence the visual buffer can act as a form of VSWM by temporarily representing material in the form of a conscious visual image. Continued maintenance of this material, however, will place considerable demands on the central executive component, and even with this 'executive maintenance' the image will become degraded over time. It would therefore be much more effective to maintain as much information as possible in short-term stores which are functionally separate from the visual buffer, and which can rehearse material without placing significant demands on the executive component. In terms of mental synthesis, we argue that the phonological loop fulfils this function by maintaining the identity of the presented symbols until all of them can be represented in a combined pattern within the visual buffer. The visual cache also operates as a back-up store for the buffer by storing previous stages of the synthesis process in a non-image based form. For instance, in the example trial described previously a participant might imagine combining the triangle, square and circle into a church tower, but then abandon this approach in favour of an alternative pattern. Although the visual image of the three symbols combined as a church tower would no longer be represented within the visual buffer, sufficient information would be retained in the visual cache to allow for it to be regenerated back into the buffer at a later stage if required. The visual cache could also store the appearance of any presented symbols that could not be imaged on the basis of a verbal description alone.

This revised model of VSWM avoids the difficulty encountered by the original version of the visuo-spatial sketchpad of assigning the storage of conscious mental images and sequential visual patterns to a single representational medium. As discussed previously, Kosslyn's computational model also deals with this problem by assigning the storage of sequentially presented visual material to a pattern activation subsystem which is both functionally and structurally distinct from the visual buffer. Although there is considerable overlap of proposed function between Kosslyn's pattern activation subsystem and Logie's visual cache, they are not synonymous. In Kosslyn's model the pattern activation subsystems are involved not only during the storage of sequential visual information, but also in the generation of mental images within the visual buffer and during high-level perceptual processing such as object recognition. In contrast, the visual cache is conceived as a passive storage system whose function is almost exclusively the temporary retention of visually based material. Although this material may be used as part of ongoing mental imagery or perception, the visual cache itself remains functionally distinct from these additional cognitive processes.

It is clear that more research will be needed before the precise operation and constraints of the different components of working memory during mental imagery can be specified further. However, the multi-component model of mental synthesis depicted in Figure 2.3 does have the advantage of being able to generate quite specific empirical predictions concerning the effects of different secondary tasks and conditions on the performance of mental synthesis. As an example, synthesis with hard-to-name symbols should involve the visual cache much more than the phonological loop, and therefore retention errors should become more visually rather than phonologically based. Also, stimulus support during synthesis (such as drawing or sketching) should reduce or eliminate the involvement of the loop because under these circumstances there is no requirement to maintain symbol identity.

FUTURE DIRECTIONS: WHAT IS THE INNER SCRIBE?

There remains a great deal of theoretical uncertainty concerning the nature and function of the active spatial component of the working memory system. This includes issues such as the precise mechanism by which spatial information is encoded and maintained within short-term memory, and also the extent to which different cognitive tasks may draw on the spatial component for successful completion. The published literature on this topic contains three broad claims about the role of the spatial component. The first claim is that the spatial component is involved during the encoding and maintenance of sequences of spatial locations. The second claim is that the component is involved during a wider range of spatial tasks, including the dynamic manipulation and transformation of visual mental images. The third claim, made most recently by Logie in his revised 1995 model of VSWM, is that the spatial component is responsible for the active rehearsal of material stored in the passive visual component of the working memory system.

The first claim is supported by the most empirical evidence. Early research made use of a spatial task devised by Brooks (1967) that requires participants to encode and retain sequences of locations using a mental image of a 4×4 matrix. Baddeley et al. (1975) found that a concurrent tracking task disrupted recall on the matrix task, but had no significant effect on a comparable verbal memory task. Quinn and Ralston (1986) asked participants to complete the matrix task while moving their arms in directions either compatible or incompatible with the encoding of locations in the mental matrix, and found that only incompatible arm movements produced disruption, even if the participants did not initiate the movements themselves. Moreover, incompatible movements only produced disruption if they occurred as the sequence of locations were being encoded, with no disruption taking place if the movement was restricted to just a retention interval (Quinn, 1988, 1991). Smyth and Pendleton (1989) have accounted for this by arguing that it is only the initial encoding of the locations in the matrix task which requires the operation of the spatial component, after which information is retained in the form of a static visual pattern that is immune to disruption from concurrent movement. Evidence for involvement of the spatial component during the actual retention of spatial locations has come from studies that have examined performance on the Corsi blocks task (De Renzi & Nichelli, 1975; Milner, 1971). Smyth, Pearson and Pendleton (1988) have reported that concurrent four-key tapping produced significant interference with participants' recall on the Corsi task, while performing concurrent sequences of body movements did not. Taken together this evidence suggests that the cognitive system responsible for the encoding and retention of spatial locations may be closely related to the cognitive systems that plan and control physical movements to external spatial targets. However, the extent to which this mechanism relies on implicit motor processes remains unclear. Alternative explanations have included a rehearsal system based on shifts in spatial attention (Smyth & Scholey, 1994), or even the involvement of much more generalised attentional resources (Klauer & Stegmaier, 1997).

The claim that the spatial component is involved in a wider range of spatial tasks than just the short-term retention of location has been made more recently than the first, but is nonetheless supported by a growing body of experimental evidence. The previous section has already discussed the finding that concurrent spatial tapping appears to disrupt individuals' ability to mentally synthesise objects using imagery (Pearson et al., 1999a). In addition to this, selective interference from concurrent spatial tasks has also been reported with mental rotation of abstract shapes (Logie & Salway, 1990); mental animation of static mechanical figures (Sims & Hegarty, 1997), mental scanning of maps (Pearson, 1999), and the encoding of relative size during mental comparison tasks (Engelkamp, Mohr & Logie, 1995). These studies suggest that the cognitive system(s) responsible for the encoding of spatial relations and for the dynamic manipulation of representations within the visual buffer overlap considerably with the cognitive system(s) involved during the planning and production of movement, although the importance of actual motor processes in this relationship is again unclear.

A final claim made for the spatial component is that it acts as a rehearsal mechanism for material represented within the passive visual store component of VSWM (Baddeley, 1986; Logie, 1995). This hypothesis suggests that there is a clear symmetry between the cognitive structure of verbal and visuo-spatial working memory, with both systems comprising passive stores in which material is maintained by the operation of an active rehearsal mechanism. In the case of verbal short-term memory phonological traces stored in the 'phonological store' component are continuously rehearsed by an articulatory control process closely linked to the production of speech. Anything that blocks the operation of this rehearsal process, such as continuous articulatory suppression, rapidly leads to forgetting as material in the phonological store decays (Baddeley, 1986; Baddeley et al., 1975). Logie (1995) has proposed that the spatial 'inner scribe' component performs a similar function in VSWM, by continuously rehearsing material stored in the visual cache using processes closely linked to the planning of movement. If this hypothesis is correct then a concurrent spatial suppression task should interfere with visual short-term memory in the same way that articulatory suppression interferes with verbal recall. However, this prediction does not appear to be supported by the available empirical evidence. As discussed previously, concurrent movement only disrupts performance of the Brooks matrix task if it occurs during the encoding of the spatial sequences, but not if it occurs during a retention interval in which the matrix is maintained as a static visual pattern (Quinn, 1988, 1991). Furthermore, it has been reported that concurrent spatial secondary tasks do not significantly disrupt the short-term retention of colour (Logie & Marchetti, 1991), shape (Tresch, Sinnamon & Seamon, 1993), static patterns (Morris, 1987), or remove visual similarity effects during the recall of drawings (Longoni & Scalisi, 1994). Vecchi, Monticellai and Cornoldi (1995) have also reported an experiment that examined performance of an active spatial processing task in conjunction with varying the load on the passive visual store (using a matrix span procedure). Increases in visual load were found to have minimal disruptive effects on performance of the active spatial task, which again is not consistent with the theory that visual rehearsal is dependent upon active spatial processes.

Considered together this evidence seems to suggest that the spatial component of working memory is involved both during the encoding and retention of sequences of spatial locations, and also during more general spatial encoding and dynamic transformations of material within the visual buffer. However, the spatial component does not appear to be responsible for the rehearsal of material stored within the visual cache. Taking all of this into account, a model is presented in Figure 2.4 that suggests how the inner scribe component may be linked to a Visual Cache–Visual Buffer (VC–VB) account of the visuo-spatial sketchpad. As discussed previously, in this model the visual buffer is essentially a similar structure to the buffer described in Kosslyn's computational model. All representations within this buffer are experienced by an individual as a conscious mental image, and can be generated either from representations stored in long-term visual memory, loaded directly from the perceptual systems in the form of visual traces, or else novel images can be created and synthesised via the operation

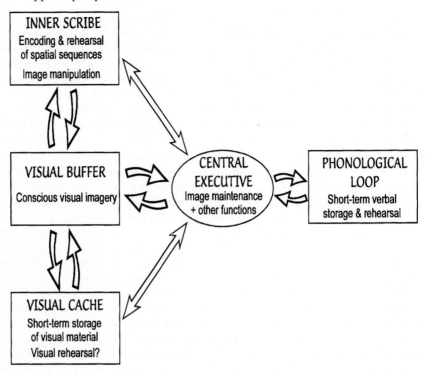

Figure 2.4 Diagram representing how the inner scribe, central executive and phonological loop are related to a VC–VB model of the visuo-spatial sketchpad.

of the central executive and the inner scribe. Once an image is generated into the buffer it will begin to decay extremely rapidly, but if necessary the image can be maintained by using executive resources continually to regenerate the image and preserve it from decay.

Operations utilising the visual buffer are supported by the visual cache, which acts as a temporary back-up store for representations that are no longer being maintained in the form of a conscious mental image. In contrast to the visual buffer, the cache has the ability to store multiple visual representations. If a cognitive task requires that this material is converted back into a conscious image (e.g., during the recall stage of pegword mnemonics), then the contents of the cache will provide the basis for the generation of a new representation in the visual buffer. However, material stored in the visual cache can be accessed directly for some tasks without any involvement of the visual buffer. Therefore, because the visual cache and visual buffer are functionally separate from each other one system can become damaged while another remains intact, suggesting potential dissociations occurring between imagery processes and visual short-term memory in head-injured patients. For instance, Riddoch (1990) has reported a patient who was able to copy letter and letter-like forms accurately over a retention interval of up to ten seconds, but was severely impaired on imagery tasks such as judging whether named letters contained curves in their upper-case form (i.e., 'q' compared to 'e' in upper-case). In contrast, Hanley et al. (1991) have described a patient who was impaired in the temporary retention of visual information during tasks such as imagery mnemonics and short-term memory for unfamiliar faces, but showed no impairment in making visual and spatial judgements about information already stored in long-term memory (i.e., relative size comparisons for pairs such as 'toothbrush–banana'; similarity judgements for shapes of countries etc.).

The inner scribe component is involved during the encoding of spatial locations and the short-term retention of spatial sequences such as occurs during the Corsi blocks task, and this can happen independently of activity in the visual buffer and visual cache. However, the visual buffer will become involved during the retention of spatial sequences if participants employ a cognitive strategy in which they visualise the to-be-remembered sequences as conscious mental images. The scribe will also interact with material represented within the visual buffer during dynamic image operations such as rotation, scanning, and mental synthesis. However, in this model it has no direct connection with either the maintenance of visual images in the buffer (which are maintained by the central executive) or the maintenance of visual material in the visual cache. This model therefore requires the existence of a visual rehearsal mechanism that is functionally separate from spatial working memory, but at this stage the method by which such a mechanism might operate remains unclear, and further research will be required to explore this possibility further. It may be valuable to consider Kosslyn's computational model in this respect, as a rehearsal mechanism could be linked to the operation of the pattern activation subsystems that he describes (Kosslyn, 1994).

On a cautionary note, the demonstration of selective spatial interference effects for both spatial working memory tasks and for spatial imagery tasks such as mental rotation and scanning does not necessarily mean that a single common mechanism underlies the performance of both. This is especially true considering the bewildering variety of different secondary tasks that have been labelled with the common term 'spatial suppresser', including four-key tapping (Smyth et al., 1988), eight-key tapping (Pearson et al., 1999a), auditory non-visual tracking (Baddeley & Lieberman, 1980), visual tracking (Quinn & McConnell, 1996), auditory localisation (Bruyer & Scailquin, 1998), arm movements (Quinn & Ralston, 1986), and eye movements (Andrade, Kavanagh & Baddeley, 1997). Faced with such a diversity of experimental paradigms any attempts to generalise across studies must be cautious, and ultimately it may prove better to consider the spatial component of working memory as consisting of a number of inter-linked but separable processes rather than a single unitary mechanism.

SUMMARY

Recent theoretical and methodological developments in the study of visuo-spatial working memory have led to considerable advances in our under-standing of how the sketchpad might contribute to the overall functioning of the working memory system, but the precise relationship between working memory and mental imagery has remained difficult to clarify. In this chapter I have argued that the original characterisation of the visuo-spatial sketchpad as a system responsible for the generation and manipu-lation of visuo-spatial images may be inappropriate, and that one potential alternative is to consider a Visual Cache–Visual Buffer model in which the visual cache is functionally separate from the medium in which conscious visual images are represented. Not only can this model better account for experimental and neuropsychological data which suggest a dissociation between conscious visual imagery and non-image based visual short-term memory, but it can also provide a more detailed account of cognitive processes that may underlie performance of imagery tasks such as creative synthesis or pegword mnemonics. In some respects this account can be superior to that offered by alternative theories such as Kosslyn's compu-tational model of imagery. Because there is no equivalent of the phono-logical loop within the computational model it has difficulty in offering an explanation for how verbal encoding and verbal rehearsal may interact with the discovery of novel properties within visual images. The computational model also does not directly specify the cognitive mechanism that actually directs activity within the visual buffer, and even taking into account its current weaknesses, the concept of the central executive can be used to make a contribution in this area.

Much still remains unclear in our understanding of the visuo-spatial sketchpad, including the nature of the rehearsal mechanism that maintains material within the visual cache, and also the means by which this material is represented. However, even at this stage the model can be usefully applied to understanding a complex cognitive activity such as mental synthesis, and I hope that in time it will provide a better framework for specifying cognitive processes in areas such as conceptual design than reliance on verbal proto-cols alone.

BACKGROUND READING

Richardson, J. T. E. (1999). *Imagery*. Hove, UK: Psychology Press.

Provides a good introduction to current mental imagery research.

Logie, R. H. (1995). *Visuo-Spatial Working Memory*. Hove, UK: Lawrence Erlbaum Associates Ltd.

Reviews the empirical evidence for VSWM and proposes Logie's revised model discussed in this chapter.

Helstrup, T. & Logie, R. H. (Eds., 1999). *Imagery in working memory and in mental discovery. The European Journal of Cognitive Psychology*, *11* (whole no. 3). Hove, UK: Psychology Press.

A special issue of the *European Journal of Cognitive Psychology* that contains a good range of papers discussing current issues in both imagery and visuo-spatial working memory.

REFERENCES

Anderson, R. E. & Helstrup, T. (1993). Visual discovery on mind and on paper. *Memory and Cognition*, *21*, 283–293.

Andrade, J., Kavanagh, D. & Baddeley, A. (1997). Eye movements and visual imagery: a working memory approach to the treatment of post-traumatic stress disorder. *British Journal of Clinical Psychology*, *36*(2), 209–223.

Atkinson, R. C. & Shiffrin, R. M. (1968). Human memory: A proposed system and its control processes. In K. W. Spence & J. T. Spence (Eds.), *The Psychology of Learning and Motivation, Vol. 2* (pp. 89–195). London: Academic Press.

Avons, S. E. & Mason, A. (1999). Effects of visual similarity on serial report and item recognition. *Quarterly Journal of Experimental Psychology*, *52A*(1), 217–240.

Baddeley, A. D. (1966). Short-term memory for word sequences as a function of acoustic, semantic and formal similarity. *Quarterly Journal of Experimental Psychology*, *18*, 362–365.

Baddeley, A. D. (1986). *Working Memory*. Oxford: Oxford University Press.

Baddeley, A. D. (1988). Imagery and working memory. In M. Denis, J. Engelkamp, and J. T. E. Richardson (Eds.), *Cognitive and Neuropsychological Approaches to Mental Imagery* (pp. 169–180). Dordrecht: Martinus Nijhoff.

Baddeley, A. D., Grant, W., Wight, E. & Thomson, N. (1975). Imagery and visual working memory. In P. M. A. Rabbit & S. Dornic (Eds.), *Attention and Performance, V* (pp. 205–217). London: Academic Press.

Baddeley, A. D. & Hitch, G. J. (1974). Working memory. In G. Bower (Ed.), *The Psychology of Learning and Motivation, Vol. VIII* (pp. 47–90). New York: Academic Press.

Baddeley, A. D. & Lieberman, K. (1980). Spatial working memory. In R. S. Nickerson (Ed.), *Attention and Performance, VIII* (pp. 521–539). Hillsdale, NJ: Lawrence Erlbaum Associates Inc.

Baddeley, A. D. & Logie, R. H. (1992). Auditory imagery and working memory. In D. Reisberg (Ed.), *Auditory Imagery* (pp. 179–197). Hillsdale, NJ: Lawrence Erlbaum Associates Inc.

Barcelo, F., MartinLoeches, M. & Rubia, F. J. (1997). Event-related potentials during memorization of spatial locations in the auditory and visual modalities. *Electroencephalography and Clinical Neuropsychology*, *103*(2), 257–267.

Baron, R. J. (1985). Visual memories and mental images. *International Journal of Man–Machine Studies*, *23*, 275–311.

Bexton, W. H., Heron, W. & Scott, T. H. (1954). Effects of decreased variation in the sensory environment. *Canadian Journal of Psychology*, *8*, 70–76.

Bower, G. H. (1973). How to . . . uh . . . remember! *Psychology Today*, *7*, 62–67.

Brandimonte, M. & Gerbino, W. (1993). Mental image reversal and verbal recoding: when ducks become rabbits. *Memory and Cognition*, *21*, 23–33.

Brandimonte, M., Hitch, G. J. & Bishop, D. (1992). Verbal recoding of visual stimuli impairs mental image transformations. *Memory and Cognition*, *20*, 449–455.

Brooks, L. R. (1967). The suppression of visualisation by reading. *Quarterly Journal of Experimental Psychology*, *19*, 289–299.

Bruyer, R. & Scailquin, J.-C. (1998). The visuo-spatial sketchpad for mental images: testing the multicomponent model of working memory. *Acta Psychologica*, *98*, 17–36.

Burgess, N. & Hitch, G. J. (1992). Towards a network model of the articulatory loop. *Journal of Memory and Language*, *31*(4), 429–460.

Cocude, M. (1988). Generating and maintaining visual images: The incidence of individual and stimulus characteristics. In M. Denis, J. Engelkamp & J. T. E. Richardson (Eds.), *Cognitive and Neuropsychological Approaches to Mental Imagery* (pp. 213–222). Dordrecht: Martinus Nijhoff.

Cowan, N. (1993). Activation, attention, and short-term memory. *Memory and Cognition*, *21*, 162–167.

De Renzi, E. & Nichelli, P. (1975). Verbal and nonverbal short-term memory impairment following hemispheric damage. *Cortex*, *11*, 219–353.

Engelkamp, J., Mohr, G. & Logie, R. H. (1995). Memory for size relations and selective interference. *European Journal of Cognitive Psychology*, *7*(3), 239–260.

Farah, M. J., Hammond, K. M., Levine, D. N. & Calvanio, R. (1988). Visual and spatial mental imagery: dissociable systems of representation. *Cognitive Psychology*, *20*, 439–462.

Finke, R. & Slayton, K. (1988). Explorations of creative visual synthesis in mental imagery. *Memory and Cognition*, *16*, 252–257.

Finke, R., Ward, T. B. & Smith, S. M. (1992). *Creative Cognition: Theory, research, and applications*. Cambridge, MA: MIT Press.

Ghiselin, B. (1952). *The Creative Process*. New York: Mentor.

Glasgow, J. & Papadias, D. (1992). Computational imagery. *Cognitive Science*, *16*, 355–394.

Goldschimdt, G. (1989). Problem representation versus domain of solution in architectural design teaching. *Journal of Architectural and Planning Research*, *6*(3), 204–215.

Guariglia, C., Padovani, A., Pantano, P. & Pizzamiglio, L. (1993). Unilateral neglect restricted to visual imagery. *Nature*, *364*, 235–237.

Hanley, J. R., Young, A. W. & Pearson, N. A. (1991). Impairment of the visuo-spatial sketchpad. *Quarterly Journal of Experimental Psychology*, *43A*, 101–125.

Helstrup, T. & Anderson, R. E. (1991). Imagery in mental construction and decomposition tasks. In R. H. Logie & M. Denis (Eds.), *Mental Images in Human Cognition* (pp. 229–240). Amsterdam: North-Holland.

Helstrup, T. & Anderson, R. E. (1996). On the generality of mental construction in imagery: when bananas become smiles. *European Journal of Cognitive Psychology*, *8*(3), 275–293.

Hue, C. & Ericsson, J. R. (1988). Short-term memory for Chinese characters and radicals. *Memory and Cognition, 16*, 196–205.

Intons-Peterson, M. J. (1996). Linguistic effects in a visual manipulation task. *Psychologische Beitrage, 38*(3/4), 251–278.

Kerr, N. H. (1983). The role of vision in 'visual imagery' experiments: evidence from the congenitally blind. *Journal of Experimental Psychology: General, 112*, 265–277.

Klauer, K. C. & Stegmaier, R. (1997). Interference in immediate spatial memory: shifts of spatial attention or central-executive involvement? *Quarterly Journal of Experimental Psychology, 50A*(1), 79–99.

Kosslyn, S. M. (1974). *Constructing visual images: An exercise in neo-mentalism.* PhD dissertation.

Kosslyn, S. M. (1978). Measuring the visual angle of the mind's eye. *Cognitive Psychology, 10*, 356–389.

Kosslyn, S. M. (1980). *Image and Mind.* Cambridge, MA: Harvard University Press.

Kosslyn, S. M. (1983). *Ghosts in the Mind's Machine.* New York: Norton.

Kosslyn, S. M. (1987). Seeing and imaging in the cerebral hemispheres: a computational approach. *Psychological Review, 94*, 148–175.

Kosslyn, S. M. (1994). *Image and Brain: The resolution of the imagery debate.* Cambridge, MA: MIT Press.

Kosslyn, S. M., PascualLeone, A., Felician, O., Camposano, S., Keenan, J. P., Thompson, W. L., Ganis, G., Sukel, K. E. & Alpert, N. M. (1999). The role of Area 17 in visual imagery: convergent evidence from PET and rTMS. *Science, 284*(5411), 167–170.

Kosslyn, S. M. & Shwartz, S. P. (1977). A simulation of visual imagery. *Cognitive Science, 1*, 265–295.

Kosslyn, S. M. & Shwartz, S. P. (1978). Visual images as spatial representations in active memory. In E. M. Riseman & A. R. Hanson (Eds.), *Computer Vision Systems.* New York: Academic Press.

Logie, R. H. (1986). Visuo-spatial processing in working memory. *Quarterly Journal of Experimental Psychology, 38A*, 229–247.

Logie, R. H. (1995). *Visuo-Spatial Working Memory.* Hove, UK: Lawrence Erlbaum Associates Inc.

Logie, R. H., Della Sala, S., Wynn, V. & Baddeley, A. D. (2000). Visual similarity effects in immediate verbal serial recall. *Quarterly Journal of Experimental Psychology, 53A*(3), 626–646.

Logie, R. H. & Marchetti, C. (1991). Visuo-spatial working memory: Visual, spatial, or central executive? In R. H. Logie & M. Denis (Eds.), *Mental Images in Human Cognition* (pp. 105–115). Amsterdam: North-Holland.

Logie, R. H. & Pearson, D. G. (1997). The inner eye and the inner scribe of visuo-spatial working memory: evidence from developmental fractionation. *European Journal of Cognitive Psychology, 9*(3), 241–257.

Logie, R. H. & Salway, A. F. S. (1990). Working memory and modes of thinking: A secondary task approach. In K. Gilhooly, M. Keane, R. Logie & G. Erdos (Eds.), *Lines of Thinking: Reflections on the psychology of thought, Vol. 2* (pp. 99–113). Chichester, UK: Wiley.

Longoni, A. M. & Scalisi, T. G. (1994). Developmental aspects of phonemic and visual similarity effects — further evidence in Italian children. *International Journal of Behavioral Development*, *17*(1), 57–71.

McConnell, J. & Quinn, J. G. (2000). Interference in visual working memory. *Quarterly Journal of Experimental Psychology*, *53A*(1), 53–67.

Mellet, E., Tzourio, N., Denis, M. & Mazoyer, B. (1995). A positron emission tomography study of visual and mental spatial exploration. *Journal of Cognitive Neuroscience*, *7*(4), 433–445.

Milner, B. (1971). Interhemispheric differences and psychological processes. *British Medical Bulletin*, *27*, 272–277.

Morris, N. (1987). Exploring the visuo-spatial scratch pad. *Quarterly Journal of Experimental Psychology*, *39A*, 409–430.

Morris, R. G. & Morton, N. (1995). Not knowing which way to turn: A specific image transformation impairment dissociated from working memory functioning. In R. Campbell & M. A. Conway (Eds.), *Broken Memories: Case studies in memory impairment* (pp. 170–194). Oxford: Blackwell.

Morton, N. & Morris, R. G. (1995). Image transformation dissociated from visuo-spatial working memory. *Cognitive Neuropsychology*, *12*, 767–791.

Paivio, A. (1975). Neomentalism. *Canadian Journal of Psychology*, *29*, 263–291.

Pearson, D. G. (1999). Mental scanning and spatial processes: a role for an inner scribe? *Current Psychology of Cognition*, *18*(4), 564–573.

Pearson, D. G. & Logie, R. H. (2000). Working memory and mental synthesis. In S. O'Nuallain (Ed.), *Spatial Cognition: Foundations and applications* (pp. 347–359). Amsterdam: John Benjamins Publishing Company.

Pearson, D. G., Logie, R. H. & Gilhooly, K. (1997). The role of working memory and stimulus support during mental synthesis. In T. Helstrup & R. H. Logie (Eds.), *Proceedings of the Sixth European Workshop on Imagery and Cognition*, 21. Oslo: The Norwegian Academy of Science and Letters.

Pearson, D. G., Logie, R. H. & Gilhooly, K. (1999a). Verbal representations and spatial manipulation during mental synthesis. *European Journal of Cognitive Psychology*, *11*(3), 295–314.

Pearson, D. G., Logie, R. H. & Gilhooly, K. (1999b). Conference paper 'Creative synthesis and executive resources: The impact of computer-based stimulus support'. *Proceedings of The British Psychological Society*, *7*(1), 44.

Pearson, D. G., Logie, R. H. & Green, C. (1996). Mental manipulation, visual working memory, and executive processes. *Psychologische Beitrage*, *38*, 324–342.

Phillips, W. A. & Christie, D. F. M. (1977). Components of visual memory. *Quarterly Journal of Experimental Psychology*, *29*, 117–133.

Purcell, A. T. & Gero, J. S. (1998). Drawings and the design process. *Design Studies*, *19*(4), 389–430.

Pylyshyn, Z. W. (1973). What the mind's eye tells the mind's brain: a critique of mental imagery. *Psychological Bulletin*, *80*, 1–24.

Pylyshyn, Z. W. (1981). The imagery debate: analogue media versus tacit knowledge. *Psychological Review*, *87*, 16–45.

Pylyshyn, Z. W. (1984). *Computation and Cognition*. Cambridge, MA: MIT Press.

Quinn, J. G. (1988). Interference effects in the visuo-spatial sketchpad. In M. Denis, J. Engelkamp & J. T. E. Richardson (Eds.), *Cognitive and Neuropsychological Approaches to Mental Imagery* (pp. 181–189). Dordrecht: Martinus Nijhoff.

Quinn, J. G. (1991). Towards a clarification of spatial processing. *Quarterly Journal of Experimental Psychology*, *47A*, 465–480.

Quinn, J. G. & McConnell, J. (1996). Irrelevant pictures in visual working memory. *Quarterly Journal of Experimental Psychology, 49A*(1), 200–215.

Quinn, J. G. & McConnell, J. (1999). Manipulation of interference in the passive visual store. *European Journal of Cognitive Psychology, 11*(3), 373–389.

Quinn, J. G. & Ralston, G. E. (1986). Movement and attention in visual working memory. *Quarterly Journal of Experimental Psychology, 38A*, 689–703.

Reisberg, D. (1996). The nonambiguity of mental images. In C. Cornoldi, R. H. Logie, M. A. Brandimonte, G. Kaufmann & D. Reisberg (Eds.), *Stretching the Imagination: Representation and transformation in mental imagery*. New York: Oxford University Press.

Riddoch, M. J. (1990). Loss of visual imagery: a generation deficit. *Cognitive Neuropsychology, 7*, 249–273.

Salamé, P. & Baddeley, A. D. (1982). Disruption of short-term memory by unattended speech: implications for the structure of working memory. *Journal of Verbal Learning and Verbal Behaviour, 21*, 150–164.

Sims, V. K. & Hegarty, M. (1997). Mental animation in the visuo-spatial sketchpad: evidence from dual-task studies. *Memory and Cognition, 25*(3), 321–332.

Smith, J. D., Reisberg, D. & Wilson, M. (1992). Subvocalization and auditory imagery: Interactions between the inner ear and the inner voice. In D. Reisberg (Ed.), *Auditory Imagery* (pp. 95–119). Hillsdale, NJ: Lawrence Erlbaum Associates Inc.

Smyth, M. M., Pearson, N. A. & Pendleton, L. R. (1988). Movement and working memory: patterns and positions in space. *Quarterly Journal of Experimental Psychology, 40A*, 497–514.

Smyth, M. M. & Pendleton, L. R. (1989). Working memory for movements. *Quarterly Journal of Experimental Psychology, 41A*, 235–250.

Smyth, M. M. & Scholey, K. A. (1994). Interference in spatial immediate memory. *Memory and Cognition, 22*, 1–13.

Suwa, M. & Tversky, B. (1996). What architects see in their sketches: Implications for design tools. In *CHI 96 Companion*. Vancouver, BC, Canada: Association for Computing Machinery.

Tresch, M. C., Sinnamon, H. M. & Seamon, J. G. (1993). Double dissociation of spatial and object visual memory: evidence from selective interference in intact human subjects. *Neuropsychologia, 31*, 211–219.

Vecchi, T., Monticellai, M. L. & Cornoldi, C. (1995). Visuo-spatial working-memory — structures and variables affecting a capacity measure. *Neuropsychologia, 33*(11), 1549–1564.

Verstijnen, I. M., van Leeuwen, C., Goldschimdt, G., Haeml, R. & Hennessey, J. M. (1998a). Sketching and creative discovery. *Design Studies, 19*(4), 519–546.

Verstijnen, I. M., van Leeuwen, C., Goldschimdt, G., Haeml, R. & Hennessey, J. M. (1998b). Creative discovery in imagery and perception: combining is relatively easy, restructuring takes a sketch. *Acta Psychologica, 99*, 177–200.

Walker, P., Hitch, G. J. & Duroe, S. (1993). The effect of visual similarity on short-term memory for spatial location: implications for the capacity of visual short-term memory. *Acta Psychologica, 83*(3), 203–224.

Watson, J. D. (1968). *The Double Helix*. New York: New American Library.

Wolford, G. & Hollingsworth, S. (1974). Evidence that short-term memory is not the limiting factor in tachistoscopic full-report procedure. *Memory and Cognition, 2*, 796–800.

3   The contribution of working memory to conscious experience

Jackie Andrade

Several influential authors have closely identified short-term or working memory with consciousness. William James (1918, pp. 643–689) described memory as a way of bringing back past conscious experiences. In the case of primary memory, there is nothing to bring back because 'it was never lost; its date was never cut off in consciousness from that of the immediately present moment' (1918, p. 647). He argued that our 'effective' consciousness is of material that is retained in primary memory. Likewise, Atkinson and Shiffrin explicitly stated that they 'tend to equate the short-term store with "consciousness", that is, the thoughts and information of which we are currently aware can be considered part of the contents of the short-term store' (1971, p. 83). Baddeley argued that consciousness 'operates through working memory' (1993, p. 21). This chapter introduces some key issues in consciousness studies and discusses the use of the WM model to guide research into conscious experience.

The scientific study of conscious experience is an issue of intense debate. Historically, behaviourists such as Watson (1913) argued that scientists could not and should not study consciousness. From the 1950s onwards, cognitive psychologists overturned the behaviourist ban on consciousness research and explored a range of conscious behaviours such as focused attention (e.g., Broadbent, 1958) and controlled processing (e.g., Norman & Shallice, 1980, 1986; Shiffrin & Schneider, 1977). The central executive of working memory has grown out of this research thus, for example, Baddeley (1986, pp. 224–253) used Norman and Shallice's (1980, 1986) supervisory attentional system as a prototype for the central executive. Chalmers (1996) characterises explaining these conscious behaviours as the very difficult 'easy problem' of consciousness. The even more difficult 'hard problem', according to Chalmers, is to explain why consciousness feels the way it does, or rather, to explain why it feels like anything at all.

Why is explaining conscious experience a hard problem? Imagine looking at a bowl of large ripe strawberries. Your abilities to recognise that they are strawberries, to know they are a type of fruit, to decide to eat one, all pose complex questions for psychology. Current theories of object recognition, semantic memory and decision making help answer those questions but they reveal nothing about why, when we encounter strawberries, we experience redness and a particular sweet summery smell. These qualitative aspects of consciousness, or 'qualia', are hard to explain because there is nothing about our cognitive processing that necessitates the experience that accompanies it. Other aspects of cognition may be reduced to neural activity but conscious experience cannot. It is conceivable that a computer or a zombie can know everything that we know about strawberries and respond to them in an identical way, without ever experiencing them. Indeed, people with the condition known as blindsight can respond quite accurately to visual stimuli yet report no sensation of seeing them (Weiskrantz, 1986).

Conscious experience is also a problem because it is private. Independent, verifiable observation is a keystone of science but we cannot observe someone else's conscious experience. When early Introspectionists claimed that they could or could not think without imagery, the ensuing Imageless Thought controversy was irresolvable because no objective observer could get inside their heads and determine whose report of their mental experience was correct and whose was not. Indeed, to do so would make no sense because from Descartes onwards we have assumed that our conscious experience is indubitable. If both sides in the imageless thought debate were correct, must we assume that conscious experience is too lawless a topic for scientific study? In this chapter I will argue that conscious experience can be studied, that people's reports of their conscious experience can be reliable, predictable and sometimes counter-intuitive, and that research into the cognitive psychology of conscious experience has applications outside the laboratory. I will argue that working memory has proved a useful tool for guiding research into one aspect of consciousness experience, namely vividness of mental imagery, but is not itself an adequate theory of consciousness.

MENTAL IMAGERY AS CONSCIOUS EXPERIENCE

Mental imagery seems a prototypical example of conscious cognition, providing a way of experiencing fictitious events and re-experiencing remembered events. Yet many imagery researchers have largely ignored the experiential aspects of imagery in favour of studying topics such as the similarities between imagery and perception (e.g., Kosslyn, 1994; Segal & Fusella, 1970; Shepard & Metzler, 1971), the nature of the representations underlying visual images (e.g., Anderson, 1978; Pylyshyn, 1973), and the contribution of imagery to verbal learning (e.g., Brooks, 1967; Paivio, 1986). Exceptions include work by Marks (1977) and others on the relationship of individual differences in vividness of imagery to other aspects of cognitive performance.

In contrast to cognitive psychology research, self-reported conscious experience is an important source of data in clinical psychology. For example, recurrent and intrusive images of a traumatic event are a diagnostic symptom of post-traumatic stress disorder (DSM-IV; American Psychiatric Association, 1994). Sometimes these images are so vivid and lifelike ('flash-backs') that people feel they are re-living the event. Brett and Ostroff (1985) argued that imagery was an important factor in the maintenance of post-traumatic stress disorder, triggering avoidance of potentially stressful situations as well as raising anxiety levels. Imagery is used in treatment of anxiety disorders. Imaginal exposure (Wolpe, 1958), in which clients visual-ise fear-provoking situations, is an effective treatment for phobias, causing habituation to the phobic stimulus without the distress caused by in vivo exposure. Imaginal exposure is also effective for treating post-traumatic stress disorder (e.g., Devilly & Spence, 1999). Understanding the cognitive processes underlying vivid imagery may help develop better clinical ther-apies. The next sections of this chapter report some research that aims to bridge the gap between the cognitive study of imagery and the clinical use of imagery. The working memory model has been a valuable tool throughout this research.

THE ROLE OF WORKING MEMORY IN VIVID IMAGERY

Secondary tasks which load the phonological loop, for example concurrent articulation, disrupt auditory imagery as well as verbal short-term memory (Smith, Wilson & Reisberg, 1996). Secondary visual or spatial tasks disrupt visual imagery as well as visual short-term memory. Indeed, as discussed in the previous chapter, current conceptualisations of visuo-spatial working memory have developed through studies of visual imagery as much as through studies of visual memory. Logie, Zucco and Baddeley (1990) demonstrated mutual, modality-specific interference between imagery and short-term memory tasks, suggesting that both make demands on the limited-capacity slave systems of working memory. These studies measured performance on imagery-based tasks. Alan Baddeley and I used similar dual task methods to investigate the role of working memory in parti-cipants' experience of imagery (Baddeley & Andrade, 2000). We began with the simple hypothesis that vivid imagery reflects a rich representation in the appropriate slave system of working memory. We predicted that loading the visuo-spatial sketchpad would selectively reduce the vividness of visual images whereas loading the phonological loop would reduce the vividness of auditory images.

Our experimental procedure on each trial was as follows:

- An imagery stimulus was presented. This could be the actual stimulus that participants were required to image, for example a novel pattern or short tune, or a written verbal cue for an image derived from infor-mation in long-term memory, for example 'imagine a clown juggling' or

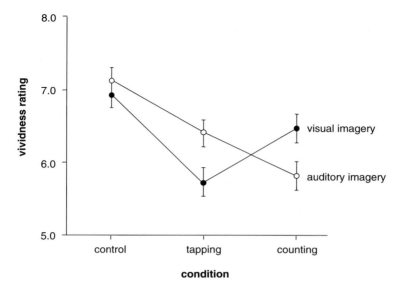

Figure 3.1 Combined data from five experiments showing effects of spatial and verbal concurrent tasks (tapping and counting respectively) on mean rated vividness of visual and auditory imagery, with standard error bars.

'imagine the sound of people laughing'. Participants were instructed to form an image of the stimulus.

- During a 6s retention interval, participants tried to maintain as vivid an image as possible.
- At the end of the retention interval, they rated the vividness of their image on a 0 to 10 scale, where 0 meant that they had no image at all and 10 meant that their image was as clear and vivid as normal hearing or vision.

This procedure was repeated with different imagery stimuli and with concurrent tasks intended to load the sketchpad or phonological loop. Participants were not asked to remember their images (except in Experiment 1), simply to report how vivid they seemed.

As predicted, a concurrent spatial task (tapping a pattern on a keyboard) or visual task (dynamic visual noise, i.e., watching a pattern of flickering dots, see Quinn & McConnell, 1996) selectively reduced the reported vividness of visual images. A concurrent verbal task (counting aloud) selectively reduced the vividness of auditory images (see Figure 3.1). We observed this cross-over interaction when participants were required to image recently presented patterns and tunes and when their images were generated from long-term memory.

Although the interaction between image and secondary task modality was reliable, it tended to be small. Varying the degree to which long-term memory could support imagery generally had a larger effect on vividness. Images of meaningful stimuli such as complete pictures were more vivid than images of nonsense stimuli such as pictures that had been cut up and rearranged. Images of static scenes and repetitive sounds (e.g., a sunset, a clock ticking) were rated as more vivid than images of dynamic scenes and changing sounds (e.g., people running to catch a train, the sound of a zoo at feeding time). Images of ordinary, everyday scenes and sounds were rated as more vivid than bizarre scenes and sounds (e.g., an elephant eating peas, a duck and a chicken debating). A questionnaire indicated that most people expect the opposite, that bizarre and dynamic images will be more vivid than ordinary and static images.

On the basis of these findings, we hypothesised that vivid imagery has two components, a long-term memory component and a working memory component. Repeatedly retrieving sensory information from long-term memory may result in a reasonably vivid image. Challenging the amount of relevant information that can be retrieved in the time available, for example by requiring imagery of bizarre situations, reduces the vividness of the resulting image. Conversely, vividness is increased by reducing the amount of information needed to create a lifelike image, by requiring imagery of simple rather than complex scenes. Working memory enhances vividness in two ways. Active maintenance of information in the slave systems produces an image that is more lifelike because it is continuous. It also allows retrieved information to be recombined and manipulated to create images of novel situations or to elaborate recollected events. For example, if we try to imagine a cat climbing a tree, we may only have a faint recollection of seeing our own cat climb a tree but this faint recollection can be combined in the visuo-spatial sketchpad with generic information about cats and trees, to form a more vivid image. A vivid image therefore requires retrieval of detailed sensory information from long-term memory (or from perception, in the case of very recently presented stimuli) and maintenance or manipulation of that information in the slave systems of working memory.

Whereas we aimed to identify the cognitive processes involved in vivid imagery, others have investigated the content of vivid images. For example, Cornoldi and colleagues tested whether focusing on different aspects of images affected overall ratings of vividness. They found that colour, context, detail, shape or contour, genericity (the extent to which the image represents a generic rather than specific object), and saliency all contributed to vividness ratings. The size of the contribution varied with task conditions, leading Cornoldi et al. to conclude that although vividness may be defined in part as a combination of shape, colour etc., to some extent it 'appears to be a primitive construct corresponding to an immediate subjective experience' (Cornoldi et al., 1992, p. 106). We propose that information about colour, shape and so on is retrieved from long-term memory during a typical imagery task. Working memory provides a workspace for combining that information to create novel, generic or dynamic images according to the task demands. Further, we suspect that an implicit evaluation of the ease of retrieving the relevant information, and of combining it in the manner required, contributes to the general subjective experience of vividness.

EMOTIONAL IMAGERY AND THE VISUO-SPATIAL SKETCHPAD

David Kavanagh and I were interested in applying this analysis to the vivid and often distressing imagery reported in conditions such as post-traumatic stress disorder (PTSD). As mentioned in the introduction to this chapter, people with PTSD often report flashbacks to the traumatic event that are so vivid they feel they are re-living it. These flashbacks are intrusive — once triggered, they seem beyond conscious control. In terms of our two-component analysis of imagery, it appears that retrieval of the relevant sensory information from long-term memory is highly automated, being rapid, complete and resistant to interference. However, the working memory component of traumatic imagery may be more prone to interference, in which case secondary tasks that load the visuo-spatial sketchpad may have a clinical use in treating PTSD.

Our first step was to examine whether emotional changes accompanied changes in image vividness (Andrade, Kavanagh & Baddeley, 1997). To do this, we tested an unselected sample who were asked to rate the vividness of visual images triggered by emotive photographs or personal memories, and to rate their emotional response to those images. We used a predominantly spatial task (tapping a pattern on a keyboard out of sight) and a task providing visual as well as spatial interference (making lateral eye movements to monitor a target appearing on alternate sides of a computer screen). As predicted, both tasks reduced the vividness of visual images, whereas a verbal task (counting aloud) had no effect. When participants recollected happy or distressing experiences, concurrent eye movements reduced their emotional responses as well as reducing image vividness (see Figure 3.2). The tapping task had smaller effects, perhaps because it required only spatial processing whereas the eye movements tasks combined visual and spatial processing.

We chose eye movements as a secondary task because rapid lateral eye movements are a central feature of a treatment for PTSD called Eye Movement Desensitisation-Reprocessing (EMDR; Shapiro, 1989a, 1991). In the original form of EMDR, the client concentrates on the traumatic memory while generating eye movements to track the therapist's finger, which moves rapidly from side to side. Shapiro (1989b) claimed dramatic effects of EMDR, including 'complete desensitization of 75–80% of any individually treated trauma-related memory in a single 50-minute session'

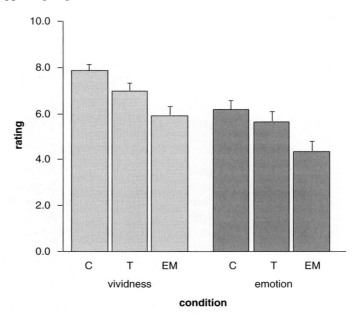

Figure 3.2   Mean vividness of imagery and strength of emotion ratings for personal recollections in dual task conditions, with standard error bars. C = control, i.e., no concurrent task, T = concurrent spatial tapping, EM = concurrent saccadic eye movements.

(p. 221). Case studies by other authors have supported Shapiro's claim (e.g., Lipke & Botkin, 1992; McCann, 1992) but larger scale clinical trials and experimental studies suggest that the eye movement component of EMDR contributes little to its efficacy (Boudewyns & Hyer, 1996). Even Shapiro (1995) no longer holds that eye movements are essential to EMDR, but without eye movements, EMDR is not substantially different from conventional imaginal exposure treatment.

This left us with a puzzle. Imaginal exposure is thought to work partly through habituation to the distress associated with imagery of the traumatic stimulus (Mackintosh, 1987). If eye movements and other visuo-spatial tasks reduce this distress, as our study suggested, then they should impede habituation rather than assist it. As a solution to this puzzle, we suggested that reducing distress in the early stages of treatment may help to maintain a stepwise exposure protocol. Stepwise exposure protocols minimise distress and maximise treatment compliance by focusing on relatively benign images in the early stages of treatment, before progressing to more distressing images. They are difficult to implement with PTSD clients because the relatively benign images used in the early stages tend automatically to elicit full-blown, distressing and vivid images of the trauma. We proposed that eye movements make these intrusive images less distressing, effectively

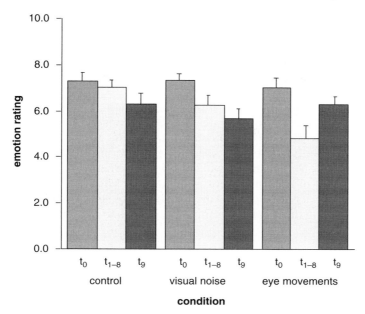

Figure 3.3 Mean strength of emotion ratings at baseline (t_0), during eight exposure trials (t_{1-8}), and at one week follow-up (t_9), with no concurrent task (control), dynamic visual noise, or lateral eye movements during the exposure phase (± standard error).

adding another step in the stepwise protocol (Kavanagh, Freese, Andrade, & May, 2001).

To begin testing this hypothesis, Kavanagh et al. assessed whether eye movements reduce distress at the expense of also reducing desensitisation to emotive images. Undergraduate volunteers selected happy and distressing personal memories and provided baseline vividness and emotion ratings for each. To mimic treatment, they then underwent 'exposure' in which they repeatedly visualised and rated each memory. During exposure, the visualisation task was performed alone (control condition), or with visual interference (dynamic visual noise), or with concurrent lateral eye movements. One week later, participants returned for a follow-up session in which they imaged each memory and again rated its vividness and emotionality.

Compared with the imagery-alone control condition, concurrent eye movements reduced participants' ratings of image vividness and emotion during 'exposure'. Visual interference had an intermediate effect. Vividness and emotion ratings were lower at follow-up than at baseline and did not differ across conditions (see Figure 3.3). This is a preliminary demonstration of eye movements reducing emotional responses to images during 'treatment', without impeding long-term desensitisation to those images. The amount of desensitisation in this study was relatively small, which was not surprising considering the low number of imaginal exposure trials and our use of a non-clinical sample. With more distressing recollections, more exposure trials or a greater degree of interference with imagery, we may have observed differential effects of condition on desensitisation. The finding is interesting nonetheless because it shows that we can temporarily alter conscious experience of emotive imagery without altering the underlying emotional processes that lead to habituation. Eye movements may therefore help clients to tolerate imaginal exposure during treatment sessions without affecting the outcome of treatment. We predict that clients with predominantly auditory images, for example remembering the sound of a crash or people screaming, will benefit from articulatory suppression in the early stages of imaginal exposure treatment. Thus interfering with the appropriate slave system of working memory may help preserve a stepwise protocol, making imaginal exposure a more humane treatment for severely distressed clients.

EVALUATION OF THE WORKING MEMORY MODEL AS A TOOL FOR RESEARCHING EMOTIONAL IMAGERY

Strengths of the WM model

The simplicity of the working memory model made it easy to step from laboratory research to an analysis of EMDR treatment for anxiety disorders, and then to begin testing the accuracy of our analysis in further laboratory studies. Our conclusion, that tasks which load the visuo-spatial sketchpad are a potential response aid in imaginal exposure treatments for anxiety disorders, is potentially important because it draws attention away from eye movements *per se* and towards exploring other tasks that may be more effective because they impose greater or smaller loads on working memory. Using the working memory model also prompted us to rule out a general interference effect by testing the effect of articulatory suppression on emotional visual imagery (Andrade et al., 1997).

Weaknesses of the WM model

Daniel Heap and I (unpublished data) recently investigated the role of the central executive in vividness of imagery. Experiment 1 showed that a putative central executive load, concurrent logical reasoning, substantially reduced rated vividness of imagery, with comparable effects on auditory and visual imagery. Participants in Experiment 2 were asked to generate visual images such as those used by Baddeley and Andrade (2000) and multi-modal images. The multi-modal images were scenes such as 'a bonfire and fireworks' where both the auditory and visual aspects were salient. Participants were asked to rate the overall vividness of the image, considering all the modalities represented in the image. With no concurrent task, the visual and multi-modal images were rated as equally vivid. With a concurrent spatial load, the visual images became less vivid than the multi-modal images. Conversely, with the central executive load, the multi-modal images were less vivid than the visual images.

The lack of specification of central executive function can be problematic, both for choosing experimental tasks and for interpreting data. We chose the logical reasoning task because it was used by Baddeley and Hitch (1974) as a task which loaded working memory and, as their data subsequently showed, had little verbal short-term memory requirement. However, as it is a complex task, like many tasks used to load executive function, our data could be interpreted as showing an effect of task difficulty rather than a selective central executive involvement in imagery. If we accept the logical reasoning task as an executive load, then our data suggest that multi-modal imagery is particularly demanding of central executive resources. They raise questions about the role of the central executive in imagery. We propose that the large effect of the executive load on multi-modal imagery reflects the need to combine sensory information stored temporarily in the visuo-spatial sketchpad and phonological loop. However, both experiments also suggest that executive processes are important for vivid imagery even when there is no requirement to blend information from the two slave systems. Our study did not address whether the important processes were those of retrieving sensory information from long-term memory, of actively maintaining that information as a conscious representation, or of preventing competing information becoming conscious. All these processes may be part of a general central executive (e.g., see Baddeley, 1996) but two areas of vagueness in the working memory model make it difficult to predict specific effects of central executive loads on vivid imagery. The first weakness of the model from this viewpoint is that it does not clearly specify the role of the central executive in rehearsal mechanisms. David Pearson, in the preceding chapter, suggests that the central executive plays a critical part in actively maintaining conscious visual representations during imagery tasks. The second weakness is the uncertainty about the unitary nature of the central executive — should imagery researchers seek to interfere selectively with image maintenance, retrieval from long-term memory, or blending of auditory and visual representations, or should they explore the effects of more general central executive loads on imagery?

The working memory model has another weakness for investigating emotional imagery, namely that it offers no explanation of the relationship between memory and emotion. To explore further the effect of secondary tasks on habituation to traumatic images, we need an account of the link between image vividness and image emotionality. Working memory offers no such account, nor was it ever intended to, therefore future researchers in this area may need to turn to a broader theory such as Barnard's Interacting Cognitive Subsystems (Barnard, 1985, 1999; see chapter 12, this volume).

Competing approaches

Kosslyn's (1994) theory of visual imagery, described by David Pearson in the preceding chapter, offers strong competition to the WM model as an explanation of visual imagery. Both theories propose that images are stored in a short-term buffer, the visual buffer in Kosslyn's theory and the visuo-spatial sketchpad in working memory. The extent to which this buffer is considered an active, conscious process varies. Kosslyn assumes that the visual buffer is passive, material in it being acted upon by attentional image transforming processes. Pearson argues for a passive visual cache serving a temporary storage function, plus a visual buffer. Representations in the visual buffer are conscious and subject to transformation by central executive processes. Baddeley's (1986) concept of the visuo-spatial sketch-pad seems less clear: the phonological loop and visuo-spatial sketchpad were proposed as storage systems supporting the central executive, but the assumption that the visuo-spatial sketchpad is involved in visual imagery raises the question of whether it is involved in all aspects of imagery, including image generation and manipulation, or whether some imagery tasks are performed by the central executive. In contrast, Kosslyn specifies the processes involved in visual imagery in sufficient detail for them to be implemented on a computer. As a description of the cognitive processes involved in visual imagery, Kosslyn's theory is far more comprehensive than working memory and has the advantage that it clearly links imagery with perception.

However, Kosslyn's theory has some drawbacks as a tool for researching imagery. His theory only concerns visual imagery but it seems likely that auditory and visual imagery have processes in common. Many people report that they can imagine sounds and scenes simultaneously. Kosslyn's theory gives no directions for researching multi-modal imagery whereas the working memory model points to exploring interactions between image modality and secondary task modality as a starting point for researching the shared and separate aspects of visual and auditory imagery. The research by Baddeley and Andrade described above showed consistent cross-over interactions that we took to be the signature of working memory involvement in imagery.

Future of the WM model for vividness of imagery research

One could argue that the WM model has done little more than point us towards using dual task methods to research imagery. However, although this was our starting point, the model offers more extensive guidance for future research. It raises questions about how the memory processes of temporary storage and rehearsal contribute to imagery. Does maintenance of a vivid image require rehearsal or merely storage capacity? How do rehearsal mechanisms contribute to imagery of dynamic scenes? How does the central executive interact with the slave systems during image generation and manipulation? These questions provide a stimulus for future research but under-specification of the model makes some of them hard to address. Future use of the WM model for imagery research will benefit from a more detailed specification of central executive function and of visuo-spatial rehearsal processes. However, the current simplicity of the model has been advantageous for starting to tease apart the cognitive processes underlying emotional imagery and desensitisation treatments.

EVALUATION OF THE WORKING MEMORY MODEL AS A TOOL FOR RESEARCHING CONSCIOUSNESS

The strengths of the WM model for researching consciousness are partly due to its central place in cognitive psychology. This strong foundation means that discoveries from WM-guided research into conscious phenomena will be more easily integrated into our current knowledge of cognition. Understanding how consciousness arises from and interacts with other aspects of cognition is potentially more useful than a theory of consciousness alone. A weakness of the WM model is that, although short-term memory has been equated with consciousness, the relationship or identity with consciousness is not specified in the model. Another weakness is that demonstrating a role of working memory in conscious phenomena is not the same as showing that working memory immediately causes those phenomena. This problem is not unique to working memory, as discussed below.

Strengths and weaknesses of the WM model

The research reported in this chapter shows that conscious experience — in this case vividness of mental imagery — can be studied using conventional techniques such as dual task methods. The results were consistent, sometimes counter-intuitive (showing that volunteers were not just responding to the demand characteristics of the experiments), and supported the hypothesis that images would be most vivid when they were maintained in the appropriate slave system of working memory.

Although we have shown that loading the subsystems of working memory alters immediate conscious experience, it would be wrong to infer from this that working memory offers a good model of conscious experience. It is a useful tool for consciousness research, helping conceptualise the cognitive processes needed for consciousness. In this vein, Baddeley (1993) presents a speculative framework for thinking about consciousness. He considers the evolutionary significance of abilities to bind together information from different sensory channels, to retrieve and reflect upon information stored in long-term memory, and to use such information to imagine the future. These are abilities which have been attributed to working memory. They are also examples of what Block calls 'Access Consciousness' (1995), rather than of conscious experience. Baddeley's framework offers no explanation of why they are associated with the conscious experiences of perceiving, remembering or imagining. Although we have found that working memory processes enhance image vividness, we still cannot explain why representations maintained in working memory are conscious at all. The 'hard problem' remains a hard problem.

Can the WM model help answer easier questions about consciousness? For example, can we say that, because images are more vivid if held in the slave systems, then working memory is the seat of consciousness? This is an instance of a pervasive problem in consciousness research. Much of this research aims to identify neural correlates of consciousness, i.e., those brain processes that are always active during consciousness of a particular stimulus and never active in the absence of consciousness. The problem is that any aspect of consciousness has many correlates. For those who favour 'multiple drafts' accounts of consciousness, where consciousness is the combined effect of widespread brain activity at any moment (Dennett, 1991), identifying the many correlates of consciousness is a satisfying outcome of research. However, for those who want to know which aspect of neural activity is most essential for consciousness, there is the problem of identifying which of many correlates is the 'proximal cause' (e.g., Hardcastle, 2000, p. 261), the one that most immediately causes conscious experience. Working memory research raises a similar problem. It has helped identify some cognitive correlates of consciousness but we do not yet know which correlate is the proximal cause of, say, conscious experience of imagery. Finding that manipulations of working memory alter consciousness does not imply that working memory is consciousness. Working memory processes may simply contribute to conscious processing occurring elsewhere, just as opening one's eyes causes consciousness of daylight because of mediating cognitive processes, and not because the eyes are the seat of consciousness. In the case of mental imagery, reducing the quality of representation in the slave systems may mean that there is less information to feed other conscious processes.

It may be more tempting to think of the central executive as the seat of consciousness because it is involved in many aspects of conscious cognition such as selective and focused attention, decision making, strategy selection. However, from an evolutionary viewpoint, it seems essential that consciousness is a stimulus-driven process as well as the result of top-down executive processing. Work on attentional biases in anxiety (e.g., Mathews, May, Mogg & Eysenck, 1991) shows that threatening or other salient stimuli 'grab' attention even when they are irrelevant to the task in hand. Sometimes these stimuli break through to consciousness, as when we hear someone mention our name in a noisy environment, even though we are attending to another conversation (Moray, 1959). It seems implausible that a central executive busy sharing resources, switching strategies and focusing attention can also be responsible for our conscious experience of salient stimuli in a background of unattended, task-irrelevant noise. However, it could be the case that the salient stimulus becomes a content of the central executive because of lower level attentional processes concerned with perceptual selection rather than control of attention. Future attempts at answering questions such as 'Can we be conscious of a stimulus that is not currently stored or processed in working memory?' and 'Can we be conscious of stimuli in the slave systems of working memory but not currently subject to executive processing?' may help clarify the relationship between working memory, attention and consciousness.

Competing approaches

Baars has addressed exactly this issue. He suggests that 'Working memory is closely associated with conscious experience, though not identical to it' (Baars, 1997a, p. 175). He describes attention as a mechanism for controlling access to consciousness (Baars, 1997b). Working memory and attention are both sets of processes which enable consciousness. Baars (1997a) encourages us to think of consciousness in terms of a theatre. Just as unseen workers help run a real theatre, dress the actors, cue their lines and so on, so the unconscious processes of syntax analysis, visual boundary analysis, semantic processing etc. are the stagehands of the theatre of consciousness. There are actors on the stage but we only see the actor currently in the spotlight. Working memory is the stage of consciousness, representations in working memory are the actors on the stage. Any of the actors could step into the spotlight but they wait until chosen by the stage director. Likewise the contents of working memory compete to become conscious but usually fail unless selected by central executive processes. Thus the central executive controls which of the potentially conscious representations in the slave systems of working memory becomes conscious, but it is not consciousness itself. It is the theatre director, not the leading performer. Baars' analysis raises the question of who or what sees the actor in the spotlight? His answer is everyone else — that 'actor' is now public property. Conscious representations are available to other processes, whether those processes be fringe conscious (on the stage, in working memory, but not illuminated) or unconscious (stagehands behind the scenes). Consciousness breaks the modularity of mind, enabling us to evaluate information, discuss our thoughts, report our feelings and beliefs.

In Baars' framework, central executive processes strongly influence conscious experience, for example by keeping imaginal representations sufficiently active that they remain conscious, or by inhibiting other information so it does not gain the spotlight. John Teasdale and his colleagues (Teasdale et al., 1995) demonstrated an example of this, observing that when a task had been practised enough for it to be performed automatically, the relaxation of executive control was associated with a change in conscious experience, namely an increase in daydreaming.

Future of the WM model for consciousness research

Baars' framework suggests that one way forward for working memory research is to divorce attention and consciousness from the executive tasks of strategy selection, task co-ordination, retrieval from long-term memory, binding together of visual and auditory information into single coherent representation, etc. The central executive has enough to do managing the actors without having to move the spotlight. Perhaps it is unparsimonious to hypothesise a spotlight of consciousness as well as a central executive? I think not, because 'executive' tasks are separable, and do not always mutually interfere (Lehto, 1996; see chapters 11 and 13 in this volume). Before equating the central executive with consciousness, we need to decide which central executive we are talking about.

CONCLUSION

Working memory has been valuable for exploring the cognitive correlates of consciousness, those cognitive processes which underlie conscious experience. To understand working memory is to understand some of the necessary conditions for consciousness, although it does not help explain why those conditions produce conscious experience. The simplicity of the working memory model, and the fact that it incorporates both visual and verbal processes, make it easy to apply to real life situations. An important question for future research is whether we are always conscious of the contents of working memory. If we are, the most parsimonious explanation might be that working memory is the set of processes which produce the function and experience we call consciousness. An additional 'spotlight' of consciousness may in that case be unnecessary. However, Pearson's analysis of visual imagery suggests that non-conscious representations stored in the visual cache aid the creation of a conscious image but are not themselves conscious. If this analysis is correct, then we need to explain the mechanism by which the contents of working memory become conscious. Future research should examine how working memory relates to attention and consciousness, rather than trying to subsume those phenomena within the WM model.

ACKNOWLEDGEMENTS

I am grateful to David Kavanagh, John Towse and David Pearson for their helpful comments on earlier drafts of this chapter.

BACKGROUND READING

Baars, B. (1988). *A Cognitive Theory of Consciousness*. New York: Cambridge University Press.
Baars, B. (1997). *In the Theater of Consciousness: The workspace of the mind*. New York: Oxford University Press.

These books expound the theatre metaphor of consciousness and explain Baars' Global Workspace theory of consciousness.

Hardcastle, V. G. (2000). How to understand the N in NCC. In T. Metzinger (Ed.), *Neural Correlates of Consciousness: Empirical and conceptual questions* (pp. 259–264). Cambridge, MA: MIT Press.

This chapter discusses the conceptual problem of identifying proximal causes of consciousness.

REFERENCES

American Psychiatric Association (1994). *Diagnostic and Statistical Manual of Mental Disorders*, 4th edition. Washington, DC: American Psychiatric Press.
Anderson, J. R. (1978). Arguments concerning representations from mental imagery. *Psychological Review*, 89, 249–277.
Andrade, J., Kavanagh, D. & Baddeley, A. D. (1997). Eye-movements and visual imagery: a working memory approach to the treatment of post-traumatic stress disorder. *British Journal of Clinical Psychology*, 36, 209–223.
Atkinson, R. C. & Shiffrin, R. M. (1971). The control of short-term memory. *Scientific American*, 225, 82–90.
Baars, B. (1997a). *In the Theater of Consciousness: The workspace of the mind*. New York: Oxford University Press.
Baars, B. (1997b). Some essential differences between consciousness and attention, perception, and working memory. *Consciousness and Cognition*, 6, 363–371.
Baddeley, A. D. (1986). *Working Memory*. Oxford: Oxford University Press.
Baddeley, A. D. (1993). Working memory and conscious awareness. In A. F. Collins, S. E. Gathercole, M. A. Conway & P. E. Morris (Eds.), *Theories of Memory* (pp. 11–28). Hove, UK: Lawrence Erlbaum Associates Ltd.
Baddeley, A. D. (1996). Exploring the central executive. *Quarterly Journal of Experimental Psychology*, 49A, 5–28.
Baddeley, A. D. & Andrade, J. (2000). Working memory and the vividness of imagery. *Journal of Experimental Psychology: General*, 129(1), 126–145.

Baddeley, A. D. & Hitch, G. J. (1974). Working memory. In G. Bower (Ed.), *The Psychology of Learning and Motivation, Vol. VIII* (pp. 47–90). New York: Academic Press.

Barnard, P. J. (1985). Interacting cognitive subsystems: A psycholinguistic approach to short-term memory. In A. Ellis (Ed.), *Progress in the Psychology of Language, Vol. 2* (pp. 197–258). London: Lawrence Erlbaum Associates Ltd.

Barnard, P. J. (1999). Interacting Cognitive subsystems: Modelling working memory phenomena within a multiprocessor architecture. In A. Miyake & P. Shah (Eds.), *Models of Working Memory: Mechanisms of active maintenance and executive control* (pp. 298–339). Cambridge, UK: Cambridge University Press.

Block, N. (1995). On a confusion about a function of consciousness. *Behavioral and Brain Sciences, 18*, 227–247.

Boudewyns, P. A. & Hyer, L. (1996). Eye movement desensitization and reprocessing (EMDR) as treatment for post-traumatic stress disorder (PTSD). *Clinical Psychology and Psychotherapy, 3*, 185–195.

Brett, E. A. & Ostroff, R. (1985). Imagery and post-traumatic stress disorder: an overview. *American Journal of Psychiatry, 142*, 417–424.

Broadbent, D. E. (1958). *Perception and Communication.* Oxford: Pergamon Press.

Brooks, L. R. (1967). The suppression of visualization by reading. *Quarterly Journal of Experimental Psychology, 19*, 289–299.

Chalmers, D. (1996). *The Conscious Mind.* Oxford: Oxford University Press.

Cornoldi, C., de Beni, R., Cavedon, A., Mazzoni, G., Giusberti, F. & Marucci, F. (1992). How can a vivid image be described? Characteristics influencing vividness judgements and the relationship between vividness and memory. *Journal of Mental Imagery, 16*(3–4), 89–108.

Dennett, D. (1991). *Consciousness Explained.* Boston: Little, Brown & Co.

Devilly, G. J. & Spence, S. H. (1999). The relative efficacy and treatment distress of EMDR and a cognitive behavioral trauma treatment protocol in the amelioration of posttraumatic stress disorder. *Journal of Anxiety Disorders, 13*, 131–157.

Hardcastle, V. G. (2000). How to understand the N in NCC. In T. Metzinger (Ed.), *Neural Correlates of Consciousness: Empirical and conceptual questions* (pp. 259–264). Cambridge, MA: MIT Press.

James, W. (1918). *The Principles of Psychology, Vol. I.* London: Macmillan & Co. Ltd. (Original work published 1890.)

Kavanagh, D., Freese, S., Andrade, J. & May, J. (2001). Effects of visuo-spatial tasks on desensitization to emotive memories. *British Journal of Clinical Psychology, 40*.

Kosslyn, S. M. (1994). *Image and Brain: The resolution of the imagery debate.* Cambridge, MA: MIT Press.

Lehto, J. (1996). Are executive function tests dependent on working memory capacity? *Quarterly Journal of Experimental Psychology, 49A*(1), 29–50.

Lipke, H. J. & Botkin, A. L. (1992). Case studies of eye movement desensitisation and reprocessing (EMD-R) with chronic post-traumatic stress disorder. *Psychotherapy, 29*, 591–595.

Logie, R. H., Zucco, G. M. & Baddeley, A. D. (1990). Interference with visual short-term memory. *Acta Psychologica, 75*, 55–74.

Mackintosh, N. J. (1987). Neurobiology, psychology and habituation. *Behaviour Research and Therapy, 25*, 81–97.

Marks, D. F. (1977). Imagery and consciousness: a theoretical review from an individual differences perspective. *Journal of Mental Imagery*, *1*, 275–290.

Mathews, A., May, J., Mogg, K. & Eysenck, M. (1991). Attentional bias in anxiety: selective search or defective filtering? *Journal of Abnormal Psychology*, *99*, 166–173.

McCann, D. L. (1992). Post-traumatic stress disorder due to devastating burns overcome by a single session of eye movement desensitization. *Journal of Behaviour Therapy and Experimental Psychiatry*, *23*(4), 319–323.

Moray, N. (1959). Attention in dichotic listening: affective cues and the influence of instructions. *Quarterly Journal of Experimental Psychology*, *11*, 56–60.

Norman, D. A. & Shallice, T. (1980). Attention to action: Willed and automatic control of behavior. *University of California San Diego CHIP Technical Report no. 99.*

Norman, D. A. & Shallice, T. (1986). Attention to action: Willed and automatic control of behavior. In R. J. Davidson, G. E. Schwartz & D. Shapiro (Eds.), *Consciousness and Self-regulation* (pp. 1–18). New York: Plenum.

Paivio, A. (1986). *Mental Representations: A dual coding approach.* Oxford: Oxford University Press.

Pylyshyn, Z. W. (1973). What the mind's eye tells the mind's brain. *Psychological Bulletin*, *80*, 1–24.

Quinn, J. G. & McConnell, J. (1996). Irrelevant pictures in visual working memory. *Quarterly Journal of Experimental Psychology*, *49A*(1), 200–215.

Segal, S. J. & Fusella, V. (1970) Influence of imaged pictures and sounds on detection of visual and auditory signals. *Journal of Experimental Psychology*, *83*, 458–464.

Shapiro, F. (1989a). Eye movement desensitization: a new treatment for post-traumatic stress disorder. *Journal of Behaviour Therapy and Experimental Psychiatry*, *20*, 211–217.

Shapiro, F. (1989b). Efficacy of the eye movement desensitization procedure in the treatment of traumatic memories. *Journal of Traumatic Stress Studies*, *2*, 199–223.

Shapiro, F. (1991). Eye movement desensitization and reprocessing procedure: from EMD to EMDR — A new model for anxiety and related trauma. *Behaviour Therapist*, *14*, 133–135.

Shapiro, F. (1995). *Eye Movement Desensitization and Reprocessing: Basic principles, protocols and procedures.* New York: Guilford.

Shepard, R. N. & Metzler, J. (1971). Mental rotation of three-dimensional objects. *Science*, *171*, 701–703.

Shiffrin, R. M. & Schneider, W. (1977). Controlled and automatic human information processing: II. Perceptual learning, automatic attending, and a general theory. *Psychological Review*, *84*, 127–190.

Smith, J. D., Wilson, M. & Reisberg, D. (1996). The role of subvocalization in auditory imagery. *Neuropsychologia*, *33*, 1433–1454.

Teasdale, J. D., Dritschel, B. H., Taylor, M. J., Proctor, L., Lloyd, C. A., Nimmo-Smith, I. & Baddeley, A. D. (1995). Stimulus-independent thought depends on central executive resources. *Memory and Cognition*, *23*, 551–559.

Watson, J. B. (1913). Psychology as the behaviorist views it. *Psychological Review*, *20*, 158–177.

Weiskrantz, L. (1986). *Blindsight: A case study and its implications*. Oxford: Oxford University Press.

Wolpe, J. (1958). *Psychotherapy by Reciprocal Inhibition*. Stanford, CA: Stanford University Press.

4 Language processing and working memory: A developmental perspective

Anne-Marie Adams and Catherine Willis

The central problem in accounting for the acquisition of language is to explain how a child is able to master the extremely complex series of rules that prescribe the possible combinations of linguistic elements making up the language to which the child is exposed. The response from the nativist tradition has been to propose that the linguistically described rule system is so complex that learning it presents an impossible task and hence at least some description of these rules must be innately given (e.g. Chomsky, 1965, 1986). The child is therefore characterised as a passive recipient of language experience and acquirer of linguistic knowledge. Constructivist approaches to language acquisition offer alternative accounts which propose a more active role for the child (see Messer, 1994 for an overview). Such approaches attribute significance to factors external to the child, for example aspects of the linguistic experience such as the surface form of the language, including its prosodic and phonological nature, the social context and the pragmatic functions of communication. Factors internal to the child are also considered to be instrumental in language acquisition, for example the individual's relative sensitivity to the physical form of the language, thereby emphasising skills such as phonological perception and prosodic awareness (e.g. Vihman, 1996), and their preferred manner of relating language to experience (e.g. Nelson, 1973).

This emphasis on the child's experience of the language input and the role of features internal to the child in learning a language, compels a description of the underlying cognitive mechanisms and resources that these imply. Such a description, together with a statement of how these factors may impinge on language learning, would constitute an information-processing account of language development. To date, however, very little research investigating language development has focused on describing the putative underlying cognitive processes.

The present chapter considers whether working memory, specifically the fractionated account originally proposed by Baddeley and Hitch (1974) and later developed by Baddeley (1986), offers a valid account of the cognitive processes which may underlie language acquisition. The chapter begins by presenting evidence of an association between the phonological component of the fractionated model of working memory (henceforth PWM) and children's language development, and introduces the proposal that this association reflects the role of PWM in the long-term learning of phonological representations. The concordance between this proposed role and some constructivist models of language acquisition is highlighted. We then consider possible alternative accounts of the association, including the converse view that the association reflects the influence of mechanisms of the language system on verbal short-term memory task performance. A further possible account, that the association between PWM and language may reflect limitations in a more general working memory resource is assessed using evidence from a competing (typically North American) tradition of working memory research. Finally, the efficacy of the fractionated model is evaluated through the central questions of this volume.

PHONOLOGICAL MEMORY AND THE ACQUISITION OF LINGUISTIC KNOWLEDGE

The association between PWM and language development

The model of short-term memory proposed by Baddeley and Hitch in 1974 was postulated as a working memory — a short-term memory that is heavily involved in everyday cognitive functioning. The model comprises three distinct components: the visuo-spatial sketchpad, the phonological loop and the central executive (see chapter 1). Very early in the endeavour to determine the areas of everyday cognitive functioning in which working memory was involved, researchers examined the intuitive proposal that the phonological component of working memory (PWM) was implicated in processing speech. Although work with adults indicated that PWM was not involved in skilled language processing (e.g. Shallice, 1988 for a review), recent studies have shown a strong and reliable association between PWM and language skills in children. Indeed much evidence has been accrued to support the contention that PWM may play an important role in *learning* language (see Baddeley, Gathercole & Papagno, 1998 for a review). Illustrative studies that have investigated the association between PWM and language development including both vocabulary and morpho-syntactic knowledge in children are presented next.

Children's phonological memory skills are associated with their vocabulary knowledge, such that children who perform better on PWM tasks also tend to have better receptive and expressive vocabularies (Adams & Gathercole, 1995, 2000; Gathercole & Adams, 1993, 1994; Gathercole, Hitch, Service, & Martin, 1997). Children grouped on the basis of their PWM performance also demonstrate differences in their knowledge of morpho-syntactic constructions, again evident in both their comprehension and production of language. Willis (1997) showed that four-year-old children with better PWM understood a wider range of syntactic constructions than did children with poorer PWM. Groups of children aged between three and five years similarly classified as having either relatively good or poor PWM, could also be distinguished in terms of their morpho-syntactic profiles (Adams & Gathercole, 1995, 2000). The speech of children with relatively good PWM comprised longer utterances, in terms of the mean number of morphemes per utterance, and included a wider range of syntactic constructions than did the speech of children classified as having relatively poor PWM skills. There is also some evidence, albeit inconclusive, that this association may not extend to the visuo-spatial component of the fractionated model of working memory (Adams & Gathercole, 2000).

Despite the wide variation in language abilities seen in these studies, none of the children were identified as having problems with language development — all had language skills that were appropriate for their age. Similar associations between PWM and language development are, however, also evident in children with disordered language development (e.g. Gathercole & Baddeley, 1990; Gillam, Cowan & Day, 1995; Montgomery, 1996). Although beset by problems of the heterogeneity of the samples and issues of the appropriate comparison group, the PWM deficit of such children has proved to be a robust finding. It may also be that this language/memory association persists in a broader range of developmental conditions (see chapter 6, this volume).

The role of PWM in the long-term learning of phonological representations

What mechanisms might underpin this association between PWM and language development? Baddeley et al. (1998) concluded that this relationship reflected differences in the quality of temporary phonological representations that could be maintained in working memory, since the construction of long-term phonological representations depended on such temporary storage. While accepting that an exact account of the mechanism by which such long-term knowledge may be consolidated remains unspecified, they drew comparisons with the Brown and Hulme (1996) computational model of verbal short-term memory whereby both computational and evolutionary advantage may be gained by postulating a temporary representational system which is able to represent experiences rapidly so that they can be compared to prior knowledge. This affords not only the ability to identify novel stimuli which diverge from long-term representations, but also an efficient means of learning the consistencies in the environment without the need to consolidate every aspect of each experience.

How might this mechanism be influential in morpho-syntactic development? Just as PWM may be required to consolidate long-term phonological representations of new lexical items in vocabulary acquisition, similar processes may be available which detail the phonological form of syntactic constructions. Speidel (1989, 1993; Speidel & Herreshoff, 1989) proposed that variations in the efficiency of interdependent articulatory and phonological memory processes governed the child's ability to imitate and create long-term memory phonological representations of morpho-syntactic constructions produced by adults. These representations are then used as templates for the syntactic structure of intended utterances. Language development was proposed to reflect both the quantity and the quality of this corpus of grammatical forms. By this account, children with better PWM would be able to imitate, create and commit to long-term memory, lengthier and more exact representations of the speech they hear. The evidence that children who have better PWM skills not only understand a greater number of syntactic constructions in comprehension tasks, but also include a wider range of syntactic constructions in their spontaneous speech is entirely consistent with this view.

How long-term phonological knowledge may affect language development

PWM may therefore be involved in the construction of long-term phonological representations which underpin the acquisition of both lexical and morpho-syntactic forms. However, learning the purported complex series of abstract rules that dictate the permissible forms of linguistic elements is often presented as a qualitatively different task. Nevertheless, some constructivist theories of language acquisition do argue that the child's ability to attend to the surface structure of the language they hear, and perhaps more importantly to retain this phonological information, plays an instrumental role in 'bootstrapping' the child to syntactic competence. A sample of such work from a range of theoretical perspectives on language acquisition is presented next.

Construction grammar

Rather than proposing that language merely reflects abstract knowledge of the rules of formal linguistics, construction grammar (e.g. Goldberg, 1995) proposes that all the elements of linguistic form are represented as diverse items (constructions) within a single lexicon. Thus the lexicon contains not only lexical items as commonly proposed (words) but also bound morphemes and phrase structures. A corollary of this assertion is that a single mechanism is postulated to underlie the acquisition of both words and grammar (for empirical evidence consistent with this view see Marchman & Bates, 1994). Thus an ability to retain the phonological form of the language input may underpin not only lexical development but morpho-syntactic knowledge in the form of constructions too.

Connectionist learning

Connectionist accounts of language acquisition also propose that children's progression towards performance which more accurately reflects adult linguistic patterns may be explicable in terms of general principles of learning without the need to stipulate prior (i.e. innate) knowledge of linguistic categories or rules. For example the network of Plunkett and Marchman (1993) accounted for both lexical and grammatical development within a single learning mechanism. These findings can also be interpreted as attributing a central role in language development to the acquisition of a body of knowledge about the surface form of language. In the Plunkett and Marchman (1993) model, the characteristic shift from early competence with both regular and irregular forms of the past tense to overgeneralisation of the suffix with overextensions to irregular forms, was dependent on the size of the lexicon the system had acquired. This pattern was explained in terms of a 'critical mass' hypothesis — when and only when the data set is sufficiently large to extract general patterns, does a pattern of language use (overgeneralisation) appear which suggests the application of linguistic rules. Language acquisition may therefore be explicable in terms of the general principles of a gradual learning mechanism which results in long-term memory representations of the input from which linguistic competance may be derived. The hypothesised role of PWM in the acquisition of long-term phonological knowledge should perhaps be considered as one account of this learning mechanism.

Distributional analysis of language

The importance of experience with and knowledge of the surface form of language is emphasised in yet another perspective on language acquisition. There is increasing evidence that it may be possible to derive linguistic knowledge from a statistical analysis of the language input. Although previously believed to be a prohibitively complex task, Saffran, Newport and Aslin (1996) demonstrated that when learning an artificial language, adults were able to take account of the differences in transitional probabilities between sequences of sounds within words compared to those which spanned word boundaries. Adults were therefore able to discriminate sequences of sounds which formed words even when presented with only acoustic input and no other cues to word boundaries. Saffran et al. (1996) proposed that similar distributional analytic techniques may be available to infants, who certainly do prefer to listen to the prosodic and syntactic patterns of their native language over those of other languages (Jusczyk, Friederici, Wessels, Svenkerud, & Jusczyk, 1993), and that these skills would aid the acquisition of certain aspects of morphology. Thus distributional analyses of language may also be interpreted as evidence that sensitivity to and the ability to exploit the phonological form of language, which allows one to derive long-term knowledge (even if implicit) about its consistencies and regularities, may be an important feature of language acquisition.

Unanalysed holistic phrases

Naturalistic assessments of child language have provided empirical evidence that for some children their utterances may simply be the repetition of unanalysed holistic phrases, and that this may be one route to gaining linguistic competence (Pine & Lieven, 1993; Lieven, Pine & Baldwin, 1997). Pine and Lieven (1993) proposed that some of the phrases children produced were merely imitated and therefore unanalysed (i.e. they had not been constructed using syntactic rules), since there was little evidence of their productive use across a range of lexical items. Lieven et al. (1997) suggested that the syntactic constructions represented by such phrases were only gradually generalised to other appropriate lexical items. In their account of language acquisition, therefore, grammatical development evolves from a corpus of rote-learned phrases. It is entirely possible that PWM may be required to construct and retain long-term representations of such unanalysed phrases.

To summarise, the phonological component of the fractionated model of working memory is indeed a potentially viable account of how a corpus of grammatical constructions, perhaps evident in the holistic phrases identified in children's speech, may be learned. Phonological working memory may also serve as the mechanism which determines the rate of acquisition or representational quality of phonological knowledge that is crucial in distributional analyses of language and hypothesised in connectionist models of the language acquisition process.

COMPETING INTERPRETATIONS OF THE ASSOCIATION BETWEEN PWM AND LANGUAGE

The influence of long-term knowledge on PWM

Thus far our interpretation of the association between PWM and language has been that a child with an impaired ability to retain phonological information in short-term memory is likely to be at a disadvantage when trying to learn new words and syntactic constructions. A plausible alternative, however, is that poor language skills impair performance in verbal short-term memory tasks (e.g. van der Lely & Howard, 1993; Howard & van der Lely, 1995). In support of this position performance on PWM tasks has indeed been shown to be influenced by long-term knowledge at both the lexical (Hulme, Maughan & Brown, 1991) and the sub-lexical (Gathercole, 1995) level. This suggests that aspects of PWM tasks other than their mnemonic component should be considered when analysing the relationship between these tasks and language development. For example, the language difficulties of children with disordered language development may originate in phonological processing difficulties (e.g. the ability to perceive, combine or articulate phonemes) and be a direct cause of their poor PWM performance (Snowling, Chiat & Hulme, 1991).

Investigation of this position from within the fractionated working memory tradition, whilst not discounting the importance of phonological processing skills and long-term knowledge in supporting PWM performance, has generally concluded that a substantial proportion of the PWM/language association rests on the ability to maintain phonological representations in short-term memory. This work has been conducted with children both with disordered (Edwards & Lahey, 1998; Gillam, Cowan & Marler, 1998) and non-disordered language development (Gathercole et al., 1997; Gathercole, Hitch, Service, Adams & Martin, 1999).

To illustrate the point one such study will be described in more detail. Gathercole and Pickering (1999) employed a technique devised to obtain separate estimates of the extent to which the serial recall of words and non-words of both high- and low-probability phoneme combinations reflected (a) the capacity of the phonological store, and (b) the contribution of long-term knowledge of lexical items and the phonotactic probabilities of the language (Gathercole, Frankish, Pickering & Peaker, 1999). Children grouped in terms of their vocabulary knowledge (either relatively good or relatively poor) were assessed on these serial recall tasks. The extent to which performance on these tasks varied as a function of vocabulary ability was assessed. The groups differed only on recall performance that could be attributed to the capacity of the phonological store, not to that attributed to long-term lexical or phonotactic knowledge. Together the evidence suggests that the association between PWM and vocabulary knowledge, for the most part, reflects individual differences in PWM that may influence vocabulary development, rather than the beneficial effects of the commensurately greater lexical and phonotactic knowledge on non-word recall.

Commonality of processes

A more radical interpretation of the relationship between language development and the ability to perceive, produce and retain phonological information is that the association arises because processing and storage required in PWM tasks are those same operations that principally exist to process speech. Thus rather than asking how a separate PWM system might support language development, the question can be reversed to ask what are the mnemonic capabilities of the speech system and what purpose in language comprehension and production might these serve?

Researchers working within the fractionated tradition have not remained impervious to the implications of the influence of other forms of knowledge on the contents of the phonological store. Indeed the influence of long-term knowledge on the retention capacity of the phonological store is accepted (Baddeley & Logie, 1999) and attempts have been made to adapt the model to account for such findings. For example Gathercole and Martin (1996) proposed that the ability to store phonological information for short periods of time emerges directly as a byproduct of the speech input processing system. The integrity of the fractionated model, however, requires that the temporary storage of such information remains functionally separate from the processing of long-term phonological information as accomplished by the central executive.

Models of verbal short-term memory (STM) have been proposed, however, which account for such performance on the basis of the processing and storage capabilities of the language system (Barnard, 1985, 1999; Monsell, 1984; Saffran & Martin, 1990). For example within Barnard's Interacting Cognitive Subsystems (ICS) model, the individual subsystems that underlie the processing of speech include implicational, propositional, morphonolexical and articulatory subsystems (crudely, translating ideas into meanings represented as sounds and then to speech). Each subsystem can represent, store and recode information. This model does not postulate storage components (the phonological loop) independently of the system which processes such information, nor a separate limited-capacity processing resource (the central executive), since capacity limitations within the ICS model result from the efficiency of the functioning and the interactions between the subsystems (see also chapter 12, this volume).

Currently the evidence of merely an association between language development and performance in verbal STM tasks is insufficient to decide between these two accounts. Children who perform better in verbal STM tasks may also demonstrate better language skills either because they have a larger PWM which allows them to create better long-term memory (LTM) phonological representations that are advantageous in spoken language production, or because the representational and 'memory record' or re-representational processes of the cognitive subsystems involved in language are more efficient. These two models have previously been judged to be highly compatible (Barnard, 1999; Shah & Miyake, 1999); however, one factor on which they can be discriminated is the need to postulate functionally separate systems for storage and controlled processing. Since this aspect of the fractionated model is directly relevant to an alternative account of the nature of the relationship between working memory and language, it will be considered after this account has been introduced.

AN ALTERNATIVE ACCOUNT OF THE WORKING MEMORY/LANGUAGE ASSOCIATION: WORKING MEMORY CONSTRAINTS ON LINGUISTIC PROCESSING

The preceding sections considered how PWM might be involved in learning the phonological form of various aspects of the language from which knowledge of linguistic structure might be derived. However, other research suggests a rather different role that working memory might play in language development. In such accounts limited resources are presumed available to process all aspects of language (e.g. semantic, syntactic and phonological). These limitations extend beyond the storage function of PWM and suggest constraints in more general cognitive processing resources. The association between PWM and language may therefore represent only one feature of a wider link between working memory and language development.

Resource limitations in children's speech processing

Within developmental psycholinguistics, researchers (e.g. Crystal, 1987; Gerken, 1991; Valian, 1991) have postulated that children's speech incompletely represents 'legal' syntactic requirements because the accumulated complexity of the target utterance, in terms of message formulation, syntax assembly and lexical selection, exceeds the child's currently available processing resources. Similar accounts of resource limitations constraining children's speech have been developed within cognitive psychology. Bock (1982) proposed a model of adult speech production in which the utterance content was constructed in five 'arenas' (referential, semantic, phonological, phonetic and motor-assembly). Although the resources available to construct the utterance were considered to be limited it was regarded that, in skilled speakers, processes other than those that took place in the referential arena (deciding what to say), for example accessing the relevant syntactic and phonological information, were relatively automatic processes. These processes were therefore not demanding of the limited cognitive resources. Whilst not primarily intended as a developmental account, Bock did propose that lower level processes such as word production might only achieve automatisation with development and thus during childhood such phonological processing would make demands on the limited resources available to process speech. Since the entirety of the resources was limited, directing some of these resources to lower level processing would deprive resources needed to construct, for example, referential aspects of the utterance.

A similar account of an interaction between the requirement to actively process phonological information and to construct other aspects of the utterance is outlined in Speidel's model of language development presented earlier. In this model too, constructing an utterance is proposed to require cognitive resources whose totality is finite. Assembling an utterance using a stored template of a syntactic construction, however, is suggested to be less demanding of these resources than constructing an utterance from scratch. The child with a more comprehensive storehouse of the phonological form of syntactic constructions may be able to apply these in their speech, thereby freeing resources to incorporate increased complexity in other aspects of the utterance.

Levelt (1992) proposed that automatically accessible long-term phonological representations (lexemes) may be an important part of skilled speech output. However, an unfamiliar phonological form, such as a foreign word or a non-word, may not have an automatically accessible long-term phonological representation. Evidence from both neuropsychology (Bub, Black, Howell & Kertesz, 1987; Caramazza, Miceli & Villa, 1986) and connectionist models of speech (Hartley & Houghton, 1996) indicates what may happen if these long-term representations are not automatically available. Specifically, producing unfamiliar phonological forms in the absence of automatically accessible long-term phonological representations requires the formation of a temporary phonological representation on which the articulatory specifications for output can be based. The developmental analogue is that since children may have fewer and less-completely specified LTM phonological representations of lexical items, PWM may be required to maintain this information and that this limits the complexity of the utterances that they can produce. Such evidence of trade-offs in processing complexity has indeed been found in the speech production skills of very young children. For example Streim and Chapman (1987) noted that increased lexical availability (prior naming) was associated with longer and more fluent utterances and Nelson and Bauer (1991) showed that the phonetic complexity of words was reduced when they were included in more complex utterances.

To summarise, it has been proposed that in the absence of automatically accessible knowledge of the phonological form of lexical items or syntactic constructions, resources from a limited pool, otherwise used to formulate other aspects of the utterance, must be employed to construct a phonological specification during speech production. We have already noted that it seems entirely plausible that PWM may play a role in the acquisition of such long-term phonological representations and thus that children with better PWM skills might be expected to have a wider range of lexical and morpho-syntactic knowledge on which to draw. However, these 'processing' accounts maintain that it is the availability of such knowledge which affects the resources available to compose all other aspects of the utterance, that underpins the association between PWM and language. The resources postulated to constrain language processing are therefore not pre-designated to the processing of phonological information, but support every aspect of message construction. Can such interactions between the resources required to create and maintain specifically phonological representations and the resources for processing and integrating other forms of information be accommodated within the fractionated model? Within the original formulation (Baddeley & Hitch, 1974) there were flexible boundaries between storage in the slave systems and the processing resources of the central executive. More recently, however, the evolution of the concept of the central executive has seen storage and processing encapsulated within the specific systems (Baddeley & Logie, 1999). Models of working memory which do not maintain such a clear distinction have, however, been proposed.

Integrated accounts of working memory

Interactions or resource trade-offs between the storage and processing of information are the central feature of an alternative tradition of working memory research, often referred to as 'unitary' and here termed 'integrated' models of working memory (see Miyake & Shah, 1999 for an overview). Integrated accounts of working memory can be most easily contrasted with the fractionated model in that modality-specific storage systems, functionally separate from the processing resources of the central executive are not postulated in such models. Rather, working memory is proposed to reflect the totality of resources that are available to support both the processing and short-term storage of information (e.g. Daneman & Carpenter, 1980; Just & Carpenter, 1992; although see Towse & Houston-Price, chapter 11, this volume, for difficulties with this view). The paradigm used to assess integrated working memory is the complex span task and although various versions of this task exist, all share the central premise that material must be simultaneously processed and stored.

The computational CC READER model (Just & Carpenter, 1992) was designed to simulate experimental data from a variety of populations which demonstrated associations between individual differences in complex span and language comprehension (Carpenter, Miyake & Just, 1994). In this model both storage (e.g. maintaining lexical items until they can be integrated with later-occurring related items) and processing (e.g. assigning thematic roles) are supported by a single common resource 'activation'. Since the model operates in parallel, such that processing is conducted at different levels of language analysis simultaneously (e.g. syntactic, semantic and referential), and since both storage and processing are demanding of activation resources, capacity constraints are highly influential in determining comprehension abilities.

Whilst not strictly an integrated model, since working memory capacity is a unitary attentional resource, the model of Engle and his colleagues (Engle, Kane & Tuholski, 1999) nevertheless also employs the complex span task as an index of working memory. Working memory, in Engle's model, comprises both long-term memory representations activated above a certain threshold (construed as short-term memory) and working memory capacity, a domain-free, limited-capacity controlled attention which achieves and maintains the activation of these representations. Although a mechanism for trade-offs between storage and processing exists, since individual differences in knowledge and the routinisation of procedures or skills for a specific task are postulated (e.g. verbal rehearsal may only be attention demanding and thus deplete working memory capacity in children), the major determinant of performance on complex span tasks and hence its association with everyday cognitive activities is the capacity for controlled attention. The primary discriminating feature of this model from the fractionated model is that representations in working memory are LTM representations activated above a certain threshold rather than a functionally separate system.

Single resource theories of working memory, although appearing to align most closely with resource limitations outlined in theories of language processing, have not gone unchallenged. Caplan and Waters (1999) maintained that the evidence does not in fact support an account in which a single common resource supports language comprehension, and alternatively propose separate subsystems of working memory for interpretive (syntactic analysis) and post-interpretive (operating on the assigned meaning) processing. They review evidence which demonstrates that in adults, only the latter form of processing is related to working memory as indexed by the complex span task. Their suggestion that working memory might not be related to the assignment of syntactic structure since such processing is highly practised and therefore automatic in adults, is analogous to the distinction made previously between novice and skilled speakers. Indeed a similar proposition of differential developmental relationships between working memory and syntactic parsing has been made (Romani, 1994). Thus the question still remains as to whether working memory is related to language comprehension in children.

Working memory as a limiting factor in children's language comprehension

In contrast to the abundance of research investigating associations between working memory and language comprehension in adults, relatively little work has examined the relationship in children. In addition, just as in the adult literature, investigations in children have tended to focus on text comprehension (e.g. Yuill, Oakhill & Parkin, 1989). There is, however, some evidence that in children, spoken language comprehension is related to complex span performance. Daneman and Blennerhasset (1984) demonstrated an association between preschool children's ability to understand spoken language and their performance on a verbal complex span task. However, listening span was assessed as the ability to recall the presented sentences because the children tended to repeat the entire sentence rather than just the sentence-final words. A conservative assessment of the study might therefore be that it merely shows that children who are better able to understand language are also better at repeating sentences. Engle, Carrulo and Collins (1991) did, however, demonstrate in older children that both listening comprehension, indexed as the ability to comply with verbally presented directions and reading comprehension were predicted by complex span performance.

The overriding impression of this area, however, is of a rather sparse and unbalanced picture, especially the way in which research within each tradition of working memory (fractionated and integrated) has tended to focus on a particular language skill (production and comprehension respectively). We have recently tried to bring these two traditions together to systematically investigate the relationship between working memory and children's language skills.

Comparing the association between children's language development with both fractionated and integrated models of working memory

Adams, Bourke and Willis (in preparation) examined whether individual differences in children's speech skills were specifically related to the ability to store phonological information or the resources available to process linguistic information. We examined the contribution of performance on tasks specific to each of the components of the fractionated model, and a composite processing and storage task, to individual differences in four- and five-year-old children's spoken language comprehension and production abilities. Thus we assessed PWM, visuo-spatial WM, and specific functions ascribed to the central executive (Baddeley, 1996), specifically dual task coordination, sustained attention and the ability to search and retrieve information from LTM. Integrated working memory was indexed by a listening complex span task. Using hierarchical regression techniques Adams, Bourke and Willis (1999) reported that, after controlling for general ability, the best independent predictor of performance on a standardised test of the development of spoken language comprehension was verbal fluency, a measure of the hypothesised function of the central executive to retrieve information from LTM. The data relating to language production have yet to be fully analysed, but preliminary analyses from a subset of the data revealed that in contrast to comprehension, performance on a standardised test of the development of language production was best predicted by PWM. In both the analyses of comprehension and production when the effects of general cognitive ability had been controlled neither visuo-spatial WM nor complex span were significant predictors of language skills. This suggested that the fractionation of working memory into modality-specific storage systems, and the designation and assessment of specific functions of attentional control assigned to the central executive, contribute explanatory power and appear to be theoretically useful distinctions.

It has been proposed (Baddeley & Logie, 1999) that in adults the central executive may play a role in comprehension by activating relevant LTM representations which might include not only lexical items but also more complex semantic concepts and inferences. The specific link between verbal fluency and comprehension concords well with this proposed function of the central executive. In contrast, a major factor in individual differences in children's production of speech seems to be the influence of PWM on the availability or quality of the LTM representations of the phonological form of lexical items and syntactic constructions. Although further analyses must be conducted on these data and caution should be exercised until the results have been replicated, such patterns of associations provide intriguing indications of the complexity of the links between working memory resources and language development.

EVALUATING THE FRACTIONATED WORKING MEMORY MODEL

The strengths and weaknesses of the fractionated working memory model for research into language development can be evaluated on two levels. In the next section we consider the strengths and weaknesses of information processing accounts of language development in general, and in the following section we evaluate the fractionated model of working memory as a specific candidate.

The need for an information-processing account of language development

Applying models of working memory to the quest for an information-processing account of language development might provide a number of benefits. First, it would allow investigation of the basis of individual differences in language acquisition, both in terms of the age at which significant milestones are achieved and in the characteristics of the language that children produce, aspects which tend to be overlooked in the essentially descriptive linguistic accounts (Bates, Bretherton & Snyder, 1988). Second, an information-processing account of language development would provide a useful instrument in the evaluation of constructivist theories of language acquisition. Third, greater understanding of the cognitive skills underlying language development would have important implications for the assessment and treatment of developmental disorders of language (e.g. Stackhouse & Wells, 1997). However, even if PWM were to be identified as the means by which children establish long-term phonological representations of lexical items and syntactic constructions, it would still face difficulties common to many constructivist accounts. In particular constructivist accounts must specify exactly how the child moves from knowledge specific to the input to the abstract knowledge of grammar and syntactic proficiency of the adult. PWM may be a useful first step towards this goal, explaining how children acquire the corpus of information from which syntactic proficiency is later derived.

Strengths and weaknesses of the fractionated model of working memory as an information-processing account of language development

The principal issue addressed in this chapter is whether working memory affords an accurate model of the limitations in processing resources that constrain language development. The first part of the chapter reviewed evidence which suggested that PWM is specifically related to the acquisition of long-term knowledge of the phonological form of language, and identified hypothesised roles for such knowledge in a number of theoretical perspectives on the nature of language acquisition. The mechanism through which PWM could foster LTM representations is most clearly (although not definitively, see above), articulated in the fractionated model. Baddeley et al. (1998) argued that a STM discriminable from the long-term store is necessary to acquire new phonological information. It is difficult to see how this function (i.e. its essential role in the construction of long-term memory representations) could be accommodated in models in which working memory comprises LTM representations activated above a certain threshold (e.g. Engle et al., 1999). Although a potential contender, Barnard's ICS model too does not fully specify how LTM representations might be established on the basis of temporary storage, because it is not clear exactly how the system might identify and overcome instances of discrepant mappings between subsystems. For example how the system would learn the implicational and propositional mappings to novel sound sequences (essentially acquire the meaning of new words) (Barnard, 1999).

The second part of the chapter considered the extent to which long-term phonological knowledge may help maximise the resources available to process the remaining aspects of an utterance. Phonological working memory did share unique variance with children's spoken language skills; however, at present it is not clear, given the functional specialisation of storage and processing in the fractionated model, how resources required to *create* and maintain temporary phonological representations impinge on the processing resources of the central executive. Although integrated models of working memory which explicit focus on such trade-offs between storage and processing resources might have appeared to offer a viable model of these capacity limitations, a direct comparison revealed that the measure of these integrated resources was less successful than assessments of individual components of the fractionated model in explaining individual differences in children's language production skills. One possible amendment to the fractionated model (see also chapter 11, this volume) is to suggest that some processing may be accomplished within the slave systems (e.g. Barnard, 1999), a proposal that would, however, emasculate the central executive.

The ultimate aim of our research is a description of the cognitive resources which may impede or facilitate language development. In the studies described previously, a function ascribed to the central executive of the fractionated model (verbal fluency) was also an independent predictor of children's comprehension skills, whilst a different component of this model, PWM, was the best predictor of their production skills. It is this specificity of the fractionated model, to indicate particular processes affecting comprehension and production skills, that appeals to the present authors. The theoretical detail of the attentional functions of the central executive, which may be directly applicable to mechanisms in language processing, combined with the assessment techniques related to explicit working memory functions, in our opinion, render the fractionated model the most potentially rewarding framework within which to proceed towards this goal (see chapter 5 in this book for a similar argument). Difficulties with the complex span task, both concerning the generality of its theoretical underpinning, and likely multiple task composition (Engle et al., 1999; chapter 11, this volume) suggest this paradigm may be less productive.

Nevertheless, despite the fractionated model's relative superiority in an initial investigation, there is clearly much work to do before we can equate the putative cognitive resources underlying children's language development with working memory as construed in this model. At a conceptual level there is a surprising degree of concordance between models of working memory. Complex span may reflect either the operation of STM and controlled attention (Engle et al., 1999) or PWM and the central executive (Baddeley & Logie, 1999). The reverse may also be true — specific PWM and central executive tasks may reflect STM and aspects of controlled attention. To be accepted as *the* model of working memory that underpins language development, the fractionated model needs to provide convincing evidence that, as a model of working memory resources, its concept of the central executive is preferable to models of controlled attention (Engle et al., 1999) or the functioning and interaction of discriminable subsystems (Barnard, 1999). As proponents of the fractionated model readily admit (Baddeley & Logie, 1999), the empirical evidence is not yet available to make these choices. It is the opinion of the present authors therefore, that whilst noting the theoretical concordance, currently other factors (e.g. the nature of the final goal and measurement specificity) should inform the choice of model to adopt in future investigations.

Conclusions

One of the major strengths of the fractionated working memory model is in providing a mechanism for the long-term learning of phonological representations which may form the building blocks for language development. Weaknesses do remain, however. Some of these relate more generally to information-processing accounts of language development, for example how one moves from linguistic knowledge specific to the input to abstract knowledge of syntactic structure. Other difficulties are specific to the fractionated model and pertain to how storage requirements may impinge on the processing resources of the central executive. Nevertheless, in the opinion of the current authors, the greater specificity of the fractionated model may be more useful in deriving predictions which might guide future research into the cognitive components of language acquisition.

Future directions for working memory research

Research investigating the relationship between language development and working memory is in its very early stages and a number of fundamental issues should be addressed in future research. First, one important caveat must be noted. None of the above studies have directly assessed the effect of individual differences in children's working memory abilities during the on-line processing of either the comprehension or the production of speech. This makes it impossible to decide whether the association reflects the role of specifically PWM in *acquiring* syntactic knowledge, or the implications of such knowledge during the *processing* of language. Our research priority is therefore to assess the relationship between children's working memory skills and their on-line comprehension and production of language. Second, the postulation of specific functions of the central executive and techniques to directly assess them is a recent advance. A great deal of work is required to validate both the assessment techniques and their theoretical basis, particularly in terms of their application to children. Of immediate concern is the replication of the results of the Adams et al. (1999, in preparation) studies.

The tenor of our research has been to return to the original impetus for working memory, its function in everyday cognitive activities. The question of the validity of various models of working memory is thus rephrased to enquire about the mnemonic properties of the language system and the nature of the controlling or attentional resources that are required to comprehend and produce language during development. We have attempted to identify areas of concordance between research on working memory and research into the acquisition of language, which indeed have largely continued in isolation of one another. We hope to have demonstrated that although a great deal remains to be explained, such interdisciplinary work may prove to be a fruitful endeavour.

ACKNOWLEDGEMENTS

This work was supported by Grant R000222200 from the Economic and Social Research Council. We are grateful to Louise Phillips, Peter Lovatt and Carmel Houston-Price for helpful comments on a previous draft of this chapter.

BACKGROUND READING

Baddeley, A., Gathercole, S. & Papagno, C. (1998). The phonological loop as a language learning device. *Psychological Review, 105,* 158–173.

A comprehensive review of the evidence relating phonological short-term memory to language skills from a range of populations.

Caplan, D. & Waters, G. S. (1999). Verbal working memory and sentence comprehension. *Behavioral and Brain Sciences, 22,* 77–126.

This paper argues that the working memory system used in syntactic processing is not the same as that measured by standard working memory measures. Combined with its associated commentary from the fields of working memory, psycholinguistics and the authors' response, this paper provides a thorough overview of the current issues in this area.

Messer, D. J. (1994). *The Development of Communication: From social interaction to language.* Chichester: John Wiley & Sons.

An eminently readable introduction to critical issues in the understanding of language development including evidence from a wide range of perspectives.

REFERENCES

Adams, A.-M., Bourke, L. & Willis, C. (1999). Working memory and spoken language comprehension in young children. *International Journal of Psychology, 34*(5/6), 364–374.

Adams, A.-M., Bourke, L. & Willis, C. (in preparation). Language processing and working memory: Differential relationships with children's receptive and expressive language.

Adams, A.-M. & Gathercole, S. E. (1995). Phonological working memory and speech production in preschool children. *Journal of Speech and Hearing Research, 38,* 403–414.

Adams, A.-M. & Gathercole, S. E. (2000). Limitations in working memory: implications for language development. *International Journal of Language and Communication Disorders, 35*(1), 95–117.

Baddeley, A. D. (1986). *Working Memory.* Oxford: Oxford University Press.

Baddeley, A. D. (1996). Exploring the central executive. *Quarterly Journal of Experimental Psychology, 49A*(1), 5–28.

Baddeley, A., Gathercole, S. & Papagno, C. (1998). The phonological loop as a language learning device. *Psychological Review, 105*(1), 158–173.

Baddeley, A. D. & Hitch, G. (1974). Working memory. In G. A. Bower (Ed.), *The Psychology of Learning and Motivation, Vol. 8* (pp. 47–48). New York: Academic Press.

Baddeley, A. D. & Logie, R. H. (1999). Working memory: The multiple-component model. In A. Miyake & P. Shah (Eds.), *Models of Working Memory: Mechanisms of active maintenance and executive control* (pp. 28–61). Cambridge, UK: Cambridge University Press.

Barnard, P. (1985). Interacting cognitive subsystems: A psycholinguistic approach for short-term memory. In A. E. Ellis (Ed.), *Progress in the Psychology of Language, Vol. 2* (pp. 197–258). Hillsdale, NJ: Lawrence Erlbaum Associates Inc.

Barnard, P. (1999). Interacting cognitive subsystems: Modelling working memory phenomena within a mulitprocessor architecture. In A. Miyake & P. Shah, (Eds.), *Models of Working Memory: Mechanisms of active maintenance and executive control* (pp. 298–339). Cambridge, UK: Cambridge University Press.

Bates, E., Bretherton, I. & Snyder, L. (1988). *From First Words to Grammar: Individual differences and dissociable mechanisms.* New York: Academic Press.

Bock, J. K. (1982). Toward a cognitive psychology of syntax: information processing contributions to sentence formulation. *Psychological Review, 89*(1), 1–47.

Brown, G. D. A. & Hulme, C. (1996). Non-word repetition, STM and word age-of-acquisition: A computational model. In S. E. Gathercole (Ed.), *Models of Short-term Memory* (pp. 129–148). Hove, UK: Psychology Press.

Bub, D., Black, S., Howell, J. & Kertesz, A. (1987). Speech output processes and reading. In M. Coltheart, G. Sartori & R. Job (Eds.), *The Cognitive Neuropsychology of Language* (pp. 79–110). Hove, UK: Lawrence Erlbaum Associates Ltd.

Caplan, D. & Waters, G. S. (1999) Verbal working memory and sentence comprehension. *Behavioral and Brain Sciences, 22*, 77–126.

Caramazza, A., Miceli, G. & Villa, G. (1986). The role of the (output) phonological buffer in reading, writing, and repetition. *Cognitive Neuropsychology, 3*(1), 37–76.

Carpenter, P. A., Miyake, A. & Just, M. A. (1994). Working memory constraints in comprehension: Evidence from individual differences, aphasia and aging. In M. A. Gernsbacher (Ed.), *Handbook of Psycholinguistics.* London: Academic Press.

Chomsky, N. (1965). *Aspects of the Theory of Syntax.* Cambridge, MA: MIT Press.

Chomsky, N. (1986). *Knowledge of Language: Its nature, origins and use.* New York: Praeger.

Crystal, D. (1987). Towards a 'bucket' theory of language disability: taking account of interaction between linguistic levels. *Clinical Linguistics and Phonetics, 1*, 7–22.

Daneman, M. & Blennerhassett, A. (1984). How to assess the listening comprehension skills of prereaders. *Journal of Educational Psychology, 76*(6), 1372–1381.

Daneman, M. & Carpenter, P. A. (1980). Individual differences in working memory and reading. *Journal of Verbal Learning and Verbal Behaviour, 19*, 450–466.

Edwards, J. & Lahey, M. (1998). Nonword repetitions of children with specific language impairment: exploration of some explanations for their inaccuracies. *Applied Psycholinguistics, 19*, 279–309.

Engle, R. W., Carullo, J. J. & Collins, K. W. (1991). Individual differences in working memory for comprehension and following directions. *Journal of Educational Research, 84*, 253–262.

Engle, R. W., Kane, M. J. & Tuholski, S. W. (1999). Individual differences in working memory capacity and what they tell us about controlled attention, general fluid intelligence, and other functions of the prefrontal cortex. In A. Miyake & P. Shah (Eds.), *Models of Working Memory: Mechanisms of active maintenance and executive control* (pp. 102–134). Cambridge, UK: Cambridge University Press.

Gathercole, S. E. (1995). Is nonword repetition a test of phonological memory or lexical knowledge? It all depends on the nonwords. *Memory and Cognition, 23*(1), 83–94.

Gathercole, S. E. & Adams, A.-M. (1993). Phonological working memory in very young children. *Developmental Psychology, 29*, 770–778.

Gathercole, S. E. & Adams, A.-M. (1994). Children's phonological working memory: Contributions of long-term knowledge and rehearsal. *Journal of Memory and Language, 33*, 672–688.

Gathercole, S. E. & Baddeley, A. D. (1990). Phonological memory deficits in language disordered children: is there a causal connection? *Journal of Memory and Language, 29*, 336–360.

Gathercole, S. E., Frankish, C. R., Pickering, S. J. & Peaker, S. H. (1999). Phonotactic influences on serial recall. *Journal of Experimental Psychology: Learning, Memory, and Cognition, 25*, 84–95.

Gathercole, S. E., Hitch, G. J., Service, E. & Martin, A. J. (1997). Short-term memory and new word learning in children. *Developmental Psychology, 33*, 966–979.

Gathercole, S. E., Hitch, G. J., Service, E., Adams, A.-M. & Martin, A. J. (1999). Phonological short-term memory and vocabulary development: further evidence on the nature of the relationship. *Applied Cognitive Psychology, 13*, 65–77.

Gathercole, S. E., & Martin, A. J. (1996). Interactive processes in phonological memory. In S. E. Gathercole (Ed.), *Models of Short-Term Memory* (pp. 73–100). Hove, UK: Psychology Press.

Gathercole, S. E. & Pickering, S. J. (1999). Estimating the capacity of phonological short-term memory. *International Journal of Psychology, 34*(5/6), 378–382.

Gerken, L. (1991). The metrical basis for children's subjectless sentences. *Journal of Memory and Language, 30*, 431–451.

Gillam, R. B., Cowan, N. & Day, L. (1995). Sequential memory in children with and without language impairment. *Journal of Speech and Hearing Research, 38*, 393–402.

Gillam, R. B., Cowan, N. & Marler, J. A. (1998). Information processing by school-age children with specific language impairment: evidence from a modality effect paradigm. *Journal of Speech and Hearing Research, 41*, 913–926.

Goldberg, A. E. (1995). *Constructions: A Construction Grammar Approach to Argument Structure*. Chicago: University of Chicago Press.

Hartley, T. & Houghton, G. (1996). A linguistically-constrained model of short-term memory for nonwords. *Journal of Memory and Language, 35*, 1–31.

Howard, D. & van der Lely, H. K. J. (1995). Specific language impairment in children is *not* due to a short-term memory deficit. *Journal of Speech and Hearing Research, 38*(2), 466–472.

Hulme, C., Maughan, S. & Brown, G. D. A. (1991). Memory for familiar and unfamiliar words: evidence for a long-term memory contribution to short-term memory span. *Journal of Memory and Language, 30*, 685–701.

Jusczyk, P. W., Friederici, A. D., Wessels, J. M., Svenkerud, V. Y. & Jusczyk, A. M. (1993). Infant's sensitivity to the sound patterns of native language words. *Journal of Memory and Language, 32*, 402–420.

Just, M. A. & Carpenter, P. A. (1992). A capacity theory of comprehension: individual differences in working memory. *Psychological Review*, *99*, 122–149.

Levelt, W. J. M. (1992). Accessing words in speech production: stages, processes and representations. *Cognition*, *42*, 1–23.

Lieven, E. V. M., Pine, J. M. & Baldwin, G. (1997). Lexically-based learning and early grammatical development. *Journal of Child Language*, *24*, 187–219.

Marchman, V. A. & Bates, E. (1994). Continuity in lexical and morphological development: a test of the critical mass hypothesis. *Journal of Child Language*, *21*, 339–366.

Messer, D. (1994). *The Development of Communication: From social interaction to language*. Chichester: Wiley.

Monsell, S. (1984). Components of working memory underlying verbal skills: A 'distributed capacities' view. In H. Bouma & D. G. Bouwhuis (Eds.), *Attention and Performance X: Control of language processes* (pp. 327–350). Hove, UK: Lawrence Erlbaum Associates Ltd.

Montgomery, J. W. (1996). Sentence comprehension and working memory in children with specific language impairment. *Topics in Language Disorders*, *17*(1), 19–32.

Nelson, K. (1973). Structure and strategy in learning to talk. *Monographs of the Society for Research in Child Development*, *38*.

Nelson, L. K. & Bauer, H. R. (1991). Speech and language production at age 2: evidence for trade-offs between linguistic and phonetic processing. *Journal of Speech and Hearing Research*, *34*, 879–892.

Pine, J. M. & Lieven, E. V. (1993). Reanalysing rote-learned phrases: individual differences in the transition to multiword speech. *Journal of Child Language*, *20*, 551–571.

Plunkett, K. & Marchman, V. (1993). U-shaped learning and frequency effects in a multi-layered perception: implications for child language acquisition. *Cognition*, *38*, 43–102.

Romani, C. (1994). The role of phonological short-term memory in syntactic parsing: a case study. *Language and Cognitive Processes*, *9*(1), 29–67.

Saffran, E. M. & Martin, N. (1990). Short-term memory impairment and sentence processing: A case study. In G. Vallar & T. Shallice (Eds.), *Neuropsychological Impairments of Short-term Memory* (pp. 428–447). Cambridge: Cambridge University Press.

Saffran, J. R., Newport, E. L. & Aslin, R. N. (1996). Word segmentation: the role of distributional cues. *Journal of Memory and Language*, *35*, 606–621.

Shah, P. & Miyake, A. (1999). Models of working memory: An introduction. In A. Miyake & P. Shah (Eds.), *Models of Working Memory: Mechanisms of active maintenance and executive control* (pp. 1–27). Cambridge, UK: Cambridge University Press.

Shallice, T. (1988). *From Neuropsychology to Mental Structure*. Cambridge, UK: Cambridge University Press.

Snowling, M., Chiat, S. & Hulme, C. (1991). Words, nonwords and phonological processes: some comments on Gathercole, Willis, Emslie & Baddeley. *Applied Psycholinguistics*, *12*, 369–373.

Speidel, G. E. (1989). Imitation: A bootstrap for learning to speak? In G. E. Speidel & K. E. Nelson (Eds.), *The Many Faces of Imitation in Language Learning* (pp. 151–179). New York: Springer Verlag.

Speidel, G. E. (1993). Phonological short-term memory and individual differences in learning to speak: a bilingual case study. *First Language*, *13*, 69–91.

Speidel, G. E. & Herreshoff, M. J. (1989). Imitation and the construction of long utterances. In G. E. Speidel & K. E. Nelson (Eds.), *The Many Faces of Imitation in Language Learning* (pp. 181–197). New York: Springer Verlag.

Stackhouse, J. & Wells, B. (1997). *Children's Speech and Literacy Difficulties: A psycholinguistic framework*. London: Whurr Publishers Ltd.

Streim, N. W. & Chapman, R. S. (1987). The effects of discourse support on the organisation and production of children's utterances. *Applied Psycholinguistics*, *8*, 55–66.

Valian, V. (1991). Syntactic subjects in the early speech of American and Italian children. *Cognition*, *40*, 21–81.

van der Lely, H. K. J. & Howard, D. (1993). Children with specific language impairment: linguistic impairment or short-term memory deficit? *Journal of Speech and Hearing Research*, *36*, 1193–1207.

Vihman, M. M. (1996). *Phonological Development: The origins of language in the child*. Oxford: Blackwell.

Willis, C. S. (1997). *Working memory and children's language processing*. Unpublished PhD thesis, Lancaster University, UK.

Yuill, N., Oakhill, J. & Parkin, A. (1989). Working memory, comprehension ability and the resolution of text anomaly. *British Journal of Psychology*, *80*, 351–361.

5   The working memory model in adult aging research

Louise H. Phillips and Colin Hamilton

In this chapter we examine the empirical evidence for adult age changes in the components of the Baddeley and Hitch working memory model, and highlight some methodological and theoretical issues raised by the study of age differences in working memory. Baddeley (1996, p. 19) argues that 'ageing may be an interesting and productive variable to study within the context of working memory'. The idea that adult age changes in the available capacity of working memory underlie deficits in reasoning and language abilities has been extremely influential. However, the majority of work in this area has conceptualised working memory in terms of a general limited-capacity system, rather than using the notion of the Baddeley and Hitch three component model (WM model) with specialised subsystems for the maintenance of verbal and visuo-spatial information.

In the aging literature, the usual view of working memory is that age differences reflect a decrease in the amount of cognitive resources that can be shared out to deal with competing task demands. This maps onto the predominant limited-resource model of working memory in the North American literature. In the current chapter we will not discuss in detail the research that largely utilises this resource capacity approach to working memory, but will instead concentrate on research specifically relevant to the WM model. In the aging literature particularly, this notion of working memory is closely tied in to other conceptions of limitations on information-processing, such as attentional capacity and processing speed (Salthouse, 1991). Salthouse (e.g. 1992) has argued that slowed speed of processing information underlies the decline in capacity of working memory with age. Evidence from statistical partialling techniques suggests that age-related variance in working memory can largely be explained in terms of processing speed at both the beginning and end of the lifespan (Chuah & Maybery, 1999; Kail & Salthouse, 1994; Salthouse, 1992).

The WM model has been utilised less in aging research than limited general resource models. However, the WM model does have promise as a tool for understanding adult aging because it allows the possibility of a functional account of exactly how and why cognitive changes occur with age, rather than the basic assertion that age differences are 'resource' differences. It seems appropriate that we should try to seek cognitive models of the effects of cognitive aging, rather than relying solely on neurobiological models, which are often the endpoint of the processing speed theories. The highly specified nature of the WM model compared to the rather nebulous concept of 'working memory capacity' also allows for specific predictions to be tested experimentally, rather than having to rely upon statistical partialling techniques. As will be outlined below, there are also problems with the use of the WM model to study aging — in particular, the general nature of aging deficits across a range of cognitive tasks may raise questions about the parsimony of using a multicomponent model as an explanation.

Many studies indicate age-related changes in measures of working memory. However, the magnitude and nature of age differences in working memory appear inconsistent across studies, and are influenced strongly by the type of test used in ways which are not yet fully explained (Baddeley, 1996). Baddeley (1996) argues that it is precisely because the effects of age on working memory appear inconsistent and challenging to explain that aging may be an interesting variable to study in respect of the working memory model. In this chapter we outline evidence for age-related changes in the various components of working memory, outline the methodological techniques that have generally been used in this area, and then evaluate the usefulness of the WM model in aging research.

THE EFFECTS OF ADULT AGE ON THE INDIVIDUAL COMPONENTS OF THE BADDELEY AND HITCH WORKING MEMORY MODEL

Phonological loop

The phonological loop, or verbal buffer system, is the best specified component of the working memory model. There is considerable evidence to support the idea that this system comprises an articulatory rehearsal mechanism based on inner speech, and a phonological store. There has been a lot of interest in the effects of adult age on verbal working memory, particularly in relation to language processing (see e.g. chapters 3–5 and 8–9 in Light & Burke, 1988). Relatively few studies have used the WM model to investigate normal adult age differences in verbal processing. One aspect of the functioning of the phonological loop that has been examined in relation to age is the rate of articulation. Articulation rate is likely to influence the number of items that can be rehearsed, and hence memory span. There is evidence that as children get older there is a strong relationship between quickening speech rates and verbal memory span (Hulme, Thomson, Muir, & Lawrence, 1984). It has been argued (Kynette, Kemper, Norman, & Cheung, 1990) that slowed articulation rates may cause impairments of verbal short term memory and language processing in older adults. Gerhand (1994) found that adult age differences in digit span could be entirely explained by statistically removing variance due to articulation rate, which was considerably slower in older adults. This raises the question as to whether articulation rate is an indicator of a more general speed of information-processing factor which underlies age differences (Chuah & Mayberry, 1999; Kail, 1993; Smyth & Scholey, 1996). Chuah and Maybery (1999) present evidence that in children, age-related improvements in short-term memory are best explained in terms of a domain-independent increase of processing speed, rather than changes in articulatory rate having a specific impact upon verbal memory. The role of processing speed in adult age differences in the operation of a phonological rehearsal mechanism has not been fully explored.

The functioning of the phonological loop can be examined through the 'unattended speech effect', in which the presentation of task-irrelevant speech-related sounds interferes with the ability to retain verbal information (Salamé & Baddeley, 1982). Rouleau and Belleville (1996) examined the functioning of the phonological loop in older adults by testing whether there were age differences in the effects of irrelevant speech on verbal memory. They hypothesised that older adults should be adversely affected by irrelevant speech because older people often report difficulty in filtering out background noise in everyday situations. Rouleau and Belleville reported a general age effect on verbal memory, with older adults recalling fewer digits. There was however no interaction between age and the effects of irrelevant speech, suggesting no particular age-related difficulty in dealing with task-irrelevant noise.

A further method of examining the phonological loop is through the use of concurrent articulatory suppression (e.g. the participant repeatedly saying 'the' while performing another task) which is argued to prevent subvocal rehearsal of verbal information. Gerhand (1994) gave a digit span task to old and young adults both with and without concurrent articulatory suppression. There were significant age differences in digit span in the single task condition, but no age differences in digit span during concurrent articulatory suppression, i.e. when subvocal rehearsal was prevented. It was therefore concluded that slow subvocal rehearsal may underlie age differences in simple verbal memory tasks.

Overall the evidence suggests that slowed articulation rates may impair verbal memory in older adults. Otherwise the operation of the articulatory loop remains relatively intact with age. The experiments outlined above highlight the value of the WM model in aging research: it allows investigation of well-specified cognitive processes (e.g. articulatory rehearsal) and how they change.

Visuo-spatial sketchpad

Very little research has directly examined the effects of age on the visuo-spatial sketchpad, the visuo-spatial buffer component of working memory.

However, age differences favouring younger adults have been reported on a number of imagery tasks which are thought to rely upon the visuo-spatial slave system. A large number of studies have shown older adults to be slower and less accurate at tasks of mental rotation (e.g. Cerella, Poon, & Fozard, 1981). Dror and Kosslyn (1994) looked at the effects of adult aging on tasks of image generation, scanning and rotation. They argue that there are substantial age differences in the ability to rotate images and activate stored images. In contrast there was little age effect on the ability to generate or scan images. In relation to the WM model it is likely that most of these tasks have some executive component, making it difficult to distinguish whether age differences on the tasks are specifically related to the operation of the sketchpad or the central executive. More data relevant to the distinction between central executive and visuo-spatial sketchpad changes with age are presented below in the section on studies comparing different aspects of the model.

There are no age differences in the benefit found for remembering concrete (imageable) versus abstract words (Dirkx & Craik, 1992), suggesting that both young and old adults spontaneously make use of visual imagery. However, it may be the case that younger adults can use imagery processes more efficiently than old. Dirkx and Craik report that when given a list of words to learn younger adults remembered considerably more than old. In contrast, when given word lists to learn during a simultaneous visual interference task the age difference was non-significant, suggesting that the younger group was making more effective use of imagery during the single task condition (Dirkx & Craik, 1992). Taken together with the results reported above for age differences in the effects of articulatory suppression, this suggests that both verbal and visual rehearsal processes may be involved in age differences in remembering verbal material. However, there are still very few studies which address changes in visuo-spatial sketchpad functioning with age, and it would be of particular interest to investigate the role of both verbal and visuo-spatial rehearsal in age differences in different types of memory paradigm.

Central executive

Baddeley (1986) has argued that the central executive component of working memory is particularly impaired in older adults compared to the verbal and visuo-spatial slave systems, and increasing evidence has been gathered which supports this viewpoint. A number of paradigms have been designed specifically to explore central executive functioning. 'Keeping track' tasks are proposed to tap the 'memory-updating' facility of working memory (Morris & Jones, 1990). Keeping track of information has been shown to decline with age (Dobbs & Rule, 1989). Another task argued to depend heavily on the central executive component of working memory is the production of random strings of numbers (Baddeley, 1986). Producing random output demands repeated inhibition of stereotyped automatic sequences (Baddeley, 1986), and thus places considerable demands on executive processes. There is evidence that older subjects produce less randomly distributed strings of digits than their younger counterparts (Van der Linden, Bregart, & Beerten, 1994). Also, older adults are less able to produce random sequences of tapping responses (Phillips, Gilhooly, Logie, Della Sala, & Wynn, submitted). However, there is still insufficient knowledge about how younger and older adults are performing these random generation tasks to be confident that the age differences reflect poorer inhibition for example, and not poorer understanding of the task demands.

The most widely used model of central executive function is based on the Norman and Shallice (1986) supervisory attentional system. This model suggests that the central executive is involved in a range of cognitive control processes such as planning, monitoring, and inhibition of inappropriate stimuli or responses. Further, this links the central executive to the operation of the frontal lobes of the brain. There has been a considerable amount of recent literature on aging devoted to the relationship between age, the frontal lobes and executive functioning (e.g. Moscovitch, 1994; Parkin, 1997; West, 1996). The frontal lobes show evidence of deterioration earlier, and more rapidly in response to aging than any other brain area (Coffey et al., 1992; Coleman & Flood, 1987; Raz, Gunning, Head, Dupuis, & Acker, 1998). There is substantial evidence of adult age differences in performance on neuropsychological tests argued to assess executive function such as the Wisconsin Card Sort test, verbal fluency and the Stroop test (see e.g. Rabbitt, 1997). However, poor performance on these tests may reflect age changes in other factors such as lower level information-processing characteristics rather than executive deficits (Phillips, 1999; Uttl & Graf, 1997).

It is difficult to distinguish empirically between 'processing resource' and 'central executive' theories of aging because both predict fairly general and widespread cognitive deficits with age. One example of this is the Stroop task, where colour words are printed in different colour inks, and in the ink-naming conditions the tendency to read the colour name must be suppressed while the ink colour is named (e.g. the answer to YELLOW would be 'black'). Executive decline with age would be predicted to cause poorer inhibition of the inappropriate response. This should then cause age-related slowing on the colour ink naming condition of the Stroop task compared to the easier task of reading the colour word. Equally though, the processing speed theory would predict greater age-related slowing on the colour-ink naming condition, because there are more processing components to be slowed. Verhaeghen and De Meersman (1998) reviewed twenty studies of age effects on the Stroop task, and concluded that 'the apparent age-sensitivity of the Stroop interference effect appears to be merely an artefact of general slowing' (p. 120).

It is difficult to isolate the effects of age on the central executive without also assessing the impact of age upon slave system operation. Some studies have compared the effects of age on the central executive component with age effects on slave systems, and this research is considered in more detail below. One question that is likely to occupy aging researchers in the future is the extent and nature of fractionation in the central executive, and whether there are differential age trajectories of the various executive functions. As it stands, the WM model could fit in with many different patterns of executive function fractionation. A number of correlational studies have attempted to determine how executive functions might be segregated (e.g. Gnys & Willis, 1991; Miyake et al., 2000; Robbins et al., 1998). However, there seems so far to be little agreement amongst these studies as to the pattern of executive fractionation. Further, there is little clear-cut neuropsychological evidence of localised brain areas associating with particular types of executive deficit. More detailed studies of the nature of executive changes with age, particularly if they shed light on the cognitive processes underlying older adults poor performance on particular executive tests, may increase understanding of the nature and interactions of the various functions of the central executive.

STUDIES COMPARING THE EFFECTS OF AGE ON DIFFERENT COMPONENTS OF THE MODEL

The usefulness of the WM model as a research tool lies partly in its multicomponential nature. A few studies have utilised this to investigate whether age differences in working memory might be particularly attributable to individual components within the model. Salthouse (1994) offers some data to test the model in aging research. Salthouse, Kausler, and Saults (1988) looked at age differences in verbal and spatial memory, using the same stimuli in both cases, but different forms of recall. Very similar degrees of age decline were found in both tasks, and Salthouse (1994) argues that this indicates similar rates of age deterioration of both phonological loop and spatial scratchpad systems. However, both verbal and spatial span tasks presumably make reasonable demands on the central executive, so it is difficult to ascertain from this type of data the extent to which individual components from the WM model may change with age.

A number of other studies have examined age differences in components of working memory in more detail. Two main methodologies have been used — correlational and experimental — and the rest of this section is divided according to the type of methodology used. First, research studies using correlational techniques to partial out variance due to particular working memory components are examined. Two different experimental approaches are considered: looking at age effects when the load placed on particular components of working memory is *reduced*, and the dual task approach, where the load on particular components is *increased*.

The correlational approach

Resource hypotheses propose that individuals differ in the amount of fundamental cognitive resources (e.g. processing speed) available. It is therefore not possible to directly manipulate the main explanatory variable, as speed is proposed to reflect a fundamental limitation on processing. However, statistical techniques can simulate this manipulation: for explanations of the logic of this procedure see Hertzog and Dixon (1996) and Salthouse (1991). There are problems with the use of statistical control methods that should be borne in mind when interpreting results. The data obtained are correlational, and therefore assumptions about causality must be treated with caution. Also, these partialling techniques assume that the effects of age and working memory are additive and linear, and do not usually test for interactions between age and resource limitations (Hertzog & Dixon, 1996). There are a number of different statistical techniques to look at the reduction in shared variance between age and reasoning ability once memory measures are partialled out, but as yet no established method of testing for the probability that such a reduction occurred due to chance factors. It is therefore a matter of judgement as to whether a particular magnitude of reduction in variance is meaningful, i.e. 'significant'.

Although very many aging studies use correlational approaches to examine the role of working memory in age changes in cognition, few have done so with the intention of examining the components of the WM model. Fisk and Warr (1996) attempted to distinguish the effects of age on the phonological loop and central executive components of working memory using correlational techniques. They assessed central executive functioning using ability to generate random strings of letters (measured using various indices of randomness), and phonological loop function using measures of digit span and word span. They investigated whether age differences in measures of working memory (computation span and reading span tasks that demand simultaneous processing and storage) could be explained in terms of phonological loop or central executive functioning. Using hierarchical regression, it was revealed that age differences in working memory could not be explained by differences in the phonological loop measures, but could partially be explained by differences in central executive measures.

It is interesting to note that in the Fisk and Warr study, age differences in the working memory measures were poorly explained by a task which appears relatively similar in format to the criterion working memory span measures (the articulatory loop measure of word span), and relatively well explained by performance on a task which appears extremely dissimilar in format and task requirements (random generation). This supports the argument that age differences in relatively difficult working memory tasks are more related to central executive than phonological loop functioning. Fisk and Warr also assessed processing speed using simple perceptual comparison tasks. They found that processing speed was a good predictor of age differences in working memory span, and conclude that speed of perception may underlie age differences in executive functioning which in turn influence working memory span.

It would be interesting to see this methodology applied to a wider range of tasks, in particular visuo-spatial measures, to examine the relationships between indices of slave system performance, executive functioning, and target memory tasks. However, it is important that the validity of the purported measures of working memory components is established. Future research in this area may clarify further the role of specific visuo-spatial or verbal mechanisms in age changes in memory and reasoning. For example, it would be interesting to know whether age differences in spatial span are specifically attributable to spatial rehearsal rate or more general information-processing rate, as has been reported for developmental changes in spatial memory in children (Chuah & Maybery, 1999).

Experimental manipulations of working memory — the central executive versus slave systems

Work in this area uses experimental modifications of working memory paradigms to investigate age effects on different components of the WM model. A series of studies carried out by Morris, Gick and Craik examined the effects of age on various manipulations of verbal memory paradigms (e.g., Craik, Morris, & Gick, 1990; Morris, Craik, & Gick, 1990). The tasks used were mostly based on the 'sentence span' task, where sentences have to be verified while simultaneously remembering words. Various manipulations of complexity were carried out, but only some showed significant age interactions, i.e. much poorer performance by older adults under the more complex conditions. There was no age interaction with storage complexity, i.e. older adults were not differentially affected by the inclusion of more words to be remembered. It was therefore argued that age differences in verbal working memory do not reflect limitations on the phonological loop. An increase in processing complexity, in terms of the grammatical complexity of the sentences was generally associated with much poorer performance by older adults. It was argued that these results indicate that with age 'both the capacity and flexibility of the central executive are impaired to some degree' (Craik et al., 1990, p. 264). They further argue that while there was little age difference in the efficiency of the articulatory rehearsal mechanism, younger participants were more effective at augmenting phonological loop functioning using central executive function. This suggests that older adults rely more on articulatory rehearsal than young, particularly when executive processes are loaded.

Next, the effects of age on visual and spatial memory are considered in relation to the respective roles of the central executive and slave systems of working memory. Recent research carried out at the Universities of Northumbria and Teeside is relevant to the distinction between different aspects of the visuo-spatial sketchpad and central executive components in age differences in working memory. Logie and Pearson (1998) found that children mature faster on tasks of visual span (e.g. retaining abstract visual matrix patterns) compared to the spatial span (such as the Corsi block test in which participants are required to retain a sequence of spatial locations). This has been interpreted in relation to a more detailed model of the visuo-spatial sketchpad (Logie, 1995) in which a visual cache stores primarily visual information and a spatially orientated inner scribe retains information about movement sequences (see chapter 2, this volume). Coates, Sanderson, Hamilton and Heffernan (1999) replicated the result that children appeared to improve faster on the visual matrix task compared to the Corsi spatial task. They also found that older adults performed significantly more poorly than young adults on both the Corsi and matrix tasks, suggesting age-related decline in both spatial and visual memory.

In terms of interpreting age differences in these tasks in relation to the WM model it is unclear the extent to which different components might be involved. Matrix and Corsi tasks were not designed to isolate components of the working memory model, and therefore age differences in performance could be due to demands upon the slave components or the more generic central executive resources in the model. There is preliminary evidence (Hamilton, Heffernan, & Coates, 1999) that concurrent verbal fluency (a task thought to tap executive processes) interferes with both Corsi and visual matrix span tasks. The increase of pattern complexity in the matrix tasks affords the possibility that participants will be able to form sophisticated representations of the pattern, a visual 'chunking' process which could underlie the developmental change seen in their data. Also, active spatial rehearsal could be employed to maintain the pattern representation. Such rehearsal methods might load the executive component of working memory. The requirement in the Corsi block task for sequential order representation may make significant demands upon executive processes (Farand & Jones, 1996; Smyth & Scholey, 1996).

Further research (Hamilton et al., 1999) has used a componential approach (Farah, 1984), to produce cognitive tasks suitable for all age groups which tap the known components of visuo-spatial working memory (Logie, 1995). This research involved the construction of working memory tasks that were relatively free of executive demands and made specific demands upon the slave systems. To assess visual memory, a task was developed where spot size was memorised. There was an initial brief exposure of a spot, followed by a maintenance interval, followed by the representation of a spot that was either the same size or different. The size step was reduced from 50 per cent through to 5 per cent, with twenty trials at each spot size. The use of a simple, single stimulus reduces the requirement for a complex representation. For the spatial task, a procedure with movement trajectory was developed. A spot of light moved obliquely across the VDU screen then disappeared for 4 seconds (the maintenance interval),

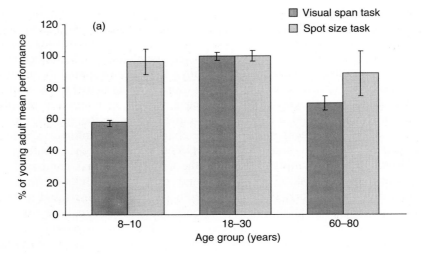

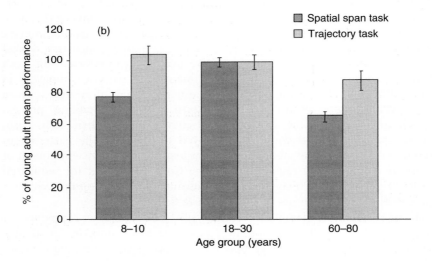

Figure 5.1 The effects of age on accuracy of (a) visual and (b) spatial memory
measures.

then reappeared either moving in the same trajectory direction or on a
different trajectory. The change in direction varied, in steps, from 27° to 4.5°
with twenty trials at each level. This procedure assesses short-term memory
for spatial movement without the sequential order component inherent in
Corsi blocks.

Figure 5.1 shows the performance of children (aged 8–10), young adults
(aged 18–30) and older adults (aged 60–80) on the visual tasks (traditional

matrix span, and size comparison) and the spatial tasks (Corsi blocks, and trajectory test). In terms of the visual tasks, children and older adults performed more poorly on the matrix span task compared to the young adults. However, there was no significant difference between the age groups in terms of performance on the judgement of spot size task. A similar pattern was seen in terms of the spatial measures: substantial age differences on the spatial span test, but no significant age differences on the trajectory test. We suggest that the poorer performance of children and older adults on the spatial and matrix tests mainly reflects the executive demands of those tasks. This supports the argument (Baddeley, 1986) that age differences in working memory are mostly attributable to the central executive rather than slave systems.

The technique of reducing the load upon particular working memory components and examining the resulting age effects is a promising way of investigating the nature of age differences. However, there are some problems with this approach too. Any task manipulation in which executive demands are reduced is almost certain to decrease the complexity of the task in terms of the number of information-processing elements to be carried out. A manipulation that reduces the number of information-processing stages involved in a task would be predicted by processing speed theory to reduce age differences. There is also an issue of how to interpret any particular experimental comparison. For example, in the research outlined above the trajectory task differs in many ways from the Corsi blocks task, so caution must be exercised in drawing strong conclusions about the comparison. Any individual task manipulation will be open to a number of different interpretations, so it would be useful to see more studies carrying out a range of manipulations to examine age interactions.

Using dual task methodology to examine the effects of aging on working memory

In this technique, experimental manipulations are used to load particular components of the WM model (see chapter 1 in this book). Dual task methodology has been widely used to examine the involvement of individual components of the WM model in a range of cognitive tasks. Relatively few studies have extended the dual task methodology to look at age differences in working memory. In those studies that do follow this method it has been argued that if age differences in a primary task are due to a particular component of the working memory model, there should be a significant interaction between age and the presence of particular dual tasks in predicting performance, such that older adults show larger dual task effects. Feyereisen and Van der Linden (1997) looked at the effects of age, articulatory suppression and pattern tapping on the ability to encode verbal and non-verbal materials. They found that interference effects were greater in older than younger adults. In general, the same modality specific interference effects were found in young and old participants (i.e. articulatory suppression affected verbal memory, pattern tapping affected spatial memory). There was no evidence of a qualitatively different pattern of interference between tasks in young and old adults.

Maylor and Wing (1996) looked at the effects of a range of secondary tasks on the ability to maintain postural balance with age. Older adults generally had less stable posture, and were particularly impaired when they also had to perform a concurrent spatial memory task or backwards digit recall. Older adults did not show particularly impaired balance when they had to perform concurrent verbal random generation, silent counting or counting backwards in threes. There were no interactions between age and being seated or standing in predicting performance on any of the secondary tasks. Maylor and Wing argue that older adults did not show excessively poor balance when carrying out tasks involving the articulatory loop or central executive components of working memory, and attribute the age decrements in balance to deterioration of the visuo-spatial scratchpad component of working memory.

Age, dual tasks and the Tower of London

In a series of experiments described by Phillips et al. (submitted), we looked at the effects of age and a range of dual tasks on performance of the Tower of London (TOL), a task proposed to measure executive function (Shallice, 1982), and which activates the frontal lobes of the brain (Owen, 1997). In the TOL, coloured disks must be moved one by one from an initial state to match a goal state (see Figure 5.2).

A range of dual tasks were used in parallel with the TOL, to investigate which aspects of the WM model were involved in age differences in performance. There is experimental evidence that these dual tasks load particular components of the WM model, rather than providing a general load on cognitive processing (Baddeley, Emslie, Kolodny, & Duncan, 1998; Evans & Brooks, 1981; Farmer, Berman, & Fletcher, 1986; Gilhooly, Logie, Wetherick, & Wynn, 1993). To load the phonological loop, articulatory suppression was used, in this case saying the numbers one to ten aloud, at a rate of one number per second. To load both the phonological loop and central executive components, verbal random generation of digits was used. Spatial pattern tapping was used to load the spatial maintenance component of working memory. Random spatial tapping was used to load both central executive resources and the visuo-spatial scratchpad (Baddeley et al., 1998). Thirty-six young (aged between 18–30) and thirty-six older adults (aged 60–78) took part in the experiment, and completed the TOL task and dual tasks alone, or in combination. A more detailed outline of the methodology used here for the Tower of London and dual tasks is described in Phillips et al. (submitted).

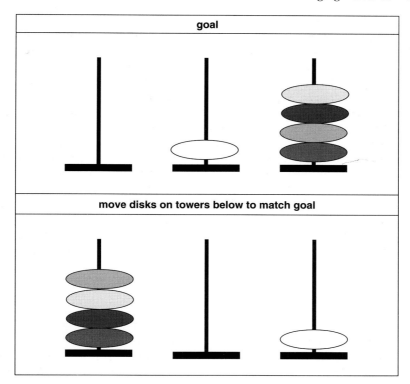

Figure 5.2   The Tower of London task.

Older adults were generally less efficient on the TOL, taking longer to execute a plan, and solving fewer trials in the minimum moves possible. Differing patterns of dual task decrements were seen in younger and older participants. For the younger group verbal random generation caused fewer TOL trials to be solved correctly, but no other dual tasks costs were significant. In contrast, for the older group, articulatory suppression, pattern tapping and random tapping caused fewer trials to be solved correctly, but the effect of random number generation just failed to reach significance. This suggests that different components of working memory may be utilised by young and old on the TOL task. Analysis of secondary task performance was also carried out: in particular the ability to maintain steady time intervals of verbal or tapping responses, and a redundancy measure which indicates randomness of responses produced on the number generation and random tapping tasks. Results showed that for younger participants there were no dual task costs on the verbal secondary tasks when performed along with the TOL. However, the younger group did show less ability to maintain steady inter-response intervals on the tapping tasks during performance of the TOL, and a less random pattern of taps under dual task conditions. For the older adults, there was poorer ability to maintain inter-response intervals at a steady pace for all four secondary tasks during concurrent TOL performance, but no dual task effect on the randomness of responses produced. A qualitatively different pattern of dual task effects was therefore seen in young and old groups. However, this pattern cannot be straightforwardly interpreted as an age-related deficit of a particular component of the working memory model.

It can be noted that the task interference patterns for younger participants were relatively specific: TOL performance was only affected by random number generation, while in terms of performance on the secondary tasks themselves only the spatial tasks showed dual task interference. In contrast, for the older group there were generally quite high levels of dual task interference seen on most performance indicators. There are two possible explanations of this finding in relation to the three-component working memory model. First, all components of the model may be affected by age: this would explain why performance was affected across all of the secondary tasks. Second, age may affect the ability to carry out any two tasks which are fairly cognitively demanding, and this may reflect executive or attentional decline.

There have been contrasting views about whether there are indeed general age-related costs in the ability to co-ordinate multiple tasks. There are often age differences in dual task performance when the two tasks involved both require complex or demanding processing (McDowd & Craik, 1988). However, when the two tasks are simple or automatic, the increased age deficit in co-ordination may not occur. Craik et al. (1990) argue that where one of two competing tasks involve rehearsal that can safely be allocated to slave systems there tends to be relatively little interference. In contrast, if two competing tasks require consistent switching of attention from one to the other age deficits tend to occur. In the current TOL results, where all of the secondary tasks require the control of response intervals, it seems likely that both primary and secondary tasks may be attentionally demanding.

The extent to which the secondary tasks outlined above load specific components of the working memory model in older adults can be called into question (Phillips et al., submitted). Older adults were generally much poorer than young in single task conditions at producing random sequences of responses. It may be that older adults have problems in understanding the task requirements of random generation, and the nature of randomness in such tasks. In relation to random number generation, there was a non-significant trend for older adults to produce more randomly distributed responses when performing random generation along with the TOL as compared to single task randomness. Perhaps in the single task condition they were using relatively effortful but ineffectual strategies to generate responses that were not particularly random.

Younger people showed greater interference effects with random tapping compared to pattern tapping; in contrast the older adults showed greater interference effects with pattern tapping as compared to random tapping. However, there may be problems with the characterisation of pattern tapping as a task which loads the visuo-spatial buffer component of working memory, while random tapping loads both the spatial buffer and the central executive. Tapping out a sequenced pattern is likely to make at least some demands on executive function, in order to carry out the motor planning and control aspects of the task. Indeed, pattern tapping has been used in the neuropsychological literature as an executive task (Martin, Wiggs, Lalonde, & Mack, 1994). If older participants were not using effortful and effective search and inhibition strategies to produce a random sequence of taps during the control random tapping task, then random tapping might in some sense have less executive load than the pattern tapping task, in which the sequence of responses must be controlled.

This may also relate to the results of Maylor and Wing (1996) where they argue that the significant age decrements in postural stability caused by spatial memory and backwards digit span (but not random number generation) indicate a role for the visuo-spatial scratchpad (but not the central executive) in maintaining posture on old age. If random number generation is not operating as a high executive-loading task for the older adults, and both spatial memory and backwards span load executive processes, an alternative interpretation of Maylor and Wing's results is that age deficits in postural stability are attributable to central executive dysfunction.

Using dual task methodology allows detailed hypotheses about the nature of age differences in a range of tasks to be assessed. However, as can be seen from the preceding discussion the results obtained are not always straightforward to interpret. Relatively few experimental studies have been carried out which look at age effects on a range of dual tasks and it is clear that more detailed small scale manipulations of the range of dual tasks used are necessary before the results can be clearly interpreted. Currently, our understanding is poor of how people perform individual secondary tasks and which cognitive components they load; this is particularly true of older populations.

SOME GENERAL POINTS ABOUT AGE AND WORKING MEMORY

There has been relatively little literature which directly investigates the effects of age on components of the WM model, however, some tentative conclusions can be drawn, as follow.

Age differences in working memory do not appear to be due to deficits in basic storage capacity. There is evidence from verbal memory studies that incrementing storage requirements does not impact age differences, while other increments of task dimensions do interact with age (e.g. Craik et al.,

1990). This suggests that the phonological loop and visuo-spatial sketchpad components of working memory *may* be largely unaffected by age. This is also supported by the data reported above on visual/spatial memory and the central executive (e.g. Hamilton et al., 1999). However, slowing of aspects such as articulation rate or visual scanning speed might cause some degradation of the functioning of these components of working memory. There is still debate about the extent to which slowing of slave system operation with age represents specific or general processing speed deficits.

Older people perform poorly on many measures of executive function, but this should be interpreted with caution.   There is considerable evidence that older adults perform more poorly on tasks which involve central executive function such as the Stroop test, random generation, and verbal fluency. However, this data must be interpreted carefully because there is evidence that e.g. age differences in Stroop performance might reflect general slowing rather than an inhibition deficit (Uttl & Graf, 1997; Verhaeghen & De Meersman, 1998), and age differences in fluency may reflect peripheral slowing rather than poor strategy generation (Phillips, 1999). There is also evidence that age differences in working memory capacity (Salthouse, 1992) and random generation ability (Fisk & Warr, 1996) may be explained by statistically partialling out variance in measures of perceptual or cognitive speed.

Dual task studies suggest rather general impairment with age.   Using a range of dual tasks to examine age differences in working memory components produced results that suggest that dual task performance is impaired generally with age. There appear to be some qualitative differences in the operation of working memory components between young and older adults: but in order to interpret these, greater knowledge about dual tasks costs in young and old on a wider range of tasks is needed. Also, the cognitive constituents of secondary tasks such as pattern tapping and random generation need to be better understood in both younger and older populations.

ISSUES

Finally, we address specifically the four questions identified in chapter 1.

What are the strengths of the WM model?

The WM model is potentially useful in aging research because it makes explicit a framework that can be used to test for potential fractionation in age differences in cognition. Most research into cognitive aging relies on correlational approaches, and the WM model allows the possibility of experimental manipulations which might throw light on age differences in cognition. Specific predictions can be made, although (as often is the case in aging research) the obtained results from different studies may not fit neatly with specific components of the model. The WM model has such a large and rich background literature exploring theoretical and methodological issues that it is very useful to plunder for tried and tested experimental paradigms. There is also a range of specific hypotheses that can be generated from the knowledge of how the WM model operates, which can sometimes be specifically contrasted with predictions made from the general resource theories.

The model is also appealing in that it provides a cognitive-level explanation for cognitive phenomena, unlike many other predominant models of aging. Other current theories ultimately draw their predictions from biology, e.g. the information-loss model (Myerson, Hale, Wagstaff, Poon, & Smith, 1990) or the frontal-lobe hypothesis of aging (West, 1996); or alternatively from social factors such as cultural stereotypes (Levy & Langer, 1994) or environmental complexity (Zec, 1995). There are clearly links between the working memory model and brain functioning, e.g. the current interest in the executive component of working memory fits in well with the substantial evidence that age changes in the brain particularly affect the dorsolateral prefrontal cortex. However, these are not the impetus behind the functional predictions made about task performance.

What are the weaknesses of the WM model for this area?

Generality of age deficits

Much of the evidence for age changes in cognition suggests rather general deficits across different modalities. Salthouse (1994, p. 537) argues of the WM model that 'to the extent that significant age differences exist in each of the hypothesized components, this framework may not be very useful for differentiating, and potentially localising the source of, age-related effects in working memory'. There is also age-related slowing on almost any measurable index from the WM model, whether speed of articulating sentences, random generation, or rotation of mental images (Dror & Kosslyn, 1994; Kynette et al., 1990). Although these findings can be interpreted within the model by arguing that there are age-related changes in both slave systems and the central executive, this does not appear particularly parsimonious.

For example, a strength of the dual task methodology in exploring the working memory model in young adults is the pattern of dissociations that can be found such that some secondary tasks interfere with some primary tasks in an interesting and interpretable manner. However, there is a danger when using the dual task methodology in aging research that older adults will show increased dual task costs compared to young adults on all secondary tasks. If this is the case, the results become uninterpretable, because they could reflect so many different scenarios: age effects on all aspects of the working memory model, age effects on the control of dual task processes, decreases in processing speed, etc.

Poor specification of the role of processing

Another weakness of the model is the lack of specification as to how and where processing (i.e. transformation, manipulation and integration of material) is carried out. In the aging literature a number of authors argue that age differences in working memory and reasoning are attributable to decreased efficiency in carrying out transformation of information, while the capacity for storage remains intact (e.g. Craik & Jennings, 1992). It is not clear in the working memory model whether cognitive processing is carried out in the central executive or slave systems, or indeed whether separate systems for some types of processing need to be considered.

Underspecification of central executive

Very many authors have argued that age differences in cognition are attributable to executive dysfunction, and this has often been linked to the central executive component of the WM model. However, it is still not clear what specific predictions this makes about cognitive performance, because there has been inadequate delineation of which processes the central executive carries out and which processes it does *not* carry out. From early conceptions of the central executive and its role in memory tasks it was argued that the executive could intervene to carry out rehearsal whenever the slave systems became overloaded. However, it is not clear whether executive-controlled rehearsal would be of a qualitatively different nature from slave system rehearsal. Subsequently, the functioning of the central executive has become linked to the Norman and Shallice Supervisory Attentional System. However, this has not led to much agreement about which functions can and cannot legitimately be considered 'executive', or agreed paradigms for the assessment of executive function. Nor is there any palpable consensus about how executive functions might be fractionated.

What are the competing models in the field?

General resource models: working memory capacity and processing speed

The predominant characterisation of working memory in the aging litera-ture is of a general limited-capacity storage and processing system. Perhaps surprisingly there has been relatively little theoretical discussion in this literature as to what in cognitive terms such a general working memory resource comprises and what exactly age differences reflect. One of the most influential interpretations of age effects on working memory capacity is that of differences in processing speed (Salthouse, 1992). The theory that age changes in cognition are best conceptualised in terms of decreases in the general speed of information processing has been extremely influential. This theory proposes that age-related declines in performance on all cognitive tests can be explained in terms of general declines in the speed at which task components can be carried out. This means that the more complex the task, the greater the age difference, because there are more cognitive components to be slowed. The major way of testing this theory has been to examine the effects of statistically partialling out variance due to processing speed measures from age variance in other tests of cognitive performance. Using this method, there is evidence that age variance in working memory measures can be largely explained by measures of processing speed (e.g. Fisk & Warr, 1996; Salthouse, 1994). However, there are problems with this technique of testing for the role of processing speed: for example, the measures used in such studies to assess information-processing speed (e.g. reaction time, copying tasks) are unlikely to be pure measures of speed, and often do not intercorrelate well amongst themselves.

The processing speed model need not contradict the WM model in relation to aging. Older adults may be slower at all of the processes involved in working memory (e.g. articulatory rehearsal, inhibition, etc). In this case, the WM model might help to predict what the effects of slowed processing might be: e.g. slowed articulatory rehearsal should cause poorer performance on verbal memory tests.

Also, the processing speed model makes little in the way of predictions about aging and specific patterns of cognitive performance such as complexity effects. Morris et al. (1990) show that older adults are differentially affected by some complexity manipulations and not others. While their results can be clearly interpreted by the WM model as age invariance in articulatory loop function but age differences in central executive function, the processing speed model could only put forward the rather weak argument that some manipulations of complexity are more complex than others.

Distributed 'continuum' model

An alternative view which has been proposed by Cornoldi and Vecchi (Cornoldi, 1995; Cornoldi & Vecchi, 2000; Vecchi, Phillips, & Cornoldi, 2000) is that working memory processes vary according to: (1) the nature of the to-be-processed information and (2) the amount of active information processing required. At the level of passive or automatic processing, different types of information are processed independently, reflecting the different sensory modalities of the material. At this level, cognitive systems are relatively autonomous and domain-specific. In contrast, more active information processing utilises domain-independent processes, and interconnections between different sensory systems. The model therefore includes a vertical continuum reflecting the amount of active processing required by a task, dependent on the requirements for information manipulation, co-ordination, and integration. Even relatively passive tasks, such as verbal or spatial span, may require some sort of active processing, probably in the form of mental rehearsal. However, active processing demands are low and they can be positioned close to the passive pole of the continuum. When the information has to be transformed, modified or integrated, then a higher amount of active processing is required. The interrelations between different types of tasks represented by the horizontal continuum increase as the active processing demands rise. For example, following this approach, the phonological storage component of the WM model can be conceptualised instead as a relatively passive mechanism to represent modality-specific information, while the articulatory rehearsal component employs more active cognitive processes.

There is evidence that age-related changes in working memory may be unaffected by variation in the horizontal (modality) dimension. In contrast age differences in working memory may be determined by the amount of active processing that a task requires (Vecchi et al., 2000). There is generally age-stability on tasks of relatively passive short-term memory; but age-related decline on active tasks loading working memory (for review see Craik & Jennings, 1992). Salthouse, Mitchell, Skovoronek, and Babcock (1989) devised tasks that discriminate between *passive* recall of segments in a unique stimulus and *active* integration of segments in a 4×4 matrix. Older participants did not show any deficit in the passive task, but were significantly poorer at the active task. A similar result was obtained by Morris et al. (1990) in a sentence analysis task: though the oldest participants required longer to perform the task, the presence of a passive interfering task impaired both groups to the same extent. This suggests that age changes are linked to tasks which demand active, central processes of cognition.

One potential problem with the distributed continuum model is that it revolves around the distinction between active and passive processing, yet in practice this distinction is difficult to crystallise. Does the active/passive distinction depend mainly on the role of consciousness of cognitive operations, or on the degree of executive control? Further, some relatively dynamic tasks, such as visual scanning (Dror & Kosslyn, 1994) and trajectory tracking (data presented above) are not affected by age — should these tasks be considered active or passive?

What is the future for the WM approach in this field?

Development of techniques which improve assessment and fractionation of the central executive component of working memory (e.g. Miyake et al., 2000) may help to address the currently unanswered issue of whether age affects all or only some aspects of executive functioning. Further to this, there is a need to undertake task-analysis in order to identify tasks with selective demands upon the slave and executive systems. Should these tasks be identified, then age changes in working memory component efficacy can be more accurately described. This also applies to more selective development of dual tasks that clearly tap specific working memory components, in both young and old populations. Until these methodologies are fully developed we are left with a difficulty in interpreting the majority of aging findings within the model. One approach to this problem would be the development and validation of tasks in which there are manipulations to both increase and decrease the load on individual components of working memory. This could be used to examine in detail under what conditions age differences occurred. Especially in relation to aging, care must be taken to construct such tasks so that performance is not time-constrained, otherwise age differences will almost inevitably be found.

It would also be helpful to have better reconciliation between the results found within the Baddeley and Hitch WM model and those found within the more widely used perspective in aging research — that of working memory capacity deficits. These 'resource' models of working memory predict well the pattern of age differences in cognition using statistical control techniques. A typical result would be that age differences in working memory predict well age variance in reasoning tasks such as Raven's Matrices (Salthouse, 1993). However, in terms of cognitive psychological theory the nature and effects of age differences in working memory capacity are still rather underspecified. There is scope for greater cross talk and possibly differentiation between these capacity theories and in particular our understanding of how the central executive component of working memory operates.

Finally . . .

The WM model has not been the predominant approach to working memory in aging research. The model offers promise as a way to unravel at a cognitive level some of the phenomena of age-related cognitive change and provide a qualitative insight into working memory which can complement the speed of processing and resource centred approaches in the field.

BACKGROUND READING

There are very few articles that review or describe in general terms the effects of adult aging on the Baddeley and Hitch working memory model. These recommended references are therefore just a selection of the experimental studies described in this chapter.

Craik, F. I. M., Morris, R. G., & Gick, M. L. (1990). Adult age differences in working memory. In G. Vallar & T. Shallice (Eds.), *Neuropsychological Impairments of Short-term Memory* (pp. 247–267). New York: Cambridge University Press.

Fisk, J. E., & Warr, P. (1996). Age and working memory: the role of perceptual speed, the central executive, and the phonological loop. *Psychology and Aging, 11,* 316–323.

Maylor, E. A., & Wing, A. M. (1996). Age differences in postural stability are increased by additional cognitive demands. *Journal of Gerontology: Psychological Sciences, 51B,* 143–154.

Salthouse, T. A. (1994). The aging of working memory. *Neuropsychology, 8,* 535–543.

REFERENCES

Baddeley, A. D. (1986). *Working Memory.* Oxford: Oxford University Press.

Baddeley, A. D. (1996). Exploring the central executive. *Quarterly Journal of Experimental Psychology, 49A,* 5–28.

Baddeley, A. D., Emslie, H., Kolodny, J., & Duncan, J. (1998). Random generation and the executive control of working memory. *Quarterly Journal of Experimental Psychology, 51A,* 819–852.

Cerella, J., Poon, L., & Fozard, J. L. (1981). Mental rotation and age reconsidered. *Journal of Gerontology, 36,* 620–624.

Chuah, Y. M. L., & Maybery, M. T. (1999). Verbal and spatial short-term memory: common sources of developmental change? *Journal of Experimental Child Psychology, 73,* 7–44.

Coates, R., Sanderson, K., Hamilton, C. J., & Heffernan, T. (1999). Identifying differential processes in visuo-spatial working memory. *Proceedings of The British Psychological Society, 7,* 38.

Coffey, C. E., Wilkinson, W. E., Parashos, I. A., Soady, S. A. R., Sullivan, R. J., Patterson, I. J., Figiel, G. S., Webb, M. C., Spritzer, C. E., & Djang, W. T. (1992). Quantitative cerebral anatomy of the aging human brain: a cross-sectional study using magnetic resonance imaging. *Neurology, 42,* 527–536.

Coleman, P. D., & Flood, D. G. (1987). Neuron numbers and dendritic extent in normal aging and Alzheimer's disease. *Neurobiology of Aging, 8,* 521–545.

Cornoldi, C. (1995). Memoria di lavoro visuospaziale. In F. Marucci (Ed.), *Le Immagini Mentali.* Roma: La Nuova Italia.

Cornoldi, C., & Vecchi, T. (2000). Mental imagery in blind people: The role of passive and active visuo-spatial processes. In M. Heller (Ed.), *Touch, representation, and blindness.* Oxford: Oxford University Press.

Craik, F. I. M., & Jennings, J. M. (1992). Human memory. In F. I. M. Craik & T. A. Salthouse (Eds.), *The handbook of aging and cognition* (pp. 51–110). Hillsdale, N.J.: Lawrence Erlbaum Associates Inc.

Craik, F. I. M., Morris, R. G., & Gick, M. L. (1990). Adult age differences in working memory. In G. Vallar & T. Shallice (Eds.), *Neuropsychological impairments of short-term memory* (pp. 247–267). New York: Cambridge University Press.

Dirkx, E., & Craik, F. I. M. (1992). Age-related differences in memory as a function of imagery processing. *Psychology and Aging, 7*, 352–358.

Dobbs, A. R., & Rule, B. G. (1989). Adult age differences in working memory. *Psychology and Aging, 4*, 500–503.

Dror, I. E., & Kosslyn, S. M. (1994). Mental imagery and aging. *Psychology and Aging, 9*, 90–102.

Evans, J. S. B. T., & Brooks, P. G. (1981). Competing with reasoning: a test of the working memory hypothesis. *Current Psychological Research, 1*, 139–147.

Farah, M. J. (1984). The neurological basis of mental imagery. *Cognition, 18*, 245–272.

Farand, P., & Jones, D. (1996). Direction of report in spatial and verbal serial short term memory. *Quarterly Journal of Experimental Psychology, 49A*, 140–158.

Farmer, E. W., Berman, J. V. F., & Fletcher, Y. L. (1986). Evidence for a visuo-spatial scratch-pad in working memory. *Quarterly Journal of Experimental Psychology, 38A*, 675–688.

Feyereisen, P., & Van der Linden, M. (1997). Immediate memory for different kinds of gestures in younger and older adults. *Cahiers de Psychologie Cognitive, 16*, 519–533.

Fisk, J. E., & Warr, P. (1996). Age and working memory: the role of perceptual speed, the central executive, and the phonological loop. *Psychology and Aging, 11*, 316–323.

Gerhand, S. (1994). *Processing speed and cognitive aging*. Unpublished MSc thesis, Aberdeen University, Aberdeen.

Gilhooly, K. J., Logie, R. H., Wetherick, N. E., & Wynn, V. (1993). Working memory and strategies in syllogistic reasoning tasks. *Memory & Cognition, 21*, 115–124.

Gnys, J. A., & Willis, J. G. (1991). Validation of executive function tasks with young children. *Developmental Neuropsychology, 7*, 487–501.

Hamilton, C. J., Heffernan, T., & Coates, R. (1999). What develops in visuo-spatial working memory development? *Proceedings of The British Psychological Society, 7*, 127.

Hertzog, C., & Dixon, R. A. (1996). Methodological issues in research on cognition and aging. In F. Blanchard-Fields & T. M. Hess (Eds.), *Perspectives on cognitive change in adulthood and old age*. New York: McGraw Hill.

Hulme, C., Thomson, N., Muir, C., & Lawrence, A. (1984). Speech rate and the development of short-term memory span. *Journal of Experimental Child Psychology, 38*, 241–253.

Kail, R. (1993). Processing time changes globally at an exponential rate during childhood and adolescence. *Journal of Experimental Child Psychology, 56*, 254–265.

Kail, R., & Salthouse, T. A. (1994). Processing speed as a mental capacity. *Acta Psychologica, 86*, 199–225.

Kynette, D., Kemper, S., Norman, S., & Cheung, H. (1990). Adults word recall and word repetition. *Experimental Aging Research, 16*, 117–121.

Levy, B., & Langer, E. (1994). Aging free from negative stereotypes: successful memory in China and among the American deaf. *Journal of Personality and Social Psychology, 66*, 989–997.

Light, L. L., & Burke, D. M. (Eds.). (1988). *Language, memory and aging*. Cambridge: Cambridge University Press.

Logie, R. H. (1995). *Visuo-spatial working memory*. Hove, UK: Lawrence Erlbaum Associates Ltd.

Logie, R. H., & Pearson, D. G. (1998). The inner eye and the inner scribe of visuo-spatial working memory: evidence from developmental fractionation. *European Journal of Cognitive Psychology*, *9*, 241–257.

Martin, A., Wiggs, C. L., Lalonde, F., & Mack, C. (1994). Word retrieval to letter and semantic cues: a double dissociation in normal subjects using interference tasks. *Neuropsychologia*, *32*, 1487–1494.

Maylor, E. A., & Wing, A. M. (1996). Age differences in postural stability are increased by additional cognitive demands. *Journal of Gerontology: Psychological Sciences*, *51B*, 143–154.

McDowd, J. M., & Craik, F. I. M. (1988). Effects of aging and task difficulty on divided attention performance. *Journal of Experimental Psychology: Human Perception and Performance*, *14*, 267–280.

Miyake, A., Friedman, N. P., Emerson, A. H. W., Witzki, A. H., Howerter, A., & Wager, T. D. (2000). The unity and diversity of executive functions and their contribution to complex 'frontal lobe' tasks: a latent variable analysis. *Cognitive Psychology*, *41*, 49–100.

Morris, N., & Jones, D. M. (1990). Memory updating in working memory: the role of the central executive. *British Journal of Psychology*, *81*, 111–121.

Morris, R. G., Craik, F. I. M., & Gick, M. L. (1990). Age differences in working memory tasks: the role of secondary memory and the central executive system. *Quarterly Journal of Experimental Psychology*, *42A*, 67–86.

Moscovitch, M. (1994). Cognitive resources and dual-task interference effects at retrieval in normal people: the role of the frontal lobes and medial temporal lobes. *Neuropsychology*, *8*, 524–534.

Myerson, J., Hale, S., Wagstaff, D., Poon, L. W., & Smith, G. A. (1990). The information-loss model: a mathematical theory of age-related cognitive slowing. *Psychological Review*, *97*, 475–487.

Norman, D. A., & Shallice, T. (1986). Attention to action: willed and automatic control of behaviour. In R. J. Davidson, G. E. Schwartz, & D. Shapiro (Eds.), *Consciousness and self-regulation* (Vol. 4, pp. 1–18). New York: Plenum Press.

Owen, A. M. (1997). Cognitive planning in humans: neuropsychological, neuro-anatomical and neuropharmacological perspectives. *Progress in Neurobiology*, *53*(4), 431–450.

Parkin, A. J. (1997). Normal age-related memory loss and its relation to frontal lobe dysfunction. In P. M. A. Rabbitt (Ed.), *Methodology of frontal and executive function* (pp. 177–190). Hove, UK: Psychology Press.

Phillips, L. H. (1999). Age and individual differences in letter fluency. *Developmental Neuropsychology*, *15*, 249–267.

Phillips, L. H., Gilhooly, K. J., Logie, R. H., Della Sala, S., & Wynn, V. E. (submitted). Age, working memory and the Tower of London task. *Memory*, *7*, 209–231.

Rabbitt, P. M. A. (1997). *Methodology of frontal and executive function*. Hove, UK: Psychology Press.

Raz, N., Gunning, F. M., Head, D., Dupuis, J. H., & Acker, J. D. (1998). Neuro-anatomical correlates of cognitive aging: evidence from structural magnetic resonance imaging. *Neuropsychology*, *12*(1), 95–114.

Robbins, T. W., James, M., Owen, A. M., Sahakian, B. J., Lawrence, A. D.,

McInnes, L., & Rabbitt, P. M. A. (1998). A study of performance on tests from the CANTAB battery sensitive to frontal lobe dysfunction in a large sample of normal volunteers: implications for theories of executive functioning and cognitive aging. *Journal of the International Neuropsychological Society, 4*, 474–490.

Rouleau, N., & Belleville, S. (1996). Irrelevant speech effect in aging: an assessment of inhibitory processes in working memory. *Journal of Gerontology: Psychological Sciences, 51*, 356–363.

Salamé, P., & Baddeley, A. D. (1982). Disruption of short-term memory by unattended speech: implications for the structure of working memory. *Journal of Verbal Learning and Verbal Behaviour, 21*, 150–164.

Salthouse, T. A. (1991). *Theoretical perspectives on cognitive aging.* Hillsdale, NJ: Lawrence Erlbaum Associates Inc.

Salthouse, T. A. (1992). Influences of processing speed on adult age differences in working memory. *Acta Psychologica, 79*, 155–170.

Salthouse, T. A. (1993). Influence of working memory on adult age differences in matrix reasoning. *British Journal of Psychology, 84*, 171–199.

Salthouse, T. A. (1994). The aging of working memory. *Neuropsychology, 8*, 535–543.

Salthouse, T. A., Kausler, D. H., & Saults, J. S. (1988). Investigation of student status, background variables, and the feasibility of standard tasks in cognitive aging research. *Psychology and Aging, 3*, 29–37.

Salthouse, T. A., Mitchell, D. R. D., Skovoronek, E., & Babcock, R. L. (1989). Effects of adult age and working memory on reasoning and spatial abilities. *Journal of Experimental Psychology: Learning Memory and Cognition, 15*, 507–516.

Shallice, T. (1982). Specific impairments of planning. *Philosophical Transactions of the Royal Society of London B, 298*, 199–209.

Smyth, M. M., & Scholey, K. (1996). Serial order in spatial immediate memory. *Quarterly Journal of Experimental Psychology, 49A*, 159–177.

Uttl, B., & Graf, P. (1997). Color–word Stroop test performance across the adult life span. *Journal of Clinical and Experimental Neurospychology, 19*, 405–420.

Van der Linden, M., Bregart, S., & Beerten, A. (1994). Age related differences in updating working memory. *British Journal of Psychology, 84*, 145–152.

Vecchi, T., Phillips, L. H., & Cornoldi, C. (2000). Individual differences in visuo-spatial working memory: The effects of age, gender and blindness. In M. Denis, C. Cornoldi, R. H. Logie, M. de Vega, & J. Engelkamp (Eds.), *Imagery, language and visuo-spatial thinking.* Hove, UK: Psychology Press.

Verhaeghen, P., & De Meersman, L. (1998). Aging and the Stroop effect: a meta-analysis. *Psychology and Aging, 13*, 120–126.

West, R. L. (1996). An application of prefrontal cortex function theory to cognitive aging. *Psychological Bulletin, 120*(2), 272–292.

Zec, R. F. (1995). The neuropsychology of aging. *Experimental Gerontology, 30*, 431–442.

6 Applying the working memory model to the study of atypical development

Chris Jarrold

The working memory model proposed by Baddeley and Hitch (1974), and subsequently modified by Baddeley (1986), has provided the theoretical basis for a considerable body of research examining memory in typically developing children (see Gathercole, 1998). The model has been less often applied to the study of working memory in individuals showing atypical development (though see Hulme & Mackenzie, 1992). Nevertheless, there are good reasons for attempting to extend the scope of the model in this direction. The purpose of this chapter is to outline the ways in which the working memory model can inform this type of research, by explaining deficits seen in memory and learning in various atypical groups. In doing this, alternative explanations of these memory deficits will be considered and contrasted against the working memory account. In particular, the question of whether working memory deficits are a fundamental cause of learning disability, or rather arise as a consequence of more general learning difficulties, will be addressed. This will highlight the problems involved in applying the working memory model in this area, some of which stem from attempting to use what is essentially an adult model to describe developmental data. Given these problems, the final section of the chapter will consider ways in which the model might be usefully developed in the future to provide a more dynamic and interactive model of atypical working memory development.

THE STRENGTHS OF THE WORKING MEMORY MODEL FOR EXPLORING ATYPICAL DEVELOPMENT

Broadly speaking there are two ways in which the working memory model can further our understanding of atypical development. First, it provides a framework for describing and explaining deficits in working memory functioning that might be seen in individuals with developmental disorders. By appropriately characterising working memory deficits we not only further our understanding of the difficulties experienced by an individual or a population group, but we may also be able to suggest ways in which memory abilities may be improved. Second, the fact that working memory has been shown to be important in the development of other cognitive abilities allows us to predict how broader problems in cognitive functioning might arise as a result of particular working memory impairments.

Characterising deficits

Given that the working memory model consists of three distinct subsystems — the phonological loop, the visuo-spatial sketchpad, and the central executive — one would expect that individuals with developmental disorders might show three specific types of working memory deficit, each being the result of breakdown or dysfunction within one of these components. There is evidence that particular populations are associated with impairments in verbal and visuo-spatial short-term memory. Both specific language impairment (SLI) and Down syndrome are conditions which have been linked with a phonological loop deficit. For example, Gathercole and Baddeley (1990a) found that individuals with SLI showed impaired non-word repetition ability (which they argue provides a pure test of verbal short-term memory) relative to vocabulary matched controls. Similarly, Jarrold and Baddeley (1997) showed that individuals with Down syndrome had poorer digit spans than controls with equivalent vocabulary levels, despite all groups having comparable Corsi spans. Specific impairments to the visuo-spatial sketchpad have also been reported. Wang and Bellugi (1994) have argued that individuals with Williams syndrome, a relatively rare genetic condition (see Mervis, 1999 for details) may suffer from a specific visuo-spatial sketchpad deficit. This is based on individuals' poor performance on the Corsi span task (Milner, 1971), a test that assesses participants' short-term memory for a series of sequentially presented spatial locations. Similarly, Cornoldi, Dalla Vecchia and Tressoldi (1995) found that individuals with 'low visuo-spatial intelligence' performed more poorly on a 'Corsi-like' spatial short-term memory task than language matched controls.

Other conditions have been linked to executive deficits. 'Executive dysfunction' is thought to be a characteristic of autism, attention deficit hyperactivity disorder (ADHD), and Tourette's syndrome (see Pennington & Ozonoff, 1996). However, here the term 'executive' is applied in the context of control of action rather than of control of memory. There is little doubt that individuals with these disorders suffer from the problems of inhibition, planning and set-shifting that would follow from an impairment to the kind of executive underpinning Norman and Shallice's (1986) model of behavioural control, but this is not the same as saying that these groups have impaired executive control of working memory. Although modelled on Norman and Shallice's 'supervisory attentional system', there is no reason to assume that Baddeley's (1986) central executive is necessarily involved in action selection (cf. Lehto, 1996). A working memory central executive deficit would be reflected in problems of dual memory task performance, and there has, in fact, been relatively little work of this nature with these particular groups.

Instead stronger evidence for an executive memory impairment among individuals with learning disability comes from an approach which has more in common with the 1974 than the 1986 conception of the central executive. This early view of the executive as 'a limited capacity "workspace" which can be divided between storage and control processing demands' (Baddeley, 1986, p. 76) was consistent with a broader (and generally North American) tradition of defining working memory as the process of storing and manipulating information (Daneman & Carpenter, 1980; Turner & Engle, 1989). Central to this approach is the use of the 'complex span task' (e.g., Case, Kurland & Goldberg, 1982; Daneman & Carpenter, 1980) in which participants have to remember a number of items of information while carrying out simultaneous processing. For example, in Daneman and Carpenter's (1980) 'reading span' task participants read a series of sentences while maintaining in memory the final word of each sentence; the maximum number of words that can be recalled under these circumstances determines the participant's span. A number of studies, reviewed in the following sub-section, have shown that individuals with particular learning difficulties have difficulties on these kinds of tasks. Further, Swanson (1993a) has argued that individuals with learning difficulty have generally reduced executive resources, which is shown by their poor performance on these complex span tasks.

The working memory model therefore provides a framework for describing some of the specific memory problems that are observed in certain developmental disorders, and perhaps in learning disability in general. An additional advantage is that aspects of the model are theoretically developed, as a result of empirical work with normal adults, with typically developing children, and with neuropsychological patients. We know a reasonable amount about the normal workings of the phonological loop (e.g., Baddeley, 1986), and are beginning to learn about the details of visuo-spatial sketchpad functioning (e.g., Logie, 1995, chapter 4); although the central executive remains, in Baddeley's terms, something of 'a pool of residual ignorance' (Baddeley, 1996, p. 12). Consequently, the working memory model has the potential to explain deficits to the slave systems in some detail. The model offers a basis for structured experimentation to explore short-term memory deficits, and suggests methods of intervention which might improve these deficits.

For example, the phonological loop is itself thought to consist of two separable components, the phonological store, and the process of subvocal rehearsal (see Baddeley, 1986). Subvocal rehearsal of information offsets forgetting from the store by refreshing the phonological trace. Given that the loop consists of these two subsystems, one can ask whether the phonological loop deficits observed in individuals with SLI or in Down syndrome are caused by problems in either storage or in rehearsal. Verbal short-term memory deficits in Down syndrome have typically been viewed in terms of problems of rehearsal. Hulme and Mackenzie (1992, pp. 89–91) argue that the relatively poor verbal short-term memory of individuals with Down syndrome reflects a failure to rehearse among this group (it is important to note that these authors argue that this deficit is not specific to Down syndrome, but is also seen in other individuals with severe learning difficulties). This suggestion has prompted a number of intervention studies aimed at training rehearsal in Down syndrome (Broadley & MacDonald, 1993; Broadley, MacDonald & Buckley, 1994; Comblain, 1994; Laws, MacDonald & Buckley, 1996; Laws, MacDonald, Buckley, & Broadley, 1995) which have met with mixed success (see Jarrold, Baddeley & Phillips, 1999). In contrast, Gathercole and Baddeley (1990a) have argued that the verbal short-term memory deficit observed in SLI is unlikely to be due to a specific rehearsal problem. They found that their groups of individuals with SLI and controls differed in verbal short-term memory, despite having comparable speech rates. In addition, all groups showed word length effects — a potential indication that rehearsal is occurring (though see Cowan, Day, Saults, Keller, Johnson & Flores, 1992). As a result Gathercole and Baddeley instead suggest that their group may be suffering from impairment to the phonological store.

Recent research suggests that the visuo-spatial sketchpad may also be further subdivided. Logie (1995, pp. 126–131) argues that the sketchpad consists of a passive, visual storage component, and an active, spatial maintenance component. These are termed the 'visual cache' and the 'inner scribe' respectively. Potential evidence for these two subcomponents of the sketchpad comes from evidence of different patterns of disruption of visuo-spatial short-term memory by concurrent tasks which are either visual or spatial in nature (Logie & Marchetti, 1991; Quinn & McConnell, 1996; Tresch, Sinnamon & Seamon, 1993). However, at present there is only mixed evidence that individuals with learning disability who appear to suffer from visuo-spatial short-term memory deficits show selective impairments along these lines. This comes from studies which have contrasted performance on the Corsi span task with that seen on pattern span tests (see Phillips & Christie, 1977), in which to-be-remembered items are presented simultaneously in a visual array rather than in a spatial sequence. One might argue that the Corsi task is likely to place heavier demands on a spatial rehearsal system than pattern span tests, as the 'path' linking spatial positions needs to be remembered. Jarrold, Baddeley and Hewes (1999) showed that individuals with Williams syndrome showed comparable levels of impairment on these two tasks. However, Cornoldi et al. (1995) found that their individuals with low visuo-spatial intelligence were less impaired on a pattern-span type test than they were on a Corsi-like task. This might suggest that these participants, unlike individuals with Williams syndrome, suffer from relatively greater problems in active spatial rehearsal.

Predicting deficits

Arguably the most relevant feature of the working memory model for the study of learning disability comes from the predictive power of the model. Baddeley, Gathercole and Papagno (1998) have recently reviewed the evidence to suggest that the phonological loop plays a role in language acquisition. One might also suggest that visuo-spatial short-term memory deficits might lead on to problems in the long-term acquisition of visual and spatial knowledge (Hanley, Young & Pearson, 1991), though as yet we lack a detailed theoretical account of exactly why and how this would occur, and there is little empirical evidence for such a link. Nevertheless, a strong prediction made by the working memory model is that individuals with a phonological loop impairment should have deficits in language acquisition, and in the development of vocabulary in particular. A more tentative suggestion is that a deficit in visuo-spatial short-term memory might lead on to problems for long-term learning of visual and spatial information. One might argue that the conditions highlighted above provide evidence for both of these predictions. Specific language impairment is, by definition, associated with particular problems in language acquisition. There is also evidence that individuals with Down syndrome tend to have language abilities that are delayed relative to their non-verbal skills (see Chapman, 1995; Gunn & Crombie, 1996). Similarly, the two groups associated with potential visuo-spatial sketchpad deficits both have visuo-spatial skills which are delayed relative to language skills. Again this is a 'necessary' feature of individuals with low visuo-spatial intelligence, and, broadly speaking, individuals with Williams syndrome suffer from specific visuo-spatial problems (see Jarrold, Baddeley & Hewes, 1998).

Central executive deficits would also be expected to have broader consequences related to the long-term learning and maintenance of information. As noted above, complex span tasks have been used to study central executive functioning in atypical populations. One of the motivations for this work was Daneman and Carpenter's (1980) finding that performance on their complex span task predicted reading comprehension in adults. Given this association one would expect a low complex span score to be an indication of reading difficulties in children. This has been demonstrated in a number of studies which have employed children classed as being either 'poor readers' or 'reading disabled' and which have shown that these groups are impaired on versions of the Daneman and Carpenter task (Nation, Adams, Bowyer-Crane & Snowling, 1999; Siegel & Ryan, 1989; Yuill, Oakhill & Parkin, 1989; though see Stothard & Hulme, 1992). Other studies have employed an alternative complex span task in which series of dots have to be counted with the successive totals being held in mind for later recall (Case et al., 1982). Both Siegel and Ryan (1989) and Hitch and McAuley (1991) have shown that this task is sensitive to 'arithmetic' difficulties in children (see also McLean & Hitch, 1999).

The studies reviewed briefly in this subsection show that there appears to be an association between particular working memory deficits and specific patterns of learning disability. One important implication of this is that these particular learning disabilities might be the direct result of working memory deficits. However, although these patterns of strengths and deficits in long-term knowledge and ability are consistent with the working memory viewpoint, they also prompt alternative explanations of the links between long-term and working memory skills (see also chapter 4, this volume). These are the accounts to which we will now turn our attention.

COMPETING MODELS

Verbal short-term memory deficits as a consequence of specific impairments in speech perception and speech production

In a comprehensive review of verbal short-term memory deficits among children with a variety of learning difficulties, Hulme and Roodenrys (1995) suggest that such deficits 'are typically a consequence of more general language difficulties' (p. 393). These authors accept that verbal short-term memory deficits are seen among certain individuals with learning difficulties, but reject the view that these deficits are the cause of other problems in language acquisition. For example they argue that: 'Short-term memory deficits, in the absence of other difficulties, probably do not have important general effects on cognitive development' (p. 392). Instead their position, and that of other authors (e.g., Snowling, Chiat & Hulme, 1991; Van der Lely & Howard, 1993), is that language difficulties and verbal short-term memory problems co-exist in populations such as Down syndrome and SLI because they are linked by underlying factors. In particular, these authors suggest that difficulties in speech production and speech perception might simultaneously give rise to poor verbal short-term memory ability and long-term problems in language development.

The potential impact of problems in speech production and speech perception can be illustrated with reference to the two conditions previously noted as being associated with verbal short-term memory deficits (see also Avons & Hanna, 1995; Raine, Hulme, Chadderton & Bailey, 1991; Waters, Rochon & Caplan, 1992). It is certainly the case that individuals with Down syndrome often have speech production difficulties, and Hulme and Mackenzie (1992, chapter 4) found that a sample of individuals with Down syndrome had slower speech rates than typically developing controls matched for verbal mental age. A reduced speech rate might give rise to reduced verbal memory span for two reasons. First, the efficiency of subvocal rehearsal is thought to be constrained by rehearsal rate (e.g., Baddeley, Thomson & Buchanan, 1975; Schweickert & Boruff, 1986). Second, speech rates will determine the speed with which individuals can output a verbal response to a serial recall task, which in turn will affect the extent of any forgetting which occurs during outputting of list items (cf. Cowan et al., 1992; Dosher & Ma, 1998). To some extent the question of whether speech production problems should be viewed as separate from, or intrinsic to, phonological loop functioning is a theoretical one. Hulme and Roodenrys (1995) would argue that speech is a more general and fundamental process than verbal short-term memory. However, rate of articulation is a key aspect of the working memory model, and as such a rehearsal deficit in Down syndrome could certainly be phrased in terms of a phonological loop impairment.

A clearer contrast between these accounts is seen in the case of individuals with SLI. Much of the evidence for a verbal short-term memory deficit in this population comes from these individuals' poor performance on tests of non-word repetition (Bishop, North & Donlan, 1996; Gathercole & Baddeley, 1990a). Although nonword repetition is thought to require verbal short-term memory — individuals have to maintain an accurate phonological representation of the novel word in order to repeat it correctly — it also depends on the ability to encode and produce the phonological information presented. Snowling, Goulandris, Bowlby and Howell (1986) have argued that poor performance on this task might therefore arise as a result of problems of phonological awareness and/or speech production difficulties (see also Bowey, 1996; Snowling et al., 1991; Van der Lely & Howard, 1993; Wells, 1995; and replies by Gathercole, 1995a; Gathercole & Baddeley, 1995, 1997; Gathercole, Willis & Baddeley, 1991). In addition there is evidence that individuals with SLI show poor phonological awareness skills (Kahmi, Lee & Nelson, 1985), raising the possibility that this, rather than a memory deficit *per se*, might underlie their poor performance on non-word repetition tasks.

Working memory deficits as a consequence of learning difficulties

The above account provides a specific explanation of the co-occurrence of certain language problems and verbal short-term memory deficits. However, one can easily extend this position to make a more radical, and yet entirely plausible, suggestion; namely that poor working memory performance in individuals with developmental disorders or with learning disability is simply a reflection of these individuals' more general learning difficulties.

According to this account, individuals perform poorly on a digit span test, not primarily because it assesses verbal short-term memory, but because it has a strong verbal component. Similarly, poor Corsi span performance would not be viewed as indicating a specific visuo-spatial sketchpad deficit, but would simply reflect the fact that the task is essentially visuo-spatial in nature. Consequently, an individual whose language skills are relatively impaired in comparison to their general visuo-spatial abilities is likely to perform relatively poorly on a digit span task. The opposite profile of general abilities is likely to lead to an apparent deficit on the Corsi span task. This analysis is entirely consistent with the data from the various populations highlighted in the previous section. Individuals with Down syndrome and with specific language impairment who show poor verbal short-term memory ability, also have relatively poor verbal skills. Individuals with Williams syndrome and individuals with low visuo-spatial intelligence have relatively delayed visuo-spatial abilities.

The same line of argument can be applied to the studies of central executive functioning which have employed complex span tasks. Because these tasks are explicitly designed to tap processing and storage it is conceivable that individual variation in performance might arise from either of these aspects of the test (Dixon, LeFevre & Twilley, 1988; Waters & Caplan, 1996). One clear constraint on performance is likely to be the efficiency with which the individual can perform the processing operations of each task (Case et al., 1982; Daneman & Carpenter, 1980). Consequently, it is quite possible that an individual with reading difficulties will perform poorly on a Daneman and Carpenter task, even one presented auditorily, because of the requirement to process and comprehend the sentence (Baddeley, Logie, Nimmo-Smith & Brereton, 1985; Nation et al., 1999). Similarly, an individual with arithmetic difficulties may struggle with the counting span task simply because it involves counting items (Hitch & McAuley, 1991).

To some extent these arguments 'turn the working memory account on its head' (Snowling, et al., 1991). The working memory position, outlined in the previous section, is that working memory deficits lead to certain specific learning disabilities, while the suggestion made here is that it is the pattern of long-term learning difficulties which constrains working memory performance. Clearly, any correlation between working memory performance and learning disability is consistent with either account. The crucial question is therefore whether these apparent working memory deficits are a cause or a consequence of the pattern of learning difficulties associated with each of these conditions. The full importance of this question, and the ways in which it can be addressed, will be considered in the final section of this chapter.

WEAKNESSES OF THE WORKING MEMORY MODEL

The accounts described in the previous section share two particular features. First, they suggest that poor memory performance, when seen among individuals with learning disability, might not be due to a primary working memory impairment. Instead it may either reflect general problems in the domain in which memory is being assessed, or more specific deficits which themselves give rise to both poor working memory performance and generalised learning difficulties. Second, and by direct implication, these accounts argue that working memory deficits are not the cause of other cognitive problems. These points, in turn, raise questions for the working memory account. Although one can characterise poor memory performance in terms of phonological loop, visuo-spatial sketchpad, or central executive impairments, these alternative accounts challenge the validity of this approach. In addition, they question the sense of interpreting other cognitive impairments as the consequence of working memory deficits. This section of the chapter will consider the extent to which the working model is undermined by these criticisms.

A failure to characterise deficits

If an adult, neuropsychological patient was shown to have a digit span of only one item, then it would be tempting to conclude that they suffered from a phonological loop deficit. This conclusion would only be warranted, though, if it could also be shown that this deficit was specific, and did not arise as a result of other, more general deficits. Exactly the same holds for the study of children with atypical development. However, and as the previous section has highlighted, in this research area the extent of learning disability shown by any individual or population group also needs to be accounted for. This poses a potential problem for the working memory approach, but one that is not necessarily insurmountable (see the following section). It is theoretically possible that individuals might show impaired digit span even when any language impairments are accounted for. Similarly, it is at least conceivable that individuals might have impaired Corsi spans even allowing for generally poor visuo-spatial abilities.

What is far less clear is whether an individual could be shown to have an impaired complex span once level of processing efficiency on the task was controlled for. Indeed one might argue that these tests never provide an adequate measure of the central executive, but only of the ease with which an individual can read or process sentences or count patterns of dots (cf. Hitch & Towse, 1995; Towse & Hitch, 1995; Towse, Hitch & Hutton, 1998). A key question, therefore, is whether performance on complex span tasks is determined by the specific processing requirements of the task, or by more general constraints on processing efficiency which operate across domains. Only the latter is consistent with the view that the central executive, which is by nature a domain-general system (Baddeley, 1986), is involved in complex span tasks. In fact the data which might answer this question are somewhat mixed. Siegel and Ryan (1989) showed that reading disabled children were impaired on complex span tasks that required either verbal or non-verbal processing (see also Swanson, 1993a), while Swanson, Ashbaker and Lee (1996) found that the significant correlation between verbal complex span performance and reading ability observed in a sample of children with general learning disability was eliminated by partialling out individual differences in mathematical ability. However, Nation et al. (1999) found a deficit in poor text comprehenders on a verbal complex span task only. The two studies which have assessed children with arithmetic difficulties on complex span tasks requiring either verbal or non-verbal processing (Hitch & McAuley, 1991; Siegel & Ryan, 1989) both found that individuals' difficulties were restricted only to the latter type of task. One way of reconciling these apparently contradictory findings is to accept that performance on any complex span task is likely to be determined by multiple factors (Dixon et al., 1988; Just & Carpenter, 1992; Kane, Conway & Engle, 1999; Waters & Caplan, 1996). It appears quite clear that individuals with a specific processing problem will perform poorly on a task that taps that kind of processing. However, this does not preclude the possibility that they also have generally inefficient processing, arising as a result of central executive dysfunction, which affects performance on any task that has conjoint processing and storage requirements (Kane et al., 1999; Swanson, 1993b).

As discussed, if a working memory deficit can be reliably demonstrated then an advantage of the model is that it has the potential to do more than simply re-describe impaired performance; its theoretical framework allows for an explanation of exactly how poor working memory performance might arise. However, the model can only succeed in this if the functions of its component subsystems are properly specified. This can be judged at three successive levels of theoretical specification. One can ask whether there is a theoretical account of the functioning of a subsystem, whether there is a developmental account of how functioning of that system typically changes with age, and whether there is a framework for explaining how functioning might break down in atypical development. Clearly, for the study of working memory deficits among children with learning difficulties the model needs to be specified at all of these three levels.

Of the three subcomponents of the working memory model, the central executive is arguably the least theoretically developed (Baddeley, 1995, 1996). The merits of complex span tasks as potential indices of central executive functioning have already been discussed in some detail, but an additional concern is exactly how these measures square with current conceptions of the executive. Even if one accepts that these tasks do require concurrent processing and storage, and that they are not solely limited by specific processing abilities, it remains unclear how task performance should be interpreted within the framework of the 1986 model, which ascribes no capacity for storage to the central executive (Baddeley, 1993; see chapter 1, this volume). Similarly, although there are clearly articulated accounts of how the function of a limited-capacity executive might develop — either in terms of increases of processing efficiency with age (Case, 1985, chapter 16) or of total capacity (e.g., Halford, Maybery, O'Hare & Grant, 1994; Swanson, 1996, 1999; Turner & Engle, 1989) — we lack an accepted account of how the executive in Baddeley's (1986) model develops with age. Research into the executive deficits shown by individuals with Alzheimer's disease (e.g., Baddeley, Logie, Bressi, Della Sala & Spinnler, 1986) has provided evidence of the ways in which the central executive might break down in adults. Although this can certainly inform research with children with learning disabilities, one cannot assume that atypical development will show the same patterns of impairment as seen in adult neuropsychological cases.

We have, perhaps, a slightly better understanding of the workings of the visuo-spatial sketchpad (e.g., Logie, 1995, chapter 4). As noted earlier, it is thought that the sketchpad might fractionate into visual and spatial sub-components, with information being maintained in memory by a process of spatial rehearsal. However, this is a model of adult functioning, and although we know that visuo-spatial short-term memory performance develops with age (Isaacs & Vargha-Khadem, 1989; Logie & Pearson, 1997; Orsini, 1994; Pickering, Gathercole & Hall, 2001; Wilson, Scott & Power, 1987), we again have no clear theoretical account of this development. Consequently, we also lack a framework for explaining how visuo-spatial short-term memory might be impaired in atypical development.

In contrast, not only are there well-developed models of phonological loop functioning in adults, but there is also an account of how verbal short-term memory performance improves in typically developing children. The argument is that verbal short-term memory increases in line with increased speech rates as individuals develop, leading to more rapid and more efficient rehearsal (e.g., Hulme, Thomson, Muir, & Lawrence, 1984; Nicolson, 1981). Clearly this prompts an immediate explanation of impaired verbal short-term memory among individuals with learning disability, in terms of rehearsal-related deficits. However, as outlined in the earlier section on Competing Models, the evidence for deficits in rehearsal processes among individuals with verbal short-term memory deficits is mixed. This may in fact reflect a problem with this account of verbal short-term memory development. A number of authors have suggested that typically developing individuals do not engage in rehearsal before the age of seven (Flavell, Beach & Chinsky, 1966; Gathercole, Adams & Hitch, 1994; Henry, 1991a; see Gathercole, 1998 for a review of this evidence). Nevertheless children's verbal short-term memory shows clear developmental improvement before this age. In addition, there is evidence to suggest that the difference between younger and older children's verbal short-term memory spans cannot be wholly explained in terms of differences in rehearsal efficiency (Henry, 1991b; Hitch, Halliday & Littler, 1989, 1993; Hulme & Muir, 1985; Roodenrys, Hulme & Brown, 1993). If one accepts these arguments, then something other than rehearsal speed must be the determinant of verbal short-term memory performance before seven, and rehearsal efficiency may not be an important constraint on performance even after this age.

Consequently, a rehearsal model of phonological loop functioning may be surprisingly ill-equipped to explain developmental change in verbal short-term memory and, by extension, verbal short-term memory deficits in children with learning disabilities. One alternative view is that speech rates predict verbal spans in children because of output effects on recall performance (cf. Cowan et al., 1992; Dosher & Ma, 1998). According to this account impaired verbal short-term memory would arise as a result of articulation difficulties. However, as noted above, there is evidence that children with SLI show impaired verbal short-term memory, even when their speech is as efficient as that of controls (Gathercole & Baddeley, 1990a). This has led, perhaps rather by default, to the suggestion that these individuals suffer from an impairment to the phonological store component of the loop. Once again though, there is not a clear theoretical explanation of what this amounts to. There are a number of models of adult verbal short-term memory which do not rely on rehearsal to explain performance (e.g., Brown & Hulme, 1995; Burgess & Hitch, 1992; Henson, 1998; Neath & Nairne, 1995; Page & Norris, 1998). However, very few of these models have been applied to the development of verbal short-term memory (see Brown, Vousden, McCormack & Hulme, 1999 for an exception).

A failure to predict deficits

As discussed, a potential strength of the working memory account as far as the study of learning disability is concerned, comes from its ability to predict impairments that will follow as a consequence of working memory deficits. However, a weakness of the model is that there is really only reasonable empirical support and theoretical justification for the importance of the phonological loop in long-term learning. Although it has been suggested that the visuo-spatial sketchpad may play a role in acquisition of long-term visual-knowledge there has been little, if any, research into this possibility. This might be because it is unclear what a visuo-spatial analogue to vocabulary acquisition would be. Vocabulary is a crystallised measure which represents the amount of information that an individual has acquired over time. In contrast, most available measures of visuo-spatial functioning in children do not assess crystallised visuo-spatial knowledge, but instead tap more fluid visuo-spatial ability. Certainly a clearer conception of visuo-spatial learning is needed before this kind of research can progress.

In addition, even the role of the phonological loop in the acquisition of aspects of language is open to criticism. The earlier section on Competing Models outlined how the observed links between verbal short-term memory and language ability can equally be viewed in terms of language level constraining verbal short-term memory performance. Showing a relationship between these two domains (Adams & Gathercole, 1995, 1996; Gathercole & Adams, 1994; Gathercole & Baddeley, 1990b; Michas & Henry, 1994; Service, 1992; Service & Kohonen, 1995) does not indicate the direction of causality between them, and consequently does not decide between the two accounts considered here. One might argue that the evidence from adult patients with acquired verbal short-term memory impairments shows that such deficits can exist in the absence of general language or phonological problems (e.g., R. Martin & Breedin, 1992; though see N. Martin, Saffran & Dell, 1996), and that they lead on to specific deficits in acquiring novel phonological information. However, the relevance of this point may be limited to adult cases. It may well be that there are strong interrelations between language and short-term memory in children which become less important with development (see following section).

There is a sense in which the evidence from complex span tasks shows that these are really quite accurate and specific predictors of learning disability. However, and as already discussed, this seems to be because the processes involved in these tasks overlap with the learning disability itself. Therefore, although these tasks might be sensitive indices of specific problems, this does not necessarily imply that central executive deficits are the cause of these problems. Instead it seems that if central executive deficits do play any role in determining complex span performance then this is likely to be a general one, which will be reflected in rather generalised learning difficulties (Swanson, 1993a).

These points show that the predictive power of the working memory account can be questioned, and that some of the evidence for the importance of the phonological loop in language acquisition can be interpreted in support of alternative accounts. This is not to say that these alternative theories and the working memory model are inseparable. The final section of the chapter will consider ways in which these accounts can be tested against each other, and the ways in which the working memory model needs to be developed to provide a better description and explanation of short-term memory deficits seen in individuals with learning disabilities.

THE FUTURE OF THE WORKING MEMORY APPROACH

The previous section has shown that although the working memory model provides a potential framework for describing, explaining and predicting deficits associated with atypical development, it is not without its weaknesses. Some of these follow from a lack of theoretical specification of the functioning of its subcomponents. In particular, there is a need for more detailed accounts of the development of the workings of these subsystems in children. Without accepted models of typical development one cannot properly characterise short-term memory deficits which may be associated with atypical development.

To some extent these weaknesses in the model reflect the fact that it was originally designed to cope with adult data. A currently popular view among developmental psychologists is that adult neuropsychological models are inappropriate for the study of both typical and atypical development (e.g., Bishop, 1997; Karmiloff-Smith, 1997). A first concern is that adult models are 'static' and do not attempt to capture the development of cognitive functioning; consequently they struggle to deal with developmental change shown in children. A second, related issue is that although neuropsychological models accept the possibility of functional re-organisation, they underestimate the extent of neural plasticity in atypical development. Given that the brain is more likely to re-organise the location of functional specialisation in younger as opposed to older individuals (see Elman, Bates, Johnson, Karmiloff-Smith, Parisi & Plunkett, 1996, chapter 1), it is argued that individuals suffering from brain dysfunction from birth are much more likely to develop compensatory organisation of function than are adults who suffer discrete lesions later in life. Finally, current developmental models emphasise the interactions which occur between developing systems, while accepting that these systems may become increasingly discrete and modularised with time (Elman et al., 1996, chapter 7; Karmiloff-Smith, 1992, pp. 165–168).

Although certainly valid, there is a danger of over-playing these criticisms. Developmental and adult cognitive neuropsychology are not qualitatively different sciences. Adult neuropsychology requires general explanations of a deficit to be ruled out before a specific hypothesis can be advanced. In the same way, studies of atypical development just need to take into account developmental factors in order to show that performance is not simply delayed, but rather deviates from what would typically be expected. It would also be incorrect to label the working memory model as an entirely static system; this chapter began by noting that it has been applied to the study of development since its conception. Nevertheless, the future of the working memory model in this research area rests on an increased acceptance of the importance of these developmental issues. This will lead to two immediate benefits, which will be outlined below. First, an acceptance of the importance of developmental factors such as age and level of intelligence will lead to empirical studies which provide appropriate tests of the working memory account. Second, developmental theories of working memory functioning will provide the tools with which to explore these deficits further. Looking further ahead, an increased emphasis on the possibility of interactions between systems — even systems which appear to be independent in adults — may allow for an integration of apparently contradictory theories.

Future approaches

The accounts outlined in the earlier section on Competing Models show how poor working memory performance might arise as a consequence of more general learning difficulties. In order to demonstrate that a particular population group really does have a fundamental and specific working memory deficit this alternative explanation therefore needs to be ruled out.

An obvious way of doing this is to account for the additional factors that constrain task performance either by matching the group in question to control samples on the basis of these measures, or by statistically accounting for any group differences in them. In the case of assessments of short-term memory performance, mental age will be a key measure to control for, as a short-term memory deficit which persists under these conditions cannot simply be the result of a group having low intelligence. More importantly, if it is the case that verbal short-term memory performance is constrained by language level, then matching groups for level of language attainment should equate verbal short-term memory performance. Consequently, when impairments in verbal short-term memory are observed relative to groups equated for verbal ability then this amounts to good evidence for a specific phonological loop deficit. One would also wish to control specifically for the individual's levels of phonological awareness, given the claims that this is an important determinant of verbal short-term memory performance. By analogy, claims of visuo-spatial short-term memory deficits can only be accepted if there is evidence that these deficits are greater than one would expect given the level of visuo-spatial ability shown by a particular population. In the case of complex span tasks specific measures of the speed and accuracy of processing on the task should be assessed (e.g., Towse & Hitch, 1995; Towse et al., 1998; Waters & Caplan, 1996). Although these measures can be taken directly from the task it is arguably more appropriate to assess individual differences in processing speed in a separate test which is not confounded by any storage requirements (cf. Russell, Jarrold & Henry, 1996).

It should be noted that this general approach is already in use in this area. Gathercole and Baddeley (1990a) found that their sample of individuals with SLI showed poorer verbal short-term memory than controls matched for verbal mental age (though see Van der Lely & Howard, 1993). Similar results have been obtained for individuals with Down syndrome (Jarrold, Baddeley & Hewes, 1999). The position is less clear when we consider the causal precedence of visuo-spatial short-term memory and long-term learning difficulties. Vicari, Brizzolara, Carlesimo, Pezzini and Volterra (1996) found that individuals with Williams syndrome were impaired on a Corsi test relative to controls matched for non-verbal ability. Jarrold, Baddeley and Hewes (1999) found that matching for general levels of visuo-spatial ability equated the performance of individuals with Williams syndrome and controls on visuo-spatial short-term memory tests, although the Williams syndrome individuals did show a selective impairment on visuo-spatial short-term memory tests when both verbal and non-verbal mental age differences between groups were accounted for statistically. In their study of visuo-spatial short-term memory among individuals with low spatial intelligence, Cornoldi et al. (1995) matched controls for verbal ability only. In the absence of a study matching for level of visuo-spatial functioning it seems entirely plausible that this particular group of individuals perform poorly on a Corsi span test simply because they have relatively poorer visuo-spatial abilities than typically developing individuals. Similarly, Hitch and McAuley (1991) found that although their group of individuals with arithmetical difficulties were impaired on Case et al.'s (1982) counting span task, they were similarly impaired on a simple test of counting efficiency. Again these results highlight the continued need for appropriate assessment and control of measures of intelligence and ability in this research.

Even if one is able to show that a certain population suffers from a specific working memory deficit, which is not simply a consequence of either their general or specific learning difficulties, this does not in itself prove that this working memory deficit is the cause of any other cognitive difficulties. However, there are again ways in which this, predictive, aspect of the working memory account can be tested empirically. Longitudinal studies have the potential to determine the causal direction of the relationship between two developing domains (though see Bowey, 1996). Longitudinal designs have been employed to examine the relationships between verbal short-term memory and vocabulary in typically developing children (Gathercole & Baddeley, 1989; Gathercole, Willis, Emslie & Baddeley, 1992), but this method has yet to be extended to the study of atypical development. An alternative approach, which again has not been fully investigated as yet, would be to examine working memory among individuals of the same level of ability (for example vocabulary level) who have acquired that level of ability at different rates. Under the working memory account those individuals who, for example, acquire vocabulary at a relatively rapid pace must do so by virtue of relatively superior verbal short-term memory. In contrast, if vocabulary constrains verbal short-term memory performance then individuals of the same vocabulary level should have the same verbal short-term memory skills, regardless of the rate of vocabulary development. This approach is conceptually equivalent to matching groups for level of verbal mental age. However, it has the advantage of providing a test of the predictive power of the working memory account within, rather than across populations.

Future models

The need for models which explain how working memory develops with age has already been highlighted. To a large extent, therefore, the future for research into working memory deficits in children with learning disability or developmental disorders depends on theoretical advances in other areas. At present some aspects of the working memory model lack a fully developed theoretical account of adult performance. Where models of adult functioning exist, they need to also take on the challenge of explaining why working memory abilities improve with age. However, the start of this section emphasised the danger of simply viewing developmental models as slightly elaborated versions of adult accounts. In particular, developmental models need to accept the possibility (and it is only a possibility and not a necessity) that systems interact and develop together even if they end up as discrete modules in adulthood. A major theme of this chapter is that there are links between working memory deficits and other cognitive impairments. The working memory account predicts that short-term memory deficits should have broader consequences for long-term learning, while at the same time we know that a child's long-term knowledge does play a role in constraining their short-term memory performance (Gathercole, 1995b; Gathercole, Frankish, Pickering & Peaker, 1999; Gathercole, Willis, Emslie, & Baddeley, 1991; Roodenrys et al., 1993; Thorn & Gathercole, 1999). Underestimating the extent of these links might actually weaken the working memory approach. For example, although matching individuals for level of long-term learning provides an appropriate test of the working memory account, this test is a very conservative one. This is because the account predicts that working memory deficits are likely to cause problems in acquiring the very long-term knowledge on which the groups are matched. Consequently, by controlling for level of learning one may be 'matching away' some of the deficit that one is trying to detect (Bishop, 1992, 1997).

It may therefore be over-simplistic to ask whether working memory deficits are either a consequence or a cause of learning difficulties, or to expect a clear 'yes' or 'no' answer to such a question; in atypical development these two options may not be entirely distinguishable. Instead of a modular conception of working memory, in which the slave systems responsible for storing information are separated from long-term knowledge, what may be needed in future is a model which makes explicit the reciprocal interaction between these domains. In actual fact, advocates of both the working memory model and alternative accounts (see above) already accept this (Bowey, 1996; Gathercole, Willis, Emslie & Baddeley, 1991, 1992). However, these alternative positions are still generally viewed as contrasting rather than complementary explanations of the available data. This perhaps reflects the fact that concepts such as phonological awareness and phonological short-term memory are, in some sense, distinguishable in adults. However, if it is the case that these distinctions are less meaningful in children, then a synthesis between these accounts may be possible (see Gathercole & Martin, 1996 for an example). Of course this will lead to a blurring of the edges of the modules in the adult neuropsychological model of working memory. This should not be viewed as a weakening of the model. Instead it would strengthen the model's ability both to explain and predict the consequences of any deficits in working memory and related systems in children showing atypical development.

ACKNOWLEDGEMENTS

Chris Jarrold is supported by a grant from the Medical Research Council awarded to Alan Baddeley and Susan Gathercole. I am very grateful to Louise Phillips, John Towse and colleagues in my own department for their helpful comments on previous drafts of this chapter.

BACKGROUND READING

Baddeley, A., Gathercole, S. & Papagno, C. (1998). The phonological loop as a language learning device. *Psychological Review*, *105*, 158–173.

A detailed example of how working memory may impact on long-term learning.

Hulme, C. & Roodenrys, S. (1995). Practitioner review: Verbal working memory development and its disorders. *Journal of Child Psychology and Psychiatry*, *36*, 373–398.

A review of the evidence for the counter-position: that apparent working memory deficits are a consequence of learning disability.

Engle, R. W., Kane, M. J. & Tuholski, S. W. (1999). Individual differences in working memory capacity and what they tell us about controlled attention, general fluid intelligence, and functions of the prefrontal cortex. In A. Miyake & P. Shah (Eds.), *Models of working memory: Mechanisms of active maintenance and executive control* (pp. 102–134). Cambridge: Cambridge University Press.

The initial and final sections of this chapter provide a clear and detailed coverage of the various factors that might influence performance on complex span tasks.

REFERENCES

Adams, A. M. & Gathercole, S. E. (1995). Phonological working memory and speech production in preschool children. *Journal of Speech and Hearing Research*, *38*, 403–414.

Adams, A. M. & Gathercole, S. E. (1996). Phonological working memory and spoken language development in young children. *The Quarterly Journal of Experimental Psychology*, *49A*, 216–233.

Avons, S. E. & Hanna, C. (1995). The memory-span deficit in children with specific reading disability: Is speech rate responsible? *British Journal of Developmental Psychology*, *13*, 303–311.

Baddeley, A. D. (1986). *Working memory*. Oxford: Oxford University Press.

Baddeley, A. (1993). Working memory or working attention. In A. Baddeley & L.

Weiskrantz (Eds.), *Attention: Selection, awareness, and control. A tribute to Donald Broadbent* (pp. 152–170). Oxford: Clarendon Press.

Baddeley, A. (1995). Working memory. In M. S. Gazzaniga (Ed.), *The cognitive neurosciences* (pp. 755–764). Cambridge, MA: Bradford/MIT Press.

Baddeley, A. D. (1996). The concept of working memory. In S. E. Gathercole (Ed.), *Models of short-term memory* (pp. 1–27). Hove, UK: Psychology Press.

Baddeley, A., Gathercole, S. & Papagno, C. (1998). The phonological loop as a language learning device. *Psychological Review, 105*, 158–173.

Baddeley, A. D. & Hitch, G. J. (1974). Working memory. In G. Bower (Ed.), *The psychology of learning and motivation* (pp. 47–89). New York: Academic Press.

Baddeley, A., Logie, R., Bressi, S., Della Sala, S. & Spinnler, H. (1986). Dementia and working memory. *The Quarterly Journal of Experimental Psychology, 38A*, 603–618.

Baddeley, A., Logie, R., Nimmo-Smith, I. & Brereton, N. (1985). Components of fluid reading. *Journal of Memory and Language, 24*, 119–131.

Baddeley, A. D., Thomson, N. & Buchanan, M. (1975). Word length and the structure of short-term memory. *Journal of Verbal Learning and Verbal Behavior, 14*, 575–589.

Bishop, D. V. M. (1992). The underlying nature of specific language impairment. *Journal of Child Psychology and Psychiatry, 33*, 1–64.

Bishop, D. V. M. (1997). Cognitive neuropsychology and developmental disorders: uncomfortable bedfellows. *The Quarterly Journal of Experimental Psychology, 50A*, 899–923.

Bishop, D. V. M., North, T. & Donlan, C. (1996). Nonword repetition as a behavioural marker for inherited language impairment: Evidence from a twin study. *Journal of Child Psychology and Psychiatry, 37*, 391–403.

Bowey, J. A. (1996). On the association between phonological memory and receptive vocabulary in 5-year-olds. *Journal of Experimental Child Psychology, 63*, 44–78.

Broadley, I. & MacDonald, J. (1993). Teaching short term memory skills to children with Down's syndrome. *Down's Syndrome: Research and Practice, 1*, 56–62.

Broadley, I., MacDonald, J. & Buckley, S. (1994). Are children with Down's syndrome able to maintain skills learned from a short-term memory training programme? *Down's Syndrome: Research and Practice, 2*, 116–122.

Brown, G. D. A. & Hulme, C. (1995). Modeling item length effects in memory span: No rehearsal needed. *Journal of Memory and Language, 34*, 594–621.

Brown, G. D. A., Vousden, J. I., McCormack, T. & Hulme, C. (1999). The development of memory for serial order: A temporal-contextual distinctiveness model. *International Journal of Psychology, 34*, 389–402.

Burgess, N. & Hitch, G. J. (1992). Toward a network model of the articulatory loop. *Journal of Memory and Language, 31*, 429–460.

Case, R. (1985). *Intellectual development: Birth to adulthood*. New York: Academic Press.

Case, R., Kurland, D. M. & Goldberg, J. (1982). Operational efficiency and the growth of short-term memory span. *Journal of Experimental Child Psychology, 33*, 386–404.

Chapman, R. S. (1995). Language development in children and adolescents with Down syndrome. In P. Fletcher & B. MacWhinney (Eds.), *Handbook of child language* (pp. 641–663). Oxford: Blackwell.

Comblain, A. (1994). Working memory in Down's syndrome: Training the rehearsal strategy. *Down's Syndrome: Research and Practice, 2,* 123–126.

Cornoldi, C., Dalla Vecchia, R. & Tressoldi, P. E. (1995). Visuo-spatial working memory limitations in low visuo-spatial high verbal intelligence children. *Journal of Child Psychology and Psychiatry, 36,* 1053–1064.

Cowan, N., Day, L., Saults, J. S., Keller, T. A., Johnson, T. & Flores, L. (1992). The role of verbal output time in the effects of word length on immediate memory. *Journal of Memory and Language, 31,* 1–17.

Daneman, M. & Carpenter, P. A. (1980). Individual differences in working memory and reading. *Journal of Verbal Learning and Verbal Behavior, 19,* 450–466.

Dixon, P., LeFevre, J.-A. & Twilley, L. C. (1988). Word knowledge and working memory as predictors of reading skill. *Journal of Educational Psychology, 80,* 465–472.

Dosher, B. A. & Ma, J. J. (1998). Output loss or rehearsal loop? Output-time versus pronunciation-time limits in immediate recall for forgetting-matched materials. *Journal of Experimental Psychology: Learning, Memory and Cognition, 24,* 316–335.

Elman, J. L., Bates, E. A., Johnson, M. H., Karmiloff-Smith, A., Parisi, D. & Plunkett, K. (1996). *Rethinking innateness: A connectionist perspective on development.* Cambridge, MA: Bradford Books/MIT Press.

Flavell, J. H., Beach, D. R. & Chinsky, J. M. (1966). Spontaneous verbal rehearsal in a memory task as a function of age. *Child Development, 37,* 283–299.

Gathercole, S. E. (1995a). Nonword repetition: More than just a phonological output task. *Cognitive Neuropsychology, 12,* 857–861.

Gathercole, S. E. (1995b). Is nonword repetition a test of phonological memory or long-term knowledge? It all depends on the nonwords. *Memory and Cognition, 23,* 83–94.

Gathercole, S. E. (1998). The development of memory. *Journal of Child Psychology and Psychiatry, 39,* 3–27.

Gathercole, S. E. & Adams, A. M. (1994). Children's phonological working memory: Contributions of long-term knowledge and rehearsal. *Journal of Memory and Language, 33,* 672–688.

Gathercole, S. E., Adams, A. M. & Hitch, G. J. (1994). Do young children rehearse? An individual differences analysis. *Memory and Cognition, 22,* 201–207.

Gathercole, S. E. & Baddeley, A. D. (1989). Evaluation of the role of phonological STM in the development of vocabulary in children: A longitudinal study. *Journal of Memory and Language, 28,* 200–215.

Gathercole, S. E. & Baddeley, A. D. (1990a). Phonological memory deficits in language disordered children: Is there a causal connection? *Journal of Memory and Language, 29,* 336–360.

Gathercole, S. E. & Baddeley, A. D. (1990b). The role of phonological memory in vocabulary acquisition: A study of young children learning new words. *British Journal of Psychology, 81,* 439–454.

Gathercole, S. E. & Baddeley, A. D. (1995). Short-term memory may yet be deficient in children with language impairments: A comment on van der Lely & Howard (1993). *Journal of Speech and Hearing Research, 38,* 463–472.

Gathercole, S. E. & Baddeley, A. D. (1997). Sense and sensitivity in phonological memory and vocabulary development: A reply to Bowey (1996). *Journal of Experimental Child Psychology, 67,* 290–294.

Gathercole, S. E., Frankish, C. R., Pickering, S. J. & Peaker, S. (1999). Phonotactic influences on short-term memory. *Journal of Experimental Psychology: Learning, Memory and Cognition, 25,* 84–95.

Gathercole, S. E. & Martin, A. (1996). Interactive processes in phonological memory. In S. E. Gathercole (Ed.), *Models of short-term memory* (pp. 73–100). Hove, UK: Psychology Press.

Gathercole, S. E., Willis, C. & Baddeley, A. D. (1991). Nonword repetition, phonological memory, and vocabulary: A reply to Snowling, Chiat, and Hulme. *Applied Psycholinguistics, 12,* 375–379.

Gathercole, S. E., Willis, C., Emslie, H. & Baddeley, A. D. (1991). The influence of number of syllables and wordlikeness on children's repetition of nonwords. *Applied Psycholinguistics, 12,* 349–367.

Gathercole, S. E., Willis, C. S., Emslie, H. & Baddeley, A. D. (1992). Phonological memory and vocabulary development during the early school years: A longitudinal study. *Developmental Psychology, 5,* 887–898.

Gunn, P. & Crombie, M. (1996). Language and speech. In B. Stratford & P. Gunn (Eds.), *New approaches to Down syndrome* (pp. 249–267). London: Cassell.

Halford, G. S., Maybery, M. T., O'Hare, A. W. & Grant, P. (1994). The development of memory and processing capacity. *Child Development, 65,* 1338–1356.

Hanley, J. R., Young, A. W. & Pearson, N. A. (1991). Impairment of the visuo-spatial sketch pad. *The Quarterly Journal of Experimental Psychology, 43A,* 101–125.

Henry, L. A. (1991a). The effects of word length and phonemic similarity in young children's short-term memory. *The Quarterly journal of Experimental Psychology, 43A,* 35–52.

Henry, L. A. (1991b). Development of auditory memory span: The role of rehearsal. *British Journal of Developmental Psychology, 9,* 493–511.

Henson, R. N. A. (1998). Short-term memory for serial order: The start–end model. *Cognitive Psychology, 36,* 73–137.

Hitch, G., Halliday, M. S. & Littler, J. E. (1989). Item identification time and rehearsal as predictors of memory span in children. *The Quarterly Journal of Experimental Psychology, 41A,* 321–327.

Hitch, G. J., Halliday, M. S. & Littler, J. E. (1993). Development of memory span for spoken words: The role of rehearsal and item identification processes. *British Journal of Developmental Psychology, 11,* 159–169.

Hitch, G. J. & McAuley, E. (1991). Working memory in children with specific arithmetical learning difficulties. *British Journal of Psychology, 82,* 375–386.

Hitch, G. J. & Towse, J. (1995). Working memory: What develops? In F. Weinert & W. Schneider (Eds.), *Memory development: State-of the art and future directions* (pp. 3–21). Mahwah, NJ: Lawrence Erlbaum Associates Inc.

Hulme, C. & Mackenzie, S. (1992). *Working memory and severe learning difficulties.* Hove, UK: Lawrence Erlbaum Associates Ltd.

Hulme, C. & Muir, C. (1985). Developmental changes in speech rate and memory span: A causal relationship? *British Journal of Developmental Psychology, 3,* 175–181.

Hulme, C. & Roodenrys, S. (1995). Practitioner review: Verbal working memory development and its disorders. *Journal of Child Psychology and Psychiatry, 36,* 373–398.

Hulme, C., Thomson, N., Muir, C. & Lawrence, A. (1984). Speech rate and the development of short-term memory span. *Journal of Experimental Child Psychology*, *38*, 241–253.

Isaacs, E. B. & Vargha-Khadem, F. (1989). Differential course of development of spatial and verbal memory span: A normative study. *British Journal of Developmental Psychology*, *7*, 377–380.

Jarrold, C. & Baddeley, A. D. (1997). Short-term memory for verbal and visuospatial information in Down's syndrome. *Cognitive Neuropsychiatry*, *2*, 101–122.

Jarrold, C., Baddeley, A. D. & Hewes, A. K. (1998). Verbal and non-verbal abilities in the Williams syndrome phenotype: Evidence for diverging developmental trajectories. *Journal of Child Psychology and Psychiatry*, *39*, 511–524.

Jarrold, C., Baddeley, A. D. & Hewes, A. K. (1999). Genetically dissociated components of working memory: Evidence from Down's and Williams syndrome. *Neuropsychologia*, *37*, 637–651.

Jarrold, C., Baddeley, A. D. & Phillips, C. (1999). Down syndrome and the phonological loop: The evidence for, and importance of, a specific verbal short-term memory deficit. *Down Syndrome Research and Practice*, *6*, 61–75.

Just, M. A. & Carpenter, P. A. (1992). A capacity theory of comprehension: Individual differences in working memory. *Psychological Review*, *99*, 122–129.

Kahmi, A. G., Lee, R. & Nelson, L. (1985). Word, syllable, and sound awareness in language-disordered children. *Journal of Speech and Hearing Disorders*, *49*, 169–177.

Kane, M. J., Conway, A. R. A. & Engle, R. W. (1999). What do working memory tests really measure? *Behavioral and Brain Sciences*, *22*, 101–102.

Karmiloff-Smith, A. (1992). *Beyond modularity: A developmental perspective on cognitive science*. Cambridge, MA: Bradford Books/MIT Press.

Karmiloff-Smith, A. (1997). Crucial differences between developmental cognitive neuroscience and adult neuropsychology. *Developmental Neuropsychology*, *13*, 513–524.

Laws, G., MacDonald, J. & Buckley, S. (1996). The effects of a short training in the use of a rehearsal strategy on memory for words and pictures in children with Down syndrome. *Down's syndrome: Research and Practice*, *4*, 70–78.

Laws, G., MacDonald, J., Buckley, S. & Broadley, I. (1995). Long-term maintenance of memory skills taught to children with Down's syndrome. *Down's Syndrome: Research and Practice*, *3*, 103–109.

Lehto, J. H. (1996). Are executive function tests dependent on working memory capacity? *The Quarterly Journal of Experimental Psychology*, *49A*, 29–50.

Logie, R. H. (1995). *Visuo-spatial working memory*. Hove, UK: Lawrence Erlbaum Associates Ltd.

Logie, R. H. & Marchetti, C. (1991). Visuo-spatial working memory: Visual, spatial or central executive. In R. H. Logie & M. Denis (Eds.), *Mental images in human cognition* (pp. 105–115). Amsterdam: Elsevier.

Logie, R. H. & Pearson, D. G. (1997). The inner eye and the inner scribe of visuospatial working memory: Evidence from developmental fractionation. *European Journal of Cognitive Psychology*, *9*, 241–257.

Martin, N., Saffran, E. M. & Dell, G. S. (1996). Recovery in deep dysphasia: Evidence for a relation between auditory-verbal STM capacity and lexical errors in repetition. *Brain and Language*, *52*, 83–113.

Martin, R. C. & Breedin, S. D. (1992). Dissociations between speech-perception and phonological short-term memory deficits. *Cognitive Neuropsychology*, *9*, 509–534.

McLean, J. F. & Hitch, G. J. (1999). Working memory impairments in children with specific arithmetic learning difficulties. *Journal of Experimental Child Psychology*, *74*, 240–260.

Mervis, C. B. (1999). The Williams syndrome cognitive profile: Strengths, weaknesses, and interrelations among auditory short term memory, language, and visuo-spatial constructive cognition. In R. Fivush, W. Hirst & E. Winograd (Eds.), *Essays in honor of Ulric Neisser* (pp. 193–227). Mahwah, NJ: Lawrence Erlbaum Associates Inc.

Michas, I. C. & Henry, L. A. (1994). The link between phonological memory and vocabulary acquisition. *British Journal of Developmental Psychology*, *12*, 147–163.

Milner, B. (1971). Interhemispheric differences in the localisation of psychological processes in man. *Cortex*, *27*, 272–277.

Nation, K., Adams, J. W., Bowyer-Crane, C. A. & Snowling, M. J. (1999). Working memory deficits in poor comprehenders reflect underlying language impairments. *Journal of Experimental Child Psychology*, *73*, 139–158.

Neath, I. & Nairne, J. S. (1995). Word-length effects in immediate memory: Overwriting trace decay theory. *Psychonomic Bulletin and Review*, *2*, 429–441.

Nicolson, R. (1981). The relationship between memory span and processing speed. In M. Friedman, J. P. Das & N. O'Connor (Eds.), *Intelligence and learning* (pp. 179–183). New York: Plenum Press.

Norman, D. A. & Shallice, T. (1986). Attention to action: Willed and automatic control of behaviour. In R. J. Davidson, G. E. Schwartz & D. Shapiro (Eds.), *Consciousness and self-regulation* (pp. 1–18). New York: Plenum Press.

Orsini, A. (1994). Corsi's block-tapping test: Standardization and concurrent validity with WISC-R for children aged 11 to 16. *Perceptual and motor skills*, *79*, 1547–1554.

Page, M. P. A. & Norris, D. (1998). The primacy model: A new model of immediate serial recall. *Psychological Review*, *105*, 761–781.

Pennington, B. F. & Ozonoff, S. (1996). Executive functions and developmental psychopathology. *Journal of Child Psychology and Psychiatry*, *37*, 51–87.

Phillips, W. A. & Christie, D. F. M. (1977). Components of visual memory. *The Quarterly Journal of Experimental Psychology*, *29*, 117–133.

Pickering, S. J., Gathercole, S. E. & Hall, M. (2001). Development of memory for pattern and path: Further evidence for the fractionation of visual and spatial short-term memory. *The Quarterly Journal of Experimental Psychology*, *54A*, 397–420.

Quinn, J. G. & McConnell, J. (1996). Irrelevant pictures in visual working memory. *The Quarterly Journal of Experimental Psychology*, *49A*, 200–215.

Raine, A., Hulme, C., Chadderton, H. & Bailey, P. (1991). Verbal short-term memory span in speech-disordered children: Implications for articulatory coding in short-term memory. *Child Development*, *62*, 415–423.

Roodenrys, S., Hulme, C. & Brown, G. (1993). The development of short-term memory span: Separable effects of speech rate and long-term memory. *Journal of Experimental Child Psychology*, *56*, 431–442.

Russell, J., Jarrold, C. & Henry, L. (1996). Working memory in children with autism and with moderate learning difficulties. *Journal of Child Psychology and Psychiatry*, *37*, 673–686.

Schweickert, R. & Boruff, B. (1986). Short-term memory capacity: Magic number or magic spell? *Journal of Experimental Psychology: Learning, Memory and Cognition, 12,* 418–425.

Service, L. (1992). Phonology, working memory and foreign-language learning. *The Quarterly Journal of Experimental Psychology, 45A,* 21–50.

Service, E. & Kohonen, V. (1995). Is the relation between phonological memory and foreign-language learning accounted for by vocabulary acquisition? *Applied Psycholinguistics, 16,* 155–172.

Siegel, L. S. & Ryan, E. B. (1989). The development of working memory in normally achieving and subtypes of learning disabled children. *Child Development, 60,* 973–980.

Snowling, M., Chiat, S. & Hulme, C. (1991). Words, nonwords, and phonological processes: Some comments on Gathercole, Willis, Emslie, and Baddeley. *Applied Psycholinguistics, 12,* 369–373.

Snowling, M., Goulandris, A., Bowlby, M. & Howell, P. (1986). Segmentation and speech perception in relation to reading skill: A developmental analysis. *Journal of Experimental Child Psychology, 41,* 489–507.

Stothard, S. E. & Hulme, C. (1992). Reading comprehension difficulties in children. *Reading and Writing, 4,* 245–256.

Swanson, H. L. (1993a). Working memory in learning disability subgroups. *Journal of Experimental Child Psychology, 56,* 87–114.

Swanson, H. L. (1993b). Executive processing in learning-disabled readers. *Intelligence, 17,* 117–149.

Swanson, H. L. (1996). Individual and age-related differences in children's working memory. *Memory and Cognition, 24,* 70–82.

Swanson, H. L. (1999). What develops in working memory? A life span perspective. *Developmental Psychology, 35,* 986–1000.

Swanson, H. L., Ashbaker, M. H. & Lee, C. (1996). Learning-disabled readers' working memory as a function of processing demands. *Journal of Experimental Child Psychology, 61,* 242–275.

Thorn, A. S. C. & Gathercole, S. E. (1999). Language-specific knowledge and short-term memory in bilingual and non-bilingual children. *The Quarterly Journal of Experimental Psychology, 52A,* 303–324.

Towse, J. N. & Hitch, G. J. (1995). Is there a relationship between task demand and storage space in tests of working memory capacity? *The Quarterly Journal of Experimental Psychology, 48A,* 108–124.

Towse, J. N., Hitch, G. J. & Hutton, U. (1998). A reevaluation of working memory capacity in children. *Journal of Memory and Language, 39,* 195–217.

Tresch, M. C., Sinnamon, H. M. & Seamon, J. G. (1993). Double dissociation of spatial and object visual memory: Evidence from selective interference in intact human subjects. *Neuropsychologia, 31,* 211–219.

Turner, M. L. & Engle, R. W. (1989). Is working memory capacity task dependent? *Journal of Memory and Language, 28,* 127–154.

Van der Lely, H. K. J. & Howard, D. (1993). Children with specific language impairment: Linguistic impairment or short-term memory deficit? *Journal of Speech and Hearing Research, 36,* 1193–1207.

Vicari, S., Brizzolara, D., Carlesimo, G. A., Pezzini, G. & Volterra, V. (1996). Memory abilities in children with Williams syndrome. *Cortex, 32,* 503–514.

Wang, P. P. & Bellugi, U. (1994). Evidence from two genetic syndromes for a dissociation between verbal and visual-spatial short-term memory. *Journal of Clinical and Experimental Neuropsychology, 16*, 317–322.

Waters, G. S. & Caplan, D. (1996). The measurement of verbal working memory capacity and its relation to reading comprehension. *The Quarterly Journal of Experimental Psychology, 49A*, 51–79.

Waters, G., Rochon, E. & Caplan, D. (1992). The role of high-level speech planning in rehearsal: Evidence from patients with apraxia of speech. *Journal of Memory and Language, 31*, 54–73.

Wells, B. (1995). Phonological considerations in repetition tasks. *Cognitive Neuropsychology, 12*, 847–855.

Wilson, J. T. L., Scott, J. H. & Power, K. G. (1987). Developmental differences in the span of visual memory for pattern. *British Journal of Developmental Psychology, 5*, 249–255.

Yuill, N., Oakhill, J. & Parkin, A. (1989). Working memory, comprehension ability and the resolution of text anomaly. *British Journal of Psychology, 80*, 351–361.

7 Neural working memory

Richard Henson

The working memory (WM) model of Baddeley and Hitch (1974) has proved hugely influential in neuropsychological and, more recently, neuro-imaging investigations of working memory. In the present chapter, I aim to illustrate this influence via three distinctions made by the WM model: the distinction between 1) verbal and visuo-spatial information, 2) storage and rehearsal, and 3) maintenance and manipulation.

The WM model postulates separate memory systems for maintaining verbal and visuo-spatial information: the phonological loop (PL) and the visuo-spatial sketchpad (VSSP) respectively. Temporary storage of a phono-logical representation of an unfamiliar telephone number, for example, would engage the PL, whereas maintenance of an image of its visual appearance would engage the VSSP.

Maintenance of information in the WM model comprises two com-ponents: passive storage of information, subject to loss by decay or inter-ference over time, and active rehearsal, which preempts such loss. Within the PL for example, storage is subserved by the phonological store and rehearsal is subserved by the articulatory control process. For a telephone number, storage might correspond to some representation of the digits and their order, and rehearsal would correspond to the common strategy of (subvocally) repeating the sequence of digits to oneself.

The third component of the WM model, the central executive (CE), is engaged when information must be manipulated. Whereas maintenance simply entails keeping information in mind in the absence of an external stimulus, manipulation refers to the further transformation or 're-represen-tation' of the information being maintained. Manipulation is rarely strictly defined; rather it is often used to refer to any working memory process that involves more than simple maintenance. An example of manipulation would be the process of reordering the digits in the telephone number (e.g., in descending numerical order).

The main argument in the present chapter is that these distinctions are respected at the functional anatomical level. In other words, the proposal is that the components of the WM model are realised by distinct brain regions. The main evidence for this claim derives from studies of acquired deficits following localised brain damage (data from developmental disorders or diffuse brain diseases are not discussed here). Converging evidence comes from recent neuroimaging studies of healthy individuals performing working memory tasks. Whether or not this functional segregation is ultimately valid is less relevant however: the purpose of the argument is to illustrate how any brain–behaviour mapping must begin with a successful theory of the behavioural phenomena, in this case, the WM model.

Finally, additional results from neuropsychological and neuroimaging studies will be mentioned that are not well captured by the WM model. These include, for example, the distinction between visual object and visual spatial information and between different types of manipulation, such as monitoring, generating strategies, selecting competing information and planning. These distinctions are used to address the remaining aims of this book, regarding the weaknesses and future of the WM model.

MAINTENANCE OF VERBAL VERSUS VISUO-SPATIAL MATERIAL

The verbal–visuo-spatial distinction appears to correspond to a hemispheric lateralisation, with regions of the left hemisphere subserving maintenance of verbalisable material and regions of the right hemisphere subserving maintenance of non-verbalisable, visuo-spatial material. This left–right lateralisation of verbal–spatial working memory originates from neuropsychological studies. De Renzi and Nichelli (1975), for example, found that a group of patients with left hemisphere lesions was impaired on several verbal working memory tasks relative to both a group of healthy controls and a group with right hemisphere lesions. Conversely, the right hemisphere group was impaired on several spatial working memory tasks relative to the left hemisphere group (though the difference was not reliable in this case).

Group studies like these are bolstered by single-case studies, such as Patient P.V. (Vallar & Baddeley, 1984), who was severely impaired on verbal working memory tasks but performed normally on spatial working memory tasks, and Patient E.L.D. (Hanley, Young, & Pearson, 1991), who was impaired on spatial working memory tasks but performed normally on verbal working memory tasks. P.V. suffered from a large stroke-induced lesion of the left hemisphere, whereas E.L.D. suffered from an aneurysm-induced haematoma in the right Sylvian Fissure (the sulcus joining A to F in the lower panel of Figure 7.1). Importantly, neither patient was impaired

Figure 7.1   Approximate location of brain regions in (a) left and (b) right hemispheres typically associated with working memory. A=inferior parietal, B=Broca's (inferior premotor), C=premotor, D=superior parietal, E=cerebellum, F=ventrolateral prefrontal, G=dorsolateral prefrontal, H=anterior occipital, I=inferior temporal.

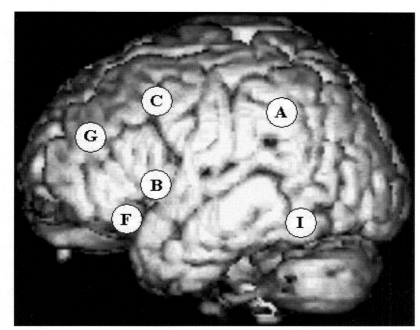

(a)

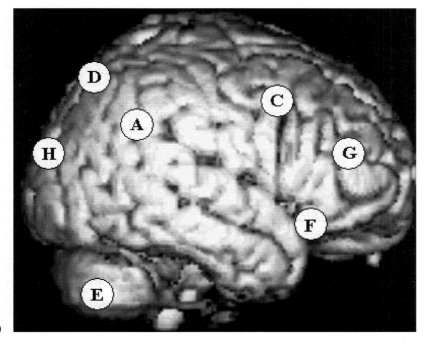

(b)

on verbal or spatial non-working memory tasks, such as tests of perception, or tests of long-term memory for previously learned verbal or spatial information. Data from these patients thus comprise a double dissociation between brain regions subserving verbal and spatial working memory.

This lateralisation of working memory has been bolstered by recent neuroimaging studies. A common test of maintenance in working memory is the Sternberg task (Sternberg, 1969). Participants in this task are presented with a memory set of typically 3–9 stimuli, which are then removed for several seconds before the appearance of a single probe stimulus. Their goal is to decide whether or not the probe stimulus was one of the stimuli in the memory set. To isolate brain areas involved in maintenance from those involved in perceptual or motor components of the task, functional images obtained during the Sternberg task are contrasted with those obtained in a control task in which the memory set and probe item are presented simultaneously, alleviating any memory requirement (first three tasks shown in Figure 7.2).

Using a verbal Sternberg task, Awh et al. (1996) reported significant activations in several left hemisphere regions, including inferior and superior parietal cortex (BA 7/40), inferior frontal cortex (BA 44; Broca's area) and premotor cortex (BA 6) — see Figure 7.1. (A Brodmann Area, BA, is a brain region distinguished by its cytoarchitecture, i.e. the nature and distribution of different cell types, Brodmann, 1909.) Similar regions were implicated by Paulesu, Frith, and Frackowiak (1993b), who compared two Sternberg tasks: one using letters and one using non-verbalisable symbols. This left hemisphere network of inferior frontal, parietal and motor areas (plus right cerebellum) is a consistent finding in studies of maintenance in verbal working memory (Smith & Jonides, 1997). Note however that, though the activations in these studies are generally stronger on the left than right, they are often bilateral. The functional significance of activation in homologous areas of the right hemisphere is unknown: it might be task-relevant (even if not necessary, given the neuropsychological evidence), or it might simply reflect spill-over of activity from the left hemisphere via cortico-callosal connections.

Activations in visuo-spatial maintenance tasks are often seen in homologous regions of the right hemisphere. Jonides et al. (1993), for example, reported activations in right inferior parietal cortex (BA 40), right premotor cortex (BA 6) and right inferior frontal cortex (BA 47) when comparing a spatial Sternberg task with its perceptual-motor control. The only additional activation was in anterior extrastriate occipital cortex (BA 19), an area often associated with visual imagery (Kosslyn et al., 1993). Comparable findings were reported by Smith, Jonides and Koeppe (1996) and Paulesu et al. (1993a) in direct comparisons of visuo-spatial versus verbal Sternberg tasks. Unlike the Jonides et al. comparison, however, the Paulesu et al. task required maintenance of abstract, visual form, with little or no requirement for spatial information. This raises an important question as to whether the visual aspects of working memory can be dissociated from spatial aspects.

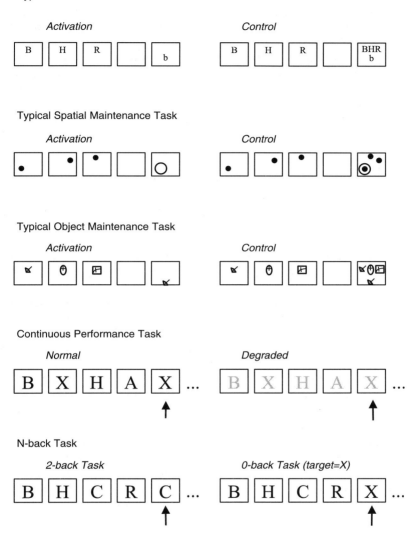

Figure 7.2 Examples of typical maintenance and manipulation tasks used in neuroimaging.

MAINTENANCE OF VISUAL OBJECT VERSUS VISUAL SPATIAL INFORMATION

Though a distinction between visual and spatial information is not made explicit in the original WM model (given that behavioural dissociations between visual and spatial maintenance are rarely clear cut; Baddeley, 1986;

see chapter 2, this volume), it has been an important distinction within the neuroscientific community.

The dissociation in the visual processing of object and spatial information is clearest in electrophysiological research on nonhuman primates. A ventral stream from occipital cortex to inferior temporal cortex appears specialised for object information and a dorsal stream from occipital cortex to inferior parietal cortex appears specialised for spatial information (Mishkin, Ungerleider, & Macko, 1983; though see Milner & Goodale, 1993). These 'what versus where' streams may continue into prefrontal cortex, where cells have been found that fire only when information must be retained during a delay following stimulus offset. Specifically, it has been argued that prefrontal cells ventrolateral to the principal sulcus code for object information during a delay, whereas prefrontal cells within and dorsolateral to the principal sulcus code for spatial information during a delay (Wilson, Scalaidhe, & Goldman-Rakic, 1993).

Similar dissociations might be expected in the functional anatomy of human working memory. Levine, Warach and Farah (1985) for example reported a double dissociation between two patients, one of whom had problems imagining visual features such as the shape of a spaniel's ears, but had no problem describing routes or locating towns on maps, and the other of whom had the opposite pattern of deficit. The first patient had bilateral temporo-occipital damage, whereas the second had bilateral parieto-occipital damage. Consistent with a dorsal spatial route, lesions to right parietal cortex are associated with the neglect syndrome (Bisiach, 1993), an apparent loss of visual information from one side of space (usually the left). Though these deficits concern long-term memory and perception, rather than working memory *per se*, they support a ventral–dorsal visual–spatial distinction in humans. Selective impairment of short-term visual maintenance was reported by Warrington and Rabin (1971). They described patients with left posterior damage who had deficits in a visual span task using random strings of letters, digits, lines or curves. The patients were less impaired when the strings of letters approximated words, and unimpaired on auditory digit span tests. Patients with right posterior damage did not show the same pattern of impairment. These data suggest the existence of a (sublexical) visual store in posterior left cortex.

Neuroimaging evidence supports such a spatial–object distinction, though the distinction also tends to be lateralised to the left for object information and to the right for spatial information. Smith and Jonides (1994) for example compared the spatial version of Sternberg task used by Jonides et al. (1993) with an object version that used abstract shapes (and for which spatial location was irrelevant; Figure 7.2). When contrasted with the spatial version, the object version revealed activations that were predominantly left-lateralised, including premotor cortex (BA 6), inferior parietal cortex (BA 40) and inferior temporal cortex (BA 37). The former two regions were close to those associated with verbal working memory tasks (see above), suggesting that participants were verbally recoding the abstract shapes. The inferior temporal region is consistent with the non-human primate data suggesting a specific role for this area in processing object information (e.g., Desimone & Gross, 1979) and the deficits following left posterior lesions in humans (Warrington & Rabin, 1971). A more direct comparison of object and spatial information was made by Smith et al. (1995). Participants were presented with two abstract shapes and, following a 3 second delay, a single probe shape prompting a yes–no response. In the test of object working memory, the task was to decide whether the probe matched one of the memory set in shape (regardless of its location on the screen). In the test of spatial working memory, the task was to decide whether the probe matched one of the memory set in its location (regardless of its shape). Thus identical stimuli were presented in both cases; the only difference was the task instruction. The areas more active in the object task than spatial task were left posterior parietal cortex and left inferior temporal cortex, a subset of the areas implicated in the Smith and Jonides (1994) study. The areas more active in the spatial task were again right inferior frontal, right posterior parietal, right anterior occipital and right premotor cortices. Other studies comparing visual object versus visual spatial working memory have been reported by McCarthy et al. (1996) and Belger et al. (1998).

Courtney, Ungerleider, Kell and Haxby (1997) used rapid fMRI scanning of a delayed-matching-to-sample task, in order to identify areas whose activity was sustained during the delay between the sample and test stimuli (i.e., reflected mnemonic rather than perceptual or motor components of the task). These areas included right inferior occipital cortex (BA 18/19), and bilateral ventral (BA 45/47) and dorsal (BA 46) lateral frontal cortex. The inferior occipital activation is consistent with the Smith et al. (1995) studies of object maintenance, though the opposite lateralisation may reflect the fact that Courtney et al.'s objects were faces rather than abstract pictures.

The above dissociations are suggestive of separate neural systems for object and spatial working memory, with an inferior temporo-occipital specialisation for maintenance of visual object information, and a right parietal specialisation for maintenance of visual spatial information. Neuro-imaging studies are yet to find evidence for the ventral–dorsal object–spatial dissociation of prefrontal cortex suggested by some nonhuman primate research however (see Owen, 1997; Petrides, 1994). The dorsolateral pre-frontal activations associated with manipulation in human working memory tasks are, if anything, dissociated (lateralised) for verbal versus spatial information, rather than spatial versus object information, and the evidence for an object–spatial distinction is not as clear as that for a verbal–visuo-spatial distinction. Indeed, the results from human imaging experiments are often difficult to interpret because participants are able to label abstract objects, allowing use of a verbal working memory system. One possible solution, adopted in a long-term memory study by Owen, Milner, Petrides and Evans (1996b), is to require discrimination of two very similar pictures of a familiar, nameable object: because the same verbal label is likely to be applied, successful discrimination requires use of more detailed visual object memory. Furthermore, little research has attempted to distinguish spatial from visual maintenance by examining spatial working memory tasks using auditory stimuli.

YET OTHER MATERIAL-SPECIFIC STORES?

It is possible that yet more material-specific stores will be associated with distinct brain areas. For example, there is both psychological (Crowder & Morton, 1969) and neuropsychological (Samson & Zatorre, 1992) evidence for temporary storage of precategorical, auditory information, which may be localised in right superior temporal cortex (Zatorre, Evans, & Meyer, 1994). There is also evidence for a short-lived iconic visual store (Phillips, 1974), which may reflect sustained activity in primary visual cortex, and even a short-lived motoric store in nonhuman primate motor cortex (Smyrnis, Taira, Ashe, & Georgopoulos, 1992). However, it is not clear whether these stores qualify as working memories, in the sense that information can be actively maintained or manipulated. Rather, these stores would seem to correspond to passive stores that lack a rehearsal process, as discussed below.

STORAGE VERSUS REHEARSAL

Maintenance consists of two components: passive storage and active rehearsal. The rehearsal–storage dissociation appears to reflect an anterior–posterior anatomical segregation, with storage involving posterior areas of parietal, temporal and occipital cortices and rehearsal involving areas of frontal cortex.

Verbal storage and rehearsal

For verbal material, this posterior–anterior storage–rehearsal dissociation is suggested by findings that patients with lesions in left inferior parietal cortex show dramatic verbal working memory deficits, whereas patients with lesions in inferior frontal cortex (e.g., Broca's area) show less dramatic deficits, despite considerable articulatory problems (Vallar & Shallice, 1990). This pattern can be explained if damage to inferior parietal cortex prevents verbal storage, whereas damage to inferior frontal cortex prevents rehearsal but leaves storage intact. Because patients with anterior brain damage may still be able to store verbal information for short periods of time, they would be less impaired on immediate tests of verbal working memory.

This group difference is again supported by single-case studies. Vallar, DiBetta and Silveri (1997) report a patient L.A., who had lesions in inferior parietal and superior/middle temporal areas of the left hemisphere. L.A. showed an impaired verbal memory span and no evidence of a phonological similarity effect, suggesting impaired storage. L.A. did however show an effect of articulatory suppression, suggesting that she retained the ability to rehearse. This pattern of deficit was contrasted with that of a patient T.O., who had lesions in premotor, frontal paraventricular and anterior insula areas of the left hemisphere. T.O. showed a phonological similarity effect with auditory presentation of stimuli, but no effect of articulatory suppression, suggesting intact storage but impaired rehearsal.

Many single-case studies have now been reported with a selective impairment of verbal short-term storage when material is presented auditorily (the 'auditory–verbal short-term memory syndrome', Vallar & Shallice, 1990). These patients show memory spans for auditory–verbal material of only 2–3 items, combined with normal speech perception and production, normal long-term memory, normal short-term memory for non-verbal auditory material and relatively unimpaired short-term memory for visual–verbal material. The less severe impairment in these patients when verbal material is presented visually is often attributed to use of an alternative, visuo-spatial store (see above). Despite a range of different aetiologies, the most common lesion site in these patients is left inferior parietal cortex (posterior to Wernicke's area), in a region called the supramarginal gyrus (Figure 7.1).

To distinguish storage and rehearsal in their neuroimaging experiment, Awh et al. (1996) compared a two-back verbal working memory task (see Figure 7.2) with a control task of continuous subvocal repetition of a single item. Subtraction of the control task the memory task revealed significant activation in left inferior parietal cortex (BA 40), bilateral superior parietal cortex (BA 7), bilateral supplementary motor area (BA 6), right thalamus and right cerebellum. Any difference in inferior frontal cortex (e.g., Broca's area) failed to reach significance. Using a different control of letter rhyme judgement, which is believed to require articulatory rehearsal (Besner, 1987), Paulesu et al. (1993b) reported greater relative activity in left inferior parietal cortex (BA 40) for their Sternberg task, but little difference in inferior frontal cortex (BA 44). Both studies therefore implicate left inferior parietal cortex (BA 40) in storage, which was more active in the memory tasks, and left inferior frontal cortex (BA 44) in rehearsal, which was common to both memory and articulatory control tasks. Indeed, storage of verbal information is associated with left parietal activation in almost every verbal working memory study (with the possible exception of Fiez et al., 1996, though see Jonides et al., 1998), in good agreement with the neuropsychological evidence.

A common suggestion (Jonides et al., 1996) is that the other areas activated during maintenance of verbal material, including left premotor cortex, supplementary motor cortex and right cerebellum, together with left inferior frontal cortex, comprise a network involved in speech production, consistent with the articulatory nature of rehearsal proposed by

Baddeley (1986; though see Bishop & Robson, 1989). (The activation in supplementary motor cortex and right cerebellum when Awh et al., 1996, contrasted their memory task with their repetition task may reflect additional speech processes, such as seriation, that were required in the more demanding two-back memory task.) More recent imaging studies have sought to dissociate not only brain regions involved in storage and rehearsal, but also those involved in the recoding of visual items into a phonological form, and the temporal grouping of items during rehearsal. Using the Burgess and Hitch (1999) computational model of the phonological loop for example, Henson, Burgess and Frith (2000) suggested that left inferior frontal activations are associated with the retrieval of output phonology (used in recoding), whereas left premotor activations are associated with the processes of seriation and timing of rehearsal (used in grouping). Further functional decomposition of the network of brain areas associated with maintenance of verbal information is likely to benefit from the use of such explicit models.

Visuo-spatial storage and rehearsal

Developments of the visuo-spatial sketchpad component of the WM model distinguish between storage of visual material in a visual cache and its rehearsal via an inner scribe (Logie, 1995; see chapter 2, this volume), analogous to the phonological loop. The neuropsychological and neuro-imaging evidence reviewed above suggests that the visual cache might exist in left temporo-occipital cortex. The localisation of the inner scribe is less clear however. Right parietal cortex may subserve spatial rehearsal processes, or it may subserve a spatial store that is independent of any visual object store. Moreover the precise nature of visuo-spatial rehearsal processes is far from clear. The hypothesis that visuo-spatial rehearsal corresponds to planned eye movements has little supportive evidence (Baddeley, 1986), and activations of areas associated with eye movements, such as frontal eye fields (BA 8), pulvinar nucleus, or superior colliculus, are yet to be observed in neuroimaging studies of visuo-spatial working memory. An alternative hypothesis that rehearsal of visuo-spatial information involves an internal attentional mechanism is consistent with neuroimaging studies of spatial attention, which activate similar areas of right superior parietal cortex (BA 7), independent of eye movement (Corbetta, Miezin, Shulman, & Petersen, 1993; Coull & Nobre, 1998). A tentative hypothesis is that visuo-spatial information is stored over abstract or object visual representations in occipital cortex and inferior temporal cortex respectively, which are spatially organised via associations with right parietal cortex. These representations may be refreshed by a process of sequential, selective attention via each visual-spatial association; a process that engages right superior parietal cortex (BA 7), right premotor cortex (BA 6) and right inferior frontal cortex (BA 47).

MANIPULATION

The functional anatomy of manipulation in working memory is less well defined than maintenance. Executive processes are generally associated with frontal cortex, on the basis that patients with frontal damage usually present with a general impairment in complex behavioural tasks, but not routine or automatic tasks (Shallice, 1988). Lesions to anterior and midlateral regions of prefrontal cortex for example do not normally impair maintenance: A review by D'Esposito and Postle (1999) found no evidence that patients with dorsolateral prefrontal lesions were impaired on span tasks. This suggests that manipulation is subserved by frontal regions distinct from those subserving maintenance. However, many different types of manipulation have been proposed (e.g., monitoring, updating, selecting, inhibiting) and a huge range of different tasks have been examined that involve at least one type of manipulation. Without attempting a precise definition of different types of manipulation, I concentrate below on four types of task that have been used extensively in neuropsychology and/or neuroimaging.

Monitoring tasks

Two simple tasks that combine maintenance and manipulation, and which have proved useful in neuroimaging studies, are the Continuous Performance Test (CPT) and the N-back task (Figure 7.2). Both tasks require monitoring of a continuous sequence of stimuli for the occurrence of a target that is contingent on preceding stimuli. Participants in a verbal CPT respond positively whenever a target letter (e.g., X) follows a specified context letter (e.g., A), and negatively otherwise. This task has a small maintenance component, in that the correct response to a stimulus requires memory for the prior stimulus, and a small manipulation component in order to update working memory whenever the context letter is not followed by the target letter. Participants in the N-back task respond positively whenever the current stimulus matches the stimulus N positions back in the sequence. For N>0, this task requires both maintenance of the last N stimuli (in order) and updating of these stimuli each time a new stimulus occurs (for N=0, the task is simply to respond whenever a prespecified target occurs, which requires no updating). N is often viewed as proportional to the working memory load – the demands placed on maintenance and/or manipulation processes.

Barch et al. (1997) used the CPT to distinguish the concept of working memory load from less interesting concepts like task difficulty, mental effort, or arousal. This dissociation is important given that working memory tasks typically involve greater error rates and/or longer reaction times than their control tasks. To increase the working memory load, Barch et al. lengthened the time interval between the context letter and target letter (increasing the proportion of time during a block of trials during which maintenance was required). To vary the level of task difficulty, they compared conditions in which the stimuli were visually degraded with conditions in which the stimuli were intact. Consistent with their expectations, variations in maintenance duration had no significant effect on error rates or reaction times, unlike variations in visual degradation, which increased both error rates and reaction times. Moreover, a double dissociation was observed between areas such as left dorsolateral prefrontal cortex (BA 9/46), left inferior frontal cortex (BA 6/44) and left posterior parietal cortex (BA 7/40), which showed effects of maintenance duration but no significant effect of visual degradation, and areas such as the anterior cingulate (BA 8/32) and right inferior frontal cortex (BA 44/45/47), which showed effects of visual degradation but no significant effect of maintenance duration. These results suggest that the left frontal and left parietal activations seen in verbal working memory studies are not simply an artifact of greater task difficulty.

Braver et al. (1997) varied verbal working memory load by increasing N from N=0 to N=3 in a letter-version of the N-back task. Areas in which activity was a linear increasing function of load included dorsolateral prefrontal cortex (BA 9/46), inferior frontal cortex (BA 6/44) and parietal cortex (BA 7/40), bilaterally in each case, as well as a number of left motor, premotor and supplementary motor areas (BA 4/6). Similar results were reported by Jonides et al. (1997). On the basis of the studies reviewed above, the inferior frontal, posterior parietal and motor activations are likely to reflect the network of areas involved in maintenance of verbal information (e.g., the storage and rehearsal of the most recent N letters). This would implicate the additional bilateral activation of dorsolateral prefrontal cortex in manipulation (e.g., updating of the particular letters being maintained). It would be valuable to examine the effects of increasing working memory load in the N-back task in patients with frontal damage.

Smith et al. (1996) reported activation in similar dorsolateral regions when a 3-back task was compared with a control task in which participants monitored stimuli for the occurrence of one of three target stimuli ('equating' the maintenance component). Activations of these regions were lateralised with respect to whether the 3-back task involved verbal or spatial stimuli, with greater left dorsolateral activation in the former and greater right dorsolateral activation in the latter. In a similar study, Owen et al. (1998) compared spatial and object N-back tasks with a single target control task. Although differences between the spatial and object memory-related activations were observed in posterior regions, such as posterior parietal cortex (BA 7/40) for the spatial task, and middle and anterior temporal cortex (BA 21/22/38) for the object task, the coordinates of the peaks of the bilateral dorsolateral prefrontal activations for the two tasks were within 2mm of each other. This suggests that manipulation processes are common to spatial and object working memory, unlike the apparent lateralisation of verbal and spatial manipulation processes.

An alternative method of dissociating maintenance and manipulation was reported by Cohen et al. (1997), who measured activity at four different poststimulus times during an N-back task. Areas involved in transient processes, such as perceiving stimuli and producing responses, would be expected to show an effect of poststimulus time but no effect of load (N), whereas areas involved in sustained processes such as maintenance would be expected to show an effect of load but no effect of poststimulus time. Furthermore, areas involved in manipulation processes might be expected to show an interaction between load and poststimulus time (updating the target item being a transient process that becomes more demanding as N increases). As expected, areas associated with stimulus perception, such as visual cortex, showed effects of poststimulus time, but no effect of load. Contrary to expectations, however, areas showing an effect of load but not poststimulus time included dorsolateral prefrontal cortex (BA 9/46), which, unlike the Braver et al. (1997) study, showed a nonlinear effect of load, such that activity was considerably greater for the 2- and 3-back tasks than for the 0- and 1-back tasks. The reason for this discrepancy between the two studies is not clear. It may reflect a difference in the strategies used by the two groups of participants: The jump in dorsolateral prefrontal activity between the 1- and 2-back tasks in the Cohen et al. study may reflect a strategic change between updating a single item in working memory and updating a sequence of two or more items in serial order. Nonetheless, this approach to distinguishing transient and sustained effects in working memory tasks is clearly an important methodological advance, and one that may prove valuable in teasing apart the processes of manipulation and maintenance in future studies.

Generation tasks

A task that has been used in neuropsychological, electrophysiological and neuroimaging studies is the self-ordered generation task (Milner, 1982). Participants in this task select one stimulus from a finite set such that, over trials, every stimulus has been selected once (without repetition). This task involves not only maintaining and updating information about which stimuli have already been selected, but also comparison of this information with the set of possible stimuli in order to select each new stimulus. Patients with frontal lesions are impaired at self-ordering tasks (Petrides & Milner, 1982) and analogous deficits are seen in primates with dorsolateral prefrontal lesions (Petrides, 1994).

Petrides, Alivisatos, Evans, and Meyer (1993a; Petrides, Alivisatos, Meyer, & Evans, 1993b) compared brain activity during performance of a self-ordering task with a control task in which participants responded to one of a set of stimuli that was indicated each trial. When the stimuli were abstract designs, the ordering task produced greater activation in right dorsolateral prefrontal cortex, as predicted (Petrides et al., 1993a) and supporting a right lateralisation of visuo-spatial working memory. When the stimuli were verbal (digits), the dorsolateral prefrontal activation was bilateral (Petrides et al., 1993b). This prefrontal activation did not owe simply to the self-generated nature of the ordering task: When an externally ordered condition was tested in which participants monitored a random sequence of heard digits in order to detect which digit 1–10 was omitted, the same bilateral dorsolateral prefrontal activation was observed (Petrides et al., 1993b).

Another generation task is random number generation (Baddeley, 1966), in which numbers must be generated without conforming to any rule or pattern (meaning that repetition is of course possible). Tasks like these involve not only internal monitoring of previous responses (rather than the external monitoring of the CPT and N-back tasks), but inhibition of prepotent responses and well-learned schemata. Frith, Friston, Liddle and Frackowiak (1991) reported bilateral dorsal frontal activations when generative, random key pressing was compared with reactive, stimulus-driven key pressing. Jahanshahi, Dirnberger, Fuller and Frith (2000) observed left dorsolateral activation when random number generation was compared with counting, and this activity was negatively related to indices of randomness and higher generation rates. Interestingly, right ventrolateral activation was also seen when random number generation was compared with counting, but did not correlate with randomness indices or generation rate, suggesting that this region is involved in maintenance processes unrelated to the difficulty of random generation. Surprisingly, though Alzheimer and Parkinson patients have been shown to be impaired at random generation, there have been few studies of the effects of localised frontal lesions on random generation in humans.

Other generation tasks like verbal fluency, a common clinical test of frontal lobe damage, involve selection of stimuli from much larger sets. The verbal fluency task requires generation without repetition of, for example, as many animal names (category fluency), or words beginning with a specified letter (letter fluency), as possible in a short period of time. This task involves not only monitoring but also development of new strategies to aid generation (e.g., first thinking of pets, then safari animals, etc.). Baddeley and Wilson (1988) reported that patient R. J., who suffered bilateral frontal damage, was only able to give four animal names in 60 seconds (cf. a dozen or more in controls). The PET study of Frith et al. (1991) found left dorsolateral prefrontal activation when letter fluency was compared with word repetition. Considerable evidence thus exists for a role of dorsolateral prefrontal cortex, on the left for verbal information and right for visuo-spatial material, in the manipulation processes required by generation tasks.

Dual tasks

Combining two tasks simultaneously often makes demands on working memory (Baddeley, 1986), typically requiring the switching between information appropriate for one or other task. Patients with frontal lesions tend to be disproportionately impaired at dual versus single task performance

(McDowell, Whyte, & D'Esposito, 1997), again suggesting a frontal role in these aspects of working memory.

D'Esposito et al. (1995) compared brain activity when participants performed two tasks concurrently with activity when each task was performed alone. Neither of the two tasks, a spatial rotation task and a semantic judgement task, produced significant activation of dorsolateral prefrontal cortex when performed alone; only when they were combined was significant activation of this area observed. Importantly, this activation was unlikely to owe simply to the impaired performance of both tasks when combined, because a second experiment, in which performance of the rotation task was impaired by decreasing the interval between stimuli, did not reveal any significant increase in dorsolateral prefrontal activity. However, a dual-task PET study by Klingberg (1998), using a visual and an auditory task in which participants indicated when a stimulus was of lower luminance or pitch respectively than the previous stimulus, found no cortical area that was activated specifically in the dual-task condition. Moreover, Goldberg et al. (1998) found that the dorsolateral activation associated with a Wisconsin card-sorting task was actually diminished when combined with an auditory verbal shadowing task, and Fletcher et al. (1995) found that the dorsolateral activation associated with elaborative verbal encoding was diminished when combined with a visuo-motor secondary task. One possible explanation for these results is that one or both of the tasks of Klingberg (1998), Goldberg et al. (1998) and Fletcher et al. (1995) required manipulation even when performed alone, consistent with the dorsolateral prefrontal activations observed in each case. This might leave less scope for additional dorsolateral activation when the tasks are combined, or even a decrement in dorsolateral activation when performance of both tasks suffers under dual-task conditions, as observed by Goldberg et al. (1998) and Fletcher et al. (1995).

Complex planning tasks

Shallice (1982) introduced the Tower of London task in order to test planning deficits in patients with frontal lesions. Participants in this task must rearrange a set of balls on pegs to match a specified goal state. Because of the constraints on legal movements of the balls, this task requires planning of a number of separate moves in order to attain the goal state, often via various subgoals, in the minimum number of moves. Shallice found that patients with left frontal lesions were more impaired on this task than patients with right frontal lesions. Owen, Downes, Sahakian, Polkey and Robbins (1990) however found that patients with both left and right frontal lesions were impaired on this task relative to controls. Importantly, their deficit remained even when movement execution times were subtracted, and neither type of patient was significantly impaired on the Corsi blocks test of visuo-spatial maintenance, suggesting that the deficit was confined to manipulation processes (i.e., planning). However, the site and extent of the frontal lesions in both studies were highly variable, preventing any further localisation within prefrontal cortex.

Owen, Doyon, Petrides and Evans (1996a) compared brain activity in healthy individuals performing a computerised version of the Tower of London task (indicating moves on a touch-sensitive screen) with activity when they simply touched highlighted balls (yoked to their number and speed of moves in the Tower of London condition). Activation of left dorsolateral prefrontal cortex was observed, as well as several activations in right premotor and parietal cortices that may be associated with visuo-spatial maintenance. When Baker et al. (1996) used a version of the Tower of London task in which no movement was required (participants were shown an initial and a goal state, and simply indicated the minimum number of moves from the initial to the goal state), subtraction of easy (2–3 move solutions) from difficult (4–5 move solutions) conditions revealed activation in right dorsolateral prefrontal, bilateral premotor and medial parietal cortices (though the same activations were not seen in a similar comparison by Owen et al., 1996a). These studies are at least suggestive of a dorsolateral (perhaps bilateral) prefrontal role in manipulation, even if manipulation has not yet been completely dissociated from maintenance in this task.

CONCLUSIONS

What are the strengths of the WM model?

I hope that the above review, albeit brief, illustrates how successful the WM model has been in interpreting neuropsychological evidence and guiding the design of neuroimaging experiments. Much progress has been made in the functional anatomy of human working memory, profiting from WM distinctions between verbal versus visuo-spatial information, storage versus rehearsal, and maintenance versus manipulation. Indeed, one can already attempt a preliminary mapping of WM model components onto the brain (Figure 7.3): The central executive maps to midlateral prefrontal regions, particularly left and right dorsal lateral prefrontal cortex; the phonological

Figure 7.3   A very tentative mapping of the WM model components onto the brain. PS=phonological store, AR=articulatory rehearsal, VC=visual cache, IS=inner scribe, CE=central executive. Note that the functions associated with each component are not meant to represent the only function subserved by the associated brain region; nor are these labels supposed to represent all brain regions associated with a particular function (e.g., operation of the central executive in a given task is likely to engage multiple brain regions in a functionally coherent network, including dorsolateral prefrontal cortex).

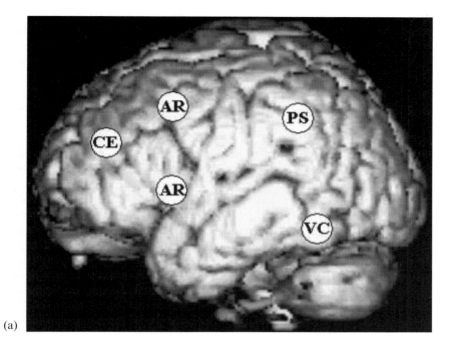

(a)

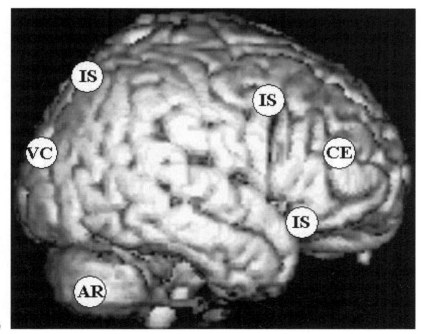

(b)

store maps to left inferior parietal cortex; the articulatory control process maps to left premotor regions (including Broca's area), left supplementary motor regions and perhaps right cerebellum; the visual cache maps to bilateral anterior occipital and/or inferior temporal regions; and the inner scribe maps to right premotor and right superior parietal regions.

What are the weaknesses of the WM model?

The main weakness of the WM model from the present perspective is its simplicity. For example, other researchers have argued for additional material-specific stores, particularly for visual object and visual spatial material. The central executive may also be fractionated by the type of material being manipulated, particularly for verbal versus visuo-spatial material. Moreover, the type of processes subserved by the central executive are not clearly defined in the WM model. The detailed task-analysis that is often required for neuroimaging studies for example is not supplied by the WM model. Though few other models fare any better (at least at a consensual level), neuroscientists clearly need a common theoretical framework with which to describe and dissociate executive (manipulation) processes.

What are the competing models?

There are few, if any, competing models of human working memory, at least that conform to a structural perspective (see chapter 10). The use of 'working memory' as a psychological construct relating to individual differences in general processing capacity for example, which has dominated North American psychological research (see chapter 1), would seem less amenable to functional anatomical fractionation. Indeed, it is difficult not to assume a structural model if one believes in functional segregation of the brain. Rather, the onus is on other models to interpret, for example, selective neuropsychological deficits.

What is the future of the WM model?

Many researchers believe that the WM model can be tested and developed without ever mapping it onto anatomy. This may or may not be the case. I believe nonetheless that future research should aim for a WM model that is mapped onto distinct brain regions, in order to make contact with the wealth of recent neuropsychological and neuroimaging data. This will be aided by a more detailed specification of the WM components, preferably through computational models that make explicit assumptions about the processes involved in the various working memory tasks (see chapter 8). A particularly important area of development is the functional decomposition of the concept of manipulation. This will address the question of whether frontal cortex is equipotential in its capacity for manipulation, or whether subregions exist with distinct functionality. Preliminary evidence exists for at least two levels of executive processes, with ventrolateral prefrontal cortex involved for comparison or selection of information in working memory, and dorsolateral prefrontal cortex involved only when additional processing is required (Owen, 1997; Petrides, 1994). In the more distant future, a successful WM model will need not only to map out functionally specialised brain regions, but also address the important question of how precisely these regions interact during performance of working memory tasks.

BACKGROUND READING

Vallar, G., & Shallice, T. (1990). *Neuropsychological Impairments of Short-term Memory*. Cambridge: Cambridge University Press.

A detailed review of verbal working memory deficits following brain damage.

Jonides, J., Reuter-Lorentz, P. A., Smith, E. E., Awh, E., Barnes, L. L., Drain, M., Glass, J., Lauber, E., Patalano, A. L., & Schumacher, E. (1996). Verbal and spatial working memory in humans. In D. Medin (Ed.), *The Psychology of Learning and Motivation* (pp. 43–88). London: Academic Press.

A review of psychological, neuropsychological and (early) neuroimaging studies of maintainance in working memory.

Owen, A. M. (1997). The functional organization of working memory processes within the human lateral frontal cortex: the contribution of functional neuro-imaging. *European Journal of Neuroscience, 9,* 1329–1339.

A review of the ventral-dorsal lateral prefrontal cortex dissociation in neuroimaging studies.

REFERENCES

Awh, E., Jonides, J., Smith, E. E., Schumacher, E. H., Koeppe, R. A., & Katz, S. (1996). Dissociation of storage and rehearsal in verbal working memory. *Psychological Science, 7,* 25–31.

Baddeley, A. D. (1966). The capacity for generating information by randomization. *Quarterly Journal of Experimental Psychology, 18,* 119–129.

Baddeley, A. D. (1986). *Working Memory*. Oxford: Oxford University Press.

Baddeley, A. D., & Hitch, G. J. (1974). Working memory. In G. Bower (Ed.), *Recent Advances in Learning and Motivation* (8th ed., pp. 47–90). New York: Academic Press.

Baddeley, A., & Wilson, B. (1988). Frontal amnesia and the dysexecutive syndrome. *Brain and Cognition, 7*(2), 212–230.

Baker, S. C., Rogers, R. D., Owen, A. M., Frith, C. D., Dolan, R. J., Frackowiak, R. S., & Robbins, T. W. (1996). Neural systems engaged by planning: a PET study of the Tower of London task. *Neuropsychologia, 34*(6), 515–526.

Barch, D. M., Braver, T. S., Nystrom, L. E., Forman, S. D., Noll, D. C., & Cohen, J. D. (1997). Dissociating working memory from task difficulty in human prefrontal cortex. *Neuropsychologia, 35,* 1373–1380.

Belger, A., Puce, A., Krystal, J. H., Gore, J. C., Goldman-Rakic, P., & McCarthy, G. (1998). Dissociation of mnemonic and perceptual processes during spatial and nonspatial working memory using fMRI. *Human Brain Mapping, 6*(1), 14–32.

Besner, D. (1987). Phonology, lexical access in reading and articulatory suppression: a critical review. *The Quarterly Journal of Experimental Psychology, 39A,* 467–478.

Bishop, D. V. M., & Robson, J. (1989). Unimpaired short-term memory and rhyme judgement in congenitally speechless individuals: implications for the notion of "articulatory coding". *The Quarterly Journal of Experimental Psychology, 41A,* 123–140.

Bisiach, E. (1993). Mental representation in unilateral neglect and related disorders: the twentieth Bartlett Memorial Lecture. *The Quarterly Journal of Experimental Psychology [A], 46*(3), 435–461.

Braver, T. S., Cohen, J. D., Nystrom, L. E., Jonides, J., Smith, E. E., & Noll, D. C. (1997). A parametric study of prefrontal cortex involvement in human working memory. *Neuroimage, 5,* 49–62.

Brodmann, K. (1909). *Vergleichende Lokalisationslehre der Grosshirnrinde in ihren Prinzipien dargelstellt auf Grund des Zellesbaues.* Leipzig: Barth.

Burgess, N., & Hitch, G. J. (1999). Memory for serial order: a network model of the phonological loop and its timing. *Psychological Review, 106*(3), 551–581.

Cohen, J. D., Perlstein, W. M., Braver, T. S., Nystrom, L. E., Noll, D. C., Jonides, J., & Smith, E. E. (1997). Temporal dynamics of brain activation during a working memory task. *Nature, 386,* 604–608.

Corbetta, M., Miezin, F. M., Shulman, G. L., & Petersen, S. (1993). A PET study of visuo-spatial attention. *The Journal of Neuroscience, 13*(3), 1202–1226.

Coull, J. T., & Nobre, A. C. (1998). Where and when to pay attention: the neural systems for directing attention to spatial locations and to time intervals as revealed by both PET and fMRI. *Journal of Neuroscience, 18,* 7426–7435.

Courtney, S. M., Ungerleider, L. G., Kell, K., & Haxby, J. V. (1997). Transient and sustained activity in a distributed neural system for human working memory. *Nature, 386,* 608–611.

Crowder, R. G., & Morton, J. (1969). Precategorical acoustic storage. *Perception and Psychophysics, 5,* 365–373.

De Renzi, E., & Nichelli, P. (1975). Verbal and non-verbal short-term memory impairment following hemispheric damage. *Cortex, 11,* 341–353.

Desimone, R., & Gross, C. G. (1979). Visual areas in the temporal cortex of the Macaque. *Brain Research, 178,* 363–380.

D'Esposito, M., Detre, J. A., Alsop, D. C., Shin, R. K., Atlas, S., & Grossman, M. (1995). The neural basis of the central executive system of working memory. *Nature, 16,* 279–281.

D'Esposito, M., & Postle, B. R. (1999). The dependence of span and delayed response performance on prefrontal cortex. *Neuropsychologia, 37*, 1303–1315.

Fiez, J. A., Raife, E. A., Balota, D. A., Schwarz, J. P., Raichle, M. E., & Peterson, S. E. (1996). A positron emission tomography study of the short-term maintenance of verbal information. *The Journal of Neuroscience, 16*, 808–822.

Fletcher, P. C., Frith, C. D., Grasby, P. M., Shallice, T., Frackowiak, R. S. J., & Dolan, R. J. (1995). Brain systems for encoding and retrieval of auditory-verbal memory: an in vivo study in humans. *Brain, 118*, 401–416.

Frith, C. D., Friston, K. J., Liddle, P. F., & Frackowiak, R. S. J. (1991). Willed action and the prefrontal cortex in man: a study with PET. *Proceedings of the Royal Society of London B, 244*, 241–246.

Goldberg, T. E., Berman, K. F., Fleming, K., Ostrem, J., Van Horn, J. D., Esposito, G., Mattay, V. S., Gold, J. M., & Weinberger, D. R. (1998). Uncoupling cognitive workload and prefrontal cortical physiology: A PET rCBF study. *Neuroimage, 7*(4), 296–303.

Hanley, R. J., Young, A. W., & Pearson, N. A. (1991). Impairment of the visuo-spatial sketchpad. *The Quarterly Journal of Experimental Psychology, 43A*, 101–125.

Henson, R. N. A., Burgess, N., & Frith, C. D. (2000). Recoding, storage, rehearsal and grouping in verbal short-term memory: an fMRI study. *Neuropsychologia, 38*(4), 426–440.

Jahanshahi, M., Dirnberger, G., Fuller, R., & Frith, C. D. (2000). The role of the dorsolateral prefrontal cortex in random number generation: a study with positron emission tomography. *Neuroimage, 12*, 713–725.

Jonides, J., Reuter-Lorentz, P. A., Smith, E. E., Awh, E., Barnes, L. L., Drain, M., Glass, J., Lauber, E., Patalano, A. L., & Schumacher, E. (1996). Verbal and spatial working memory in humans. In D. Medin (Ed.), *The Psychology of Learning and Motivation* (pp. 43–88). London: Academic Press.

Jonides, J., Schumacher, E. H., Smith, E. E., Koeppe, R. A., Awh, E., Reuter-Lorenz, P. A., Marshuetz, C., & Willis, C. R. (1998). The role of parietal cortex in verbal working memory. *The Journal of Neuroscience, 18*, 5026–5034.

Jonides, J., Schumacher, E. H., Smith, E. E., Lauber, E. J., Awh, E., Minoshima, S., & Koeppe, R. A. (1997). Verbal working memory load affects regional brain activation as measured by PET. *Journal of Cognitive Neuroscience, 9*, 462–475.

Jonides, J., Smith, E. E., Koeppe, R. A., Awh, E., Minoshima, S., & Mintum, M. (1993). Spatial working memory in humans as revealed by PET. *Nature, 363*, 623–625.

Klingberg, T. (1998). Concurrent performance of two working memory tasks: potential mechanisms of interference. *Cerebral Cortex, 8*(7), 593–601.

Kosslyn, S. M., Alpert, N. M., Thompson, W. L., Maljkovic, V., Weise, S. B., Chabris, C. F., Hamilton, S. E., Rauch, S. L., & Buonanno, F. S. (1993). Visual mental imagery activates topographically organized visual cortex: PET investigations. *Journal of Cognitive Neuroscience, 5*, 263–287.

Levine, D. N., Warach, J., & Farah, M. (1985). Two visual systems in mental imagery: dissociation of "what" and "where" in imagery disorders due to bilateral posterior cerebral lesions. *Neurology, 35*, 1010–1018.

Logie, R. H. (1995). *Visuo-spatial Working Memory*. Hove, UK: Lawrence Erlbaum Associates, Inc.

McCarthy, G., Puce, A., Constable, R. T., Krystal, J. H., Gore, J. C., & Goldman-

Rakic, P. (1996). Activation of human prefrontal cortex during spatial and nonspatial working memory tasks measured by functional MRI. *Cerebral Cortex*, 6, 600–611.

McDowell, S., Whyte, J., & D'Esposito, M. (1997). Working memory impairments in traumatic brain injury: evidence from a dual-task paradigm. *Neuropsychologia*, 35(10), 1341–1353.

Milner, A. D., & Goodale, M. A. (1993). Visual pathways to perception and action. In T. P. Hicks, S. Molotchnikoff, & T. Ono (Eds.), *Progress in Brain Research*. Amsterdam: Elsevier.

Milner, B. (1982). Some cognitive effects of frontal-lobe lesions in man. *Philosophical Transactions of the Royal Society of London*, 298, 211–226.

Mishkin, M., Ungerleider, L. G., & Macko, K. A. (1983). Object vision and spatial vision: two cortical pathways. *Trends in Neuroscience*, 6, 414–417.

Owen, A. M. (1997). The functional organization of working memory processes within the human lateral frontal cortex: the contribution of functional neuroimaging. *European Journal of Neuroscience*, 9, 1329–1339.

Owen, A. M., Downes, J. J., Sahakian, B. J., Polkey, C. E., & Robbins, T. W. (1990). Planning and spatial working memory following frontal lobe lesions. *Neuropsychologia*, 28, 1021–1034.

Owen, A. M., Doyon, J., Petrides, M., & Evans, A. C. (1996a). Planning and spatial working memory: a positron emission tomography study in humans. *European Journal of Neuroscience*, 8(2), 353–364.

Owen, A. M., Milner, B., Petrides, M., & Evans, A. C. (1996b). Memory for object features versus memory for object location: a positron emission tomography study of encoding and retrieval processes. *Proceedings of the National Academy of Sciences, USA*, 93, 9212–9217.

Owen, A. M., Stern, C. E., Look, R. B., Tracey, I., Rosen, B. R., & Petrides, M. (1998). Functional organization of spatial and nonspatial working memory processing within the human lateral frontal cortex. *Proceedings of the National Academy of Sciences, USA*, 95(13), 7721–7726.

Paulesu, E., Frith, C. D., Bench, C. J., Bottini, P. M., Grasby, P. M., & Frackowiak, R. S. J. (1993a). Functional anatomy of working memory: the visuo-spatial "sketchpad". *Journal of Cerebral Blood Flow and Metabolism*, 13, 551.

Paulesu, E., Frith, C. D., & Frackowiak, R. S. J. (1993b). The neural correlates of the verbal component of working memory. *Nature*, 362, 342–344.

Petrides, M. (1994). Frontal lobes and working memory: evidence from investigations of the effects of cortical excisions in non-human primates. In F. Boller & J. Grafman (Eds.), *Handbook of Neuropsychology* (Vol. 9, pp. 59–82). Amsterdam: Elsevier Science.

Petrides, M., Alivisatos, B., Evans, A., & Meyer, E. (1993a). Dissociation of human mid-dorsolateral from posterior dorsolateral frontal cortex in memory processing. *Proceedings of the National Academy of Sciences, USA*, 90, 873–877.

Petrides, M., Alivisatos, B., Meyer, E., & Evans, A. C. (1993b). Functional activation of the human frontal cortex during the performance of verbal working memory tasks. *Proceedings of the National Academy of Sciences, USA*, 90, 878–882.

Petrides, M., & Milner, B. (1982). Deficits in subject-ordered tasks after frontal- and temporal-lobe lesions in man. *Neuropsychologia*, 20, 249–262.

Phillips, W. A. (1974). On the distinction between sensory storage and short-term visual memory. *Perception and Psychophysics, 16,* 283–290.

Samson, S., & Zatorre, R. J. (1992). Learning and retention of melodic and verbal information after unilateral temporal lobectomy. *Neuropsychologia, 30*(9), 815–826.

Shallice, T. (1982). Specific impairments of planning. *Philosophical Transactions of the Royal Society of London, 298,* 199–209.

Shallice, T. (1988). *From Neuropsychology to Mental Structure* (Vol. 14). Cambridge: Cambridge University Press.

Smith, E. E., & Jonides, J. (1997). Working memory: a view from neuroimaging. *Cognitive Psychology, 33,* 5–42.

Smith, E. E., Jonides, J., & Koeppe, R. A. (1996). Dissociating verbal and spatial working memory using PET. *Cerebral Cortex, 6,* 11–20.

Smith, E. E., & Jonides, J. J. (1994). Working memory in humans: Neuropsychological evidence. In M. Gazzaniga (Ed.), *The Cognitive Neurosciences.* Cambridge, MA: MIT Press.

Smith, E. E., Jonides, J. J., Koeppe, R. A., Awh, E., Schumacher, E. H., & Minoshima, S. (1995). Spatial versus object working memory: PET investigations. *Journal of Cognitive Neuroscience, 7,* 337–356.

Smyrnis, N., Taira, M., Ashe, J., & Georgopoulos, A. P. (1992). Motor cortical activity in a memorized delay task. *Experimental Brain Research, 92*(1), 139–151.

Sternberg, S. (1969). Memory scanning: mental processes revealed by reaction time experiments. *American Scientist, 57,* 421–457.

Vallar, G., & Baddeley, A. D. (1984). Fractionation of working memory: neuropsychological evidence for a phonological short-term store. *Journal of Verbal Learning and Verbal Behaviour, 23,* 151–161.

Vallar, G., DiBetta, A. M., & Silveri, M. C. (1997). The phonological short-term store-rehearsal system: patterns of impairment and neural correlates. *Neuropsychologia, 35,* 795–812.

Vallar, G., & Shallice, T. (1990). *Neuropsychological Impairments of Short-term Memory.* Cambridge: Cambridge University Press.

Warrington, E. K., & Rabin, P. (1971). Visual span and apprehension in patients with unilateral cerebral lesions. *Quarterly Journal of Experimental Psychology, 23,* 423–431.

Wilson, F. A. W., Scalaidhe, S. P., & Goldman-Rakic, P. S. (1993). Dissociation of object and spatial processing domains in primate prefrontal cortex. *Science, 260,* 1955–1958.

Zatorre, R. J., Evans, A. C., & Meyer, E. (1994). Neural mechanisms underlying melodic perception and memory for pitch. *Journal of Neuroscience, 14*(4), 1908–1919.

Part III
Theoretical perspectives

8 Computational models of short-term memory: Modelling serial recall of verbal material

Mike Page and Richard Henson

One of the great achievements of the Working Memory (WM) model is that it allows a large amount of data to be fitted into a compact theoretical framework. This is particularly true in the case of the phonological sub-system of working memory as applied to the task with which it has been very directly associated, the immediate serial recall (ISR) of verbal material. In the twenty-six years since the first publication of the WM model, the conception of the phonological component of working memory, the so-called phonological loop (PL), has proved capable of being adapted to account for a variety of data from ISR tasks. These data bear on the effects of factors such as modality, phonological similarity, word length, con-current articulatory suppression and irrelevant speech and, further, on the interactions between these factors. That the general patterns embodied in such a large body of data can be summarised within a reasonably concise theoretical framework, is a tribute to a style of verbal modelling that allows models to be adapted in the face of new and constraining data, but that preserves a clear sense of the core, defining features of the theory.

The shortcomings of purely verbal theorising have nonetheless become evident. While the phonological loop, as verbally specified, supplies a framework in which overall patterns of data can be interpreted, it does not actually specify a mechanistic account of how, for example, the ISR task is actually accomplished. Neither does it seek to explain the pattern of errors that underlies differential performance under various experimental condi-tions, some of which will be discussed in what follows. Beyond being expressed in terms of the overall percentage of items correctly recalled in position, ISR data can be analysed in a number of ways. Errors can be broken down into various error types, such as transpositions (e.g., '5937' in response to stimulus list 5397), omissions (e.g., response '539-' to same stimulus) and extra-list intrusions (e.g., '5327'), and the occurrence of each type of error can itself be plotted as a function of serial position. In the case of substitution errors (e.g., transpositions, intrusions) the origin of the substituting element can itself often be surmised and the data broken down accordingly.

Such a detailed exposition of error patterns highlights a need for more quantitative models of ISR. While quantitative models of ISR had been attempted even before the advent of the WM model (e.g. Estes, 1972), none had attempted to address itself to the breadth of data resulting from the experimental manipulations listed above. One of the first models that sought to meet this challenge was that of Burgess and Hitch (1992). Burgess and Hitch, in keeping with what was then a growing trend in cognitive modelling, chose to implement their model as a connectionist network. They showed how a network of nodes could be organised to simulate aspects of human ISR performance. In fact Burgess and Hitch's (1992) model, while representing something of a milestone in the simulation of ISR, was far from being an unqualified success in the modelling of actual data — as its authors point out in their subsequent work (e.g. Burgess & Hitch, 1999), it was unable to account satisfactorily for the shape of serial position curves, and was unable to capture the intricate pattern of results associated with the phonological similarity effect (PSE), particularly that found with lists of alternating phonological confusability (Baddeley, 1968; Henson, Norris, Page & Baddeley, 1996; see below).

Both the successes and the failures of the Burgess and Hitch (1992) model were influential in encouraging a number of researchers either to develop new models of ISR, or to develop variants of models that had pre-dated Burgess and Hitch, but that initially had a more limited purview (e.g. Nairne's, 1990, feature model, later developed in Neath & Nairne, 1995, and Neath, 1999). As a result there is now a wealth of models addressing themselves to the quantitative modelling of the ISR task. While most have seen their task as being to provide a mathematical (and, in many cases, connectionist) account of ISR to complement the verbal theorising of Baddeley, Hitch and colleagues, others (notably Neath & Nairne, 1995; Neath, 1999) have used their models to question the legitimacy of the WM/ PL model. Thus the growing popularity of mathematical models has sharpened considerably debate in the area.

In this chapter we shall give brief descriptions of a number of the competing models of immediate serial recall. These will include the primacy model of Page and Norris (1998), the latest version of the Burgess and Hitch model (Burgess & Hitch, 1999), Henson's (1998) start–end model, the OSCAR model (Brown, Preece & Hulme, 2000), and Nairne's feature model (Nairne, 1990, 1999; Neath & Nairne, 1995).[1] The first four of these are essentially cast in the framework of the phonological loop component of working memory, though they differ in the ways that they simulate some of the effects found in the data. The latter model embodies a rather different approach and is motivated by some data whose interpretation, as we will see, is still the subject of some debate. In discussing the various models we will highlight certain aspects of the ISR data that we believe afford some

---

1   We will not describe the OOER model of Jones (1993) here as it has not been quantitatively specified and has been principally directed towards an account of the irrelevant speech effect rather than being more broadly applied.

leverage in discriminating between them. The areas of the data to which we will address ourselves are the effect of relatively short filled retention intervals on recall, with particular reference to the phonological similarity effect (PSE), and the pattern of between-list intrusions.

The PSE refers to the poorer serial recall of lists of phonologically confusable (e.g. rhyming) items relative to that of lists of nonconfusable items (Baddeley, 1968; Bjork & Healy, 1974; Conrad & Hull, 1964; Henson et al., 1996; etc.). In mixed lists comprising some mutually confusable items and other nonconfusable items, the confusable items still suffer, in terms of how well they are recalled in the correct position, relative to the nonconfusable items. In such lists the nonconfusable items are recalled at a level indistinguishable from that found for pure nonconfusable lists. In lists of alternating confusability, this leads to the characteristic sawtooth-shaped serial position curves that have been the target of simulation attempts for several of the models described above. A key feature of the PSE is that it dissipates over short delays during which rehearsal is prevented by a task such as articulatory suppression or naming of successive, visually presented stimuli. In several studies, strong effects of phonological similarity have been shown to dissipate over retention intervals as short as 5–7 seconds (Bjork & Healy, 1974; Estes, 1973). Note that overall serial recall performance is reduced substantially even over such short retention intervals, but not to the extent that the loss of the phonological similarity effect can be attributed to a floor in performance having been reached. For example, in the study performed by Bjork and Healy (1974), subjects were asked to recall four-consonant lists, comprising either four nonconfusable letters or two confusable and two nonconfusable letters, after filled retention intervals lasting either 1.2s, 3.2s or 7.2s. After the 1.2s retention interval there was a clear effect of phonological confusability with 77 per cent of confusable items versus 90 per cent of nonconfusable items being recalled correctly; after 3.2s the corresponding figures were 56 per cent and 64 per cent and after 7.2s they were 35 per cent and 38 per cent. Although the relevant statistical comparisons were not presented, a later analysis of the errors revealed that there is only a hint of a phonological similarity effect after 3.2s and no reliable effect after 7.2s. This was in spite of the fact that even at the longest retention interval performance was well above a chance level, which might be estimated at 25 per cent correct (i.e., 75 per cent error) if all the items were known and their order was guessed at random, or at only 8 per cent correct if guesses are assumed to have been made from the full experimental set of 12 letters.

To confirm this rapid disappearance of the phonological similarity effect, one of us (MP) has recently been involved (together with Dennis Norris and Alan Baddeley) in running a series of experiments investigating the evolution of the phonological similarity effect and the irrelevant speech effect, two effects traditionally held to rely on the use of the phonological loop, over filled retention intervals ranging from 0.75s to 12s (Norris, Page &

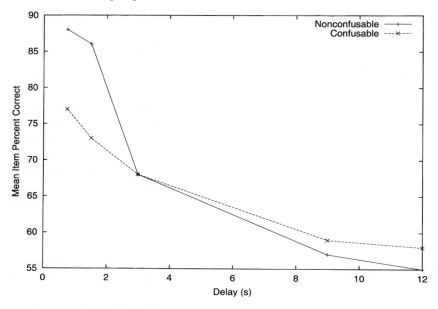

Figure 8.1   Data from Norris et al. (submitted) showing the disappearance of the
phonological similarity effect over time.

Baddeley, submitted). While space does not permit a detailed discussion of
the results here, Figure 8.1 illustrates the magnitude of the PSE as evident
in the recall of four-letter lists over a range of retention intervals. As can be
seen, the PSE is strongly evident at the shortest retention intervals but
declines rapidly such that at medium to long retention intervals the confusable items are even recalled better than the nonconfusable items (though
not reliably so; cf. Nairne & Kelley, 1999). Once again, overall levels of
performance at these longer retention intervals, though sharply reduced
relative to performance on the short intervals, are a long way from chance
performance which is at most 25 per cent. These data, together with those
in the literature, show the rapid decline of the PSE with short delays.

The data collected by Norris et al. (submitted) also allow us to look at
another type of error, namely intrusions. It has been noted by several
authors that occasionally items that were present in the previous list (i.e.,
list N-1, and probably, therefore, in the response to that list) appear in the
recall attempt for the current list (list N). Obviously this phenomenon is
best seen in the context of an experiment in which consecutive lists share no
items, as was the case for the data discussed here. Importantly, it has been
observed that there is a slight but significant tendency for these intruding
items to be recalled in the same position as they appeared in the previous
list (e.g. Estes, 1991; Henson, 1996, 1998). (Actually, the tendency is even
stronger for them to intrude in the same position as they appeared in the

Table 8.1   Data from Norris et al. (submitted) showing input and output intrusions in the recall of four-letter, visually presented lists collapsed over filled delays of 0.75s and 1.5s. Intrusions that maintain their serial position are shown in bold.

	Source position							
	Input intrusions				Output intrusions			
Recall position	1	2	3	4	1	2	3	4
1	**22**	3	8	2	**33**	0	4	1
2	5	**15**	7	8	4	**24**	5	7
3	3	12	**20**	8	5	12	**21**	18
4	9	20	18	**29**	6	19	19	**38**

Table 8.2   Data from Norris et al. (submitted) showing input and output intrusions in the recall of four-letter, visually presented lists after a filled delay of 12s. Intrusions that maintain their serial position are shown in bold.

	Source position							
	Input intrusions				Output intrusions			
Recall position	1	2	3	4	1	2	3	4
1	**52**	30	29	21	**74**	32	27	19
2	27	**44**	37	27	37	**56**	25	25
3	40	32	**41**	30	34	33	**35**	33
4	39	47	37	**69**	37	41	39	**75**

response to the previous list — see Henson, 1996.) Thus, if one assembles a matrix of intrusion errors, with the row indexing the position in the current list in which the intrusion appeared, and the column indexing the position in the previous list (response) from which the intruding item originated, one finds the numbers on the leading diagonal to be reliably higher than those found elsewhere in the matrix.

The four matrices shown in Tables 8.1 and 8.2 were generated in an experiment run by Norris et al. (submitted) in which four item lists were recalled, as before, after varying retention intervals. Because different letter sets were used on consecutive trials, the intrusions could not be misinterpreted as other types of error. Three different letter sets (BDPY, FSXQ, JHRZ) were rotated predictably making it possible that subjects learned to predict on any given trial what the four letters would be. This might explain the very low level of intrusions overall. The matrices in Table 8.1 were generated from an experiment in which the retention interval was only 0.75s or 1.5s (blocked), with performance relatively high at a mean percent correct of 82 per cent (even taking into account a phonological similarity effect). The matrices in Table 8.2 were generated from an experiment in which the retention interval, for the same set of lists, was 12s with mean percent correct of about 64 per cent. The point that we wish to highlight is that mentioned above, namely the numbers on the leading diagonal are reliably higher than those off-diagonal for both matrices. In other words, intrusions are more likely than chance to hold their position between lists, even at retention intervals (12s) at which the PSE is long gone.

So what do these data have to tell us about the plausibility or completeness of the models listed above? To address this question it is necessary to describe how each model accounts for the PSE and for positional intrusions. Unfortunately, space limitations permit only the briefest of accounts of each model and the reader is referred to the source works for a more comprehensive description. We shall begin with one of those models with which we are most familiar.

THE PRIMACY MODEL (PAGE & NORRIS, 1998)

The primacy model represents a list of items as a gradient of activation across localist connectionist representations of those items, such that the representations of items earlier in the list are more active than those of later items. This primacy gradient of activations is assumed to decay with a half-life of approximately two seconds.[2] More importantly for current purposes, the primacy gradient is assumed to be independent of the degree of phonological similarity exhibited by list items, that is, a list of phonologically similar items will be represented as a primacy gradient indistinguishable from that representing a list of nonconfusable items (other than being across a different set of localist nodes). The disruptive effect of phonological similarity is located at what can loosely be called an output stage. Items are forwarded one at a time to this output stage in an order dependent on their degree of activation, most active first, as assessed by a noisy choice-process, with suppression of previously forwarded responses preventing perseveration of the most active item. Each item forwarded to the second stage activates there a further set of item nodes. Each second-stage item node activates to a degree that is a product of two values: one represents a priming signal from the first-stage primacy gradient; the other represents the degree to which the second-stage item is phonologically similar to the item forwarded from the first stage. The priming signal ensures that the items that are activated at the second stage are likely to come from the most recent list. Naturally an item forwarded from the first stage will exhibit maximal phonological similarity to itself and will therefore be strongly

2 Note that this 2 seconds should not be confused with a similar number found by multiplying the mean number of items recalled correctly for a given list by the mean time taken for speeded articulation of a list item — this latter number has often been wrongly interpreted as the 'duration of the phonological loop'.

activated at the second stage. A competition for output ensues at this second stage. Because a nonconfusable item forwarded from the first stage does not activate any items other than itself at the second stage, it essentially passes through the second stage unscathed, performance on such items being unaffected, therefore, by whether or not the other list items are mutually confusable. By contrast, a confusable item forwarded from the first stage will activate a number of items at the second stage, in addition to itself, and one of these will occasionally win the competition for output, giving an increased probability of transposition errors specifically between confusable items. This is precisely the pattern of errors found in the data (e.g. Baddeley, 1968; Henson et al., 1996) and simulations show a very good fit between model and data. In part to justify the use of a two-stage model in which the second stage only contributes to additional errors, Page and Norris (1997) (after Ellis, 1980) have related the primacy model to models of speech production (e.g. Dell, 1986, 1988; Levelt, 1989) in which phonological errors in everyday speech are attributed to a similar two-stage process.

The primacy model is essentially an implementation of the PL (although as noted above there is nothing strictly phonological about the storage component of the primacy model) and it accounts for the rapid loss of the PSE in the same manner as does the WM model. Namely it assumes that the phonological loop (primacy gradient) is extremely labile, and decays rapidly to a point at which it is ineffective for recall. Thus while the PL is the 'system of choice' for immediate serial recall and recall after short delays, its rapid decay makes it inappropriate for recall after longer intervals. Since the PSE is consequential on the use of the loop (primacy gradient), it will not be seen at any but the shortest intervals. The idea that the phonological loop rapidly becomes unusable, or at least unusable enough to forfeit its role as the system of choice for serial recall, has been cited at various points in the development of the WM model to explain cases in which effects associated with the phonological loop have failed to be observed. For instance, Salamé and Baddeley (1986) found that for recall of lists of letters, phonological similarity effects disappeared at list length 8, having been present for shorter list lengths — a similar result had been found by Colle and Welsh (1976). Salamé and Baddeley suggested the possibility of a strategic move away from use of the phonological loop, particularly by subjects at or beyond the limit of their memory span, when performance using the phonological loop fell below a certain level. They supported this interpretation by splitting subjects into two groups based on their overall level of performance, showing that 'good' subjects continued to show the PSE for 8-item lists. Hanley and Broadbent (1987) made a similar appeal to the abandonment of the use of the phonological loop to explain the lack of an effect of irrelevant speech on recall of 9-digit lists presented auditorily under articulatory suppression (the effect was present at a shorter list length). A related account might explain the rather unusual findings of Neath, Surprenant and LeCompte (1998), who found that, contrary to the predictions of the WM model, irrelevant speech eliminated the word-length effect. A WM-based explanation would have to claim that for lists of long words and for short-word lists in the presence of irrelevant speech, subjects were encouraged to abandon the use of the phonological store, leaving the recall task to some other mechanism not sensitive to word length, phonological similarity or irrelevant speech (see Baddeley, 2000, for the same suggestion). This might explain the otherwise curious finding that for lists of long words there is absolutely no irrelevant speech effect (64 per cent correct under both IS conditions), while for short words irrelevant speech lowers mean recall by over 22 per cent (from 88 per cent to 66 per cent correct, averaged across serial position).

Of course, our phrase 'some other mechanism not sensitive to word-length, phonological similarity or irrelevant speech' (above), highlights a shortcoming of the WM model with regard to the serial recall task. The WM model, and hence the primacy model, has to propose an alternative store that is capable of performing at levels significantly above chance at times when, because of delay or, say, the effects of articulatory suppression with visual presentation, the phonological loop is no longer effective. While such a 'back-up store' has been postulated, sometimes implicitly, since the earliest days of the WM model, its nature has seldom been discussed, still less its mechanism described. In early and rather ingenious work with Ecob (Baddeley & Ecob, 1970), Baddeley suggested that for a given list of words there was simultaneous semantic and acoustic coding, with both sources contributing to performance at a short (2s), filled retention-interval but with semantic effects dominating at a longer (20s) interval. Nonetheless, recall for the semantically incompatible words was still well above chance after a 20s delay (at about 43 per cent of words correctly recalled for a 6-word list). Thus, while semantic compatibility might contribute to ordered recall (pairs of semantically compatible word-triads were recalled at about 69 per cent correct after 20s), there is still better-than-chance recall in its absence. Another potential contributor to a back-up memory is some sort of visual store. It is possible, though difficult, to obtain visual similarity effects when the phonological store is either rendered inoperative by suppression, or when unnameable objects are used as the ordered stimuli (see Logie, Della Sala, Wynn & Baddeley, 2000, and the work reviewed therein; Avons & Mason, 1999). This suggests that visual memory can aid somewhat in the retention of ordered material. A third type of memory might include some sort of positional/episodic record and we will now briefly discuss this in relation to the data on positional intrusions.

The primacy model is not able to account for positional intrusions. This is because any primacy gradient remaining from the previous trial comprises an ordered record of that trial in which the early items will always be more active than the later items, no matter what position of recall has been currently reached. Thus, on this conception of the primacy model, the first item will always be the most likely to intrude at any position on the current trial. In fact, Page and Norris (1998) note that it makes little sense to use the primacy model to explain intrusion errors. Put simply, if the primacy gradient is a model of the phonological loop, which is sufficiently labile to be ineffective after as few as 5s of intervening material, then it is unlikely to persist over the period between recall of one trial and recall of the next. To make this point even more clearly, note that the intrusion data shown in the matrices in Table 8.2 come from serial recall trials in which filled retention intervals of 12s intervened between each stimulus and its attempted recall. At such delays the phonological loop is not even operative for recall of the current trial (as evidenced by the poor performance and the lack of a PSE) let alone for recall of the previous trial. And yet positional intrusions persist. Similar data were collected by Estes (1991) who found positional intrusions for trials in which the within-trial retention interval ranged between 3 and 9s. Similarly Henson (1998) and Conrad (1960) show evidence for positional intrusions for intertrial intervals of 20–25s. Page and Norris (1998) concluded that if one's task is to model the phonological loop, then positional intrusions between trials should not be evinced in support of positional models (i.e. models that operate by the learning of position-item associations) of this labile store. Rapid loss of the PSE and the enduring presence of positional intrusions are thus linked, in the sense that the presence of both puts quite interesting constraints on potential models. We will next discuss two positional models, namely those of Burgess and Hitch (1999) and Brown et al. (2000). By their nature these are able to account in principle for positional intrusions; most have more problem accounting for the rapid loss of the PSE.

BURGESS AND HITCH (1999)

The latest version of the Burgess and Hitch model (BH, Burgess and Hitch, 1999) is a version of their original 1992 model updated to extend its scope and to improve its performance with certain data, notably recall of lists of alternating phonological confusability. Unlike the primacy model, the BH model is based on position-item associations: Each item is represented locally (i.e., by a single connectionist node) and on presentation of a given item the corresponding node is associated, via short-term weights, with a context vector representing its position in the list. Recall proceeds by reactivating each of the positional context vectors in order, at each position reading off (without noise) the most activated item. To model the detail of the phonological similarity effect, the BH model, rather like the primacy model, resorts to a second stage of processing before output is generated. The item selected at a given position of recall projects activation to the relevant units in a bank of output-phoneme units via both long-term and short-term weighted connections. Activation flows from the output-phoneme units to a bank of input-phoneme units, along fixed-weight, one-to-one connections, and from the input-phoneme units back to the items, again along long- and short-term weighted connections. There are now three inputs to each of the item units: input from the positional context vector; input from the input-phoneme nodes that for a given item node represents the phonemic similarity of that item to the item selected at the first stage of processing; and an inhibitory input that implements suppression of previously recalled (and, indeed, previously presented) items. Another selection process follows, in which the most active item is chosen (this time in the presence of noise), the relevant output is generated, and the generated item is suppressed. A detrimental effect of phonological confusability occurs when a confusable item selected at the first stage activates a number of competing items at the second stage, thus increasing the chances of a second-stage error.

Norris, Page and Baddeley (1994, 1995), and later Henson et al. (1996) and Page and Norris (1998), discussed how a two-stage process could cope with challenging data relating to lists of mixed confusability. The original Burgess and Hitch (1992) model was unable to model these data as it lacked this two-stage structure. The modified model of Burgess and Hitch (1999), however, is capable of accounting for the critical data (qualitatively at least — quantitative modelling is not attempted). When the item selected at the first stage is a nonconfusable item, it will effectively be the only item to receive a boost in activation via the output–input loop. By contrast, when the item is confusable, phonologically similar items will all receive some activation from the second stage of processing, bringing them all into the running as potential winners of the second-stage competition. Of course, like the primacy model, the BH model is somewhat vulnerable to enquiries into why the system, that is able to select the correct item noiselessly in the first stage of processing, goes to the trouble of cycling through a second stage of processing whose only apparent function is to introduce errors. As noted above, Page and Norris (1997) relate their second stage to a speech output buffer, this second stage being physically removed from the first stage rather than simply being implemented as a separate phase of processing over the same units. The Page and Norris account locates phonological confusions at the same stage of speech production at which speech errors (e.g. Spoonerisms) occur, this stage itself being motivated by considerations germane to speech production such as those relating to cross-word resyllabification. It is not clear whether the BH model could adopt a similar account while maintaining its current dynamics.

More pertinent to our current concerns, however, is the question as to whether the BH model can account for the rapid disappearance of the PSE. It appears that it cannot. Suppose that a moderate filled delay (e.g. 5–10s) is inserted between presentation and recall. At recall, the positional context will be reinstated appropriately for each position and, given that the first stage is noiseless, it is likely that the correct item will be selected; indeed it is certain, providing the long-term context-item weights do not embody long-term positional biases. Thus the first stage of processing will be largely unaffected by the delay. The second stage will also proceed as before: Activation will project to the output phonemes along the stable long-term connections and what remains of the short-term connections; from there, activation will flow to the input nodes and back to the item nodes, again via long-term and short-term connections. In this way, in the event that the item chosen at the first stage is confusable, all confusable items will receive a boost from the second stage of processing and will be better able to compete for output than they otherwise would have been. It is hard to see how the BH model can fail to predict a PSE even after significant delay. Such an effect would be due to both long- and short-term weights in the output–input phonemic loop, so even if the short-term weights have decayed completely, a PSE is still predicted by virtue of the long-term phonological weights. This is contrary to the data described above.

With regard to positional intrusions, Burgess and Hitch (1999) are successful at modelling these qualitatively, as would be expected of a position–item association model. The model predicts such positional intrusions by speculating that the short-term weights linking context to items are sufficiently long-lasting to persist somewhat between trials. It is less clear, however, that the BH model, or any similar model based on absolute position, can explain the data presented by Henson (1999) in which he showed that protrusions tend to occur between the end items of consecutive lists even if those lists are of different lengths, such that the protruding item and the item it replaces occupy different absolute positions in the list. We now turn to another model based on position–item associations, Brown et al.'s (2000) OSCAR model.

OSCAR (OSCILLATOR-BASED ASSOCIATIVE RECALL; BROWN ET AL., 2000)

The OSCAR model (Brown et al., 2000) is similar in its basic structure to Burgess and Hitch's (1992) model. It is much more explicit than the latter in describing the genesis of an appropriate time-varying context signal with which items can be associated in a serial recall task. The context signal is derived from the activation of a large number of oscillators of varying frequencies. The precise way in which the context signal is generated is rather complex but it is sufficient here to note that in general it changes such that consecutive states of the context signal are more similar to each other than are states of the context signal more distant from each other in time. Under more specific circumstances it can be arranged that a subset of the context vector repeats itself every P time steps. This causes the monotonic decrease in similarity with distance in time to be modulated such that context vectors corresponding to times separated by P time steps can be more similar to each other than items separated by either P–1 or P+1 time steps. It is this property that allows OSCAR to simulate both positional intrusions between trials and position-in-group-preserving transpositions in the recall of grouped lists. As OSCAR is a position–item association model, with the flexibility inherent in being able to decompose the positional information hierarchically (i.e. into position-in-experiment, position-in-list, position-in-group, etc.) we will assume that OSCAR is able qualitatively to account for positional intrusions. Brown et al. (2000) do model similar data from Nairne (1991), though these data refer to a task involving a list-reconstruction task that followed a delay of 2min and are therefore unlikely to bear directly on the operation of the phonological loop in immediate serial recall. Like Burgess and Hitch (1999), OSCAR has trouble accounting for the data presented by Henson (1999) relating to the dependence of intrusions on relative rather than absolute position.

The modelling of the PSE and its disappearance over short delays is more difficult for OSCAR. OSCAR is a one-stage model, by which we mean that the positional cue is directly associated with a vector representing phonological content. Page and Norris (1998) have suggested that any such model will have difficulty in modelling the data from lists of alternating confusability. Brown et al. (2000) choose not to attempt to model these data, in spite of modelling performance on the pure confusable and pure nonconfusable lists taken from the same experiment. We assume, therefore, that the alternating data do indeed prove troublesome for OSCAR. Similarly, because even delayed memory will depend on the resetting of the context vector, the generation of an associated response vector and a comparison of that vector with each of the vectors corresponding to possible responses, it must be assumed that OSCAR will fail to show the loss of the PSE found after reasonably short delays. The problem is similar to that faced by the Burgess and Hitch (1999) model: Because the position–item association mechanism is designed to be moderately long-lasting to account for the existence of positional intrusions, and because that system is identified with the phonological loop, features of the phonological loop, such as the presence of a phonological similarity effect, will also be long-lasting. This is contrary to the data.

THE FEATURE MODEL (NAIRNE, 1990; NEATH, 1999)

The feature model originated with Nairne (1990) and has since been developed by Neath and Nairne (1995) and Neath (1999) to account for word-length effects and effects of irrelevant speech respectively. In the feature model, items in memory are represented as vectors of features and are said to reside in both primary memory and secondary memory. Features belonging to items in primary memory can become degraded by retroactive interference. Specifically if item n+1 shares feature f with item n then feature f in item n's primary memory representation is overwritten by setting it to zero with a given probability. The original model (Nairne, 1990) could not deal with very well with the pattern of order errors in serial recall, predicting that local transpositions would be less common than distant transpositions, contrary to one of the most basic aspects of the ISR data. The latest version, from Neath (1999), therefore includes an ordering mechanism based on that found in the perturbation model of Estes (1972). In particular, each item in primary memory is accompanied by some positional information with this estimate of the item's list position drifting or perturbing along the position dimension with a given average drift rate applied probabilistically from moment to moment. This modified ordering mechanism allows the feature model to capture the basic pattern of transposition errors found experimentally. It also, however, calls into question Neath and Nairne's (1995) assertion, based on the previous version of the feature model, that there is no time-based decay in the ability of the model to perform ordered recall. This is because the perturbation process seems to be at least partly time-based.

Ordered recall proceeds as follows. The perturbation process gives, for each recall position, probabilities that each of the items in primary memory occupied that position. For a given position, its most likely occupant is chosen. The primary-memory representation of this item, degraded by interference, is compared with each of the undegraded item representations in secondary memory. The secondary memory item most similar to the chosen primary memory cue is then selected probabilistically using a Luce Choice Rule (Luce, 1959). Because phonologically confusable items share a comparatively large number of feature values, cueing secondary memory with any one such item will result in a larger number of secondary memory items competing for Luce selection than would compete in the case of a nonconfusable cue. This is the genesis of the PSE in the feature model. In the terminology introduced above, the model is a two-stage model that is likely to be able to model some, but not all, of the data associated with lists of mixed confusability. Importantly, however, providing the perturbation stage is not so hampered by a delay that it is performing at floor, there will continue to be a deleterious effect of phonological confusability even after long retention intervals. This is contrary to the PSE data on which we are focusing in this chapter.

The feature model has not yet been applied to modelling of between-list effects, so it is difficult to predict how it would cope with positional intrusions. Presumably the perturbation model could be used as suggested in Nairne (1991) to contain information relating to which-trial as well as to which-position-in-trial. Nairne tested a version of the perturbation model in which perturbations along the two dimensions were deemed independent — this clearly predicts the same positional gradients (scaled by overall frequency) regardless of whether an item was recalled in the correct trial or whether it intruded from a previous trial. Such a pattern was not found by Nairne (1991) and is not found in relation to the matrices shown in Tables

8.1 and 8.2 — the within-trial transposition matrices (not shown) are much more heavily weighted towards the leading diagonal than are the intrusion matrices (see also Henson, 1998). This implies that the assumption of independence would have to be dropped, and/or some effective decay of previous trials introduced, before a perturbation model could deal with the intrusion data appropriately.

THE START–END MODEL (HENSON, 1998)

We finish with the start–end model (SEM) of Henson (1998). This model postulates that as a list is presented, each of the items gives rise to a new token in short-term memory containing an episodic record of the item in its positional context. Position in this model is coded relative to the start and end of the corresponding sequence. The positional context stored in relation to a given item is therefore a two-dimensional vector expressing the item's 'degree-of-startness' and its 'degree-of-endness'. The precise way in which these measures change with list position is given by Henson (1998). Suffice to say that any list position will be expressible as a unique two-dimensional vector. The complete episodic record for a given item contains this two-dimensional vector corresponding to its position in the list (and perhaps another corresponding to its position in a group), a single number related to nonpositional contextual change and, of course, information regarding the item's identity. Recall is achieved by cueing memory with a vector corresponding to the current recall position. Episodic records in memory then activate to a degree dependent on their match with the memory cue. Naturally a given positional cue will tend to activate strongly the episodic record of the item that was located in that position, with activation of other records decreasing with their positional distance from the cued position. There will also be some activation of records corresponding to items in the same position (measured relative to start and end) in the previous lists, though overall levels of activation of such records will be lowered by their comparative lack of nonpositional contextual match. It is this latter feature that allows the SEM to capture the pattern of positional intrusions and Henson shows how these are peaked at the current within-list position, with the peaks becoming shallower for longer intertrial intervals, for both the SEM and in the data (Henson, 1998).

But does the start–end model, unlike the position–item association models to which it is most similar, account for the disappearance of the PSE over short delays? The answer is yes. The SEM is able both to model positional intrusions between trials and the fast decay of the PSE. It does this by assuming a separate, short-term store in which 'phonological' representations of verbal items are located. Each presentation and rehearsal of an item activates that item's phonological representation to a fixed degree, the activation decaying exponentially thereafter. In this way, immediately after presentation of a list, the phonological store contains a recency gradient across the representations of list items, that is, with more recently presented items more highly active (consistent with evidence for nonserial, item-probe tasks, e.g., McElree & Dosher, 1989). As in the primacy model, recall is a two-stage process. In the first stage, memory is cued and the most active item is selected. In the second stage, the selected item is matched against a set of phonological representations before a second competition determines the response. Specifically, the responses compete with a strength determined by the sum of three terms

- the degree to which the item competed in the first stage
- the phonological activation of the item multiplied by the degree to which it is phonologically similar to the item forwarded from the first stage
- a noise term.

Note that for a nonconfusable item forwarded from the first stage, the second term will be zero for every response other than that corresponding to the item itself. This is because the degree to which an item is similar to another nonconfusable item is deemed to be zero and the degree to which an item is similar to itself is deemed to be 1. Thus for a nonconfusable item forwarded from the first stage, the second term in the sum will exceed that for other nonconfusable items by the degree to which the forwarded item is active in the phonological store. In the case of a confusable item forwarded from the first stage, the second term of the sum will be nonzero for other similar items from the list, to a degree to which they are phonologically similar (a parameter between 0 and 1) and to the extent to which they are active in the phonological store. Note that if the second term were the only term taken into account, activations across phonologically similar items would form a recency gradient. This would predict distant second-stage transpositions between confusable items, as opposed to the local trans-positions found in the data. The presence of the first term in the sum must therefore outweigh this tendency by favouring items from close to the current recall position.

Henson's (1998) arrangement can explain the basic pattern of data constituting the PSE. Performance with lists of mixed confusability are correctly simulated because SEM is a two-stage model whose second stage is effectively transparent to nonconfusable items. Moreover, as the acti-vation of items in the phonological store decays, the difference between the second-stage treatment of confusable and nonconfusable items disappears. Henson (1998) postulates that the purpose of the phonological store is to act as an item memory, such that its benefits, in the form of avoidance of omissions and intrusions (achieved by boosting the response activation of the item forwarded from the first stage), outweigh its disadvantages, in the form of the PSE. It is interesting, therefore, that Henson (1998) speculates that the fast-decaying phonological store protects against item loss and is not responsible for order memory at all. Indeed, given that it forms a recency gradient, the phonological component of the SEM rather works against responses emerging in the correct order, for confusable items at least.

The start–end model is thus the only model that has explicitly simulated both positional intrusions and fast-decaying effects of phonological similarity. The primacy model (Page & Norris, 1998) predicts the rapid loss of the PSE but deliberately eschews the modelling of positional intrusions. We will finish by speculating, in a fit of authorial cooperation, that a rapprochement might be effected between the two models. This could be achieved, as Henson (1998) suggests, by 'incorporating a primacy gradient into SEM's phonological activations. This would provide an ordered phonological store that would enhance immediate serial recall, but not recall after a short delay, which would rely on SEM's positional information' (pp. 120–121).

One potential advantage of such an arrangement would lie in the modelling of the irrelevant speech effect (ISE). Recent data (Norris et al., submitted) have shown both that the size of the ISE decreases over short delays (although unlike the PSE, the effect does not disappear completely) and that irrelevant speech presented during a filled retention interval can affect performance on delayed recall of a list as much as does the same irrelevant speech presented during the list. As it stands, the SEM would have trouble simulating these data. First, because irrelevant speech has at least part of its effect on order errors then it must have its effect on the first stage of SEM. But if the effect is on the comparatively long-lasting first stage then one would expect the ISE to increase in magnitude over short delays as the strength of the positional signal weakens. This is contrary to the data. Second, the retroactive effect of irrelevant speech presented during a filled retention interval is not easily simulated by an episodic account, like that embodied in the first stage of SEM. Retrieval of episodes with positional cues should not be affected by the presence of irrelevant speech in the period between presentation and recall. By contrast, if the phonological store is deemed to contribute to correctly ordered recall, then irrelevant speech between presentation and recall might have its effect by damping down activations in this short-term store (see Norris et al., submitted; Page, in press).

The prospect of a combined model is an enticing one. A model in which order information were represented in both a reasonably long-lasting episodic store and a labile phonological store would raise interesting questions. Would it best be envisaged, as Page and Norris (1998) suggest, as primarily a phonological system dedicated to short-term recall, with a subsidiary episodic system assisting when phonological activation was weak or when episodic information was strong (as, perhaps, in grouped lists)? Or would it best be envisaged, as in Henson (1998), as primarily an episodic and positional system, supplemented by a labile phonological item store? For the sake of continuing authorial harmony, we will leave this question for another time.

SUMMARY AND CONCLUSIONS

Since the pioneering work of Burgess and Hitch (1992), a number of computational models have been implemented in an attempt to capture the full range of data relating to immediate (or near immediate) serial recall of verbal material. In nearly all cases the WM model has been used as a framework for the computational model. Even in cases where the details of the WM model have been questioned (e.g. Neath & Nairne, 1995; Neath, 1999), the models owe a good deal to the theoretical and experimental work that has flowed from Baddeley and Hitch's original (1974) paper. In this chapter, we have focused on a particular aspect of the serial recall data, highlighting the fast disappearance of the PSE and the presence of inter-trial positional intrusions. These data pose problems of varying character and of varying seriousness for most of the models that have claimed to simulate serial recall from short-term memory. Henson's (1998) start–end model is the only model that has been applied to both effects. In doing so it places a different emphasis from that of the WM model on the contribution of the phonological component of short-term memory (STM) and extends itself to intertrial effects operating at delays beyond that previously considered the upper limit of the PL's functioning. Of the models, the primacy model is perhaps closest to the classical conception of the phonological loop, possessing a fast decaying phonological store dedicated to ordered recall of verbal material and attributing later effects to a nonphonological back-up mechanism whose character is as yet rather underspecified.

Finally, in the light of the arguments presented in this chapter, we turn to addressing the four questions central to this book. First, *what are the models competing with the WM model* in the area of serial recall of verbal material? We have discussed a number of models of the process of serial recall from STM, but few of these can be said to be competing with the WM model — most represent attempts to flesh out the WM model with quantitative simulations of particular recall mechanisms. The remainder do take issue with the WM model, sometimes over very particular aspects of the data, but still locate themselves firmly in the tradition of the WM model in the questions that they ask and the data that they employ to answer them. There has been some move, particularly amongst some North American researchers (see Baddeley, 2000), to deny the distinction between short-term memory and what one might call medium-term memory (e.g. memory over several minutes). One problem with this denial is that it is often based on data from slightly changed tasks, from, for example, serial order reconstruction tasks performed after significant delay rather than serial recall tasks performed after, at most, a short delay. In our view, and for the reasons detailed in this chapter, it would be a mistake to believe that a single-store model can account for performance in both delayed reconstruction and immediate serial recall. In fact, a recent paper by Nairne, Whiteman and Kelley (1999) gives some support to our view rather than, as the authors imply, contradicting it. They show how performance on a serial recall reconstruction of five-word lists declines surprising little (from 78 per cent to 73 per cent correct) over filled delays ranging from 2s up to 96s, for lists in which a unique set of five words is used for each list. Recall was rather poorer, and the effects of decay rather more pronounced, when a fixed set of ten words was used to generate the lists, with performance equal to 74 per cent, 64 per cent and 57 per cent for delays of 2s, 8s and 24s respectively. These results certainly are suggestive of a single memory system, sensitive to intertrial proactive interference but not greatly susceptible to delay. Nonetheless, in the discussion section of the paper, the authors refer to a subsidiary study in which a 0s retention interval was used, resulting in performance of 81 per cent and 80 per cent correct for the different word and repeated word conditions, compared with a reliably lower 68 per cent and 62 per cent correct after a 2s filled delay. As Nairne, Whiteman and Kelley acknowledge, these results are at least consistent with the existence of a labile store, insensitive to proactive interference, that contributes to good performance at zero retention interval, but which is rendered ineffective by as little as a 2s delay (cf. Tehan & Humphreys, 1995).

What are the weaknesses of the WM model in the realm of serial recall of verbal material? One weakness was alluded to early in this chapter, namely, the verbal and qualitative, rather than mechanistic and quantitative, nature of the account of serial recall that the WM model offers. This is not a serious weakness, first because the WM model has traditionally been directed at a different level of analysis from the mechanistic, preferring to account for the general patterns found in the data, and, second, because the challenge to supplement the WM model with quantitative simulations has now been enthusiastically taken up. The fact that the WM model, or more specifically its phonological loop component, has been so intimately tied to the immediate serial task might be considered another weakness. But such an accusation loses its force somewhat if one really believes, as we do, that the phonological loop is specialised for immediate recall of verbal material. It is the degree of specialisation of the loop that places a fairly tight restriction on the experimental tasks that can be used to investigate it.

What are the strengths of the WM model? It gives a very good, indeed unsurpassed, qualitative account of the data in which we are interested, placed in the framework of an elegant (and easily remembered!) theory. When one comes to build, say, a connectionist model of a given process, it is far more productive to have a sound theory in mind and to attempt an implementation than to try to construct both model and theory simultaneously.

Naturally, the process of modelling can alter one's theoretical outlook, perhaps radically, in the same way as can new and unexpected data. Nonetheless, to have a sound theoretical bedrock on which to begin constructing a computer model is of very considerable advantage.

Finally, *what is the future of the WM model*, specifically with regard to verbal recall? One aspect of what we believe to be a bright future will undoubtedly be in the direction of answering the question 'What is the phonological loop for?'. It is a safe bet that the loop did not evolve so as to keep legions of experimental psychologists employed in the running of ISR experiments. Recent work by Baddeley, Gathercole and Papagno (1998) has supported the view that the loop acts as a short-term buffer that plays an important role in the acquisition of new vocabulary, a proposal that is supported by a good deal of experimental data as well as having impeccable evolutionary credentials. One of us (MP, with Dennis Norris and Nick Cumming) is currently engaged in a study of the so-called Hebb effect, in which repeated, spaced presentation of a particular list gives progressively improved recall. Future work will, we hope, give us a better idea of how, if at all, such learning is related to the learning of linguistic material. In this regard, the study of groups of patients with apparent damage to those brain areas in which the phonological loop is implemented will be of increasing importance. We look forward to future developments of the working memory model.

BACKGROUND READING

Brown, G. D. A., Preece, T. & Hulme, C. (2000) Oscillator-based memory for serial order. *Psychological Review, 107*, 127–181.

Burgess, N. & Hitch, G.J. (1999) Memory for serial order: A network model of the phonological loop and its timing. *Psychological Review, 106*, 551–581.

Henson, R.N.A. (1998) Short-term memory for serial order: The start–end model. *Cognitive Psychology, 36*, 73–137.

Neath, I. (1999) Modelling the disruptive effects of irrelevant speech on order information. *International Journal of Psychology, 34*, 410–418.

Page, M.P.A. & Norris, D. (1998) The primacy model: A new model of immediate serial recall. *Psychological Review, 105*, 761–781.

These are the source papers for the models described in this chapter.

REFERENCES

Avons, S.E. & Mason, A. (1999) Effects of visual similarity on serial report and item recognition. *Quarterly Journal of Experimental Psychology, 52A*, 217–240.

Baddeley, A.D. (1968) How does acoustic similarity influence short-term memory? *Quarterly Journal of Experimental Psychology*, 20, 249–263.

Baddeley, A.D. (2000) The phonological loop and the irrelevant speech effect: Some comments on Neath (2000). *Psychonomic Bulletin and Review*, 7(3), 544–549.

Baddeley, A.D. & Ecob, J.R. (1970) Simultaneous acoustic and semantic coding in short-term memory. *Nature*, 227, 288–289.

Baddeley, A.D. & Hitch, G. (1974) Working memory. In G.A. Bower (Ed.), *Recent Advances in Learning and Motivation, Vol. 8* (pp. 47–89). New York: Academic Press.

Baddley, A., Gathercole, S. & Papagno, C. (1998) The phonological loop as a language learning device. *Psychological Review*, 105, 158–173.

Bjork, E.L. & Healy, A.F. (1974) Short-term order and item retention. *Journal of Verbal Learning and Verbal Behavior*, 13, 80–97.

Brown, G.D.A., Preece, T. & Hulme, C. (2000) Oscillator-based memory for serial order. *Psychological Review*, 107, 127–181.

Burgess, N. & Hitch, G.J. (1992) Toward a network model of the articulatory loop. *Journal of Memory and Language*, 31, 429–460.

Burgess, N. & Hitch, G.J. (1999) Memory for serial order: A network model of the phonological loop and its timing. *Psychological Review*, 106, 551–581.

Colle, H.A. & Welsh, A. (1976) Acoustic masking in primary memory. *Journal of Verbal Learning and Verbal Behavior*, 15, 17–32.

Conrad, R. (1960) Serial order intrusions in immediate memory. *British Journal of Psychology*, 51, 45–48.

Conrad, R. & Hull, A.J. (1964) Information, acoustic confusion and memory span. *British Journal of Psychology*, 55, 429–432.

Dell, G.S. (1986) A spreading-activation theory of retrieval in sentence production. *Psychological Review*, 93, 283–321.

Dell, G.S. (1988) The retrieval of phonological forms in production: Tests of predictions from a connectionist model. *Journal of Memory and Language*, 27, 124–142.

Ellis, A.W. (1980) Errors in speech and short-term memory: The effects of phonemic similarity and syllable position. *Journal of Verbal Learning and Verbal Behavior*, 19, 624–634.

Estes, W.K. (1972) An associative basis for coding and organization in memory. In A. Melton and E. Martin (Eds.), *Coding Processes in Human Memory*. New York: Halsted Press.

Estes, W.K. (1973) Phonemic coding and rehearsal in short-term memory for letter strings. *Journal of Verbal Learning and Verbal Behavior*, 12, 360–372.

Estes, W.K. (1991) On types of item coding and sources of recall in short-term memory. In W.E. Hockley and S. Lewandowsky (Eds.), *Relating Theory and Data: In Honor of Bennet B. Murdock*. Hillsdale, NJ: Lawrence Erlbaum Associates Inc.

Hanley, J.R. & Broadbent, C. (1987) The effects of unattended speech on serial recall following auditory presentation. *British Journal of Psychology*, 78, 287–297.

Henson, R.N.A. (1996) *Short-term memory for serial order*. Unpublished doctoral dissertation, University of Cambridge.

Henson, R.N.A. (1998) Short-term memory for serial order: the start–end model. *Cognitive Psychology*, 36, 73–137.

Henson, R.N.A. (1999) Positional information in short-term memory: Relative or absolute? *Memory and Cognition*, 27, 915–927.

Henson, R.N.A., Norris, D., Page, M.P.A. & Baddeley, A.D. (1996) Unchained memory: Error patterns rule out chaining models of immediate serial recall. *Quarterly Journal of Experimental Psychology*, 49A, 80–115.

Jones, D.M. (1993) Objects, streams, and threads of auditory attention. In A.D. Baddeley & L. Weiskrantz (Eds.), *Attention: Selection, awareness and control* (pp. 87–104). Oxford: Clarendon Press.

Levelt, W.J.M. (1989) *Speaking: From Intention to Articulation*. Cambridge, MA: MIT Press.

Logie, R.H., Della Sala, S., Wynn, V. & Baddeley, A. (2000) Visual similarity effects in immediate verbal serial recall. *Quarterly Journal of Experimental Psychology*, 53(3), 626–646.

Luce, R.D. (1959) *Individual choice behavior: A theoretical analysis*. New York: Wiley.

McElree, B. & Dosher, B.A. (1989) Serial position and set-size in short-term memory: The time course of recognition. *Journal of Experimental Psychology: General*, 118, 346–373.

Nairne, J.S. (1990) A feature model of immediate memory. *Memory and Cognition*, 18, 251–269.

Nairne, J.S. (1991) Positional uncertainty in long-term memory. *Memory and Cognition*, 19, 332–340.

Nairne, J.S. & Kelley, M.R. (1999) Reversing the phonological similarity effect. *Memory and Cognition*, 27, 45–53.

Nairne, J.S., Whiteman, H.L. & Kelley, M.R. (1999) Short-term forgetting of order under conditions of reduced interference. *Quarterly Journal of Experimental Psychology*, 52A, 241–251.

Neath, I. (1999) Modelling the disruptive effects of irrelevant speech on order information. *International Journal of Psychology*, 34, 410–418.

Neath, I. & Nairne, J.S. (1995) Word-length effects in immediate memory: Overwriting trace decay theory. *Psychonomic Bulletin and Review*, 2, 429–441.

Neath, I., Surprenant, A.M. & LeCompte, D.C. (1998) Irrelevant speech eliminates the word length effect. *Memory and Cognition*, 26, 343–354.

Norris, D., Page, M.P.A. & Baddeley, A.D. (1994, July) *Serial Recall: It's all in the representations*. Paper presented at the International Conference on Working Memory, Cambridge, UK.

Norris, D., Page, M.P.A. & Baddeley, A.D. (1995) Connectionist modelling of short-term memory. *Language and Cognitive Processes*, 10, 407–409.

Norris, D., Page, M.P.A. & Baddeley, A.D. (submitted) Retrospective effects of irrelevant speech on serial recall from short-term memory. *Journal of Experimental Psychology: Learning, Memory and Cognition*.

Page, M.P.A. (in press) Connectionist models of short-term memory for serial order. In G. Houghton (Ed.), *Connectionist Models in Cognitive Psychology*. Hove, UK: Psychology Press.

Page, M.P.A. & Norris, D. (1997) Modelling immediate serial recall with a localist implementation of the primacy model. In J. Grainger & A.M. Jacobs (Eds.), *Localist Connectionist Approaches to Human Cognition*. Mahwah, NJ: Lawrence Erlbaum Associates Inc.

Page, M.P.A. & Norris, D. (1998) The primacy model: A new model of immediate serial recall. *Psychological Review*, 105, 761–781.
Salamé, P. & Baddeley, A.D. (1986) Phonological factors in STM: Similarity and the unattanded speech effect. *Bulletin of the Psychonomic Society*, 24, 263–265.
Tehan, G. & Humphreys, M.S. (1995) Transient phonemic codes and immunity to proactive interference. *Memory and Cognition*, 23, 181–191.

9   Re-evaluating the word-length effect

Peter Lovatt and Steve Avons

People can recall a sequence of short words in the correct order more accurately than they can recall a sequence of long words. This, the word-length effect, is one of the most salient features of immediate serial recall. In this chapter we shall briefly review the original evidence for the word-length effect, and how this led to the proposal of the phonological loop model of working memory. We shall then discuss more recent evidence that questions the original interpretation of the word-length effect, and strongly contests one fundamental assumption of the model. Finally, we consider some recent alternatives to the phonological loop and discuss the extent to which these recent accounts meet current requirements.

THE WORD-LENGTH EFFECT IN RELATION TO THE PHONOLOGICAL LOOP

The word-length effect describes the finding that in tests of immediate serial recall subjects are able to remember more short words than long words. Baddeley, Thomson and Buchanan (1975) carried out an extensive study investigating the effect of word length on serial recall. In several experiments they varied the number of syllables of list items, and found that both serial recall (the proportion of items recalled in the correct serial position, for a given list length) and memory span (the list length at which a given proportion of trials are recalled correctly) decreased as word length increased. This finding was confirmed using several different sets of words, and was observed with both auditory and visual presentation. The effect of syllabic word length on serial recall has been replicated many times with English-speaking adults and children, using many different word sets (e.g. Hitch, Halliday & Littler, 1989; Hulme, Thomson, Muir & Lawrence, 1984; LaPointe & Engle, 1990; Lovatt, Avons & Masterson, 2000). The results have also extended to other languages such as French (e.g. Belleville, Peretz & Arguin, 1992; Van der Linden, Coyette & Seron, 1992), Italian (e.g. Longoni, Richardson & Aiello, 1993; Vallar & Baddeley, 1984), and Hebrew (e.g. Birnboim & Share, 1995). Although rare exceptions have been reported (e.g. Cowan, Wood, Nugent & Treisman, 1997), there is over-whelming evidence that increasing the syllabic length of items reduces serial recall. However, establishing this empirical fact leaves open many questions about (a) the particular characteristics of words that generate the word-length effect, and (b) the processes that support serial recall and are influenced by these characteristics. Considering the first issue, the syllabic word-length effect could arise in at least three ways. First, long and short words may impose different storage demands on a strict phonological memory (e.g. in terms of the number of sublexical units that must be maintained). Second, since long words are pronounced more slowly, any memory system that depends on processing of real-time speech will be sensitive to the duration of these words. Third, short and long words may differ in their lexical properties, and these may become crucial if serial recall requires the identification of lexical items.

The idea that serial recall was related to the *temporal* properties of list items was first raised by Mackworth (1963). She found that serial recall was better for some materials (digits and letters) than others (colours and shapes). The materials that were more easily recalled could also be named more quickly. Mackworth proposed that items that were named slowly required more attention for encoding and storage, and that memory span was limited by attentional capacity. Although naming latency (or identification time) has been extensively studied, especially in relation to memory development (e.g. Dempster, 1981), there is now evidence that other temporal measures more closely related to the spoken duration of items are better predictors of serial recall (e.g. Dosher & Ma, 1998; Hitch et al., 1989).

The first extensive study relating serial recall to measures of speech rate was that of Baddeley et al. (1975). They showed that serial recall was proportional to reading rate across words varying in syllabic length, and from this inferred that serial recall had a limited temporal capacity, equivalent to the number of items that could be rehearsed in about 1.6–1.8s. To provide a more direct test of the duration hypothesis, Baddeley et al. (1975) devised two pools of ten disyllabic words which differed in terms of their spoken duration, and reported that serial recall was superior for the short duration items. From these original pools, two subsets of five words were selected which were matched for word frequency and number of phonemes. The superiority of serial recall in the short-duration words was confirmed, again showing a consistent relationship between serial recall and speech rate. This result would be expected if the capacity of serial recall was governed by the time taken to pronounce the list items.

Baddeley and his colleagues proposed a simple model, the *phonological loop*, to account for the word-length effect and other phenomena associated with serial recall (cf. Baddeley, 1986). The core of the model consists of two components: the *phonological store*, which holds incoming phonological information, linked to an *articulatory control process*. Item representations in the phonological store decay at a fixed rate, but are refreshed by rehearsal. In the model, rehearsal is assumed to be a real-time process resembling covert speech (Landauer, 1962). Serial recall is therefore superior for short-duration words, because more of them can be rehearsed within the decay time of the phonological store:

$$\text{serial recall capacity} = \text{decay time} \times \text{rehearsal rate}$$

The most striking feature of the phonological loop model is that serial recall is predicted using just two parameters: the decay rate of the phono-logical store and rehearsal rate for the list items. Rehearsal rate has been estimated by measuring the speech rate of sequences of list items, or the spoken duration of individual list items. The linear relationship between speech rate and serial recall across items of different lengths has proved to be remarkably consistent across studies, and the slope suggests that recall capacity corresponds to about 1.8s of speech (see Schweickert & Boruff, 1986, for a review). This is therefore the value assumed for the effective decay time of the phonological store.

Many developmental studies have shown that the slope of the serial recall/speech rate function is constant throughout development, suggesting that the increase in serial recall with age is due to an increase in speech rate, rather than increased temporal capacity of the loop. Hulme et al. (1984), for example, examined speech rate and serial recall for lists of one, two and three syllable words at ages 4, 7, 10 and 18 years. They found that all four age groups showed significant word-length effects, and that the data points of all the age groups fell on the same regression line when span was plotted against speech rate. Similar results have been obtained in many other studies (e.g. Hitch et al., 1989; Nicolson, 1981).

Studies of digit span also appear to show a relationship between speech rate and memory span across languages. Ellis and Hennelly (1980) found that Welsh digit names took longer to read than English digit names and reported that English/Welsh bilinguals showed higher digit spans in English than in Welsh. Chen and Stevenson (1988) reported higher digit spans in Chinese than American school children and found that the spoken duration of Chinese digits was shorter than the spoken duration of English digits. Similarly, Naveh-Benjamin and Ayres (1986) found that the speed of reading digits was inversely related to memory span across four languages.

In addition to the effects of word duration on serial recall, the model predicts a general correlation between individual speech rate and serial recall, since individuals with slower speech rates will rehearse fewer items during the decay time of the store. Baddeley et al. (1975) reported a strong correlation ($r = 0.68$) between measures of reading rate and serial recall, and this correlation has since been confirmed many times (e.g. Gathercole, Adams & Hitch, 1994). The correlation between serial recall and speech rate across individuals could arise in any number of ways, and does not of course imply a causal relationship between the two measures. In this regard Smyth and Scholey (1996) reported that articulation rate correlated as strongly with spatial span as it did with digit span. They therefore suggested that articulation rate was an indicator of general ability, which facilitated performance in nonspecific ways.

The strong appeal of the phonological loop model lies in its parsimony. Although very simple, it predicts a strong relationship between serial recall performance and measures of speech rate, which accounts for the variation in serial recall performance across items, across languages and across individuals, and throughout development. As a bonus, the inferred decay time of the phonological store appears to be a universal constant. However, much of the evidence for the word-length effect reduces to the frequently observed correlation between speech rate and serial recall across items. In terms of the model this correlation is explained as the effect of rehearsal rate on serial recall, operating through a phonological store that decays at a fixed rate. In the next section we critically examine this evidence.

CRITICAL EVIDENCE AGAINST THE DURATION-BASED ACCOUNT OF THE PHONOLOGICAL LOOP

The word-length effect: duration or memory load?

As explained above, Baddeley and his colleagues (e.g. Baddeley, 1986; Baddeley et al., 1975) interpreted the word-length effect as a consequence of word duration rather than the complexity of the items. This interpretation was based on two sources: (a) the linear relationship between serial recall and speech rate across syllabic word lengths, and (b) the effect of manipulating word duration independently of phonological complexity. The first of these results has been confirmed many times in adult and developmental studies, and the serial recall/speech rate slope has been reasonably consistent, although there is a suggestion that memory span measures yield smaller slope values (cf. Avons & Hanna, 1995). The finding that the duration of disyllables affects recall has also been replicated (e.g. Longoni et al., 1993; Nairne, Neath & Serra, 1997; see also Baddeley & Andrade, 1994), but to our knowledge, such replications have all used subsets of the original set of long- and short-duration items drawn up by Baddeley et al. (1975). We know that lexical properties such as word frequency and concreteness affect serial recall (e.g. Hulme, Maughan & Brown, 1991; Neath, 1997). Thus minor variations in lexical properties could potentially lead to a superiority of one set of words over another set. It is therefore critically important to ensure that the effect of word duration (across word sets matched for phonological complexity and other properties) is a general phenomenon and not an accidental property emerging from one set of items.

Several recent studies have investigated the effect of disyllable duration using new sets of items. Caplan, Rochon and Waters (1992) investigated serial recall of word lists that were matched for number of syllables and number of phonemes and differed in spoken duration. Stimuli were presented both auditorially and visually and subjects responded by pointing to pictures depicting the words presented. The short-word list was made up of words containing principally lax vowels (e.g. carrot), while the long-word list was made up of words containing principally tense vowels (e.g. sirloin). The results of this experiment failed to support the findings of Baddeley et al. (1975), as they showed superior recall for the long words. In marked contrast, using the same method Caplan et al. were able to demonstrate a clear difference in serial recall for words varying in syllabic length.

A number of criticisms have been levied against Caplan et al.'s (1992) study, concerning their materials and methods. Baddeley and Andrade (1994) failed to find consistent differences in articulation rates between Caplan's long and short words, using the technique of repeating word pairs. They also took measures of phonological similarity and concluded that Caplan et al.'s short words were more phonologically similar than their long words, and this phonological similarity may have impaired recall. But Caplan and Waters (1994) confirmed that their long- and short-word lists differed in spoken duration, as measured by the time taken to read the lists. They also demonstrated that their long and short words did not differ in phonological similarity when rated by North American subjects, and finally, they replicated their original failure to find a recall advantage for short duration words. This exchange emphasises the need to take measures of serial recall and speech rate under similar conditions and using the same subjects. Cowan (1997; Cowan & Kail, 1996) also criticised the method used in these studies, arguing that picture-pointing recall would minimise any word-length effect, based on the idea, discussed below, that serial recall is limited by output time.

We developed two new sets of short and long disyllabic words that varied on several measures of spoken duration, but which were matched on frequency, familiarity, number of phonemes, and phonemic similarity (Lovatt et al., 2000). We measured serial recall using both visual and auditory presentation and tested each kind of presentation using both spoken and pointing recall. With one word set we found superior recall with long words, and with the other set there was no difference between long and short disyllables. Performance was generally superior with pointing recall, but method of recall did not in any way interact with word duration. Thus it is unlikely that Caplan et al.'s use of picture-pointing recall masked word duration effects in disyllables. Moreover, using visual presentation and spoken recall, we were able to replicate the results of Baddeley et al. (1975, Experiment IV) using their original disyllabic word set. (The syllabic word-length effect was also confirmed using picture-pointing recall, see Lovatt, 1999.) These results consolidate the claim of Caplan et al. (1992; see also

Caplan & Waters, 1994) that there is no reliable word-duration effect for disyllabic stimuli.

Service (1998) investigated memory span for non-words, making use of the phonological structure of Finnish to control both duration and phonological complexity. In the Finnish language, there are long and short versions of vowels and consonants. Linguistically, long phonemes are regarded as equivalent to a repeated phoneme. In terms of articulation, Service argued that items containing long phonemes are no more complex than those containing equivalent short phonemes. Hence increasing the duration of phonemes in a word (/tepa/ to /te: p: a/, where e: and p: denote long phonemes) increases duration but leaves complexity constant, whereas increasing the number of phonemes (/tepa/ to /tiempa/) increases both complexity and duration. Service found that although the spoken duration of the short non-words (/tepa/) was significantly shorter than the duration of the long non-words (/te:p:a/) there was no difference in memory span between these stimuli. However, increasing phonological complexity did decrease memory span.

Zhang and Feng (1990) also reported no difference in the serial recall of short and long duration Chinese disyllables. They selected 288 words varying in duration, frequency and graphic complexity, providing 18 separate conditions. Two lists of 8 words were visually presented in each condition, so each word was shown only once in the experiment. They found that although written serial recall varied as a function of word frequency and graphic complexity there was no effect of word duration. This result must be treated with caution. One possible criticism relates to the use of unique items which may make the design insensitive to word-duration effects (discussed below). Another problem is that their long- and short-duration items were slightly confounded by phonological complexity, and on these grounds we would expect recall to be lower with long duration words. Also, the effect of graphic complexity is difficult to explain in terms of the phonological loop, unless it reflects additional delay in writing more complex characters. Nevertheless, as in the studies above, Zhang and Feng failed to show an effect of pronunciation duration with disyllabic words.

These failures to detect consistent word-duration effects in immediate serial recall suggest, contrary to previous results, that serial recall is not constrained by the spoken duration of list items, although it is robustly affected by syllabic length. The evidence to date suggests that previous accounts of an effect of word duration in disyllables arise from unexplained differences between list items in one set of words. This conclusion is tentative because typically only a small sample of items is used in any one experiment. However, experimental manipulation of word duration provides the strongest evidence that spoken duration constrains recall. If this fundamental effect is insecure, then the claim for a duration-based account of serial recall is seriously challenged, and by extension so is the claim for a phonological short-term memory limited by its own intrinsic decay rate.

Critical attention should also be directed to the studies comparing digit span and speech rate across languages. In many studies the syllabic length of digit-names varies between languages, so that these cases are equivalent to the syllabic length effect, and irrelevant to the discussion of word duration. In the case of a few languages, such as English, Welsh and Cantonese, the digit names are nearly all monosyllabic. In these cases the superiority of digit recall in English compared to Welsh, or the superiority of Cantonese, compared to English, might indicate a duration effect. But these studies are not without their difficulties. For example, although Ellis and Hennelly (1980) reported that Arabic digits could be read more quickly in English than in Welsh, correctly predicting the advantage for English in digit span, there was no such superiority when bilingual subjects *spoke* lists of English and Welsh number names. This questions the extent to which reading Arabic digits was a pure measure of articulatory duration. More recent studies have also reported differences between reading rates of numerals and number words in bilinguals, and these suggest that digit reading rates and digit span are determined by fluency rather than the spoken duration of the digit names (Chincotta, Hyona & Underwood, 1997; Chincotta & Underwood, 1997). Taken together, cross-language studies of digit span do not provide convincing evidence for word-duration effects across different languages.

To summarise, the case that serial recall is influenced by the spoken duration of items rests on a relatively small number of studies that have selected items to vary in duration or speech rate while keeping phonological complexity constant. Most of these studies are based on one set of words, and studies which have manipulated duration using other items have consistently failed to replicate the effect. As this kind of evidence is crucial for a duration-based account of serial recall, which is necessary to support decay-based theories, we now briefly consider if any other evidence supports the idea of decay in auditory-verbal short-term memory.

Decay in short-term memory

The classic method for investigating decay in short-term memory is to test memory after a short retention interval filled by a simple task that prevents rehearsal. The original study by Peterson and Peterson (1959) reported a substantial decline in performance over an interval of 18s. However, Keppel and Underwood (1962) showed that the decline with retention interval built up over trials, which is inconsistent with a pure decay explanation, but accountable in terms of proactive interference (PI). To avoid PI there are two basic experimental techniques: to study only initial trials, or to introduce new items on each trial.

When Baddeley and Scott (1971) tested subjects with only one trial they reported evidence of a slight decline of digit recall over filled intervals of up to 6s. More recently, Nairne, Whiteman and Kelley (1999) used new words on each trial, and demonstrated only a very small (but significant) loss over retention intervals from 2 to 96s. The studies agree in demonstrating relatively small effects of retention interval, although they differ in their interpretations. Based on the phonological loop model, we should expect a marked deterioration in performance with short retention intervals of a few seconds. However, the evidence from both studies is consistent with a relatively small decline in performance occurring over longer intervals of 30s or so. There is a pronounced deterioration between retention intervals of 0 and 2s in the Nairne et al. (1999) study, but in this comparison the duration of the retention interval is confounded with the effect of suppression.

A recent study by Nairne et al. (1997) found that the disyllabic word-length effect appeared only after the first few trials of testing. This result provides prima facie evidence that PI contributes to the word-length effect. However, Nairne and his colleagues proposed two alternative explanations: that rehearsal was not used on the first trial, and that first trial recall accessed long-term memory. Moreover, an earlier study by LaPointe and Engle (1990) obtained clear syllabic word-length effects when new items were introduced on each trial, a procedure that should also minimise PI. Thus there is no clear evidence at present that the word-length effect is caused by, or enhanced by, PI.

The role of rehearsal in the word-length effect

Although training children to rehearse has been shown to increase their serial recall of pictures (Keeney, Canizzo & Flavell, 1967), results from this and other developmental studies suggest that young children do not rehearse spontaneously. The age at which rehearsal first appears is disputable, as different behaviours are considered as indices of rehearsal. Taking spontaneous verbalisation as an index of rehearsal, Flavell, Beach and Chinsky (1966) found that this was present in 10-year-olds but not 5-year-olds. Bebko and McKinnon (1990), suggest that the production of automatic lip movements in response to visual stimuli is indicative of rehearsal, but such lip movements do not emerge until around 7 years. Henry and Millar (1993), however, suggested that lip movements may signify labelling rather than rehearsal. Another recently proposed criterion for rehearsal is the presence of a correlation between speech rate and memory span across individuals (e.g. Gathercole et al., 1994). Their data, based on digit span, suggests that rehearsal begins at about age 7, although the correlation between speech rate and word span has been observed in younger children (e.g. Avons, Wragg, Cupples & Lovegrove, 1998).

Syllabic word-length effects have been consistently shown in children as young as 5 years who are not generally believed to rehearse (e.g. Avons et al., 1998; Hitch, Halliday, Schaafstal & Heffernan, 1991; Hulme et al., 1984; Hulme, Silvester, Smith & Muir, 1986; Johnston, Johnson & Gray,

1987). For example, Hitch et al. (1991), showed that word-length effects were present in 5-year-olds when the stimuli were labelled by either the children or the experimenter. These results, they argue, are indicative of phonological loop mediation in 5-year-olds in short-term memory tasks in the absence of rehearsal. The word-length effect can be explained with minimal modification to the phonological loop model, by suggesting that phonological representations decay during output rather than between successive rehearsals. This issue is reviewed below. However, if the duration of spoken output determines memory span, then a correlation between speech rate and memory span will be expected, in the absence of rehearsal. The utility of this correlation as an indicator of rehearsal is therefore questioned.

The word-length effect during output

The concept of the phonological loop proposed by Baddeley (1986) suggests that the word-length effect originates from rehearsing items, and thus maintaining them in the phonological store. If this is true, then different output methods should not influence the word-length effect. However, Henry (1991), working with children, and Avons, Wright and Pammer (1994) with adults, both demonstrated that word-length effects were smaller in probed recall than in serial recall. Henry (1991) noted that, with 5-year-old children, the syllabic word-length effect disappeared altogether with probed recall, although the effect persisted under probed recall in older children. This supports the interpretation made above that word-length effects occur during serial output in young children, in the absence of rehearsal. The results are broadly consistent with the proposal that decay occurs during output, since less decay occurs when reporting one item in probed recall than when serially reporting the whole list. But Avons et al. (1994) proposed two alternative explanations for the differences observed between probed and serial recall: output interference and output buffer requirements. The first of these suggested that events occurring during recall interfere with the recall of later items. The second account proposed that an overload on an output buffer increases the word-length effect in serial recall relative to probed recall, which has fewer output demands.

The idea of decay during output was tested more directly by Cowan, Day, Saults, Keller, Johnson and Flores (1992) who proposed that if recall begins with long words, the recall of the following list items will be delayed more than if recall begins with short words. Hence the duration of those items that are recalled first critically determines the accuracy of recall. Cowan et al. (1992) showed that when the duration of disyllabic words was manipulated independently in the first and second half of each list, it was the duration of the words recalled first that determined recall. This was true for both forwards and backward recall. However, a problem for these studies was that the words used by Cowan et al. (1992) were drawn from those originally selected by Baddeley et al. (1975), and the contribution of these particular items to the generation of the disyllabic word-duration effect has been questioned throughout this article and elsewhere.

Lovatt (1999) and Lovatt, Avons and Masterson (in press) re-examined the mixed list paradigm, using other controlled sets of short- and long-duration disyllables and one set of trisyllabic words. None of these word sets showed a word-duration effect in pure lists, although the differences in spoken duration were substantial and reliable. We were also unable to find any effect of the duration of words recalled first on overall recall, or of recall of subsequent items. When the Cowan et al. (1992) words were used, the original finding was confirmed: if long words were recalled first there was a decrease in performance mainly in the latter half of the list. But in the first half of recall these long words also produced more errors. We found that if trials containing errors in the first half of recall were eliminated, no effect of first half word type on second half recall was found. However, on these error-free first-half trials the speech time of long words was significantly greater than for short words. According to Cowan (see Cowan, Keller, Hulme, Roodenrys, McDougal & Rack, 1994) increased speech time for first-half output should increase decay in the phonological store, leading to reduced performance on items output subsequently. Our results, in contrast, suggest that if speech time increases in the first half of recall and error rate is held constant, there will be no effect of first half duration on subsequent recall. This was the case for the Cowan words, for which the error rate was controlled, and for the other word sets tested, in which the error rates on first half recall did not differ between long and short words. We tentatively conclude that the apparent effect of first half word duration noted by Cowan et al. (1992) was caused by early errors in recalling the list, which then impaired subsequent recall. As with the disyllabic word-length effect, the claims arising from the use of mixed lists appear to be an artifact of a particular set of items.

Other studies have examined serial recall in direct relation to *output time*. If we discount the possibility of rehearsal during output, then the phonological loop model predicts that the duration of output at the limit of serial recall should not exceed the decay time of the loop. Dosher and Ma (1998) measured memory span and output duration for small sets of different materials (e.g. digits, letters and words) using spoken and keypress recall. They found that output time could be used to predict memory span, but output time for span-length lists was neither constant, nor consistent with the assumed decay time of 2s. Hulme, Newton, Cowan, Stuart and Brown (1999) also measured output time for span-length lists that were correctly recalled, and reported output times which varied with both word length and lexicality, and again exceeded the assumed decay time. Neither of these results is consistent with the idea that output takes place from a phonological store decaying at a fixed rate.

CURRENT ACCOUNTS OF THE WORD-LENGTH EFFECT IN SERIAL RECALL

Baddeley's (1986) phonological loop model, which we refer to as the standard model, makes predictions concerning the gross relationship between spoken word duration and serial recall. However, predictions concerning other aspects of serial recall (for example the form of serial position curves, levels of supraspan performance, or the types of errors that occur) cannot be made because the representations and processes of the standard model are not specified in sufficient detail. This limitation applies to some subsequent modifications of the standard model. For example, Gathercole and Hitch (1993) suggest that word-length effects in pre-rehearsing young children are due to a sequential readout of the contents of the phonological store, limited by the time required to convert each phonological representation into an output speech plan. They argue that as it takes longer to read out polysyllabic words (compared to monosyllabic words) this will lead to more decay of unread items in the phonological store. Hence lists of monosyllabic words are easier to recall than lists of long words. However, the nature of decay in the phonological store is not specified in sufficient detail to fully explain the phonological readout hypothesis, because it does not make explicit the nature of the function that relates levels of representational decay and the probability of recall for any given item. Similarly, due to its lack of specification, the phonological loop model is unable to account for the production of certain types of recall errors (e.g. Henson, Norris, Page & Baddeley, 1996) and serial position curves (e.g. Burgess & Hitch, 1992).

In this section we examine several models of serial recall that account for the word-length effect which are, computationally, more highly specified than the phonological loop model (e.g. Brown & Hulme, 1995; Brown, Preece & Hulme, 2000; Burgess & Hitch, 1999; Neath and Nairne, 1995; Page and Norris, 1998; see also chapter 8). A common thread that runs through these, and other computationally specified models, is the notion that the limit of immediate serial recall is determined, either explicitly or implicitly, by decay. By questioning the empirical evidence on which the decay assumption is based, the present review poses a challenge to all these models. The main ways in which the word-length effect has been modelled are described below.

The word-length effect can be described in terms of decay during maintenance, which is opposed by rehearsal, or decay during output. These processes form the basis of the Primacy Model (Page & Norris, 1998) and of the Network Model of the phonological loop (Burgess & Hitch, 1999). Performance is limited in the Primacy Model by the amount of delay between the presentation of any list item and its recall, the number of items in a list, the strength of certain node activations, and covert rehearsal rate, which is indexed by the number of rehearsals of a particular item that is possible before recall. With regards to the word-length effect the critical factors are the time interval between the presentation (or last rehearsal if the item is rehearsed) and the recall of an item, and the covert rehearsal rate. It is assumed that rehearsal occurs in real time between the presentation of each list item, and that the number of items that can be rehearsed is determined by the relationship between articulation rate and the duration of list items. This model is therefore functionally very similar to the original phonological loop, except that the primacy model distinguishes between item and order errors, and predicts that order errors will increase with delay.

Burgess and Hitch (1992, 1996, 1999) have developed a connectionist model of the phonological loop that retains many of the features of the standard model. According to the 1999 account, list items are represented by a layer of item nodes. These nodes receive input from a layer of input phoneme nodes, and also from a context signal. Item nodes send their outputs to the output phoneme nodes which are themselves hard-wired to the corresponding input phoneme nodes. When a list item is presented, the input and output phoneme nodes are activated, and the most strongly activated item node is selected by mutual competition between item nodes. The modifiable connections between the activated item node and the input phoneme, output phoneme and context signals are then strengthened. These modifiable connections preserve the information about the order and identity of list items, but their weights are subject to decay. According to this model, the word-length effect occurs because the interval between presentation and recall increases with increasing word length, during which time additional decay of the connection weights takes place. Burgess and Hitch (1999) show that this model captures the linear relationship between memory span and the speech rate of items. Thus as in the standard model, word-length effects are attributed to the duration of spoken items that are produced from decaying memory traces.

In marked contrast, the word-length effect can be specified in terms of either trace decay or interference-based processes, that are not dependent on rehearsal or decay during output. Such processes have been specified in the models of Brown and Hulme (1995) and Neath and Nairne (1995; see also Nairne, 1988, 1990). For example, Brown and Hulme model memory traces as a series of time slices (segments). Word length corresponds to the number of segments that a word has. Each segment has an activation level which decrements during the presentation and recall of other list items. The probability of an item being recalled is calculated from the product of each of its segment values, and an additional factor that reflects redintegration (re-assembly) during recall. Two factors are thought to facilitate redintegration: (a) an item's lexical status, and (b) its duration. Brown and Hulme's decay-based account suggests that word-length effects arise because long duration words occupy more time steps than short duration words and consequently suffer more *decay* at both input and output. The same processes provide an interference-based account because the strength (activation) of each segment is reduced by a fraction each time another segment is either input or output. Since long duration words contain more segments, long items suffer more from *interference*. However, whether forgetting is due to decay or interference, the probability of recalling a word is determined by the product of the level of activation of all of the segments in a word. This product will always be lower for long words than short words. Neath and Nairne (1995) suggest that an interference-based feature model is able to account for the word-length effect without recourse to representational decay or rehearsal. The feature model assumes that primary memory holds active memory representations, which are subject to interference from other primary memory representations, through a process of retroactive interference. In order to model the word-length effect, the feature model assumes that list items are divided into segments, such that longer words have more segments than shorter words. It is assumed that corrupted and segmented memory traces must be re-assembled before they can be recalled. Successful re-assembly depends on the number of segments in a word, as a segment assembly error will occur with a fixed probability at each segment. Hence long words have a lower probability of being re-assembled, and thus recalled.

Both of these models make strong claims regarding their ability to model time-independent forgetting, which would be consistent with the current review. However, in both models forgetting is dependent on the temporal duration of list items. The reason for this is that in both models the number of segments in a word is determined by either the spoken duration of items (Brown & Hulme) or by articulation rate (Neath & Nairne). To model truly time-independent forgetting the definition of a segment must be decoupled from duration and articulation rate.

The word-length effect can also be described in terms of redintegration processes occurring prior to output. Redintegration processes form part of the models of Brown and Hulme (1995) and Neath and Nairne (1995) and of the processes described by Caplan et al. (1992). Although redintegration is thought to be the restructuring of degraded (or abstract) representations prior to recall there is little agreement, or even understanding, of what limits the redintegration process. For example, Brown and Hulme suggest that long words are easier to redintegrate than short words, because the same amount of information loss in long and short words will make short words harder to identify and redintegrate based on their remaining information. However, Neath and Nairne suggest that long words are harder to redintegrate than short words, because each time a segment assembly error occurs the memory representation of a particular item is corrupted further. Because long words have more segments they will suffer the effects of more segment assembly errors and be corrupted more, and thus will be harder to recall, than short words. The redintegration processes described by Caplan et al. (1992) are not computationally specified. However, they suggest that syllabic word-length effects arise when planning motor speech gestures, rather than in their execution (see also Rochon, Caplan & Waters, 1991; Waters & Caplan, 1995). The planning process is affected by the phonological complexity of items, not their duration: more phonological features must be specified in planning to output complex words.

The findings described in the current chapter pose a new problem for models of immediate serial recall. Any complete model of immediate serial recall must define a duration-independent factor that limits recall. Clearly, any model that relies on time-based decay, either explicitly or implicitly as its principal cause of forgetting, will have difficulty simulating the full range of effects.

THE WORD-LENGTH EFFECT WITHOUT DECAY AND REHEARSAL: IS THERE A FUTURE FOR THE WORKING MEMORY MODEL?

The experimental findings reviewed in the present chapter suggest that word-length effects do not arise from a process that is limited by the spoken duration of items. These findings are not consistent with key postulates of the phonological loop that (1) the representations of long- and short-duration items decay at a fixed rate, and (2) differences in recall arise because more short duration words can be rehearsed before decay occurs.

One way to sustain the decay and rehearsal theory would be to propose that rehearsal rates are not reflected in speech rates, possibly because they represent a more abstract code. An extreme version of this theory would propose that rehearsal (or scanning, see Cowan, 1992) occurs at a constant rate for all items, but that decay rates vary, a possibility discussed by Cowan, Saults and Nugent (1997). The notion that rehearsal is not a speech-based, real-time operation runs counter to subjective reports, the operational definitions used in developmental studies, studies in which overt rehearsals predict performance (see chapter 10), and neuropsychological evidence which suggests that rehearsal requires a conversion between output and input phonology (e.g. Howard & Franklin, 1993). Secondly, the utility of this kind of model would be limited, since speech rate could not be used directly to predict serial recall. Hence much of the plausibility and power of the phonological loop model would be lost by dissociating rehearsal rates from speech rates. The same considerations apply to the closely related theory that decay occurs during output.

Another way of conceptualising the relation between speech rate and serial recall, is to propose that serial recall is limited by the capacity of a phonological output buffer, which depends on phonological complexity, and that the capacity of this buffer is one of a number of variables which determines speech rate. This approach is consistent with Caplan et al.'s (1992) proposal that serial recall is limited by output planning requirements. Although this approach could account for the presence of a syllabic length effect, and the absence of a word-duration effect, at present there is no credible and well-specified model which predicts a linear relationship between serial recall and speech rate.

OVERVIEW

The work reviewed in this chapter has largely been concerned with the role of decay and rehearsal processes, fundamental characteristics of the phonological loop, in limiting immediate serial recall. A wide range of early findings led to the assumption that representations in the phonological store were subject to decay, which could be offset by a process of rehearsal. However, the main body of research discussed in this chapter does not support this view, and suggests that immediate serial recall is not a function of time-limited decay. Evidence for this view converges from several lines of experimental research.

These findings are that: (1) differences in disyllabic word duration do not reliably produce word-length effects; (2) experimental manipulation of non-words show effects of phonological complexity but not of duration; (3) differences in digit span across languages have recently been questioned; and (4) recall is not a decreasing function of output time. These findings cast doubt on the assumption that word-length effects reflect a decaying phonological representation that is refreshed by a process of rehearsal.

This chapter has focused on evidence that does not support the phonological loop. This evidence also poses a new challenge for other models of immediate serial recall which depend, either explicitly or implicitly, on decay or the duration of list items to account for the limits of immediate serial recall. The work reviewed in this chapter does not allow us to determine the primary factor that limits immediate serial recall; however, it is clear that other factors, such as the effect of errors early in the recall sequence and output buffer characteristics, may turn out to be critical.

To conclude, the *strengths* of the phonological loop component of the WM model are that it makes clear and testable predictions concerning immediate serial recall, temporal decay, and rehearsal. The apparent relationship between these variables has been observed across a wide range of applied research. According to this chapter, the primary *weakness* of the phonological loop model is the finding that increasing the time needed to rehearse, by increasing word duration, does not reliably reduce immediate serial recall. This finding undermines the assertion that a duration-based phonological loop accounts for cross-linguistic differences in memory span, the developmental increase in memory span with age, and individual differences in speech rate and serial recall. Contemporary *competing models* of immediate serial recall are generally specified at a more detailed level than the phonological loop. However, they all, either explicitly or implicitly, adopt the assumption that time-based decay is a primary factor limiting immediate serial recall, which is disputable in light of recent data. With regards to the *future* of the phonological loop model, further careful empirical research is needed to establish what factors limit the processes underlying immediate serial recall. It is expected that this work will be most fruitful when it is balanced with the development of well-specified computational models.

BACKGROUND READING

Baddeley, A. D., Thomson, N. & Buchanan, M. (1975). Word length and the structure of short-term memory. *Journal of Verbal Learning and Verbal Behavior*, *14*, 575–589.

This paper represents the cornerstone of word-length effect research and is extensively cited. It shows that recall decreases as a function of syllabic word length and demonstrates the relationship between speech rate and memory span. Experiments 3–5 report the critical finding of a word-length effect using long- and short-duration disyllabic words that provides the most persuasive evidence for time-limited decay in short-term memory. The current review (and Lovatt et al., 2000, see below) questions the extent to which these findings are a general property of long- and short-duration disyllabic words.

Cowan, N., Day, L., Saults, J. S., Keller, T. A., Johnson, T. & Flores, L. (1992). The role of verbal output time in the effects of word-length on immediate memory. *Journal of Memory and Language*, *31*, 1–17.

According to Dosher and Ma (1998) the experiments reported in this paper present the strongest evidence for time-limited decay during output. Cowan et al. introduce a neat experimental paradigm, whereby the duration of words in each half of a list is manipulated independently, to show that the duration of list items recalled first critically determines recall.

Lovatt, P. J., Avons, S. E. & Masterson, J. (2000). The word-length effect and disyllabic words. *Quarterly Journal of Experimental Psychology*, *53A*, 1–22.

Lovatt et al. provide strong experimental evidence against the theory that immediate serial recall is influenced by time-limited decay during storage. In addition to carefully controlled experimental work this paper also highlights difficulties with the secondary evidence which is used to support a theory of time-limited decay, namely, the syllabic word-length effect, cross-linguistic comparisons, and individual differences.

REFERENCES

Avons, S. E., & Hanna, C. (1995). The memory span deficit in children with specific reading disability: Is speech rate responsible? *British Journal of Developmental Psychology, 13*, 303–311.

Avons, S. E., Wragg, C. A., Cupples, L., & Lovegrove, W. J. (1998). Measures of phonological short-term memory and their relationship to vocabulary development. *Applied Psycholinguistics, 19*, 583–601.

Avons, S. E., Wright, K. L., & Pammer, K. (1994). The word-length effect in probed and serial recall. *Quarterly Journal of Experimental Psychology, 47A*, 207–231.

Baddeley, A. D. (1986). *Working memory*. Oxford: Oxford University Press.

Baddeley, A. D., & Andrade, J. (1994). Reversing the word-length effect: A comment on Caplan, Rochon, and Waters. *Quarterly Journal of Experimental Psychology, 47A*, 1047–1054.

Baddeley, A. D., & Scott, D. (1971). Short-term forgetting in the absence of proactive interference. *Quarterly Journal of Experimental Psychology, 23*, 275–283.

Baddeley, A. D., Thomson, N., & Buchanan, M. (1975). Word length and the structure of short-term memory. *Journal of Verbal Learning and Verbal Behavior, 14*, 575–589.

Bebko, J. M., & McKinnon, E. E. (1990). The language experience of deaf children: Its relation to spontaneous rehearsal in memory in a memory task. *Child Development, 61*, 1744–1752.

Belleville, S., Peretz, I., & Arguin, M. (1992). Contribution of articulatory rehearsal to short-term memory: Evidence from a case of selective disruption. *Brain and Language, 43*, 713–746.

Birnboim, S. L., & Share, D. L. (1995). Surface dyslexia in Hebrew: A case study. *Cognitive Neuropsychology, 12*, 825–846.

Brown, G. D. A., & Hulme, C. (1995). Modelling item length effects in memory span: No rehearsal needed? *Journal of Memory and Language, 34*, 594–621.

Brown, G. D. A., Preece, T., & Hulme, C. (2000). Oscillator-based memory for serial order. *Psychological Review, 107*(1), 127–181.

Burgess, N., & Hitch, G. J. (1992). Toward a network model of the articulatory loop. *Journal of Memory and Language, 31*, 429–460.

Burgess, N., & Hitch, G. J. (1996). A connectionist model of STM for serial order. In S. E. Gathercole (Ed.), *Models of short-term memory* (pp. 51–72). Hillsdale, NJ: Lawrence Erlbaum Associates Inc.

Burgess, N., & Hitch, G. J. (1999). Memory for serial order: A network model of the phonological loop and its timings. *Psychological Review, 106*, 551–581.

Caplan, D., Rochon, E., & Waters, G. (1992). Articulatory and phonological determinants of word-length effects in span tasks. *Quarterly Journal of Experimental Psychology, 45A*, 177–192.

Caplan, D., & Waters, G. (1994). Articulatory length and phonological similarity in span tasks: A reply to Baddeley and Andrade. *Quarterly Journal of Experimental Psychology, 47A*, 1055–1062.

Chen, C., & Stevenson, H. W. (1988). Cross-linguistic differences in digit span of preschool children. *Journal of Experimental Child Psychology, 46*, 150–158.

Chincotta, D., Hyona, J., & Underwood, G. (1997). Eye fixations, speech rate and bilingual digit span: Numeral reading indexes fluency not word length. *Acta Psychologica, 97*, 253–275.

Chincotta, D., & Underwood, G. (1997). Bilingual memory span advantage for Arabic numerals over digit words. *British Journal of Psychology, 88*, 295–310.

Cowan, N. (1992). Verbal memory span and the timing of spoken recall. *Journal of Memory and Language, 31*, 668–684.

Cowan, N. (Ed.). (1997). *The development of short-term memory in childhood.* Hove, UK: Psychology Press.

Cowan, N., Day, L., Saults, J. S., Keller, T. A., Johnson, T., & Flores, L. (1992). The role of verbal output time in the effects of word-length on immediate memory. *Journal of Memory and Language, 31*, 1–17.

Cowan, N., & Kail, R. (1996). Covert processes and their development in short-term memory. In S. E. Gathercole (Ed.), *Models of short-term memory* (pp. 29–50). Hillsdale, NJ: Lawrence Erlbaum Associates Inc.

Cowan, N., Keller, T. A., Hulme, C., Roodenrys, S., McDougal, S., & Rack, J. (1994). Verbal memory span in children: Speech timing clues to the mechanisms underlying age and word length effects. *Journal of Memory and Language, 33*, 234–250.

Cowan, N., Saults, J. S., & Nugent, L. D. (1997). The role of absolute and relative amounts of time in forgetting within immediate memory: The case of tone-pitch comparisons. *Psychonomic Bulletin and Review, 4*, 393–397.

Cowan, N., Wood, N. L., Nugent, L. D., & Treisman, M. (1997). There are two word-length effects in verbal short-term memory: Opposing effects of duration and complexity. *Psychological Science, 8*, 290–295.

Dempster, F. N. (1981). Memory span: Sources of individual and developmental differences. *Psychological Bulletin, 89*, 63–100.

Dosher, B. A., & Ma, J.-J. (1998). Output loss or rehearsal loop? Output-time versus pronunciation-time limits in immediate recall for forgetting-matched materials. *Journal of Experimental Psychology: Learning, Memory and Cognition, 24*, 316–335.

Ellis, N. C., & Hennelly, R. A. (1980). A bilingual word-length effect: Implications for intelligence testing and the relative ease of mental calculation in Welsh and English. *British Journal of Psychology, 71*, 43–51.

Flavell, J. H., Beach, D. R., & Chinsky, J. M. (1966). Spontaneous verbal rehearsal in a memory task as a function of age. *Child Development, 37*, 283–299.

Gathercole, S. E., Adams, A.-M., & Hitch, G. J. (1994). Do young children rehearse? An individual-differences analysis. *Memory & Cognition, 22*, 201–207.

Gathercole, S. E., & Hitch, G. J. (1993). Developmental changes in short-term memory: A revised working memory perspective. In A. Collins, S. E. Gathercole, M. A. Conway, & P. E. Morris (Eds.), *Theories of memory* (pp. 189–209). Hove, UK: Lawrence Erlbaum Associates Ltd.

Henry, L. A. (1991). The effects of word-length and phonemic similarity in young children's short-term memory. *Quarterly Journal of Experimental Psychology, 43A*, 35–52.

Henry, L. A., & Millar, S. (1993). Why does memory span improve with age? A review of the evidence for two current hypotheses. *European Journal of Cognitive Psychology, 5*, 241–287.

Henson, R. N. A., Norris, D. G., Page, M. P. A., & Baddeley, A. D. (1996).

Unchained memory: Error patterns rule out chaining models of immediate serial recall. *Quarterly Journal of Experimental Psychology, 49A*, 80–115.

Hitch, G. J., Halliday, M. S., & Littler, J. E. (1989). Item identification time and rehearsal rate as predictors of memory span in children. *Memory and Cognition, 16*, 120–132.

Hitch G. J., Halliday, M. S., Schaafstal, A. M., & Heffernan, T. M. (1991). Speech, "inner speech", and the development of short-term memory: Effects of picture-labeling on recall. *Journal of Experimental Child Psychology, 51*, 220–234.

Howard, D., & Franklin, S. (1993). Dissociations between component mechanisms in short-term memory: Evidence from brain-damaged patients. In D. E. Meyer & S. Kornblum (Eds.), *Attention and performance XIV: Synergies in experimental psychology, artificial intelligence and cognitive neuroscience.* Cambridge, MA: MIT Press.

Hulme, C., Maughan, S., & Brown, G. D. A. (1991). Memory for familiar and unfamiliar words: Evidence for a long-term memory contribution to memory span. *Journal of Memory and Language, 30*, 685–701.

Hulme, C., Newton, P., Cowan, N., Stuart, G., & Brown, G. D. A. (1999). Think before you speak: Pauses, memory search, and trace redintegration processes in verbal memory span. *Journal of Experimental Psychology: Learning, Memory and Cognition, 25*, 447–463.

Hulme, C., Silvester, J., Smith, S., & Muir, C. (1986). The effects of word length on memory for pictures: Evidence for speech coding in young children. *Journal of Experimental Child Psychology, 41*, 61–75.

Hulme, C., Thomson, N., Muir, C., & Lawrence, A. (1984). Speech rate and the development of short-term memory. *Journal of Experimental Child Psychology, 38*, 241–253.

Johnston, R. S., Johnson, C., & Gray, C. (1987). The word-length effect in young children: The effects of overt and covert rehearsal. *British Journal of Developmental Psychology, 5*, 243–248.

Keeney, T. J., Canizzo, S. R., & Flavell, J. H. (1967). Spontaneous and induced verbal rehearsal in a recall task. *Child Development, 38*, 953–966.

Keppel, G., & Underwood, B. J. (1962). Proactive inhibition in short-term retention of single items. *Journal of Verbal Learning and Verbal Behavior, 1*, 153–161.

Landauer, T. K. (1962). Rate of implicit speech. *Perceptual and Motor Skills, 15*, 646.

LaPointe, L. B., & Engle, R. W. (1990). Simple and complex word spans as measures of working memory capacity. *Journal of Experimental Psychology: Learning, Memory and Cognition, 16*, 1118–1133.

Longoni, A. M., Richardson, J. T. E., & Aiello, A. (1993). Articulatory rehearsal and phonological storage in working memory. *Memory & Cognition, 21*, 11–22.

Lovatt, P. J. (1999). *Immediate serial recall and the word-length effect.* Unpublished Doctoral thesis, University of Essex, Colchester, UK.

Lovatt, P. J., Avons, S. E., & Masterson, J. (2000). The word-length effect and disyllabic words. *Quarterly Journal of Experimental Psychology, 53A*, 1–22.

Lovatt, P. J., Avons, S. E., & Masterson, J. (in press). Output decay in immediate serial recall: Speech time revisited. *Journal of Memory and Language.*

Mackworth, J. F. (1963). The relation between visual image and post-perceptual immediate memory. *Journal of Verbal Learning and Verbal Behavior, 2*, 75–85.

Nairne, J. S. (1988). A framework for interpreting recency effects in immediate serial recall. *Memory & Cognition, 16*, 343–352.

Nairne, J. S. (1990). A feature model of immediate memory. *Memory & Cognition, 18*, 215–269.

Nairne, J. S., Neath, I., & Serra, M. (1997). Proactive interference plays a role in the word-length effect. *Psychonomic Bulletin and Review, 4*, 541–545.

Nairne, J. S., Whiteman, H. L., & Kelley, M. R. (1999). Short-term forgetting of order under conditions of reduced interference. *Quarterly Journal of Experimental Psychology, 52A*, 241–261.

Naveh-Benjamin, M., & Ayres, T. J. (1986). Digit span, reading rate, and linguistic relativity. *Quarterly Journal of Experimental Psychology, 38A*, 739–751.

Neath, I. (1997). Modality, concreteness and set-size effects in a free reconstruction of order task. *Memory & Cognition, 25*, 256–263.

Neath, I., & Nairne, J. S. (1995). Word-length effects in immediate memory: Overwriting trace decay theory. *Psychonomic Bulletin and Review, 2*, 429–441.

Nicolson, R. (1981). The relationship between memory span and processing speed. In M. P. Freidman, J. P. Das, & N. O'Connor (Eds.), *Intelligence and learning* (pp. 179–183). New York: Plenum Press.

Page, M. P. A., & Norris, D. (1998). The primacy model: A new model of immediate serial recall. *Psychological Review, 105*, 761–781.

Peterson, L. R., & Peterson, M. J. (1959). Short-term retention of individual verbal items. *Journal of Experimental Psychology, 58*, 193–498.

Rochon, E., Caplan, D., & Waters, G. (1991). Short-term memory processes in patients with apraxia of speech: Implications for the nature and structure of the auditory verbal short-term memory system. *Journal of Neurolinguistics, 5*, 237–264.

Schweickert, R., & Boruff, B. (1986). Short-term memory capacity: Magic number or magic spell? *Journal of Experimental Psychology: Learning, Memory and Cognition, 12*, 419–425.

Service, E. (1998). The effect of word length on immediate serial recall depends on phonological complexity, not articulatory duration. *Quarterly Journal of Experimental Psychology, 51A*, 283–304.

Smyth, M. M., & Scholey, K. A. (1996). The relationship between articulation time and memory performance in verbal and visuo-spatial tasks. *British Journal of Psychology, 87*, 179–191.

Vallar, G., & Baddeley, A. D. (1984). Fractionation of working memory: Neuro-psychological evidence for a phonological short-term store. *Journal of Verbal Learning and Verbal Behavior, 23*, 151–161.

Van der Linden, M., Coyette, F., & Seron, X. (1992). Selective impairment of the "central executive" component of working memory: A single case study. *Cognitive Neuropsychology, 9*, 301–326.

Waters, G. S., & Caplan, D. (1995). What the study of patients with speech disorders and of normal speakers tells us about the nature of rehearsal. In R. Campbell & M. Conway (Eds.), *Broken memories: Case studies in memory impairment* (pp. 302–330). Oxford: Blackwell.

Zhang, W., & Feng, L. (1990). The visual recognition and capacity of STM for Chinese disyllabic words. *Acta Psychologica Sinica, 22*, 383–390.

10 A critique of the working memory model

Geoff Ward

The aim of this chapter is to try to accommodate one of the strengths of the WM model (its ability to account for performance in the immediate serial recall task) with one of its weaknesses (its inability to account for recency effects in free recall) in an alternative framework for working memory research, called the General Episodic Memory (GEM) framework. This framework assumes that all episodic memory tasks are performed by the same memory systems, and in so doing, dispenses with the central assumptions of the WM model, those of a separate short-term memory system, of limited-capacity. The main reasons for this attempt are that (1) the similarities between the immediate serial recall task and the free recall task are so great that it is unreasonable to assume that the memory mechanisms underpinning the two tasks are completely independent, and (2) the rationale for working memory, in my own mind, is at least as closely associated with explaining recency effects as it is with explaining memory span-type tasks.

THE RATIONALE FOR WORKING MEMORY

I had hoped to begin this chapter by stating that there was an agreed and straightforward rationale for working memory. Unfortunately, I am no longer certain that this is the case. As I have been re-reading the original account of the WM model (Baddeley & Hitch, 1974) and its more recent expositions (e.g., Baddeley, 1986, 1990, 1992, 1996) for this chapter, I have observed in myself a growing and uneasy tension between the way that I use the term 'working memory' in day-to-day conversation and the actual type of phenomena that the WM model purports to explain. To see whether this tension is limited only to my own understanding of the term 'working memory' and the WM model, I would like to ask you to perform a simple test. You should speak the following sentence out loud to yourself and then answer the question that it poses:

'Which words from this sentence, if any, are now in your working memory?'

You should think carefully before you answer, because this simplest of questions may provide interesting insights into your perceived rationale for working memory.

You may have answered my question by using an everyday definition of the term 'working memory'. You might use the term 'working memory' when referring to the processing extended present, in which information pertaining to the most recent, current, and prospective objects, concepts, goals, beliefs, desires, and actions are temporarily highly activated. This definition of working memory can be considered to be in the spirit of primary memory (James, 1890, p. 646), in which a distinction is made between the retrieval of 'directly intuited' objects from the 'just past' (the retrieval from primary memory) and the retrieval of 'properly recollected objects' which had 'been absent from consciousness' (retrieval from secondary memory). It would also be consistent with the Atkinson and Shiffrin (1968) view of the short-term memory store (STS), in which the most recent items could be easily recalled, recoded, or rehearsed, whereas the earlier items must be properly retrieved from long-term memory. Alternatively, you may use the term 'working memory' simply as a convenient label or 'umbrella' term (Monsell, 1984) to describe the heterogenous capacities for temporary storage in the cognitive system that are distributed over diverse cognitive subsystems (e.g., Allport, 1980a, b). If you had used any of these everyday definitions of working memory then you may be able to provide a sure and straightforward answer: that certainly the most recently perceived words, if not all the words of my question, were highly accessible in your extended processing present, and hence in your working memory.

I would like to contrast that straightforward answer, with the response that you may have been deliberating upon had you addressed my question by directly considering the WM model and what it purports to explain. It is well documented that the phonological loop component of the WM model provides a reasonably detailed account of the temporary storage and processing that occurs in the immediate serial recall task (or memory span task). Therefore, if you considered that my question was requesting that you perform something akin to an immediate serial recall task, then your response may have been that the last few seconds worth of the sentence could be accurately recalled in the correct serial order. However, it is perhaps less well documented that the WM model does not play a role in the temporary storage or processing in the recency effect (the advantage of the last items in a list) in the free recall task. That is, 'it is suggested that working memory, which in other respects can be regarded as a modified STS, does not provide the basis for recency' (Baddeley & Hitch, 1974, p. 81) or 'working memory is supposed to have both buffer-storage and control-processing functions, with recency explained by a separate mechanism' (p. 82). It follows that if you considered that my question required that you perform something more akin to a free recall task then the perceived wisdom would be that (perhaps rather surprisingly) none of the words in the sentence were currently in your working memory.

I have used this simple example to illustrate the tension that I feel when using the term 'working memory': that in my 'everyday' usage, the rationale for working memory is at least as closely associated with explaining recency effects as it is with explaining memory span-type tasks. However, the WM model (Baddeley & Hitch, 1974; Baddeley, 1986) focuses solely on the latter and does not encompass an account of recency. Perhaps part of this tension stems from the fact that many of the very same phenomena and data sets that were used as evidence for the distinction between short-term and long-term memory (the intuitive appeal of primary memory, the 2-component nature of free recall) are no longer explained when short-term memory evolved into Working Memory. Surely an account of recency effects should be at the very heart of a model that proposes to account for the temporary storage and processing of information? Can it be correct that there is no overlap between the cognitive mechanisms involved with the immediate serial recall and free recall tasks? The omission of recency from the WM model is an indicator to me that there may be something wrong. In the next sections, I investigate why the recency effects were separated from the WM model. I then provide an alternative interpretation of this data, based on the implications of some recent studies in free recall. I conclude with an alternative account of working memory, one in which general memory mechanisms underpin all episodic memory tasks.

RECENCY EFFECTS AND THE WM MODEL

The development of the WM model (Baddeley & Hitch, 1974) coincided with a time when the short-term memory store (STS) was being investigated using many different experimental methodologies. These techniques included the memory span task (Miller, 1956), the digit-probe task (Waugh & Norman, 1965), free recall (Glanzer & Cunitz, 1966), the running memory span task (Hockey, 1973), and the Brown-Peterson task (Brown, 1958; Peterson & Peterson, 1959). Despite this wide range of techniques, there was little general agreement concerning the characteristics of STS. Perhaps the most widely accepted 'signatures' of STS were the recency effect in free recall and the limitations in memory span in the immediate serial recall task.

However, these two 'signatures' of STS appeared to be affected by different variables. For example, the memory span was considered to be more active, it was affected by phonological coding, word length, and articulatory suppression, whereas the recency effect was considered more passive and not greatly affected by these variables (Baddeley, 1976; Glanzer, 1972). Thus, it was found that the size of the memory span, but not the size of the recency effect, was affected by the age, intelligence, mnemonic skill, and language processing ability of the participants.

The fate of recency effects in the WM model was decided by a series of experiments that investigated the effect of a concurrent memory span task on a range of cognitive tasks (Baddeley & Hitch, 1974). The pre-theoretical assumption was that short-term memory acted as a common working memory in which the total workload possible by humans was limited, and hence some trade-off in performance could be expected when two tasks competed for the same limited-capacity resources. Of particular interest are the results of a series of experiments which investigated the effect of concurrent digit span on the free recall of a list of 16 words (Baddeley & Hitch, 1974, 1977). In a typical experiment in this series, participants were presented with a list of 16 visual words to recall in any order at a rate of 2 seconds per word. In addition, all the participants were presented with concurrent sequences of digits at a rate of 6 digits per 4 seconds, with a 4-second recall period. The participants in the 6-digit load condition had to learn the words whilst encoding and recalling these digit sequences in the correct serial order. The free recall performance of these participants was then compared to that of a control group of participants who had to learn the words whilst repeating the digits as they were presented. Baddeley and Hitch found that there was a relatively small primacy effect and an extended recency effect in the control condition. They also found a small but significant effect of concurrent digit load on the early and middle portions of the serial position curves, but, critically, no significant effect of concurrent digit load on the recency effect. That is, there was no evidence of a trade-off between the recency effects in free recall and a concurrent 6-digit memory load. This suggested that the two signatures of STS must reflect rather different memory mechanisms. The preferred solution was that the memory span was performed by the phonological loop component of Working Memory, whereas recency must be explained by a general more passive mechanism, outside of Working Memory. In addition, the fact that there was some decrement in learning on the primacy and middle items with the concurrent digit load was interpreted as further evidence for a common, limited-capacity, Working Memory system that might also be responsible for both digit span and learning.

The distinction between the recency effects in free recall and immediate serial recall is equally apparent in accounts from alternative methodologies. For example, converging evidence against a STS account of the recency effect is obtained from the continuous distractor procedure (e.g., Tzeng, 1973; Bjork & Whitten, 1974; Glenberg, 1984; Glenberg et al., 1980). In this procedure, participants are presented with a list of items for free recall and must also perform a distractor task immediately after each studied item (which is argued to overwrite the contents of their STS). Performance throughout the serial position curve is reduced under these conditions, but critically, a significant (although reduced) recency effect is still observed. In addition, long-term recency effects can be shown in free recall tests of items such as the opponents in rugby matches or the location in which one's car was parked, which occurred over days, weeks or months (Baddeley & Hitch, 1977; Pinto & Baddeley, 1991). Clearly these recency effects can not be attributed to the direct output from a short-term store. Furthermore, it has become widely accepted that the size of the recency effects in free recall may be predicted by the ratio ($\Delta t/T$) of the inter-presentation interval (Δt) to the retention interval (T). This finding, which is known as the ratio rule, can account for the size of the recency effects under a wide range of presentation conditions, including immediate and delayed free recall, incidental learning conditions, the continuous distractor technique, and recency effects over extended time periods. For some theorists, the ratio rule reflects the greater temporal or contextual distinctiveness of the most recent items (Crowder, 1993; Genberg, 1984; Glenberg et al., 1980), whereas for others it is the result of an episodic retrieval mechanism operating on the implicit priming of the most recent items (Baddeley & Hitch, 1993). Importantly, the ratio rule only predicts recency effects, and has little or nothing to say about any primacy effects, including the primacy effects in free recall and the typical serial position curves in the immediate serial recall task (which show extensive primacy with only very limited recency).

It is also worth noting that many recent models of immediate serial recall concentrate exclusively upon explaining memory span phenomena, but say little or nothing about performance in the free recall task (e.g., Baddeley, 1986; Burgess & Hitch, 1999; Henson, 1998; Page & Norris, 1998). These models tend to assume that performance on immediate serial recall tasks are performed by separate, more active, short-term or working memory mechanisms.

Upon reflection, the distinction between the temporary storage and processing involved in free recall and immediate serial recall may seem surprising given that these two tasks may possess essentially the same input at encoding and differ only in the instructions given to the participants. More recent accounts of the WM model (Baddeley, 1986) propose that immediate serial recall is performed by the phonological loop which contains a passive phonological input store with obligatory access for auditory stimuli. Can this passive component of the phonological loop system in Working Memory really be completely separate from the passive recency-based (non-working memory) mechanism used to store the words when the participants are free to recall the items in any order? This complete theoretical distinction between the accounts of two rather similar methodologies is, in essence, the source of the tension that I referred to at the start of this chapter.

SOME INTRIGUING NEW DATA

A recent series of studies by Lydia Tan and myself (Tan & Ward, 2000) provides some new and intriguing data concerning the nature of primacy and recency effects. We re-examined the primacy and recency effects in free recall, using the overt rehearsal methodology. In this methodology, participants are asked to say out loud any words in the list that they are thinking about during the presentation of the list items. Rundus (1971) had used this methodology to show that early items in the list were well remembered and these items typically received more rehearsals than middle or later items. The traditional account of this finding (e.g., Atkinson & Shiffrin, 1968) is that the number of times that an item has been rehearsed determines the likelihood that the item will be stored and subsequently retrieved from long-term memory. In line with this account, factors that reduce the amount of rehearsal (such as incidental learning conditions, fast presentation rate, or distractor activity in the inter-presentation interval) reduce the size of the primacy effect. However, many theorists (e.g., Baddeley, 1990; Crowder, 1982) point to the large number of studies that have demonstrated that recall performance is not improved by extra rehearsals when they are massed together in a block (e.g., Craik & Watkins, 1973; Woodward, Bjork & Jongeward, 1973; Fischler, Rundus & Atkinson, 1970; Rundus, 1977).

Tan and Ward were interested in whether all these findings could be explained if one assumed that it was not solely the number of rehearsals that was the important factor, but rather that recall was affected by the number, distribution, and recency of the rehearsals. Specifically, one consequence of an early item in the list being rehearsed many times is that there is a tendency for multiple instantiations of that item to be created, and for the most recent instantiations to tend to be towards the very end of the list. When we re-plotted the standard free recall serial position curves in terms of the time at which each item was last rehearsed and by the number of items that followed the last rehearsal of each item, we found that the 'U'-shaped serial position curves were transformed into curves with large and extended recency effects, and only very modest primacy effects. In addition, the performance at delayed testing could be explained using a model of retrieval which was based on the relative discriminability of the list items. We argued that these findings supported the claim that both primacy and recency effects in free recall could be explained by a recency-based mechanism. These findings essentially replicated and extended the earlier empirical work by Brodie and colleagues (e.g., Brodie, 1975; Brodie & Murdock, 1977; Modigliani & Hedges, 1987; Rundus, 1971), but showed that both primacy and recency effects in free recall were potentially explainable in terms of the ratio rule.

Two related accounts of the ratio rule ($\Delta t/T$) are the temporal distinctiveness hypothesis (e.g., Crowder, 1982, 1989, 1993; Crowder & Neath, 1991) and the contextual retrieval hypothesis (e.g., Glenberg, 1987; Glenberg & Swanson, 1986; Glenberg et al., 1980). The principle is often illustrated using the perceptual metaphor of the appearance of a line of evenly spaced telegraph poles that recede into the distance. Through perspective, the closer telegraph poles will be more discriminable because they will appear larger and more widely spaced than telegraph poles that are further away. In terms of the temporal distinctiveness hypothesis, $\Delta t/T$ can be considered to be a kind of Weber fraction of temporal distinctiveness, such that an item will appear to be more temporally distinctive, and hence more accessible to recall if it is more recent (when T is low), and when there are no near neighbours (when Δt is high). Similarly, the contextual retrieval hypothesis (Glenberg et al., 1980; Glenberg, 1987) assumes that every study item is associated with a particular encoding context, and successful recall involves the sampling of the study context at test, followed by the successful retrieval of the study item given the study context. The similarity between encoding and test contexts will be greatest when there is a small retention interval (when T is low), and the probability that an individual item will then be accessed will depend on the specificity of the contextual cue, which will be greatest when few items share the same encoding context (when Δt is high). The metaphor is illustrated in Figure 10.1. Figure 10.1A illustrates the differing ease of retrieval within a list of ten items. Each telegraph pole represents one of the ten stimuli; the white number in the filled circle represents the order of the item on the experimenter's list.

If only the externally presented stimuli are considered, then this type of account cannot explain primacy effects, because the earliest list items will be close to the horizon and will appear small and closely spaced. However, Tan and Ward argued that the ratio rule could be extended to consider participants' rehearsals as well as the experimental presentations of the items. We observed that the primacy items were very frequently rehearsed and these rehearsals were typically well-distributed and often continued towards the end of the list. By contrast, the middle and recency items were rarely rehearsed. Figure 10.1B illustrates the perceived pattern of stimuli when both the externally presented stimuli and the participants' own rehearsals are considered. The black digits in open circles indicate the serial position on the experimenter's list of each rehearsal. It is now possible to see that when the rehearsals are also considered, the most recently experienced items tend to be both the primacy and the recency items, and hence both tend to be very discriminable at test. Thus, we suggested that the serial position curves in free recall may be explained by the operation of two types of mechanism: a rehearsal-based mechanism which repeats and reorders items, and a recency-based retrieval mechanism that is used to discriminate study items from their neighbours. Participants selectively rehearse the early items towards the end of the list, such that the most recently perceived items are the recency items embedded in rehearsals of the early list items.

A number of important implications arise from adopting a recency-based explanation of free recall. First, the explanation provides an alternative, ratio rule interpretation of Baddeley and Hitch's data (1974, Experiment 9). Figure 10.1C and 10.1D illustrate a plausible pattern of rehearsals for the control and concurrent digit load conditions, respectively. In both

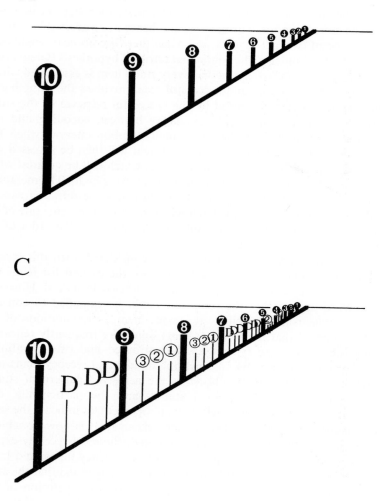

Figure 10.1 The temporal distinctiveness of a list of evenly spaced, to-be-remembered items, illustrated using the telegraph pole metaphor. Panel A illustrates the stimuli that are presented by the experimenter. The white digits in the filled circles denote the serial position of the items in the list. Panel B illustrates the stimuli that are presented by the experimenter, together with the participants' rehearsals. The black digits in the open circles denote the original serial position of the rehearsed items. Panel C illustrates the stimuli

B

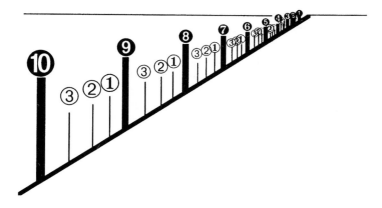

D

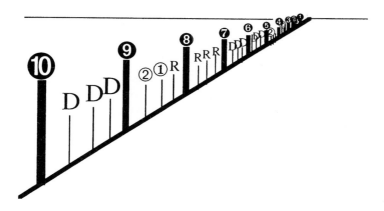

that are presented by the experimenter, together with the participants' rehearsals in the Control condition of Baddeley and Hitch (1974). The symbol D illustrates the coding in episodic memory of a digit stimulus. Panel D illustrates the stimuli that are presented by the experimenter, together with the participants' rehearsals in the concurrent working memory load condition of Baddeley and Hitch (1974). The symbol R illustrates the rehearsal of a digit stimulus as it is recalled.

conditions, participants were required to perform a free recall task while hearing sequences of digits. In the control condition (Figure 10.1C), participants had to report each digit as it was presented; whilst in the concurrent digit load condition (Figure 10.1D), participants had to recall the 6 digits in the correct serial order. As can be seen from a comparison of the figures, the distribution of the recency items is relatively unaffected by the nature of the concurrent tasks, since the recency items receive few or no rehearsals. By contrast, the concurrent tasks (listening to digits, D, and recalling the digits, R) limit the amount of rehearsal that can take place in the inter-stimulus interval. The concurrent digit load task greatly reduced the amount of selective rehearsal of the early list items to later serial positions. However, a very limited amount of rehearsal could still occur if recall was completed before the end of the 4-second recall period that follows each sequence of 6 digits. The control task of reporting the digits also reduced the amount of selective rehearsal of the early list items to later serial positions, although now the entire 4-second recall period after each digit sequence was available for rehearsal. The recency-based explanation of the free recall serial position curves therefore predicts the patterns of performance on the earlier items, which will be affected by the number, the recency, and the distribution of rehearsals of these items. Because the opportunity for rehearsal is reduced in the control condition, and reduced still further in the concurrent load condition, the performance on the earlier items will also tend to be reduced. The recency-based explanation of the free recall serial position curves also correctly predicts that recency will be relatively unaffected by the concurrent tasks. This is because the recency items in free recall are very rarely rehearsed and so the recency and distribution of these items is unchanged in the two conditions. There may be little difference between the difficulty of retrieving those recency items that are embedded in the encoding of digits and the rehearsals of earlier items (control condition), and retrieving those recency items that are embedded in the encoding and recall of sequences of digits (digit load condition).

A second implication of adopting a recency-based account of free recall is that it extends the range of different 'short-term memory' methodologies that can be explained using the ratio rule. The ratio rule is a general account of episodic memory that assumes that memory extends over a continuum, rather than assuming a need for separate STS and long-term store. It is well documented that the ratio rule can account for performance in the Brown-Peterson task (Baddeley, 1976, pp. 127–130, 1990, pp. 47–50; Crowder, 1989, 1993), and the recency effect in free recall (e.g., Baddeley, 1986, pp. 156–164; Baddeley & Hitch, 1993; Crowder, 1989, 1993). In addition, because the ratio rule essentially predicts recency, it would also have little difficulty explaining the results of the Waugh and Norman (1965) digit probe task, and the Hockey (1973) running memory span task. To this list we can now add the primacy and middle portion of the free recall task (Tan & Ward, 2000). Therefore, a second implication of the recency-based account of free recall is that it provides evidence against the fractionation of memory into short-term and long-term components (for a more extensive critique on these issues, see Melton, 1963; Craik & Lockhart, 1972; Crowder, 1982, 1989, 1993).

A third implication of adopting the ratio rule to explain the serial position curves in free recall is that it may help explain why recency and memory span are affected by different variables. In free recall, recency effects occur because the most recently presented items are already towards the end of the list, and are therefore highly discriminable and more accessible, and may be output first. However, in the memory span task, some items must be rehearsed, because the earliest (and not the most recent) list items must be output first. Therefore, one explanation for the fact that different factors affect the memory span and recency effects is that recall performance on the memory span task but not free recall requires rehearsal.

AN ALTERNATIVE PERSPECTIVE: THE GENERAL EPISODIC MEMORY MODEL

The task analysis of free recall provided by Tan and Ward raises the intriguing possibility that performance on the free recall and the immediate serial recall tasks may be underpinned by common memory mechanisms. Recall that Tan and Ward argued that the free recall task requires at least a recency-based mechanism and rehearsal. It is also possible that a third, phonological component is required for a more complete account. Similarly, the immediate serial recall task requires a phonological input store and a subvocal rehearsal process (together known as the phonological loop, Baddeley, 1986), and there is growing recognition that some additional, long-term storage component is required to accommodate the findings that memory span is greater for familiar items. In this next section, I explore the possibility that both the free recall and the immediate serial recall tasks may be modelled using the same set of cognitive components.

A candidate architecture, the General Episodic Memory (GEM) framework is presented in Figure 10.2. The GEM framework has been deliberately kept simple to encourage the reader to combine what is known about the phonological loop in immediate serial recall, and what is known about episodic memory and rehearsal in free recall. It consists of three components: a subvocal rehearsal process, a phonological store, and a general episodic memory system. The subvocal rehearsal mechanism is used to recall the most recently presented items in the correct serial order and can also be used to repeat and reorder items from episodic memory. The general episodic memory store represents items (in item memory) associated with the context(s) in which they were presented. Each presentation (or rehearsal) of an item results in the addition of an associated contextual cue to the item (the addition of a telegraph pole in context memory), and also

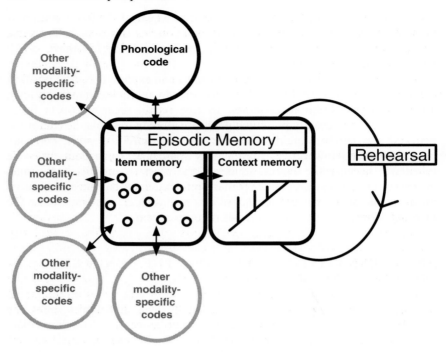

Figure 10.2   The General Episodic Memory (GEM) framework.

increments the strength of that item in item memory. The phonological store represents the phonology of verbal material, and this modality-specific information directly augments the modality-independent item information in item memory. Following Baddeley (1986), spoken verbal material has direct access to the phonological store, whereas written verbal material must be first recoded. The phonological store is just one of a number of modality-specific codes that augment the modality-independent item information.

One advantage of the GEM framework is that all explicit memory tasks are assumed to make use of common memory mechanisms. For example, both rehearsal in the free recall task and rehearsal in maintaining and outputting items in the memory span task are assumed to make use of the same subvocal rehearsal component. Since subvocal rehearsal in free recall is assumed to underpin the primacy effect, the GEM framework assumes that both the primacy effect in free recall and performance in immediate serial recall should be similarly affected by variables that affect the efficiency of rehearsal. It therefore assumes that factors that detrimentally affect rehearsal such as articulatory suppression, increased word length and irrelevant speech will have a detrimental affect on recall in both tasks.

There is some existing evidence that free recall is affected by 'phonological loop' variables, such as articulatory suppression (Richardson & Baddeley, 1975; Hanley & Thomas, 1984), word length (Craik, 1968; Watkins, 1972), and irrelevant speech (LeCompte, 1994). However, the methodological details of these studies make it difficult to determine conclusively whether the effects of the 'phonological loop' variables are greatest in the primacy portion of the serial position curves.

The GEM framework also assumes that common memory mechanisms underpin the effects of item similarity across all different memory tasks. Note that the effects of similarity may vary according to the task demands of the different tests. Free recall requires participants to recall all the items in the list in any order. Any identified similarity between items within the list may be used as a retrieval cue to help generate list members. By contrast, immediate serial recall requires participants to distinguish individual list members from their neighbours. Any identified dissimilarity between items within the list may be used to help reconstruct the original list order. These different task demands may therefore explain the apparently different effects of variables such as phonological similarity on free recall and immediate serial recall tasks. There is evidence that phonological similiarity increases performance in free recall (Bruce & Crowley, 1970; see also Wickelgren, 1965), but decreases performance in immediate serial recall (Baddeley, 1966). It may be tempting to assume that this suggests that the two tasks are underpinned by fundamentally different mechanisms. However, the GEM framework may account for the increased free recall of phonological similar lists by assuming that the phonological similarity may be used as a cue to generate candidate list members. The decreased performance in the immediate serial recall task may be explained by assuming that the phonological similarity will make it harder to discriminate the list items from each other, leading to errors in correct order.

Furthermore, periods of distractor activity immediately following the study list increase the retention interval (T) and might therefore be expected to reduce the temporal discriminability ($\Delta t/T$) of the study list items for all memory tasks, including both free and immediate serial recall. I have earlier in this chapter discussed evidence that free recall performance decreases with the filled retention interval and is sensitive to the ratio rule (e.g., Bjork & Whitten, 1974; Glanzer & Cunitz, 1966; Tan & Ward, 2000). The effect of a filled delay on the memory span task can be approximated by the Brown-Peterson task (Melton, 1963), and it is well known that serial recall performance on the Brown-Peterson task decreases with the filled retention interval, and is sensitive to the ratio rule (see, e.g., Baddeley, 1990, pp. 46–50).

Finally, the GEM framework can account for the separate characteristics of the memory span and recency effects and the apparent lack of trade-off between the two tasks in the Baddeley and Hitch (1974, 1977) studies. The GEM framework predicts the memory span task requires the subvocal rehearsal loop, whereas retrieving recency items does not. Therefore, one explanation for the different effects of variables on the two tasks is that the efficiency of rehearsing early items in a list is affected by the age, intelligence and concurrent task, whereas the retrieval of recency items is unaffected by this rehearsal because the recency items, by definition, are already at the end of the list. It is interesting to note that the GEM framework predicts that there will be a very large reduction in both primacy and recency effects in free recall, when free recall performance on its own is compared with free recall performance with concurrent memory load. This is because the GEM framework predicts that both tasks make use of the same episodic memory system and the same phonological input store in the recency portion, and the same subvocal rehearsal mechanism in the primacy portion. However, the GEM framework correctly predicts that there will be little or no trade-off between the recency effects in free recall and the memory span when the effects of concurrent memory load on free recall is compared with a digit copying control condition. The reason is that in both the concurrent load and the control task, the concurrent digits must still be processed and this common processing has an equivalent, detrimental effect on the phonological input and recency of both conditions.

THE WM MODEL AND THE GEM FRAMEWORK

In some ways the GEM framework can be seen as a combination of the phonological loop component of the WM model with the ratio rule from free recall. However, it is important to stress that the fundamental characteristics of the GEM framework are not the same as those of the WM model.

The two fundamental assumptions behind the development of the WM model were the notion that short-term memory acted as a working memory, and that the capacity of working memory was limited. Thus, 'we would like to suggest that the core of the working memory system consists of a limited capacity "work space" which can be divided between storage and control processing demands' (Baddeley & Hitch, 1974, p. 76). This assumption continues in more recent accounts of the model. For example, 'for the concept of working memory to be useful, I would wish to argue that the system should be limited in capacity, and should operate across a range of tasks involving different processing codes and different input modalities' (Baddeley, 1986, pp. 34–35).

The GEM framework does not share either of these two assumptions. First, there are no separate short-term and long-term episodic memory stores in the GEM framework. Rather, the GEM framework assumes that recall of all items is from a general episodic memory, and that the probability that an item will be accessible (in the absence of any alternative cue) is determined by the ratio rule. This issue has been discussed in more detail earlier in the chapter.

Second, the GEM framework does not assume a general-purpose, limited-capacity workspace. Rather, memory limitations arise from encoding and retrieval limitations within specific memory mechanisms, such as the three components outlined in bold in Figure 10.2, rather than storage or capacity difficulties. It is worth noting that the evidence that working memory was limited in capacity has been provided by the dual-task methodology, a methodology criticised by Allport (1980a, b) because it can result in unfalsifiable models. Consider the results of Baddeley and Hitch (1974, Experiment 9). Prior to the study there were only two generally accepted signatures of STS: memory span and recency in free recall. Even these methodologies had been criticised (e.g., Melton, 1963; Tzeng, 1973) as reflecting more general memory mechanisms. Therefore, one could argue that Baddeley and Hitch (1974, Experiment 9) provided a definitive test of whether there is a limited-capacity short-term store. If there was a limited-capacity, common STS then performance on one or both signatures of STS should decrease when the two tasks are performed concurrently. However, as we have seen, there was no trade-off in performance: recency and memory span could be performed concurrently with seemingly no loss in performance. One interpretation of this finding is that memory span and recency reflect rather different mechanisms, neither of which constitute a common short-term or working memory. Instead, Baddeley and Hitch's (1974) preferred interpretation was that short-term memory acted as a working memory which was limited in capacity, but that memory span and not recency was an STS component. That is, recency was dropped from the WM model to preserve the pre-theoretical assumption that working memory was limited in capacity. This leads to a rather worrying state of affairs, in which it no longer becomes possible to experimentally falsify the limited-capacity nature of working memory based on dual-task trade-offs. If two tasks are combined and there is no trade-off in performance then one or both tasks cannot be tapping the limited-capacity working memory system (e.g., recency). By contrast, if two different tasks are combined and there is a trade-off in performance then the two tasks must be tapping the limited-capacity working memory system (e.g., digit span, and long-term learning). That is, the limited-capacity working memory system can, post-hoc, 'explain' any pattern of results (for a related and more detailed criticism of cognitive ergonomics, see Allport, 1980a, b).

THE GEM FRAMEWORK AND WORKING MEMORY

As it is outlined in Figure 10.2, the GEM framework provides a very simplified account of the performance on episodic memory tasks. Its strength is that it attempts to unify the cognitive architecture that underpins different episodic memory tasks. Within the GEM framework, there is no separate 'working memory' store or set of stores. The number of items that can be 'held in working memory' simply reflects the fact that discrimination of episodic memory is not perfect. However, the term 'working memory' may still be a valid expression, conveying the more general 'everyday' definition that I was alluding to in the introduction. 'Working memory' may be applied as an umbrella term (Monsell, 1984), encompassing the items that are highly accessible for a variety of reasons, such as those items that have recently been experienced or are currently being rehearsed.

A more specified GEM framework would have to account for the variety of processing codes that interface with the general episodic memory beyond simply the phonological. These types of coding must clearly include the visual, visuo-spatial processing codes, as well as auditory non-speech codes, lip-reading and sign-language codes, intonation, location, and haptic codes, and so on. Although there is much to be said for the immediate inclusion of these processing codes into the GEM framework, this temptation has been resisted in order to focus attention on the possibility that immediate serial recall of verbal materials is underpinned by the same cognitive components as free recall.

In addition, the present GEM framework is deliberately underspecified about the nature of rehearsal, because there are a number of fundamental issues that are currently being explored. For example, it is unclear whether the rehearsal that occurs to maintain and reorder stimuli in free recall differs significantly from the retrieval that occurs at the time of recall (see Tan & Ward, 2000). Nevertheless, it is self-evident that rehearsal of verbal material can be performed by humans, both covertly and out loud. Rehearsal is particularly evident for visually presented verbal stimuli (e.g., written words) which are phonologically recoded. However, it also seems possible to 'rehearse' auditory presented stimuli, in such a way that some of the original characteristics of the stimulus are also rehearsed. For example, it seems as though we can rehearse what someone else has just said 'in their voice', or replay some of the last few sounds from a piece of music. Similarly, it appears possible to 'rehearse' the rooms in your house, or your route to work, or 'replay' the most recent piece of action in a football match. It remains to be seen whether these forms of 'rehearsal' are actually underpinned by verbal coding, or whether the serial order of these non-verbal stimuli (e.g., Avons, 1998; Avons & Mason, 1999; Smyth & Scholey, 1996; Jones, 1993) may be rehearsed using modality-specific, non-verbal mechanisms or common amodal mechanisms. A model of working memory that permits the replaying of the most recently perceived events may fit well with James' (1890) description of primary memory. James famously argued that the most recently encountered thoughts may be retrieved from the 'just past', regardless of the type of material (e.g., counting the strikes of a clock, recalling the most recent words in a passage of prose, recalling someone's most recent movements).

CONCLUSIONS

I started this critique of the WM model (Baddeley & Hitch, 1974; Baddeley, 1986, 1990, 1996) by stating that one of the strengths of the WM model was that the phonological loop component can account for performance on the immediate serial recall task. However, one of the most important weaknesses of the WM model is that it no longer provides an account of recency effects. In this chapter, we saw that recency effects were discarded from the WM model to maintain the pre-theoretical assumption that there was a separate short-term memory which acted as a working memory of limited-capacity. I have attempted to provide a competing account of working memory, one that assumes that working memory is an umbrella term for the most highly accessible items in general episodic memory. Central to the development of this alternative approach has been the realisation that, by considering rehearsal dynamics, it is possible to explain both the primacy and recency effects in free recall by a recency-based model of episodic memory. When the implications of this finding are fully realised, it is possible to combine aspects of the phonological loop component of the WM model with the ratio rule account of recency. A candidate model, the General Episodic Memory (GEM) framework, illustrates this alternative possibility, in which a set of common memory mechanisms underpin all episodic memory tasks, including free and immediate serial recall. It is argued that this new framework takes the best features from both accounts, but dispenses with the underlying assumptions of the WM model.

A successful WM model in the future would be one that could account for the similarities and differences between recency and rehearsal. However, if recency effects continue to fall outside the remit of the WM model, then there is a danger that the WM model will lose touch with the very same sets of data that founded STS and working memory, and that the continued application of the WM model to other tasks and populations will lead to only incomplete explanations of the temporary storage, maintenance, and processing of information that occurs in these applied areas of study.

BACKGROUND READING

Foster, J. K. & Jelicic, M. (Eds.). (1999). *Memory: Systems, process, or function?* Oxford: Oxford University Press.

An interesting series of papers looking at a complementary debate between structuralist and proceduralist accounts of memory.

Melton, A. W. (1963). Implications of short-term memory for a general theory of memory. *Journal of Verbal Learning and Verbal Behavior*, *2*, 1–21.

A classic paper in support of a continuum of episodic memory which is still worth reading (or indeed re-reading) today.

Shiffrin, R. M. (1993). Short-term memory: A brief commentary. *Memory and Cognition*, *21*, 193–197.

One of several excellent commentaries in a special issue of *Memory and Cognition* devoted to short-term memory.

REFERENCES

Allport, D. A. (1980a). Patterns and actions: Cognitive mechanisms are content-specific. In G. Claxton (Ed.), *Cognitive psychology: new directions* (pp. 26–64). London: Routledge and Kegan Paul.

Allport, D. A. (1980b). Attention and performance. In G. Claxton (Ed.), *Cognitive psychology: new directions* (pp. 112–153). London: Routledge and Kegan Paul.

Atkinson, R. C., & Shiffrin, R. M. (1968). Human memory: A proposed system and its control processes. In K. W. Spence & J. T. Spence (Eds.), *The psychology of learning and motivation, Vol. 2* (pp. 89–195). New York: Academic Press.

Avons, S. E. (1998). Serial report and item recognition of novel visual patterns. *British Journal of Psychology*, *89*, 285–308.

Avons, S. E., & Mason, A. (1999). Effects of visual similarity on serial report and item recognition. *Quarterly Journal of Experimental Psychology*, *52A*, 217–250.

Baddeley, A. D. (1966). Short-term memory for word sequences as a function of acoustic, semantic, and formal similarity. *Quarterly Journal of Experimental Psychology*, *18*, 362–366.

Baddeley, A. D. (1976). *The psychology of memory*. New York: Basic Books.

Baddeley, A. D. (1986). *Working memory*. Oxford: Clarendon Press.

Baddeley, A. D. (1990). *Human memory: Theory and practice*. Hove, UK: Lawrence Erlbaum Associates Ltd.

Baddeley, A. D. (1992). Working memory. *Science*, *255*, 556–559.

Baddeley, A. D. (1996). The concept of working memory. In S. E. Gathercole (Ed.), *Models of short-term memory* (pp. 1–29). Hove, UK: Psychology Press.

Baddeley, A. D., & Hitch, G. J. (1974). Working memory. In G. Bower (Ed.), *Recent advances in learning and motivation, Vol. VIII* (pp. 47–90). London: Academic Press.

Baddeley, A. D., & Hitch, G. J. (1977). Recency re-examined. In S. Dornic (Ed.), *Attention and performance VI* (pp. 647–667). Hillsdale, NJ: Lawrence Erlbaum Associates Inc.

Baddeley, A. D., & Hitch, G. J. (1993). The recency effect: Implicit learning with explicit retrieval? *Memory and Cognition*, *21*, 146–155.

Bjork, R. A., & Whitten, W. B. (1974). Recency-sensitive retrieval processes in long-term free recall. *Cognitive Psychology*, *6*, 173–189.

Brodie, D. A. (1975). Free recall measures of short-term store: Are rehearsal and order of recall data necessary? *Memory and Cognition, 3*, 653–662.

Brodie, D. A., & Murdock, B. B. (1977). Effect of presentation time on nominal and functional serial-position curves of free recall. *Journal of Verbal Learning and Verbal Behavior, 16*, 185–200.

Brown, J. (1958). Some tests of the decay theory of immediate memory. *Quarterly Journal of Experimental Psychology, 10*, 12–21.

Bruce, D., & Crowley, J. J. (1970). Acoustic similarity effects on retrieval from secondary memory. *Journal of Verbal Learning and Verbal Behavior, 9*, 190–196.

Burgess, N., & Hitch, G. (1999). Memory for serial order: A network model of the Phonological Loop and its timing. *Psychological Review, 106*, 551–581.

Craik, F. I. M. (1968). Two components in free recall. *Journal of Verbal Learning and Verbal Behavior, 7*, 996–1004.

Craik, F. I. M., & Lockhart, R. S. (1972). Levels of processing: A framework for memory research. *Journal of Verbal Learning and Verbal Behavior, 11*, 671–684.

Craik, F. I. M., & Watkins, M. J. (1973). The role of rehearsal in short-term memory. *Journal of Verbal Learning and Verbal Behavior, 12*, 599–607.

Crowder, R. G. (1982). The demise of short-term memory. *Acta Psychologica, 50*, 291–323.

Crowder, R. G. (1989). Modularity and dissociations in memory systems. In H. L. Roediger & F. I. M. Craik (Eds.), *Varieties of memory and consciousness: Essays in honor of Endel Tulving* (pp. 271–294). Hillsdale, NJ: Lawrence Erlbaum Associates Inc.

Crowder, R. G. (1993). Short-term memory: Where do we stand? *Memory and Cognition, 21*, 142–145.

Crowder, R. G., & Neath, I. (1991). The microscope metaphor in human memory. In W. E. Hockley & S. Lewandowsky (Eds.), *Relating theory and data: Essays in human memory in honour of Bennet B. Murdock* (pp. 111–126). Hillsdale, NJ: Lawrence Erlbaum Associates Inc.

Fischler, I., Rundus, D., & Atkinson, R. C. (1970). Effects of overt rehearsal procedures on free recall. *Psychonomic Science, 19*, 249–250.

Glanzer, M. (1972). Storage mechanisms in recall. In G. H. Bower (Ed.), *The psychology of learning and motivation: Advances in research and theory, Vol. V* (pp. 129–193). New York: Academic Press.

Glanzer, M., & Cunitz, A. R. (1966). Two storage mechanisms in free recall. *Journal of Verbal Learning and Verbal Behavior, 5*, 351–360.

Glenberg, A. M. (1984). A retrieval account of the long-term modality effect. *Journal of Experimental Psychology: Learning, Memory and Cognition, 10*, 16–31.

Glenberg, A. M. (1987). Temporal context and recency. In D. S. Gorfein & R. R. Hoffman (Eds.), *Memory and learning: The Ebbinghaus Centennial Conference* (pp. 173–190). Hillsdale, NJ: Lawrence Erlbaum Associates Inc.

Glenberg, A. M., Bradley, M. M., Stevenson, J. A., Kraus, T. A. Tkachuk, M. J., Gretz, A. L., Fish, J. H., & Turpin, B. M. (1980). A two-process account of long-term serial position effects. *Journal of Experimental Psychology: Human Learning and Memory, 6*, 355–369.

Glenberg, A. M., & Swanson, N. G. (1986). A temporal distinctiveness theory of recency and modality effects. *Journal of Experimental Psychology: Learning Memory and Cognition, 12*, 3–15.

Hanley, J. R., & Thomas, A. (1984). Maintenance rehearsal and the articulatory loop. *British Journal of Psychology, 75*, 521–527.

Henson, R. N. A. (1998). Short-term memory for serial order: The Start–End Model of serial recall. *Cognitive Psychology, 36*, 73–137.

Hockey, R. (1973). Rate of presentation in running memory and direct manipulation of input-processing strategies. *Quarterly Journal of Experimental Psychology, 25*, 104–111.

James, W. (1890). *The principles of psychology*. New York: Henry Holt and Company.

Jones, D. M. (1993). Objects, streams and threads of auditory attention. In A. D. Baddeley & L. Weiskrantz (Eds.), *Attention: selection, awareness and control* (pp. 87–104). Oxford: Clarendon Press.

LeCompte, D. C. (1994). Extending the irrelevant speech effect beyond serial recall. *Journal of Experimental Psychology: Learning, Memory and Cognition, 20*, 1396–1408.

Melton, A. W. (1963). Implications of short-term memory for a general theory of memory. *Journal of Verbal Learning and Verbal Behavior, 2*, 1–21.

Miller, G. A. (1956). The magical number seven plus or minus two: Some limits on our capacity for processing information. *Psychological Review, 63*, 81–97.

Modigliani, V., & Hedges, D. G. (1987). Distributed rehearsals and the primacy effect in single-trial free recall. *Journal of Experimental Psychology: Learning, Memory and Cognition, 13*, 426–436.

Monsell, S. (1984). Components of a working memory underlying verbal skills: A 'distributed capacities' view — A tutorial review. In H. Bouma & D. G. Bouwhis (Eds.), *Attention and performance X* (pp. 327–50). London: Lawrence Erlbaum Associates Ltd.

Page, M. P. A., & Norris, D. (1998). The primacy model: A new model of immediate serial recall. *Psychological Review, 105*, 761–781.

Peterson, L. R., & Peterson, M. J. (1959). Short-term retention of individual items. *Journal of Experimental Psychology, 61*, 12–21.

Pinto, A. Da C., & Baddeley, A. D. (1991). Where did you park your car? Analysis of a naturalistic long-term recency effect. *European Journal of Cognitive Psychology, 3*, 297–313.

Richardson, J. T. E., & Baddeley, A. D. (1975). The effect of articulatory suppression in free recall. *Journal of Verbal Learning and Verbal Behavior, 14*, 623–629.

Rundus, D. (1971). Analysis of rehearsal processes in free recall. *Journal of Experimental Psychology, 89*, 63–77.

Rundus, D. (1977). Maintenance rehearsal and single-level processing. *Journal of Verbal Learning and Verbal Behavior, 16*, 665–681.

Smyth, M. M., & Scholey, K. A. (1996). Serial order in spatial immediate memory. *Quarterly Journal of Experimental Psychology, 49A*, 159–177.

Tan, L., & Ward, G. (2000). A recency-based account of the primacy effect in free recall. *Journal of Experimental Psychology: Learning, Memory and Cognition, 26*, 1589–1625.

Tzeng, O. J. L. (1973). Positive recency effect in a delayed free recall. *Journal of Verbal Learning and Verbal Behavior, 12*, 436–439.

Watkins, M. J. (1972). Locus of the modality effect ion free recall. *Journal of Verbal Learning and Verbal Behavior, 11*, 644–648.

Waugh, N. C., & Norman, D. A. (1965). Primary memory. *Psychological Review*, *72*, 89–104.

Wickelgren, W. A. (1965). Short-term memory for phonemically similar lists. *American Journal of Psychology*, *78*, 567–574.

Woodward, A. E., Jr., Bjork, R. A., & Jongeward, R. H., Jr. (1973). Recall and recognition as a function of primary rehearsal. *Journal of Verbal Learning and Verbal Behavior*, *12*, 608–617.

11 Reflections on the concept of the central executive

John N. Towse and Carmel M. T. Houston-Price

The central executive lies at the heart of Baddeley's theory of working memory, and is frequently called upon to explain research findings. This holds true for studies in both laboratory and applied settings. What exactly does the central executive do, then? That is a surprisingly difficult question to answer. Much of this difficulty arises because the executive has been characterised in rather different ways, with these views often considered independently of each other. Furthermore, experimental data that pin the executive down are hard to come by. The present chapter reviews and brings together various interpretations of central executive functioning, while an experiment involving a novel cognitive task is described that points up the rather restrictive nature of the term 'executive capacity'. The chapter concludes by commenting briefly on the implications of a working memory model in which the executive does not play a major part.

INTRODUCTION

Are you sitting comfortably? Really? Then we'll begin.

> Once upon a time, in a land far away, a King and Queen decided to have an enormous banquet. Invitations went out to all the important people in their Kingdom. One reached a house with three offspring from former marriages; two haughty young women just like their mother and a beautiful daughter of the husband. She was called 'Cinderella' by her stepsisters, because she was made to sit among the chimney cinders. On hearing the invitation, the two sisters (who dearly longed to catch the eye of the bachelor Prince) began choosing the most flattering of their gowns and petticoats while Cinderella just tidied up around them. After they left, a fairy godmother found Cinderella in the kitchen, weeping. 'I so wanted to go to the ball,' she cried. 'And so you shall!' said the fairy godmother.
>
> The fairy godmother turned a pumpkin into a carriage, mice into footmen, Cinder's rags into enchanting clothes and finally made a pair

of perfectly moulded glass slippers. She then hurried Cinderella off to the ball — but only after issuing strict instructions not to stay after midnight, when the magic spell would end.

Cinderella's arrival at the ball caused a real stir and the Prince instantly succumbed to her beauty. He gave Cinderella his hand and throughout the evening, hardly took his eyes off her. Cinderella quite forgot herself, until suddenly, the clock struck twelve. She rose and fled. The prince, initially stunned, attempted to follow her, but to no avail. He did however find a glass slipper, which he believed she had lost in her rush to depart.

The Prince became quite inconsolable at Cinderella's disappearance and the King and Queen realised how utterly he had fallen in love. No surprise, then, that they proclaimed the Prince would marry whoever could wear the glass slipper. A gallant, handsome (and, importantly, wealthy) Prince, a great crowd flocked to court to see the slipper. Indeed, there was something of an unseemly melée as many people wanted to try and wear the slipper. But, although the Prince eagerly awaited Cinderella's return, no-one could make the slipper fit . . .

The great thing about fairy tales is that their fantastic nature gives full reign to our imagination. Pumpkin carriages, gingerbread houses, or mermaids from the sea, one is freed from the dull restrictions of reality. Another great thing about fairy tales is that everything is supposed to end happily, leaving us with a warm feeling of satisfied contentment. Is reality like this too?

In several ways, the story of the central executive turns out to be rather like the present story of Cinderella. Note the heroine is extremely beautiful, with many people captivated by her charms. The central executive is a heroine of the working memory story too, glamorous and undoubtedly special. Yet Cinderella is (at least initially) in the shadows of her stepsisters who are invited to the ball, just as the central executive has often been the poorly understood relation of the phonological loop and the visuo-spatial sketchpad. Even so, these 'slave systems' are generally deemed by researchers to be the less glamorous components of the working memory family, true to the fairy tale. The reaction to Cinderella's mysterious arrival at the ball parallels reactions to the mysterious central executive. The Prince becomes besotted with Cinderella, or at least with the image he has of her that night. Psychologists (and the Prince stands as a collective term for researchers) appear to be only mildly less obsessed by their heroine.

Perhaps most tellingly of all, as the sound of the clock fades away, the only evidence left of Cinderella is her glass slipper. Likewise, the central executive leaves little trace of itself in the aftermath of Baddeley & Hitch (1974), where the working memory framework has its roots. Nonetheless, researchers have inherited a strong and resilient faith in a central executive system and have spent considerable energy in determining the cognitive functions or phenomena that might characterise the executive. With a reaction similar to the despair of the Prince, the cognitive kingdom has been trawled for the real central executive. As the chapter will attempt to show, there have been various attempts to make the glass slipper fit, to lay claim to being the real central executive. Indeed, there is not space to detail them all here, so that for example notions of a central executive as a memory updating system, as a form of housekeeping device (Morris & Jones, 1990) will not be considered. Nonetheless, we can ask what claims have been made, and ask how will the research fits these claims. In other words, how does this psychological fairy story end? Have cognitive psychologists found their Cinderella, or was she just a dream?

Let us audition, then, several candidates for the role of central executive, allowing us to lay the foundations for answers to the book questions:

THE CENTRAL EXECUTIVE AS . . . A GENERAL-PURPOSE PROCESSOR

Many have regarded a 'general-purpose processor' as being the natural candidate for describing the central executive. After all, the central executive idea emerged from experiments linking retention with ongoing cognitive activities. Baddeley & Hitch (1974, Experiment 3) asked subjects to examine the match between sentences (for example, 'A follows B') and related stimulus pairs ('B A'). Some sentences were easier to comprehend than others. On certain trials, subjects were required to perform a secondary task at the same time. There were various types of secondary task including repetitive articulation of novel sequences (a six-digit number string) and over-learned sequences (e.g., the number sequence one to six). Comparison of these two tasks allows one to tell whether any interference is caused by overt articulation (involved in both novel and over-learned sequences) or memory demands (required only in reproducing novel sequences). Analysis revealed that the concurrent memory load of the novel sequences impaired sentence reasoning more than the other articulatory tasks. Furthermore, the size of this impairment was a function of the difficulty of the reasoning task itself. Thus, the memory load had a greater impact when the sentences were difficult.

These findings led Baddeley & Hitch (1974) to conclude that both the reasoning and memory tasks were, in part, serviced by a common cognitive system. Since other experiments by Baddeley & Hitch (1974) showed no interference when the memory load was small, they concluded that there was a dedicated system for remembering a few items (a system now referred to as the phonological loop). When the memory requirements were substantial, however, the phonological loop system could be supplemented by a general workspace that was also responsible for carrying out the reasoning task. Accordingly, the ability to perform the reasoning task is compromised under heavy memory loads, and this is especially true when the reasoning task itself is hard.

This account has come to be known as a processing-storage trade-off. Since both processing and storage functions compete for a common or general (limited-capacity) system, one task is accomplished at the expense of the other. Accordingly, an increase in memory demands impairs performance on a concurrent processing task. Similarly, as processing tasks become harder, retention abilities would be expected to decline. The logic of this scheme is attractive; it provides an effective explanation for why one is liable to forget information under situations of cognitive stress. At the same time, the phrase 'processing-storage trade-off' has unfortunate connotations, marking memory functions — storage — as distinct from processing. At the very least, one should be careful about allowing the term processing-storage trade-off to constrain our understanding of memory mechanisms.

The idea that the central executive is a general-purpose system (often one will see reference to a 'general cognitive resource') is related to the development of working memory span tasks. Indeed, although Baddeley & Logie (1999) suggested that the central executive is not a memory system, many other researchers have argued that the central executive is responsible for working memory span phenomena. In one form of working memory span task called 'reading span' (Daneman & Carpenter, 1980), the subject begins by reading two unrelated sentences. Afterwards, they recall the last word in the first sentence and the last word in the second (it is also common to provide some comprehension questions to make sure that the sentences are read for meaning). If the subject is successful at remembering the two sentence-terminal words, sets of three sentences are presented so that three words must be remembered. Sentences are added until the point where recall performance drops below some threshold value. The essence of the reading span task is that it is designed to require both 'processing' (sentence comprehension) and 'storage' (sentence-final words). Related tasks include operation span (Turner & Engle, 1989) where subjects solve arithmetic questions and remember the solutions, and counting span (Case, Kurland & Goldberg, 1982), where subjects count objects in a series of arrays and remember each total.

It is worth being aware of a certain sleight-of-hand in some accounts of working memory span. From the original Baddeley & Hitch (1974) experiments emerged the argument for a partial overlap between general processing and retention functions. However, researchers often refer to working memory capacity, as measured by working memory span tasks, as if the slave systems components did not exist. Thus, Just & Carpenter (1992) make the following assumption:

> The working memory in our theory corresponds approximately to the part of the central executive in Baddeley's theory that deals with

language comprehension. The working memory in our theory does not include modality-specific buffers, such as the articulatory loop.

(1992, p. 123)

By this account, working memory (as measured by relevant span tasks) is located exclusively within the central executive, and working memory is seen as a more 'unitary' system as a consequence. Of course, describing the theoretical landscape like this, whereby one ignores the slave systems, avoids the irritating complication of having to consider the different ways that items might be remembered. But it only does so by the apparent audacity of defining one's own rules to the memory game. While it is true that the slave systems are usually thought to have properties rather unsuitable for explaining working memory span tasks, there is considerable evidence that modality-specific systems play an important role in many recall situations (see for example chapter 1).

Various attempts, then, have been made to advance the view that working memory can be seen as a rather general, unitary, resource, within which different activities play off against each other (Engle, 1996). Adopting a similar standpoint, it has been argued that individual differences in working memory span — taken to reflect how resources are shared between processing and 'storage' — have widespread consequences. To provide some examples, individuals with large working memory spans are differentiated from those with small working memory spans in terms of general cognitive skills (Turner & Engle, 1989), the processing of ambiguous syntactic constructions (Miyake, Just & Carpenter, 1994) and the suppression of task-irrelevant information (Rosen & Engle, 1998). Working memory span is also a predictor of early reading ability in children (Leather & Henry, 1994).

While these findings are interesting and important, we are rather sceptical of the argument that these individual differences are simply due to vari-ations in 'resource-sharing capacity' (central executive capacity by another name). It is likely that there are a host of factors that differentiate high and low working memory span groups. Any one of these (and not always the same one) may influence span levels and some particular cognitive style (although see Engle, Cantor & Carullo, 1992, for an attempt to exclude some alternatives). Reports that working memory span varies in test–retest situations (Waters & Caplan, 1996) reinforce the suspicion that span performance is the result of a complex collection of behaviours.

Conceptual concerns aside, what of the experimental evidence that working memory span measures resource-sharing within a central execu-tive? Towse & Hitch (1995) approached this issue by considering whether both developmental and experimentally induced changes in children's counting span were best understood in terms of processing difficulty (as proposed by resource-sharing models), or in terms of task length. That is, when the counting task is made difficult, counting span might be low because it takes a long time to complete the processing rather than because difficult tasks require a large proportion of the shared resources. Likewise, younger children may be at a disadvantage on counting span tasks because, being slower to count objects, they have to remember the memory items for longer (as opposed to the idea that they suffer through having fewer resources to share out). The emphasis on task length is captured by a task-switching model in which information is lost as a function of the time 'switched away' from memory activities, when the individual spends time on the processing task.

The resource-sharing and task-switching models were evaluated by measuring working memory span when counting was made easy, difficult, or easy (but lengthy) — see Towse & Hitch (1995) for details of how this was achieved. The *easy* and *difficult* conditions differed in cognitive effort and completion time, so counting span differences were predicted by both models. However, for the *difficult* and *easy (but lengthy)* conditions, processing time was equated while processing difficulty was not. The resource-sharing account continues to predict span differences, while the task-switching account predicts instead that, as tasks were matched for duration, spans should be the same. In fact, this latter prediction describes the results obtained. For children in each of four age groups, span was higher in the easy condition than in the difficult condition, but span was equivalent in the difficult condition and the easy (but lengthy) condition (see Figure 11.1). This occurred even though other data showed that the difficult condition produced most errors. Thus, despite differences in difficulty, there were no differences in span. This is inconsistent with a resource-sharing model, but quite compatible with task-switching, the idea that forgetting increases with retention duration.

Subsequent experiments have presented further problems for the resource-sharing model, while confirming the importance of retention duration manipulations. Towse, Hitch & Hutton (1998) assessed children on counting span, operation span, and reading span tasks in a series of experiments. Processing efficiency did not show a consistent impairment as memory load increased, but when the task was administered in such a way that items had to be retained for longer periods of time, span was significantly reduced. Towse, Hitch & Hutton (2000) report comparable effects among adults. This combination of results, on the one hand failing to obtain a trade-off and on the other hand showing reliable effects of retention duration when overall workload is equivalent, is damaging for the notion that working memory span tasks measure a processing-storage trade-off.[1]

In summary, this section has reviewed the popular view that resource-sharing occurs in the central executive. While crucial to some descriptions

---

1   In terms of the arguments about time-based decay considered in chapter 9, it may be helpful to note that the present findings are agnostic about the underlying mechanism of forgetting, whether information degrades because of interference or time itself. These issues are taken up in more detail in the original articles.

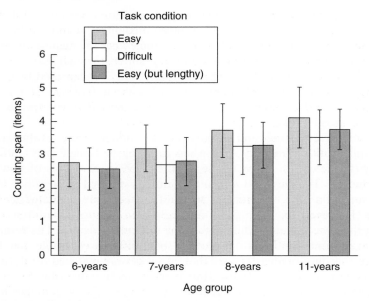

Figure 11.1   Counting span (mean values and standard deviations), redrawn from
Towse & Hitch (1995). Span scores are highest in the 'easy'
condition, and are lower in the 'difficult' and 'easy (but lengthy)'
conditions, which did not differ.

of working memory performance, the evidence for resource-sharing is not
always clear cut. Alternative explanations are rarely considered in detail
and the predictions of resource-sharing models are liable to fall down in the
face of direct tests (and for further critical analysis, see Caplan & Waters,
1999; Stoltzfus, Hasher & Zacks, 1996). While none of the current models
of working memory span (including the task-switching account) is entirely
satisfactory, it is increasingly apparent that both theoretical and computational accounts (Byrne, 1998; Kieras, Meyer, Mueller, & Seymour, 1999)
make the idea of limited resource-sharing capacity superfluous.

THE CENTRAL EXECUTIVE AS . . . A DUAL-TASK CONTROLLER

Another candidate for our Prince's attention deserves at least some consideration. It is that the central executive is important in most divided
attention tasks, where two activities are performed simultaneously. This
provides a more general variant on the idea in the previous section that the
central executive performs both 'processing' and 'memory' functions. One
feature that distinguishes the present view from that discussed previously is
a focus on the notion that each task involves an element of control and that

such control is a function of the central executive system. Also, the more relevant concern here is to account for phenomena of attention rather than retention. It is argued that mutual interference between two tasks occurs when both involve the central executive. The demands from each task places the executive under particular strain and the consequent loss of efficiency leads to degraded behaviour (for example, see Baddeley, Bressi, Della Sala, Logie & Spinnler, 1991). Thus the central executive theory is employed as an explanation for why simultaneous performance is not as good as individual performance (even if this is not always the case; see Allport, Antonis & Reynolds, 1972). Resources are shared across tasks, and when there are insufficient resources to go round, neither task is processed in an optimal fashion.

This line of reasoning certainly provides one account of dual-task interference (DTI) and was pursued in the previous section. What is surprising, however, is that there seems little discussion in the literature of alternative explanations for DTI. So it is rather ironic that DTI may arise, not because resource-sharing occurs, but because resource-sharing doesn't occur! If certain types of tasks essentially take priority within the cognitive system (possibly via mechanisms like behavioural inhibition; Neumann, 1987) and preclude concurrent activities from developing, then these concurrent activities are liable to suffer. Not only because they are delayed and therefore slowed, but also because that delay may affect the need to re-compute earlier information (for a relevant discussion, see Byrne, 1998). If this is true for both of the tasks, then interleaving or switching between them can produce weakened performance all round.

From this standpoint, DTI arises from situations where tasks do not comfortably co-exist, rather than being attributable to a common cognitive resource. In general, complex dual tasks are going to make it much harder to pinpoint the locus of interference, since with more things to do and several potential strategies available, there are more opportunities for interference. The subtle effects of temporal scheduling (particularly when models allow these effects to be non-linear) may well lead to complex task dynamics. Production-system models of working memory such as EPIC (Kieras et al., 1999) provide one example of this. To conclude, then, it is possible to challenge the resource-sharing hegemony as an explanation for DTI. One alternative has been identified very briefly. Whether this particular account is correct, however, is perhaps less important than the idea that various explanations are possible, and indeed healthy in stimulating and fuelling an evolution of theoretical frameworks.

THE CENTRAL EXECUTIVE AS . . . THE SAS

Asking someone to produce a very long string of responses (for example, digits, letters or keystrokes) in a random sequence is an unusual task. It is quite unlikely that the participant has attempted something like this before (or will attempt to do so again once outside the psychologist's lair). What lies behind the instructions to imagine drawing numbers from a hat, to imagine rolling a many-sided die? Van der Linden, Beerten & Pesenti (1998) put the case:

> According to Baddeley (1986, 1996), attempting to generate random sequences of items is an activity that places significant demands on the central executive component of working memory. Indeed, when subjects are required to produce random sequences of letter names or digits, they have to select new strategies to keep the sequence as random as possible, prevent the occurrence of schematic responses (e.g., alphabetic stereotypes, such as LMN), check that the responses are suitably random, and, if not, change the strategy. All these selection and control functions correspond exactly to the role that is assigned by Baddeley (1986) to the central executive system.
>
> (1998 p. 1)

Thus, one is encouraged to believe that random generation is a central executive task, in much the same way that articulatory suppression taps the phonological loop or visual noise taps the visuo-spatial sketchpad. Accordingly, random generation has been used concurrently with primary tasks to establish whether they have a central executive element to them (e.g., Lemaire, Abdi & Fayol, 1996; Logie, Gilhooly & Wynn, 1994). The relatively impaired random generation by Alzheimer patients (Brugger, Monsch, Salmon & Butters, 1996) would be consistent with the claim that these patients have reduced central executive capacity (see also Baddeley et al., 1991). In general, the central executive is likened to the Supervisory Attentional System (SAS) within the control of action model proposed by Norman & Shallice (1986), though as Jarrold (1997) points out, the SAS model has a rather broader scope than does the working memory executive. With respect to random generation, one view is that the central executive works at filtering out automatic, stereotyped sequences (Baddeley, 1986). A variant on this position is that the executive is responsible for activating response plans and for switching between plans so as to maintain response novelty (Baddeley, Emslie, Kolodny & Duncan, 1998).

It does not take much to establish that random generation is a difficult and demanding task. More important is, first, whether the description in the previous sentence is sufficient and second, whether random generation can be regarded as a valid measure of the central executive. A close examination suggests the answer to both questions is 'no'. It is possible to establish differences between randomisation of verbal and keypress sequences (Towse, 1998; Wagenaar, 1970) and subjects show a rather impressive ability to perform verbal and manual generation tasks simultaneously (Baddeley et al., 1998). These findings must cast doubt on the conclusion that randomisation involves some general or domain-independent system, because performance depends on what is being generated. Furthermore, factor-analytic studies converge with experimental evidence in showing there are several different facets to performance (Ginsburg & Karpiuk, 1994; Towse & Mclachlan, 1999; Towse & Neil, 1998). These task components appear to include immediate and long-term memory, attempts to choose responses with equal frequency, attempts to prevent chains of sequences and the avoidance of response repetition.

The above list of random generation processes is probably not exhaustive. Yet it does not need to be to make the point that it is not particularly satisfactory to regard random generation as a pure measure of central executive functioning. Generating random sequences involves a constellation of processes (as chapter 12 illustrates, the same can be said for the random generation of a single number). Task configurations such as the required response speed, the available response set and the response format are likely to shape the way these different processes come together in producing responses. In these terms, reference to 'central executive capacity' with respect to random generation can be no more than a mirage. For capacity is not a *determinant* of performance, rather it is an emergent *consequence* of the way many different processes interact. Thus, however much random generation might seem like a difficult central executive control task, it actually illustrates the inherent difficulties in the enterprise of segregating control functions. Complex tasks are unlikely to reveal neat demarcations of capacity constraints.

THE CENTRAL EXECUTIVE AS . . . A COORDINATION OR INTEGRATION SYSTEM

It should be increasingly apparent that the central executive construct is used when dealing with quite abstract functions — for example as a multi-purpose resource, or a device to select and control stereotyped schemata. The possibility that the central executive is a coordinating device follows similar lines. The notion that there are multiple systems within working memory that are rather circumscribed in what they can do, generates a belief that there must be some means by which information within these systems can be synchronised or coordinated. Otherwise, how does a coherent percept or representation emerge from the specialised systems? While previous sections have concentrated on the possible executive involvement in carrying out two independent tasks (i.e., dual task performance), at issue here is the mechanism which can efficiently combine working memory sub-processes.

Standard short-term memory tasks often predict reading and number skills moderately but there is nonetheless substantial unexplained variance. It follows, then, that since complex tasks such as reading and arithmetic require integrated and coordinated processing, a coordinating system might account for some remaining variance. For example, lexical, semantic, pragmatic and thematic representations need to come together (to be coordinated) to yield text comprehension. Indeed, measures of short-term memory have been thought to be relatively poor predictors of integrated cognitive tasks for the very reason that they do not simulate their complex demands (King & Just, 1991). Likewise, Swanson, Ashbaker & Lee (1996) suggest that the core deficit among learning-disabled children has more to do with coordinating memory information than the retention systems themselves (see also chapter 6).

These considerations are important; mathematics and reading undoubtedly represent complex tasks. However, neither the complexity itself, nor the idea of specialised systems for component skills, necessitates a general and supervisory coordinating device. Component processes could be self-organising (see Monsell, 1996). Alternatively, coordination mechanisms could function in quite specific ways, restricted to particular types of task. These alternatives mean that, if the notion of a coordination system is to have much scientific value, it should be possible to identify situations where the system plays some part. Several attempts have been made to do this. For example, aspects of a complex task with an element of coordination have been explored (Camos, Fayol & Barrouillet, 1999; Towse & Hitch, 1997; Yee, Hunt & Pellegrino, 1991). In the above instances, data have not supported the idea of a limited capacity coordination system, although in addition to methodological concerns, one can always question whether the particular tasks are appropriate for testing coordination skill.

One way to sum up the discussion of coordination so far is to note both the potential importance of the issue and the degree of uncertainty about its resolution. Accordingly, we recently examined whether a task that involved coordination of memory — bringing together in temporal synchrony verbal and visuo-spatial representations — provided a unique prediction of children's complex cognitive skills (Towse & Houston-Price, in press). Children were studied because their scholastic development, obviously important theoretically and practically, can be measured with standardised tests, and might be related to coordination ability in combining different memory stimuli.

The study involved computerised tasks for 5–9-year-old children. Verbal short-term memory was assessed using digit span and visuo-spatial memory using a form of Corsi span. Both of these were delivered visually on computer to minimise task differences. There was also a third memory task, combination span, where both digit and Corsi tasks were presented simultaneously. Children were asked to remember sequences of both spatial locations and digits appearing at these various locations. Measures of children's articulation rate, reading and numerical ability were also collected. Since combination span involved digit and Corsi tasks and these constituent elements were assessed separately, it was possible to determine

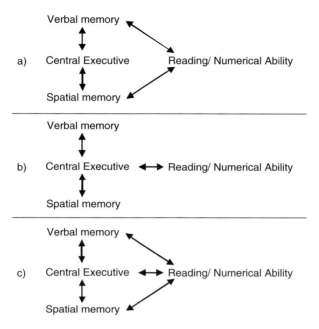

Figure 11.2   Idealised depiction of the relationships between memory systems and scholastic ability.

whether the combined task predicted scholastic ability once the component memory scores had been accounted for.

Figure 11.2 illustrates in simplified form some of the potential patterns of results (double-headed arrows are used since no causal relationship can be assumed). As represented in Figure 11.2a, the combination span task itself may not be a reliable indicator of cognitive skill, because it does not play any role in cognitive ability that cannot already be explained by its component parts. Alternatively, if reading, arithmetic and the combination task all rely on the central executive, this may be the mediating variable — represented by Figure 11.2b. A third scenario, shown as Figure 11.2c, is that both memory systems and the central executive all play an important part, producing a more complete set of interrelationships.

Figure 11.3 shows the mean span levels achieved at each age for each span task. Interestingly, while combination span scores are smaller than digit or Corsi span scores, they are by no means half these values. This is despite the observation that children must remember twice as much information for the combination span task as for the other tasks for any given span score (a combination span score of three involves three digits and three spatial positions). This certainly implies that children were using more than a single memory system to retain the different pieces of information.

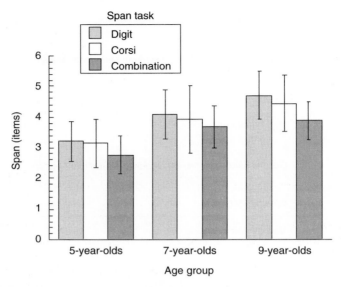

Figure 11.3   Mean span scores and standard deviations for each age group.

Cognitive ability or attainment was measured by combining children's scores from the standardised number skill and word reading tests. Data showed a significant correlation between combination span and these ability scores, $r(73) = .73$, $p<.001$. However, as Figure 11.2a illustrates, this relationship could be illusory — it may really be the digit and Corsi span parts of the test that relate to the ability scores, and the combination span test merely feeds off this by incorporating digit and Corsi elements. The key question, then, is whether, in a regression model, combination span is a significant predictor of reading and maths ability once digit span and Corsi span relationships have already been accounted for. Alternatively phrased, whether there is a partial correlation between combination span and ability controlling for age and the other variables. The significant and unique correlations between variables are shown in Figure 11.4. Whilst the pattern of data do not correspond exactly to any of the idealised predictions in Figure 11.2, it is apparent that the combination span task does indeed provide unique information about reading and number skills.

We can take these data further, however. Figure 11.4 shows a composite measure of ability derived from both reading and number tasks. The relationships between variables can be considered for reading and number skills independently. Why would one want to do this? Well, on the basis of the findings so far, one can ask whether the same coordination capacity supports both reading and number skills. That is, if coordination is the function that links combination span, reading and number, then partialling out that commonality should eliminate the relationship. Indeed, the

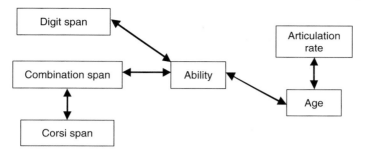

Figure 11.4   Path diagram illustrating the significant relationships between pairs of variables after controlling for all others.

combination span — reading ability correlation was no longer significant after controlling for number skill, $r(67) = .17, p>.10$. However, combination span and number skill remained correlated when reading ability was partialled out, $r(67) = .26, p<.05$. Given that number and reading are highly related, this is a strong test of the idea that there are separable elements to whatever combination span measures. Thus the significant remaining correlation is quite impressive, implying domain-specific aspects to the combination span task in addition to any domain-general component.

Has this experiment uncovered the real Cinderella? On a first reading, one might be tempted to say 'yes'. After all, combination span, a task that requires the integration or coordination of different memory information, does provide a reliable index of tasks also thought to involve processes of coordination. We suspect that many would take this as sufficient evidence of central executive involvement in combination span. However, several further issues should be borne in mind. The (albeit tentative) separation of reading and number abilities in the analysis of individual differences shows an asymmetric pattern of results, revealing that there is no simple single link between combination span (the 'central executive' task) and school ability.

A second and in many ways more important consideration is that, thus far, it has been assumed that the combination span task measures central executive coordination ability, a processing resource allowing information to be accurately integrated. It seems a reasonable enough place to start. However, based on the present results, it seems inappropriate to claim that the combination span task measures coordination capacity. Inappropriate, because it merely re-describes the results without explaining the cause of the relationship between the span task and the ability measures.

In terms of accounting for the pattern of data, there are several properties of combination span that may be important, making the task distinguishable from the digit and Corsi span elements that it is formed from. To consider some of these:

- Performance requires a balanced memory strategy — avoiding the temptation to pay too much notice to either spatial positions or numeric identities, because task success requires both dimensions to be remembered accurately.
- The speed of encoding may be important for a task with complex (multiple) aspects in a way that is not the case for simpler tests. A presentation rate of one second for either a single item or a combined item may result in quite different constraints on the child's encoding mechanisms.
- Performance may reflect the extent to which at some stage the two dimensions become associated or form a relationship in the child's mind, so that at retrieval the attributes cross-cue each other. Children who make such associative links between the two memoranda are likely to show a recall advantage.
- Strategies for recalling items and the speed at which this takes place (e.g. Cowan, 1999) may be particularly important if digit and Corsi aspects of the task are differentially sensitive to the speed at which answers are given. That is, what may be most relevant is the way children retrieve the set of answers, as opposed to the way they retain them as memory items.
- It has been reported previously that recall of cross-modal information is superior when organised by presentation modality or channel rather than by time of onset (Broadbent, 1956). Since the combination span task required recall in temporal order (the location and identity of the first item, then the location and identity of the second, etc.) children who used the most task-appropriate strategy for remembering the streams would benefit the most.

This list does not represent a comprehensive profile of the tasks, nor are we in a position to confirm which of these accounts is the most important. Discriminating between these possibilities would have to be driven by further research. The core point, however, is that the present results mark the beginning, not the end, of the quest for understanding the coordination of information in working memory. While highly interesting, the data do not show that combination span is a central executive task. Only that combination span is a memory task that uniquely predicts scholastic ability. Thus, just invoking central executive capacity as an explanation for combination span performance is insufficient, being of little help in developing an appreciation of the task. Given the specific possibilities mentioned above, a theoretical account stressing coordination capacity alone may also be rather misleading.

Framed in terms of the Cinderella story, the moral to be drawn is that in the continuous search for the foot that fits the slipper, one might forget that the real goal is not actually the foot at all, but the heroine it uniquely identifies. The Prince fell in love with Cinderella, not her arch or her instep.

Likewise, the priority must be to understand what a cognitive task entails, not to merely label it as 'executive' or otherwise. As emphasised in the section on the central executive as SAS, research ought to move beyond the idea that there is a processing resource (or even processing resources) out there, waiting to be captured by the right task. Instead, there is a need to develop an account of what the 'resources' are, to understand the principles underlying complex behaviour and their implementation. Leaving aside various methodological and analytic questions (see Towse & Houston-Price, in press), the study gives possible clues, but not answers, to these issues.

CONCLUDING REMARKS

The book's motivational questions have been addressed rather implicitly so far, through the description and evaluation of the central executive concept in its different guises. Having considered the evidence, it is now possible to respond directly to the four thematic questions. Undoubtedly, a major reason for studying the central executive is its importance to the working memory model. Many and varied vital cognitive functions have been attributed to this system. So it is paramount that researchers think seriously about the executive. A *strength* of the central executive concept is that it offers the potential to explain aspects of developmental and adult skills that have considerable practical significance in the lives of individuals. For example, in terms of reading comprehension and numerical computation. Furthermore, not only have considerable theoretical claims been made about the executive, but also at an empirical level, tests of working memory span correlate with important abilities among both children and adults.

The central executive has been thought of in several different ways. A common thread, perhaps, is that the executive is viewed within a hierarchical framework and is situated above other systems. Beyond this, however, the connections between the various functions are not as clear. From one perspective, this means that *there are rather few competing models* to the central executive because, although there are serious problems with the various conceptions of the central executive, the prospects for any overarching explanation for the processes of cognitive control do not look promising. Thus, as described here, *the main weakness* of the central executive concept lies in its attempt to be all things to all tasks, in its insistence on being a pervasive influence. This approach generates a burden that is difficult to carry. As already described, alternatives to the central executive can be, and have been proposed for specific phenomena, but they are just that: specific. It should also be apparent that we conclude that the *future* for the central executive is less than rosy. We suggest that it is time to give up on this theoretical fantasy, at least in the form it is often used. Indeed, once the central executive slipper is finally discarded, accepting it was but a temporary creation, theoretical life might take on new purpose and renewed vigour. For the research questions that prompted the executive account have not been fully answered and remain vibrant research topics.

If one accepts the conclusion that separate explanations are required for phenomena traditionally bundled together as part of executive control, then this must affect working memory theory as described elsewhere. For example, given the problems in trying to establish a coherent model of highly centralised control, it is possible to point towards the desirability of emancipating the 'slave' systems. Space does not permit a detailed treatment of how this might be implemented and in any case this would clearly go beyond the scope of a central executive chapter. In the broadest terms, though, the transformation of representations within working memory would become more self-organising and the systems involved in the maintenance and processing of information would become more elaborate. At any rate, it seems inevitable that the dissipation of power from the central executive (an argument distinct from the mere fractionation of function advocated by Baddeley et al., 1998) must have implications for researchers in other areas of working memory. No longer shackled to an executive, working memory systems would acquire the controlling power necessary to carry out their functions.

The quest for the central executive has been compared to an open-ended Cinderella story. This has allowed us, hopefully, to illustrate a number of features of current thinking about the executive construct, and to emphasise answers to the book questions. There are some attendant dangers in the approach, however. For instance, it might be tempting to read the chapter and then dismiss it as merely mischievous, as impudence. That would be unfortunate because the primary aim has been to provide a perspective on this area of working memory, a way of describing the situation that has developed. For researchers in the area, the quest for central executive functions has almost come to be the only game in town; part of our concern has been to indicate the dearth of alternative lines of thought. Another danger is that, by drawing some parallels between the Cinderella and the central executive stories, the degree of correspondence becomes exaggerated. The allegory only works up to a certain point, and the true picture of the central executive is complicated. Nonetheless, it is not just by the literal accuracy of a fairy story that it comes to be remembered, but also its message. Perhaps someone does have the happy-ever-after script for the central executive story. Just don't hold your breath waiting.

ACKNOWLEDGEMENTS

John Towse has been supported by the ESRC (grants R000236113 & R000222789) and Carmel Houston-Price has been supported by an MRC studentship. The chapter has benefited greatly from the constructive comments of several other book contributors, as well as from the encouragement of final-year students at Royal Holloway who reviewed an earlier draft.

BACKGROUND READING

Baddeley, A. (1996). Exploring the central executive. *Quarterly Journal of Experimental Psychology*, *49A*(1), 5–28.

Baddeley's review paper contains a defence of the idea of a central executive, and so offers an alternative, more positive viewpoint to the current chapter. He refers to random generation data that subsequently appeared in Baddeley et al. (1998).

Engle, R. W. (1996). Working memory and retrieval: An inhibition-resource approach. In J. T. E. Richardson, R. Engle, L. Hasher, R. Logie, E. Stolzfus, & R. Zacks (Eds.), *Working memory and cognition* (pp. 89–120). New York: Oxford University Press.

Engle focuses on the interpretation of working memory span data, and in doing so, covers a section of this important literature.

Monsell, S. (1996). Control of mental processes. In V. Bruce (Ed.), *Unsolved mysteries of the mind: Tutorial essays in cognition* (pp. 93–148). Hove: Erlbaum (UK) Taylor & Francis.

Monsell makes a number of pertinent remarks about mental control. There is a detailed account of a 'task-switching' paradigm, which requires individuals to juggle between competing task instructions. Monsell shows how a careful task analysis can take theory beyond a simple reference to 'executive control'.

Emerson, M. J., Miyake, A., & Rettinger, D. A. (1999). Individual differences in integrating and coordinating multiple sources of information. *Journal of Experimental Psychology: Learning, Memory and Cognition*, *25*(5), 1300–1321.

In the context of the combination span task described in the current chapter, Emerson et al. provide a useful contemporary discussion of integration and coordination abilities.

REFERENCES

Allport, A. D., Antonis, B., & Reynolds, P. (1972). On the division of attention: A disproof of the single channel hypothesis. *Quarterly Journal of Experimental Psychology, 24,* 225–235.

Baddeley, A. D. (1986). *Working memory.* Oxford: Clarendon Press.

Baddeley, A. D. (1992). Is working memory working? *Quarterly Journal of Experimental Psychology, 44A*(1), 1–31.

Baddeley, A. D. (1996). Exploring the central executive. *Quarterly Journal of Experimental Psychology, 49A*(1), 5–28.

Baddeley, A. D., Bressi, S., Della Sala, S., Logie, R., & Spinnler, H. (1991). The decline of working memory in Alzheimer's disease. *Brain, 114,* 2521–2542.

Baddeley, A. D., Emslie, H., Kolodny, J., & Duncan, J. (1998). Random generation and the executive control of working memory. *Quarterly Journal of Experimental Psychology, 51A*(4), 819–852.

Baddeley, A. D., & Hitch, G. J. (1974). Working memory. In G. Bower (Ed.), *The psychology of learning and motivation: Advances in research and theory* (pp. 47–90). New York: Academic Press.

Baddeley, A. D., & Logie, R. H. (1999). Working memory: The multiple component model. In A. Miyake & P. Shah (Eds.), *Models of working memory* (pp. 28–61). New York: Cambridge University Press.

Broadbent, D. E. (1956). Successive responses to simultaneous stimuli. *Quarterly Journal of Experimental Psychology, 8,* 145–152.

Brugger, P., Monsch, A. U., Salmon, D. P., & Butters, N. (1996). Random number generation in dementia of the Alzheimer type: A test of frontal executive functions. *Neuropsychologia, 34*(2), 97–103.

Byrne, M. D. (1998). Taking a computational approach to aging: The SPAN theory of working memory. *Psychology and Aging, 13*(2), 309–322.

Camos, V., Fayol, M., & Barrouillet, P. (1999). L'activité de denombrement chez l'enfant: double-tache ou procedure? *Année Psychologique, 99*(4), 623–645.

Caplan, D., & Waters, G. S. (1999). Working memory and sentence comprehension. *Behavioral and Brain Sciences, 22*(1), 77–126.

Case, R., Kurland, M., & Goldberg, J. (1982). Operational efficiency and the growth of short term memory span. *Journal of Experimental Child Psychology, 33,* 386–404.

Cowan, N. (1999). The differential maturation of two processing rates related to digit span. *Journal of Experimental Child Psychology, 72,* 193–209.

Daneman, M., & Carpenter, P. A. (1980). Individual differences in working memory and reading. *Journal of Verbal Learning and Verbal Behavior, 19,* 450–466.

Engle, R. W. (1996). Working memory and retrieval: An inhibition-resource approach. In J. T. E. Richardson, R. Engle, L. Hasher, R. Logie, E. Stolzfus, & R. Zacks (Eds.), *Working memory and cognition* (pp. 89–120). New York: Oxford University Press.

Engle, R. W., Cantor, J., & Carullo, J. J. (1992). Individual differences in working memory and comprehension: A test of four hypotheses. *Journal of Experimental Psychology: Learning, Memory and Cognition, 18,* 972–992.

Ginsburg, N., & Karpiuk, P. (1994). Random generation: Analysis of the responses. *Perceptual and Motor Skills, 79,* 1059–1067.

Jarrold, C. (1997). Pretend play in autism: Executive explanations. In J. Russell (Ed.), *Autism as an executive disorder* (pp. 101–140). Oxford: OUP.

Just, M. A., & Carpenter, P. A. (1992). A capacity theory of comprehension: Individual differences in working memory. *Psychological Review, 99*(1), 122–149.

Kieras, D. E., Meyer, D. E., Mueller, S., & Seymour, T. (1999). Insights in working memory from the perspective of the EPIC architecture for modeling skilled perceptual-motor and cognitive human performance. In A. Miyake & P. Shah (Eds.), *Models of working memory* (pp. 183–223). New York: Cambridge University Press.

King, J., & Just, M. A. (1991). Individual differences in syntactic processing: The role of working memory. *Journal of Memory and Language, 30,* 580–602.

Leather, C. V., & Henry, L. A. (1994). Working memory span and phonological awareness tasks as predictors of early reading ability. *Journal of Experimental Child Psychology, 58,* 88–111.

Lemaire, P., Abdi, H., & Fayol, M. (1996). The role of working memory resources in simple cognitive arithmetic. *European Journal of Cognitive Psychology, 8*(1), 73–103.

Logie, R. H., Gilhooly, K. J., & Wynn, V. (1994). Counting on working memory in arithmetic problem solving. *Memory & Cognition, 22*(4), 395–410.

Miyake, A., Just, M. A., & Carpenter, P. A. (1994). Working memory constraints on the resolution of lexical ambiguity: Maintaining multiple interpretations in neutral contexts. *Journal of Memory and Language, 33,* 175–202.

Monsell, S. (1996). Control of mental processes. In V. Bruce (Ed.), *Unsolved mysteries of the mind: Tutorial essays in cognition* (pp. 93–148). Hove: Erlbaum (UK) Taylor & Francis.

Morris, N., & Jones, D. M. (1990). Memory updating in working memory: The role of the central executive. *British Journal of Psychology, 81,* 111–121.

Neumann, O. (1987). Beyond capacity: A functional view of attention. In H. Heuer & A. F. Sanders (Eds.), *Perspectives on perception and action* (pp. 361–394). Hillsdale, NJ: Lawrence Erlbaum Associates Inc.

Norman, D. A., & Shallice, T. (1986). Attention to action: Willed and automatic control of behavior. In R. J. Davidson, G. E. Schwartz, & D. Shapiro (Eds.), *Consciousness and self-regulation* (Vol. 4, pp. 1–18). New York: Plenum.

Rosen, V. M., & Engle, R. W. (1998). Working memory capacity and suppression. *Journal of Memory and Language, 39,* 418–436.

Stoltzfus, E. R., Hasher, L., & Zacks, R. T. (1996). Working memory and aging: Current status of the inhibitory view. In J. T. Richardson, R. Engle, L. Hasher, R. Logie, E. Stoltzfus, & R. Zacks (Eds.), *Working memory and human cognition* (pp. 66–88). Oxford: Oxford University Press.

Swanson, H. L., Ashbaker, M. H., & Lee, C. (1996). Learning-disabled readers' working memory as a function of processing demands. *Journal of Experimental Child Psychology, 61,* 242–275.

Towse, J. N. (1998). On random generation and the central executive of working memory. *British Journal of Psychology, 89*(1), 77–101.

Towse, J. N., & Hitch, G. J. (1995). Is there a relationship between task demand and storage space in tests of working memory capacity? *Quarterly Journal of Experimental Psychology, 48A*(1), 108–124.

Towse, J. N., & Hitch, G. J. (1997). Integrating information in object counting: A role for a central coordination process? *Cognitive Development, 12*(3), 393–422.

Towse, J. N., Hitch, G. J., & Hutton, U. (1998). A reevaluation of working memory capacity in children. *Journal of Memory and Language, 39*(2), 195–217.

Towse, J. N., Hitch, G. J., & Hutton, U. (2000). On the interpretation of working memory span in adults. *Memory and Cognition, 28*(3), 341–348.

Towse, J. N., & Houston-Price, C. M. T. (in press). Combining representations in working memory: A brief report. *British Journal of Developmental Psychology*.

Towse, J. N., & Mclachlan, A. (1999). An exploration of random generation among children. *British Journal of Developmental Psychology*, *17*(3), 363–380.

Towse, J. N., & Neil, D. (1998). Analyzing human random generation behavior: A review of methods used and a computer program for describing performance. *Behavior Research Methods, Instruments & Computers*, *30*(4), 583–591.

Turner, M. L., & Engle, R. W. (1989). Is working memory capacity task dependent? *Journal of Memory and Language*, *28*, 127–154.

Van der Linden, M., Beerten, A., & Pesenti, M. (1998). Age-related differences in random generation. *Brain and Cognition*, *38*, 1–16.

Wagenaar, W. A. (1970). Subjective randomness and the capacity to generate information. *Acta Psychologica*, *33*, 233–242.

Waters, G. S., & Caplan, D. (1996). The measurement of verbal working memory capacity and its relation to reading comprehension. *Quarterly Journal of Experimental Psychology*, *49A*(1), 51–70.

Yee, P. L., Hunt, E., & Pellegrino, J. W. (1991). Coordinating cognitive information: Task effects and individual differences in integrating information from several sources. *Cognitive Psychology*, *23*, 615–680.

12 Specifying the central executive may require complexity

Jon May

The central executive (CE) component of the Baddeley & Hitch (1974) working memory (WM) model was initially intended to avoid the need for the model to deal with phenomena that went beyond the scope of short-term memory problems. The application of the model beyond laboratory tasks has inevitably brought more and more of these 'complex' aspects of task performance into play. While the general conception of the CE as an attentional organiser or contention scheduler has allowed some of these aspects to be dealt with, there remains no detailed account of how the CE is organised, how it functions, or more importantly, how it might fail to function. With the rise of interest in 'dysexecutive syndrome' this has become a critical problem for the application of the WM model.

In this chapter, I argue that the problem lies in the absence of a clear distinction in the WM model between processing and storage resources, and in the lack of detail about how the CE communicates with the slave subsystems. This has led to two possible views on the operation of the slave subsystems. They can either be conceived of as storage mechanisms that passively receive their particular form of representation from the CE, hold it, and then return it to the CE for processing; or they can actively process and modify the representations themselves, organising and elaborating the content. The latter role requires the development and application of stored knowledge by each subsystem, something that is not specified within the original conception of WM. These two views are not always recognised as being distinct by WM researchers.

An alternative approach is exemplified by Barnard (1985, 1999). The emphasis of his Interacting Cognitive Subsystems (ICS) model is upon the flow of mental representations between different levels of representation, and in the competition for processing resources within each cognitive subsystem rather than between them. This chapter follows on from the previous chapter by presenting an account of CE phenomena within the ICS model. As a more detailed description, ICS is able to make distinctions where the WM model cannot, particularly with regard to the internal functions of all subsystems and on the interchange of information between the two central subsystems. The breadth of the ICS model means that is less economical in its accounts of traditional WM tasks, but as the scope of research moves onto more complex tasks, especially the investigation of the role of the CE, a more highly specified model may be necessary.

SIMPLICITY VERSUS COMPLEXITY

As a model of the 'temporary holding and manipulation of information during the performance of a range of cognitive tasks such as comprehension, learning and reasoning' (Baddeley, 1986, p. 34) there can be no doubt that the specific model of working memory proposed by Baddeley & Hitch (1974) has proven remarkably successful and durable. It was initially able to accommodate the phenomena that its predecessors had been able to deal with, notably those of Broadbent (1958) and Atkinson & Shiffrin (1968), as well as with subsequent phenomena that they could not encompass. In its own right, it has shown its facility as a conceptual tool in generating twenty-five years worth of empirical and applied research, without too many large cracks appearing.

Part of its attractiveness for researchers is its apparent simplicity. Simplicity in a model has long been recognised as a virtue, since at least Occam's time. Complexity is seen as undesirable, because it takes researchers longer to learn to apply a complex model, and a complex model might predict multiple possible patterns of results for experiments, depending upon aspects of the testing situation that are not open to experimental control. In Dawkins' (1989) Meme analogy for the natural selection of ideas, simplicity allows both rapid reproduction (i.e., communication of a model into the heads of new researchers) and the colonisation of new niches (i.e., application to new problems). Once a problem has been identified and conceived of in terms of a simple model, it becomes almost impossible for the proponents of a complex model to persuade people to reconceive it in different terms, even if they are able to offer a richer, but more complex, account of the phenomenon. Just as grey squirrels outbreed red squirrels, and can eat nuts before they are ripe enough for the reds to digest, so simple models can prevent people learning complex models, and can provide partial answers to problems before anyone attempts to apply the complex models.

Simplicity brings penalties too, though, if it leads people to disregard or gloss over the details that are there if you look for them. Although the description of the working memory model makes it clear that (overall) it should be seen as a single, limited-capacity system, the famous 'egg and boxes' diagram dissociates verbal and visual short-term memory phenomena into two domains, with the problematic issues of their integration and control allocated to the central executive. A consequence is that some researchers focus on issues arising from problems in verbal tasks, others have concentrated on problems in the visual domain; but the relationship between the two domains is often overlooked, and some even see it as a strength that the two 'modalities' of short-term memory should be dealt with differently. It is therefore possible to find detailed connectionist models of serial digit recall tasks (as described in chapter 8), which are based solely upon the operation of the phonological loop (PL), and which make little reference to the function of the CE or the visuo-spatial sketchpad (VSSP), even though the models are based on data from visually presented tasks. Similarly, there is a programme of research into the possible fractionation of the VSSP into spatial and visual components (see chapter 2), that does not consider any implications for functionally splitting the PL in a similar fashion. A noticeable absence from the party, as John Towse and Carmel Houston-Price have described in chapter 11, has been detailed work on the central executive, despite the best efforts of Baddeley to point people in that direction (e.g., 1986, chapter 10; 1996).

Even if this separation into camps were not a problem for a model that is supposed to be unitary, the ubiquitous diagram illustrated in Figure 1.1 (chapter 1) is not a complete representation of the WM model. It is most accurately labelled as a 'simplified representation' (as is Figure 4.6 in Baddeley, 1986, p. 71). When you start to ask what the phonological loop 'does', or why the diagram has double-headed arrows between the visuo-spatial sketchpad and the central executive, but single-headed arrows between the phonological loop and the central executive, the picture becomes more complex. The phonological loop includes a pre-categorical acoustical store (PAS), which feeds into a phonological short-term store (PSS) 'which is maintained and refreshed by the process of articulation' (1986, p. 84), and which drives that same articulatory control process (ACP). The single phonological loop box, then consists of at least the PSS and the ACP, interacting in a reciprocal manner, and fulfils both storage and processing functions. The visuo-spatial sketchpad is less defined, but may be preceded by an iconic memory (analogous perhaps to the PAS), and fulfils functions for 'retaining and manipulating images' (1986, p. 143), so it too carries out both storage and processing. Taking these details into account, the specification of the WM model becomes more complicated, as Figure 12.1 attempts to show.

The representation of storage and processing within single boxes can be defended on the grounds of simplification for exposition, but it does mask a real issue. The debate as to whether processing and storage functions compete for resources is far from resolved and the WM model is, if anywhere, in the camp that sees them as independent and non-competitive. The ambiguity on this issue is problematic theoretically, because the recency effect has been attributed to the behaviour of the 'passive storage processes' of the model acting without rehearsal (e.g., 1986, p. 145), whereas patterns of item intrusion, confusion, transposition and eventual forgetting have been attributed to the active processing subcomponents becoming overloaded as span increases to the point where the processing time per item becomes longer than the time taken for them to decay significantly.

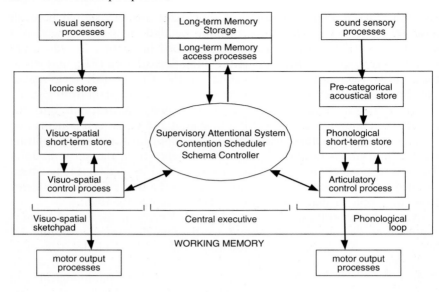

Figure 12.1   A less simplified representation of the processing and storage
resources of the Working Memory model.

A side effect of this ambiguity is a confusion about the role of the central
executive, as noted in the previous chapter. Baddeley describes it as:

> the residual area of ignorance about working memory which we are
> consistently attempting to reduce. We have assumed that the central
> executive has attentional capacities and is capable of selecting and
> operating control processes.

(1986, p. 71)

The reference to attention has subsequently been developed and related to
Norman & Shallice's (1986) Supervisory Attentional System or SAS
(Baddeley, 1996), and is worth noting here because, by elimination, it
implies that the slave subsystems do not have attentional capacities, and
that for us to attend to or be aware of the contents of short-term memory
(STM), the slave subsystems' contents must be conveyed to and processed
by the CE. This interpretation is supported by Baddeley's (1993) arguments
about WM and consciousness, which refer to experiments on thought
suppression by tasks that load the CE. There must be some communication
between the CE and the slave subsystems, after all, or the model as a whole
could hardly be unitary. The next point in this quotation, that the CE
directs the operations of the control processes, implies that it does not
directly communicate with the storage components of the slave subsystems.
This leaves the control processes responsible for rehearsal, manipulation

and conscious access of material in STM: functions that would be represented by separate processes in a more detailed model. The picture is already becoming much more complex than the simple representation would suggest, and the quotation goes on to raise the possibility of further complexity:

> We tend to assume a single central controller, but this is not essential to the model. If the control functions could be shown to be carried out by the interactions of the various cognitive subsystems, as for example Barnard (1985) suggests, we would be happy to accept this.
>
> (Baddeley, 1986, p. 71)

Despite the subtitle of his 1985 paper mentioning short-term memory, Barnard has not positioned his Interacting Cognitive Subsystems (ICS) model as a direct competitor to WM, since it is not topicalised solely upon STM phenomena, nor is it just a model of CE function. It has the more ambitious aim of describing all of human cognitive activity, and is consequently both more complex than the WM model, and less specific. Complex does not necessarily mean complicated, though: while it contains more boxes than the simplified representation of the WM model, each box has a more specific responsibility. Unlike the WM model, the internal structure of the boxes is also specified, and they are all the same, so once something has been learnt about the operation of one box, it can be applied generally. One of the surprising consequences of this approach is that, as the previous quotation intimated, CE phenomena do not require special purpose boxes, but more of the same sort of boxes. In fact, although ICS appears to be a more complex model in terms of the number of components, it may provide a simpler explanation of CE phenomena than the WM model.

HIGH-LEVEL SIMILARITIES BETWEEN ICS AND WM

An overview of Barnard's model is presented in Figure 12.2, together with a detailed view 'inside' one of the subsystems. The model works by identifying the different forms of mental representation that are required during the course of some cognitive task, and working out how the sensory information obtained from the world can be combined with and interpreted in terms of information in long-term memory, and then used to drive behavioural actions.

For those familiar with the WM model, this representation of ICS has a helpful overall similarity in its gross structure. At the top are three 'boxes' dealing with sound and speech, at first sight apparently much like the PL.

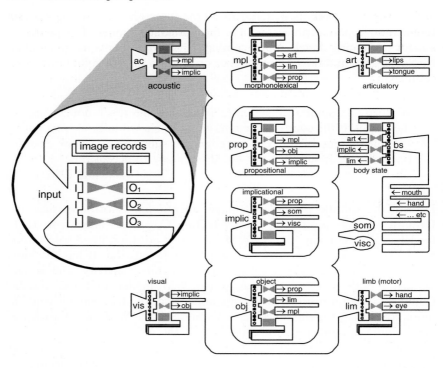

Figure 12.2   An overview of Barnard's Interacting Cognitive Subsystems (ICS), and (inset) the common internal architecture of each subsystem.

At the bottom are three boxes dealing with visuo-spatial information and motor action, again, apparently like the VSSP. Three is more complex than one, of course, but we have already seen that the PL and VSSP actually contain a lot of detail. In ICS, the leftmost 'sensory' boxes correspond somewhat to the pre-categorical levels of processing that precede the storage components of the WM model, one for acoustic sensations, the other for visual sensations. The rightmost 'effector' boxes produce articulatory and motor output, and so do somewhat more finalised work than the WM slave subsystems' control processes. In between them are abstract structural subsystems specialised for the information derived from each modality. On the right of the model is a third sensory subsystem, for Body State information, that has no direct parallel in the WM model, but which allows proprioceptive, olfactory and visceral sensations to be dealt with. In the centre of Barnard's model, where the CE would be in the WM model, appear two more boxes which will be detailed below. These two subsystems, their interactions, and the communication between them and the rest of the system, give rise to the cognitive activity that could not be accounted for solely by the slave subsystems in the WM model.

This superficial similarity between the two models is comforting but should not be pursued too far. The big difference comes in the internal structure of Barnard's boxes, shown in the inset section to the left of Figure 12.2. Each of the subsystems contain some processing capabilities, represented by the I→O and I→I channels (I=Input, and O=Output), and a storage capability, represented by the Image Records. Each subsystem can only process or store its own form of representation (that is, I), and each of its I→O processes produce a representations for another subsystem (the effector subsystems producing non-cognitive muscular commands). The I→I process 'copies' incoming representation into the subsystem's Image Record, and is, in effect, writing to long-term memory. On its own, a subsystem can do very little, but when all nine are combined into the complete system, it becomes possible for information to flow between them, and it is this flow that characterises cognition.

Because the subsystems only produce two or three output representations each, rather than all eight possible, the actual patterns of flow are much more constrained than might at first appear. Linear flows from sensation to effector output are the simplest. Sound sensations can be transformed into morphonolexical sound structures by the AC→MPL process within the acoustic subsystem. These structures can then be received by the morphonolexical subsystem, where they can be transformed into articulatory representations by the MPL→ART process. These can be received by the articulatory subsystem, and finally processed into the muscular commands necessary for speech. A similar linear flow from visual sensation, through the visuo-spatial object structures, to Limb representations, and finally motor action, can be conducted by the *VIS→OBJ: :OBJ→LIM: :LIM→Motor* sequence of processes. (The double colons in this notation indicate an exchange of representations between subsystems, and the * an exchange of information with the world via the senses or by overt behavioural responses.)

This just describes the I→O transformation processes, though. At the same time, the I→I 'copy' process within each subsystem can be active upon the representations that it is receiving, copying them (unaltered) into its own image records. Here is the vital distinction between the storage mechanisms (the image record), the process by which information is stored (the copy process) and other processing. This operation provides each subsystem with a permanent trace of everything that has ever been processed into its own representation. Importantly, the outputs of a subsystem are stored by the subsystems that receive them, not by the one that produces them. These stored records may be accessed in the future if the incoming representations are of insufficient detail or quality, or are arriving at too fast a rate for the processes to produce a stable output. In this situation, the incoming representation currently being copied into the image record by the I→I process 'revives' similar stored records that can be used as input by one of the I→O processes, instead of it using the currently arriving information directly. This revival mechanism can operate either to retrieve records stored (and perhaps abstracted) over the long term, or those that have only just arrived (giving rise to a useful mode of activity called 'buffered processing', with the phenomenological consequence of focal awareness). It is also possible for a process to disengage from the input stream completely and continue to repeatedly process a single record from the image records.

ACCOUNTING FOR STM IN ICS

In this limited description of ICS, one account of short-term memory is already possible. If a string of digits were being read to a listener, the acoustic representations would be stored in their acoustic image record and transformed to morphonolexical representations, stored there and transformed to articulatory representations, finally being stored there and used as input to the ART→speech output processes. Since the ART→speech processes are not being used to produce overt speech and shadow the presented digits, they are actually producing subvocalised output. This supports immediate production of the prepared vocalisation when it is eventually required (by the end of the presentation, perhaps, or a recall signal). While the presented list remains below the capacity of a single articulatory representation, this is all the processing that is required for STM, and all of the other processes would be available for other ('secondary') tasks. As soon as the capacity of the ART→speech processes are exceeded, though, a strategic choice must be made. Either the older material can be replaced by new material that is arriving (a good choice for a free recall task, perhaps), or the processes must disengage from the input stream and continue to rehearse the earlier material, a mode of activity equivalent to articulatory rehearsal in the WM model.

This explains recall of very short series, or recall of either the end or the start of longer lists. To account for the recall of longer lists, and how the 'strategic choice' of processing configuration is made, the two boxes in the centre of the model need to be introduced. Like the boxes described so far, they too contain I→O transformation processes, I→I 'copy' processes and image records for storage. The upper box processes propositional representations (PROP), which are semantic facts that can be derived from sentences processed by the MPL→PROP transformation, or from scenes processed by the OBJ→PROP transformation. Propositions express attributes of and relationships between entities. The lower box processes implicational representations (IMPLIC), which are high-level schematic models of the world, and which can be derived from sequences of propositions by the PROP→IMPLIC transformation, or directly from patterns in sensory representations by the AC→IMPLIC and VIS→IMPLIC transformations.

Barnard's model's origins lie in psycholinguistics, and the distinction between propositional and implicational levels of representation become clear when their roles in comprehension are considered. Where the propositions in a verbal discourse might contain several semantic facts ('I was proceeding in a north-easterly direction at a steady pace towards the suspect'), the implications that one constructs from them carry the real 'meaning' of the discourse. To a reader sharing my own culturally derived set of implicational schemas, the 'I' in this discourse has the stereotypical characteristics of a rather dim policeman: these 'facts' are not provided by the discourse, but are inferred by the PROP→IMPLIC transformation, and by revival from the implicational image record. Similarly, a propositional description of a visual scene might allow one to reconstruct it, but to understand what was happening, an implicational representation would be necessary.

The propositional subsystem is sufficient to complete the description of simple STM tasks. As well as receiving input from the morphonolexical and object subsystems, the propositional subsystem can output to them too. This allows reciprocal loops of activity to arise within the model, whereby information may be repeatedly exchanged between the propositional and the two structural subsystems. It also allows the propositional subsystem to provide the 'cue' needed to act as the key for the structural subsystems to revive records from their image records. Here we have, in ICS, the basis for the complex communication between the CE and the slave subsystems that is not specified in the simpler WM model.

Returning to the serial digit recall task, each subsystem contains two or three processes, so each subsystem can turn its representations into two or three output representations simultaneously. In this respect, they do not compete for any limited processing capacity. They are limited, though. Each process can only produce one output representation at a time, so, for example, two acoustically presented words cannot both be converted by AC→MPL into phonemic forms simultaneously, but must be dealt with serially, using the image record as a buffer. Once the representation of a word reaches the morphonolexical subsystem, however, the parallel processes MPL→ART and MPL→PROP can produce their outputs simultaneously. This means that a fourth trace of the digit sequence is laid down, in the propositional image record.

Unlike the representations being passed through the top three subsystems, the propositional representation is not temporally based. The identity of the entities in propositions is of primary importance, but there is little or no order information, apart from that afforded by the structure that the listener imposes upon the stream. By default, the first entity in a propositional stream serves as the topic of the representation, with subsequent entities being stored as an unordered predicate set. This representation can be used to provide verification about whether a candidate item was actually in the presented list (again, useful in free recall and recall of word lists), but not its position (so of limited use in serial digit recall, but helping to explain higher item than position accuracy). The first item, though, is known, and in the same way that the ART→speech processes can rehearse their records, PROP→MPL is able to rehearse this entity and to output it to the morphonolexical subsystem when recall is required. There it serves as the key to revive the matching record in the morpho-nolexical image record, and this can then be used to drive the MPL→ART transformation. Because the first few items have already been produced by ART→speech, only the latter part of the MPL→ART stream actually needs to be vocalised.

It is possible to construct this account of a STM task, even though Barnard's model is not specifically intended to be a WM model, because the content and function of the subsystems are well specified. Knowing what the subsystems do, a theorist faced with a new task or an unexplained phenomenon does not need to add new boxes with new functions, but can decide how the existing architecture can be co-ordinated to 'implement' the cognitive capabilities of interest. The price of complexity and detail in the initial model is repaid by this wider scope of applicability. The subsystems are not working memory modules, but more general processing and storage units that are involved in all cognitive operations. In this way, working memory in ICS is modelled as an intrinsic part of all cognitive activity.

EXECUTIVE FUNCTION IN ICS

The description of serial digit recall STM task was only intended to show how the various components of Barnard's model interact. Barnard (1985, 1999) provides more detail about how a variety of empirical effects arising from STM research can emerge from the ICS model. The remaining issue is how these several autonomous cognitive subsystems co-operate, and how 'strategies' of processing can be chosen to suit the task. In the WM model, this is the preserve of the CE, which presumably has stored action sequences that enable it to match the rehearsal and output operations to be conducted by the slave subsystems with an interpretation of task demands. The CE, or some additional components, must carry out a task analysis to decode the verbal task description provided by the experimenter, or more usually, recognise the task constraints about to be imposed upon it by the real situation that its owner has gotten it into. Once the task analysis and decomposition have been identified, the ongoing task performance has to be monitored and controlled, and competing tasks contended with, scheduled, and executed. The rapprochement between WM and the SAS model provides a conception of the necessary operation of the CE. As yet, the SAS model has not been fully integrated with the CE and slave subsystems. It may be that future work will explain how SAS may co-ordinate and control the slave subsystems, either directly or through the CE, but this is not yet understood.

Another solution, with a distinctly different approach, is exemplified by the ICS model. As in the WM model, the comprehension of task constraints, and judgement of their violation or fulfilment, is handled by the propositional and implicational subsystems, but strategic choice and contention scheduling are not seen as necessary operations. They are emergent features of the constraints upon processing within and flow between subsystems that themselves have no knowledge of any high-level task. Subsystems only 'know' what data they get, 'know' what they can do with it, and 'know' whether their output is being used. They are all acting locally, trying to maximise the usefulness of their local output, without being told what to do in any sense whatsoever. There is no executive in the ICS model.

The propositional and implicational subsystems are left with the role of observing planned and actual behaviour (through the representations they receive from other subsystems), assessing whether the overall goals are being met (by comparing consequences of behaviour with expectations), and if they are not, trying through a top-down feed of information into the flow (via PROP→MPL or PROP→OBJ, or perhaps even IMPLIC→ somatic* and IMPLIC→visceral*), to influence processing until the goals are met. Influence rather than control is perhaps a subtle distinction, but it is one that arises from the basic ICS model, without requiring any additional constructs, boxes, or processing routes to be added or incorporated. The propositional and implicational subsystems are 'special' in the sense that they do have a monitoring and motivating role, and so have been termed a Central Engine rather than a central executive, but they are 'ordinary' in the sense that these special roles are fulfilled by the same subsystem architecture and processing rules that govern the behaviour of the other seven subsystems. All that differs is the nature of the information that they process, and their position within the overall systemic architecture.

To appreciate the different consequences that these two approaches to co-ordination and control have, consider the case of random number generation. This is a task that has been widely used within working memory research as one that loads the central executive, that is, one that requires a high degree of monitoring and strategy choice. In the WM model, the CE of someone who is generating a random sequence of digits between, say, one and ten first selects a strategy from long-term memory (LTM) that can be used to generate a numerical sequence. The sequence is then passed through the phonological loop as part of the normal articulatory control process. Using a single strategy would not lead to a sequence fulfilling the randomness constraint, though, so at some point the CE decides to select another strategy. Perhaps the CE has a strategy for strategy selection, or maybe it is able to observe the contents of the phonological loop and detect non-randomness in the output (such as a recognisable string, or repetition, or linear incrementation). Perhaps some individuals can also recruit the VSSP with small sets of digits, using a spatial image of the ordered set of digits to ensure that they sample from both extremes in rough alternation. Co-ordination of the PL, VSSP and LTM are what the CE does, and therefore this is an intensive CE task, that can interfere with any other task requiring more than simple subspan rehearsal, and which can be impaired by increasing the set size or the production rate (because the CE cannot monitor fast enough, or select generation strategies quickly enough, or control the phonological loop and do all of the above smoothly).

The sequence of events is much the same within an ICS explanation, but the steps are more clearly allocated to specific parts of the architecture. From the verbal or visual task instructions provided by MPL→PROP or OBJ→PROP, the PROP→IMPLIC process generates the overall requirement for an absence of predictability in output as the key attribute of the task. Simultaneously, PROP→MPL recruits its image record to provide a sequence of digits, with the probability of any particular digit string being influenced by its recent processing history. This is articulated through the MPL→ART::ART→speech* processes, but internal feedback about the sequence is also produced by MPL→PROP. PROP→IMPLIC is thus able to detect any schematic patterns in the feedback stream that MPL→PROP is generating. As soon as any regularities or recognisable patterns are detected as implicational patterns of meaning (e.g., 2–4–6 conveys an even and regularly rising pattern; 7–3–5 conveys an 'oddness' pattern), IMPLIC→PROP can signal a conflict with the main task attribute, that of unpredictability, and this can interrupt the PROP→MPL generation process. PROP→IMPLIC and IMPLIC→PROP can then co-ordinate to fashion a new generation strategy from their respective image records, and this will of course be influenced by the strategy that has just been in use. Bringing this all together, if the individual had just said 'seven, three, five . . .' and had generated nine at a propositional level as the next candidate for output, the implicational pattern of 'oddness' produced by PROP→IMPLIC would cause IMPLIC→PROP to prevent it being used. To select an alternative digit quickly, the propositional attributes of this high, odd digit might be switched to produce a low, even digit, such as 2 or 4, and PROP→MPL would send that for output. MPL→PROP would return 'two' to act as the key for the next digit, reviving some personally familiar digit pattern beginning with 2 or 4.

As with the simpler example of serial digit recall, this account of random number generation in ICS involves a large number of interactions between different processes and storage components. Those components are not dedicated to the execution of this task. The propositional and implicational processes are powerful and general in scope, and random number generation is a cut-down example of their fuller role in cognition: the construction and evaluation of their owner's internal mental world and of their intended actions in the external world. The explication of random number generation is apparently complex, because it is a simple task being done by a complex architecture. Some of the odder aspects of the behaviour with this task, however, such as the general preference for the digits 3 and 7, and the avoidance of repetition, start to make sense when the wider cognitive context is taken into account.

EVIDENCE FOR THE ICS ACCOUNT

Whether the higher level description of the task produced by the WM model is preferable to the more detailed description provided by ICS depends wholly upon the purposes to which the description will be put. If the focus of interest is not the random generation task, or the particular interplay of operations required for it to occur, but its global interference with STM span, or with task co-ordination, as a whole task, then the higher level description is perfectly adequate, and is to be preferred. If the focus is upon finding out more about the operation of the CE itself, however, the more specific the description of the task the better.

Scott, Barnard & May (in press) have used the ICS account of random generation to distinguish the contribution of implicational and propositional representations in 'central executive' activity. Instead of the generation of a sequence of single digits, they asked people to generate a single, large number, between specific but wide bounds. In their first experiment, the bounds were one million to ten million. Of course, one could perform this task by producing a seven item sequence of digits, just as if the task has required people to produce 'seven random digits between one and nine', but very few people actually completed the task in this way. Instead, people tended either to produce round millions such as 'one million' or 'five million', minimally elaborated numbers such as 'one million and one', or more fully elaborated numbers such as 'one million, five hundred and twenty six thousand, three hundred and seven'. Crucially, the relative frequency of these three patterns of answer was directly influenced by minor changes in the propositional content of the task instructions.

Instructions that asked for 'a number between' or 'a random number between' produced mainly round million responses, although there were a large proportion of minimally elaborated responses for the 'random' instructions. Presumably the addition of the word 'random' cued people to produce some specific, exact number rather than a 'rough' round number. Although in reality no one number is actually more specific than any other, 'one million and one' feels more specific than 'one million', and it is this implicational quality of specificity that has been inferred as the marker of task adequacy by more people in the 'random' condition. In round million responses, the number of millions was more likely to be odd than even and was most often drawn from the lower part of the magnitude range (three or five). The randomness in these answers came from the specific million that had been chosen, just as if people had been asked for a single random digit, and had marked randomness by choosing the implicationally 'strange' numbers three or seven. In minimally elaborated responses, the answer was almost always 'one million and . . .', with the randomness coming in the elaboration. For these people, randomness was not relevant to the start of their response.

Instructions that asked people to give 'a seven figure number, that's a number between . . .' produced mainly fully elaborated responses: not seven digit strings, but fully elaborated, linguistically structured numbers. The mention of the seven figures has led people to infer that this is the main task constraint. The remaining condition asked for 'a number between one million and nine million, nine hundred and ninety nine thousand nine hundred and ninety nine'. Here the full elaboration is given so one might expect fully elaborated answers in return, but the most frequent response was a minimally elaborated answer. Specificity had been inferred, but the complexity of full elaboration was also inferred and noted as something to be avoided.

When participants are asked to do a number generation task (or indeed, any task), they generate a propositional interpretation of its content and this, in turn, constrains the generation of the more abstract implicational model of the target number. This is then used to generate a propositional representation of the target number to generate the surface MPL form of the response. The target number may be evaluated for possible discrepancy with a representation of the original question content, prior to overt articulation, but that checking will centre on the implicational understanding of the instructions, not the actual instructions. Support for this came from the surprisingly high error rate for such an apparently simple task: one in seven of the 1,293 people gave an answer that was outside the very specific bounds they had just been given.

OPENING THE BOX

The point of the one million–ten million study was not to discover how people go about coming up with random numbers, although hopefully this might be of interest to research sponsors from the gambling industry. It was to show that small variations in propositional content can have specific and systematic consequences for behaviour that only make sense if an implicational level of representation is included within the model. The research was driven by the pragmatic identification of these two levels of meaning within the central engine of ICS in order to account for psycholinguistic and emotional phenomena, and is a first step to showing that the central executive can indeed be fractioned, providing that you have a principled reason for knowing where the cracks in the box might be located.

Returning to the four questions that motivate this book, the *strengths* of the working memory model are clear. Its simplicity allows it to be understood and applied quickly, and it is directly applicable to a wide range of short-term memory phenomena, both in the laboratory and in practical, applied settings. It has proven useful in generating novel tasks that have extended our knowledge about the relationship between memory and attention in task performance, especially when dual tasks compete for cognitive resources. However, I have tried to make the case that this simplicity is more apparent than real, and is also, in the long run, the model's *weakness*, because it masks a great deal of complexity in 'real' cognitive processing. In particular, the mode of operation of the central executive, and its communication with, and control of, the slave subsystems, has allowed the model to be defined in different ways at different times. The lack of detail makes it hard to extrapolate beyond the domain of short-term memory tasks, and makes it hard to say how the model contributes to phenomena such as episodic memory, to long-term memory, or to the abstraction of rules (whether explicit or implicit). The simplicity of a parsimonious model becomes uneconomical if new models, or even new modules, must be specified for additional, related, phenomena. Every addition to a model requires all previous research findings to be reassessed, to check that the addition does not contradict earlier conclusions.

For *future development of the model* it will be necessary to identify tasks that show the central executive working in different ways, without affecting the behaviour of the slave subsystems. This will allow researchers to elucidate the structure of this 'residual area of ignorance'. With the current degree of uncertainty about which processes or storage functions reside within the central executive, and which reside with the slave subsystems, such exploration is impossible. Different behavioural outcomes cannot be attributed safely to subcomponents of the central executive, while the boundaries between it and the slave subsystems, and the communication across those boundaries, remain unspecified. ICS has been described in this chapter as an example of an approach that provides just such a specification, and which is intended to be generally applicable to all cognitive tasks rather than to be specifically limited to one domain. This does not mean that the WM model has to be discarded, or put to one side, and replaced by ICS or any other model, for they are not competitors; but it does mean that it should be recognised as being a model of short-term memory phenomena, and not of general cognitive activity. Understanding more about the structure of the components of the working memory model will allow it to be related to more general models, and will remove the need for general models to be used in situations where specific models are more economical. While it is indeed more complicated to apply a general model of cognition to short-term memory phenomena, it will prove simpler to apply a well-specified general model to the complexities of task co-ordination and control than to extend the WM model by adding new components.

BACKGROUND READING

Barnard, P. J., & May, J. (1999). Representing cognitive activity in complex tasks. *Human–Computer Interaction, 14*(1&2), 93–158.

The first half of this paper contains a comprehensive description of the ICS model. The remainder describes an expert system implementation of the 'principles' underlying the model, which was able to model a variety of human–computer interaction scenarios by reasoning about the cognitive activity that the human user would have to engage in during the inter-action.

Barnard, P. J. (1999). Interacting cognitive subsystems: Modeling working memory phenomena within a multiprocessor architecture. In A. Miyake & P. Shah (Eds.), *Models of working memory: Mechanisms of active maintenance and executive control* (pp. 298–339). Cambridge: Cambridge University Press.

This paper contains a briefer account of ICS, and in answering a number of questions arising from different views of working memory, describes the ICS account of working memory tasks, executive function, capacity limita-tions, complex cognitive activity, and the relationship of working memory to long-term memory, attention, consciousness, and neurology.

REFERENCES

Atkinson, R. C., & Shiffrin, R. M. (1968). Human memory: a proposed system and control processes. In K. W. Spence & J. D. Spence (Eds.), *The psychology of learning and motivation* (Vol. 2, pp. 89–195). New York: Academic Press.

Baddeley, A. D. (1986). *Working memory*. Oxford: Oxford University Press.

Baddeley, A. D. (1993). Working memory and conscious awareness. In A. F. Collins, S. E. Gathercole, M. A. Conway, & P. E. Morris (Eds.), *Theories of memory* (pp. 11–28). Hove: Lawrence Erlbaum Associates Ltd.

Baddeley, A. (1996). Exploring the central executive. *Quarterly Journal of Experi-mental Psychology, Section a — Human Experimental Psychology, 49A*(1), 5–28.

Baddeley, A. D., & Hitch, G. (1974). Working memory. In G. A. Bower (Ed.), *The psychology of learning and motivation* (Vol. 8, pp. 47–89). New York: Academic Press.

Barnard, P. J. (1985). Interacting cognitive subsystems: A psycholinguistic approach to short-term memory. In A. Ellis (Ed.), *Progress in the psychology of language* (Vol. 2, pp. 197–258). London: Lawrence Erlbaum Associates Ltd.

Barnard, P. J. (1999). Interacting cognitive subsystems: Modeling working memory phenomena within a multiprocessor architecture. In A. Miyake & P. Shah (Eds.), *Models of working memory: Mechanisms of active maintenance and executive control* (pp. 298–339). Cambridge: Cambridge University Press.

Broadbent, D. E. (1958). *Perception and communication*. London: Pergamon Press.

Dawkins, R. (1989). *The selfish gene*. Oxford: Oxford University Press.

Norman, D. A., & Shallice, T. (1986). Attention to action: Willed and automatic control of behaviour. In R. Davison, G. Shwartz, & D. Shapiro (Eds.), *Consciousness and self-regulation: Advances in research and theory* (pp. 1–18). New York: Plenum.

Scott, S. Barnard, P. J., & May, J. (in press). Specifying executive function in random generation tasks. *Quarterly Journal of Experimental Psychology.*

Part IV
Conclusion

13 The working memory model: Consensus, controversy, and future directions

Jackie Andrade

This chapter summarises the issues that emerge from the previous chapters, highlighting areas of consensus and of disagreement. It assesses whether the strengths of the WM model outweigh its weaknesses, and whether it looks a viable model for future research into short-term memory and general cognition. The future of the model depends not only on the balance of its own strengths and weaknesses, but also on those of competing models. I will begin by summarising the contributing authors' answers to the four questions that form the backbone of the book, and then outline a research programme to build on the strengths of the WM model while tackling its weaknesses. The summary of the contributors' answers follows the structure of the main part of the book, that is, it is split into Applied and Theoretical parts. Note that this is not a strict division, and that many theoretical issues emerge from using the model for applied research.

WHAT ARE THE STRENGTHS OF THE WM MODEL?

Strengths of the WM model from an applied perspective

The chapters in the Applied Perspectives part of the book highlight three main strengths of the WM model. Pearson and Andrade agree that one strength is the *breadth* of the model. The fact that it encompasses auditory as well as visuo-spatial processing, and manipulation as well as temporary storage of representations, makes it useful for analysing complex, real-life tasks such as creative design and emotive imagery. For example, Pearson's research on mental synthesis shows that subjects use verbal short-term memory to support their performance on what is notionally a visual imagery task. Competing models, such as Kosslyn's (1994) model of visual imagery, tend to focus on processing in a single modality and cannot capture the complex interactions between processes in different modalities. Although one could argue that breadth is gained at the expense of specificity, breadth is the more useful attribute for applied research into the cognitive processes underlying performance in real-world situations, where it is impossible to control and manipulate task conditions to the extent that one can do in laboratory tasks.

A related strength is the *specificity* of the WM model. Chapters 4–7 all cite specificity as a strength of the WM model, and indeed would like greater specificity. In contrast to the general resource models of the North American working memory tradition, the fractionated, Baddeley and Hitch model of working memory offers a framework for making specific predictions about the role of verbal and visuo-spatial storage and manipulation in other cognitive processes. By specifying separate storage and processing functions, and separate verbal and visuo-spatial subsystems, the WM model helps guide research into the specific cognitive elements of typical and atypical lifetime changes (see Jarrold for example). Phillips and Hamilton make the point that the specificity of the WM model enables researchers to go beyond correlational studies, allowing them to gather converging evidence from experimental manipulations of specific functions such as verbal rehearsal or visual short-term memory. Even though current empirical evidence favours theories which claim that general cognitive deficits (e.g., slower processing speed) underpin adult aging, the WM model guides researchers in their attempts to test and falsify such general theories. In the case of language acquisition, Adams and Willis report new data which show that different measures of working memory are not equally good predictors of language ability, showing the utility of the fractionated WM model for guiding research into the component processes of cognition. Henson also makes the point strongly that specificity is a strength, arguing that one could not use a general resource model to investigate the brain structures underlying working memory function. He discusses empirical evidence that the verbal and visual storage, rehearsal and manipulation processes proposed by the WM model are anatomically distinct as well as functionally distinct.

Another strength of the WM model may be characterised as a historical as well as an inherent strength. It is that the WM model already holds a *central place in cognitive psychology*, and there already exists a substantial body of data concerning the role of working memory in cognitive function. Andrade suggests that this is an advantage for studying consciousness because, if supported by empirical evidence, an explanation of consciousness in terms of working memory function should help us to understand the relationship between consciousness and other aspects of cognitive function. If an ultimate aim of cognitive psychology research is a grand unified theory of cognition then, all else being equal, it makes sense to tackle a new research area from a theoretical position that is already widely accepted and based on secure empirical foundations. Jarrold argues that the existing research into the role of working memory in cognition adds an extra dimension to new research into atypical development. Not only can the WM model help to characterise cognitive function in different developmental disorders, but it can also help to predict how specific working memory deficits will impinge on general cognitive function, for example the ability to learn novel information.

Strengths of the WM model from a theoretical perspective

The *simplicity* of the working memory model emerges as an important strength for the authors offering theoretical perspectives on the model. Page and Henson, Lovatt and Avons, and Ward agree that the phonological loop component of the model, in which rehearsal offsets decay of stored representations, offers a parsimonious account of immediate serial recall. As such, it explains a large body of data. One advantage of the simplicity of this model is that it provides a sound basis for constructing quantitative models of the decay and rehearsal mechanisms that underpin immediate serial recall performance. May elaborates the practical advantages of theoretical simplicity, explaining that researchers are more likely to use a model which they can rapidly comprehend and easily apply to everyday phenomena. Although arguing that the WM model is too simplistic to account for many everyday phenomena, May accepts that it provides an excellent account of the short-term memory phenomena that were its original foundation. By including the central executive component, the WM model helped researchers go beyond short-term memory to investigate, via dual task methodologies, the relationship between memory and attention. Thus the model has proved useful for explaining data from a narrow range of immediate serial recall tasks and for generating new data from a broader range of tasks and situations. However, although the territory claimed by 'working memory' rather than mere 'short-term memory' promises us a better understanding of complex cognitive skills such as reading and arithmetic, Towse and Houston-Price argue that weaknesses in the specification of the central executive mean that it has not fulfilled this promise.

WHAT ARE THE WEAKNESSES OF THE WM MODEL?

Weaknesses of the WM model from an applied perspective

All the contributors to the Applied Perspectives part of this volume argue that the model fails to fulfil its potential as a tool for making predictions and explaining phenomena because *the components of the model, and their interrelationships, are underspecified.* While addressing this issue, it is important also to bear in mind the virtues of a simple model, both in principle, as discussed above, and in practice, as illustrated by the diverse and productive range of applications of the WM model.

The central executive proves the main source of problems. Evidence of only modest correlations between different putative executive functions (e.g., Lehto, 1996; Miyake et al, 2000) and of deficits in one executive function combined with preservations in another (e.g., Baddeley, Della Sala, Papagno & Spinnler, 1997) suggest that the central executive may not be a unitary system, but until recently there has been little theoretical development of the functioning of the 'executive committee' (Baddeley, 1996). Without a framework that describes the organisation of executive function, it is impossible for researchers to develop experimental tasks which unequivocally tap a particular aspect of executive function, or even tasks which unequivocally tap the slave systems without impinging on the executive. Similarly, researchers cannot analyse the executive loads imposed by complex real-world tasks. Therefore there is a risk that central executive research reveals little more than that performance on a complex multi-componential laboratory task correlates with performance on a complex, multi-componential real-world task. Not knowing which are functions of the central executive and which are functions of cognitive systems outside working memory exacerbates the problem of determining causality, discussed by Adams and Willis, Phillips and Hamilton, and Jarrold, that is, the problem of determining whether working memory function contributes to the development of other cognitive functions or whether those other cognitive functions determine the level of working memory performance.

Not only is the nature of the central executive underspecified, but so is the relationship between the central executive and the slave systems. The separation of storage from processing is the key feature that distinguishes the Baddeley and Hitch fractionated WM model from the integrated models typical of North American working memory research, yet close inspection of the fractionated WM model reveals little about the relationship between the two functions. An issue of general concern to the contributors was the lack of specification of the role of the central executive in rehearsal. Is rehearsal purely a function of the slave systems, a function of the slave systems that is initiated and monitored by the central executive, or a function solely of the central executive? Pearson offers one answer to this question. Based on previous theorising by Kosslyn (e.g., 1983) and existing empirical evidence, he argues that the central executive helps to maintain conscious images in the visual buffer but does not contribute to maintenance of other visual representations stored in the visual cache, for which another, currently unspecified, component is required. Pearson's model offers greater specificity of the relationship between executive function, visuo-spatial short-term memory, and imagery than the original conception of the visuo-spatial sketchpad. However, until the essential functions of the central executive are clearly specified in sufficient detail for researchers to design tasks that selectively load it, the problem of specifying the relationship between the executive and slave systems will remain fairly intractable because there will be no way to corroborate or falsify hypotheses unequivocally.

Another manifestation of the underspecification of the central executive is the problem of distinguishing between rehearsal and manipulation of representations in the slave systems. Many researchers have assumed that at least manipulation is a function of the central executive (see Henson, this volume, for example). However, in the domain of visuo-spatial working memory research, the two functions have been conflated by conceptualising the visuo-spatial sketchpad as a system for the temporary storage of visuo-spatial information which is also 'capable of retaining and manipulating images' (Baddeley, 1986, p. 143). This conceptualisation suggests that the visuo-spatial sketchpad comprises processes which maintain visual representations via some rehearsal mechanism and also manipulate those representations when the task requires image transformation. If maintenance and manipulation are seen as functions of the slave systems, the WM model offers scant explanation of the finding that visuo-spatial imagery tasks often load heavily on the central executive (Salway & Logie, 1995). Pearson suggests that, contrary to the prevailing view, the central executive performs the function of maintaining conscious images whereas modality-specific processes serve to manipulate them. The neuropsychology and neuroimaging data reviewed by Henson potentially shed some light on this issue. Henson concludes that maintenance maps onto posterior temporoparietal and premotor areas, among others, whereas manipulation maps onto midlateral prefrontal regions. If these processes are anatomically separated, they may also be functionally separate. Brain imaging techniques offer promise as a way of investigating the interactions between the hypothesised subsystems of working memory. However, as Henson's analysis makes clear, cognitive theories drive brain imaging research, by helping researchers predict the functions that may be carried out by separate brain areas and by helping them select appropriate experimental and control tasks for their studies. Although neuroimaging data may render a particular theoretical viewpoint more or less tenable, they are themselves currently too theory-dependent to confirm or falsify cognitive theories in the absence of converging evidence for other sources.

The concept of working memory, as opposed to short-term memory, appeals to many applied researchers because it encapsulates the way we use temporarily stored information in general cognition. However, several authors felt that the WM model *does not help predict when working memory resources will be drawn on by other cognitive tasks*. For example, Jarrold debates whether control of action should be attributed to central executive function, as it might be if one uses Norman and Shallice's supervisory attentional system as a model of the central executive (see Baddeley, 1986, chapter 10), or whether only control of memory is a 'true' central executive function. This problem is compounded by different researchers having different views on the remit of working memory. There has been a temptation to invoke the central executive to explain any aspect of cognitive data which cannot be attributed to the phonological loop or visuo-spatial sketchpad. Although this strategy has been expedient for researchers interested in short-term memory (see Baddeley, 1996, p. 6), it has left the overall WM model untestable because the central executive remains all things to all people (see Towse & Houston-Price, chapter 11, this volume). A well-specified model of working memory should help researchers in applied domains to explain the memory and executive components of the phenomenon of interest, and to raise questions about the relationships between those components and the other cognitive processes involved. However, because the WM model is not perfectly specified, and it is not always clear which cognitive processes are not a function of working memory, researchers may have been over-inclusive in the processes they attribute to working memory. For example, Pearson criticises the assumption that the visuo-spatial sketchpad subserves short-term memory and imagery functions, when there has been little investigation of the processes common to imagery and memory, and there exists evidence that visual imagery and visual short-term memory are dissociable functions. Andrade discusses a related problem, the unsubstantiated assumption of a close or even identical relationship between working memory and consciousness. Whereas Pearson proposes a revised model of visuo-spatial working memory, containing separate but related imagery and storage functions, Andrade argues that greater progress might be made by separating the functions of attention and consciousness from working memory, and then researching the relationship of those functions to working memory.

Weaknesses of the WM model from a theoretical perspective

The preceding discussion shows that the major weakness of the WM model for applied research is the lack of specification of the functions and mechanisms of its subcomponents, and of their relationship to each other and to other cognitive processes. *Underspecification* also emerges as a problem from a theoretical perspective. For example, Page and Henson argue that, because it does not specify a mechanistic account of how immediate serial recall is actually accomplished, the WM model cannot explain the different patterns of errors that emerge when the task is performed under different conditions. Analysis of error patterns as well as of absolute performance levels is a recent trend which has been driven by attempts to implement the phonological loop as a quantitative, computational model of serial recall. Thus the failure of the model to explain error patterns in serial recall is relatively unproblematic because the model inspired the better specified computational models that in turn inspired the recording and analysis of error patterns. Although the original WM model now seems inadequate in this respect, it has served its duty as a framework for guiding research.

May argues that although simplicity is a strength of the WM model, it is also its downfall because the simple model fails to reflect the complexity of 'real' cognition and is hard to apply to phenomena outside the domain of laboratory short-term memory tasks. A broader application of the model would require the addition of extra subcomponents or processes, removing the original virtue of simplicity and potentially creating a less coherent model than one that began life as a complex model. He illustrates his argument with the finding that, when asked to generate single, large numbers, people's responses can be predictably altered by phrasing the question in ways that tap different interpretations of the task in hand (Scott, Barnard & May, in press). May argues that a model such as Interacting Cognitive Subsystems, which specifies implicational as well as propositional levels of processing, captures these data in a way which the simpler WM model cannot do. In a similar vein, Towse and Houston-Price admire the apparent simplicity of the central executive from afar but claim that, on closer inspection, there is nothing there to guide research and help explain cognitive phenomena.

Thus underspecification of the WM model means that it sometimes *fails to explain data* generated by better specified models. This failure does not unduly threaten the WM model, because its better specified competitors are typically narrower in their focus or less simple to apply. Potentially more problematic for the WM model are recent failures to demonstrate the word-length effect, discussed by Lovatt and Avons (see also the Foreword by Baddeley & Hitch). This effect is a foundation stone of the claim that real-time articulatory rehearsal processes prevent decay of representations in the phonological store. Although researchers have replicated Baddeley, Thomson and Buchanan's (1975) finding that polysyllabic words are less memorable than monosyllables, they have questioned the generality of their other finding, that disyllables which are quick to pronounce are better recalled than disyllables which take longer to say. Lovatt, Avons and Masterson (2000) failed to replicate this finding with new word sets that differed only in pronunciation time (and not phonological similarity or number of phonemes, for example), suggesting that the effect of spoken word duration in limiting serial recall is at best evanescent and that further research is needed to discover the factors which determine its appearance and disappearance. Yet it is this word-duration effect which provides the strongest evidence for a decay-based phonological store. Lovatt and Avons discuss possible explanations of the failure of word length to influence recall. One possibility is that rehearsal rate is independent of speech rate, i.e., that long words can be rehearsed just as quickly as short words even though they take longer to say aloud, but that begs the question of why speech rate correlates so strongly with serial recall performance. Another possibility is that people do not rehearse words during serial recall tasks. Lovatt and Avons discount this possibility because of evidence that people do rehearse and that rehearsal aids performance, but they also point out that children show word-length effects before the age at which they begin to rehearse spontaneously. A third possibility is that items in the phonological store are not prone to decay over time, but instead are prone to interference. This possibility potentially revives the classic debate between decay and interference as mechanisms of forgetting, and raises questions about what interferes and why.

If the notion of a decay-and-rehearsal based phonological loop is discarded, future research must determine (a) how rehearsal aids short-term memory performance, and why articulatory suppression impairs it, and (b) what constrains immediate serial recall performance if not time-based decay. Discarding the current concept of the phonological loop would necessitate a reassessment of models of visuo-spatial working memory (e.g., Logie, 1995) which, by analogy, assume a passive storage component in which representations are refreshed by active rehearsal processes. However, it would not threaten the essence of the WM model as a tripartite control and temporary storage system. The current concept of the phonological loop could be maintained if future research identifies characteristics of certain sets of words that enable them to be well recalled despite taking a relatively long time to pronounce. For example, they may be particularly easy to visualise and hence more likely to recruit the visuo-spatial sketchpad to support verbal recall, or they may be equated for total output time even though they differ in overt pronunciation time (see Dosher & Ma, 1998; Page & Norris, 1998).

HOW DOES THE WM MODEL COMPARE WITH COMPETING MODELS?

Competing models from an applied perspective

From an applied perspective, competitors to the WM model fall into three classes: *theories of cognitive functions to which working memory contributes, competing accounts of the causal pathway of cognitive development*, and *competing theories of working memory*.

Kosslyn's theory of visual imagery (e.g., Kosslyn, 1994) exemplifies a competing theory of a cognitive function which appears to involve working memory resources. Pearson and Andrade discuss Kosslyn's theory as a means of explaining and predicting mental imagery performance. Both authors agree that Kosslyn's theory is better specified than working memory, describing the processes by which images are generated, maintained and manipulated in greater detail than is possible within the present working memory framework. It also has the advantage of clearly linking imagery with perception. However, it has disadvantages as a tool for researching imagery in applied contexts. It does not extend to auditory processing and therefore offers no framework for investigating multi-modal imagery, for example, visualising a beach while imaging the sound of waves breaking, or for analysing tasks such as creative synthesis where, as

Pearson's research showed, people use verbal processes to support visual imagery. Many applied problems in cognitive psychology involve processing information from several sensory modalities therefore, as a framework for conceptualising the important issues in the target problem and for predicting the contributing cognitive processes, the WM model compares favourably with models that are better specified but narrower in scope.

Much evidence exists that working memory function correlates with cognitive performance during childhood development and adult aging. For example, Adams and Willis discuss the evidence that children's phonological working memory ability correlates with their language development, for example, their acquisition of the vocabulary of their native language. Jarrold presents evidence that specific deficits in verbal or visual working memory correlate with more general deficits in verbal or visual learning in developmental disorders like Down sydrome and Williams syndrome. Phillips and Hamilton discuss the evidence that working memory deficits correlate with the overall cognitive decline in adult aging. The problem is that these data are correlational, showing that changes in working memory function mirror the changes in other cognitive functions, rather than showing that working memory causes those changes. Competing accounts interpret these data as showing that changes in another cognitive function cause the change in working memory, or that changes in both functions are due to a common, third factor. For example, better vocabulary knowledge may cause better performance on verbal working memory tasks (Adams & Willis; Jarrold), or generally slowed processing speed may impair performance on working memory and other cognitive tasks (Phillips & Hamilton).

The problem of determining causality is common to all studies of individual differences. Some methodological techniques can help infer the direction of causality, though they cannot prove it. For example, Gathercole and Baddeley (1989) conducted a longitudinal study of young children's phonological working memory performance and vocabulary knowledge. Using cross-lagged correlations, they showed that working memory scores at age 4 predicted vocabulary knowledge at age 5, even when vocabulary knowledge at age 4 had been partialled out. Their analysis suggests that working memory development precedes vocabulary development. Bishop, North and Donlan (1996) tested the verbal working memory skills of children who had previously been diagnosed with Specific Language Impairment, which had subsequently resolved. Although their language abilities had improved to the level of normally developing children, their working memory scores remained atypically low, suggesting that a working memory deficit was fundamental to their language difficulties rather than a consequence of them. These data are at least consistent with the claim that working memory development precedes and influences language development. However, theories should be judged not only by how much data they can account for, but also by how satisfying an explanation they provide of those data. Adams and Willis discuss the mechanisms by which phonological working memory may help establish stable long-term representations of novel words. Explaining the underlying mechanisms of learning in this way helps to bolster claims that working memory contributes to language learning, rather than the converse, even when the empirical data are consistent with either interpretation. Better specification of the component processes of working memory, perhaps through the development of computational models, should increase the explanatory value of the WM model. Likewise, a better understanding of the developmental trajectory of working memory would help researchers investigate the order in which working memory and other cognitive functions emerge during childhood.

Integrated accounts of working memory, which postulate a trade-off between storage and processing demands on a single limited-capacity resource, offer major competition to the fractionated WM model in which storage and processing are functions of separate limited-capacity subsystems. Generally, contributors felt that the fractionated model compared favourably with the integrated models, for explaining the data (Adams & Willis), for characterising cognitive changes across the lifespan (Phillips & Hamilton), and for predicting which aspects of working memory function might be subserved by the same or different brain regions (Henson). Even though the evidence favouring the fractionated model over integrated models is rather sparse, there are pragmatic reasons for selecting the fractionated model as a conceptual tool for guiding research because it helps make more specific, testable predictions. However, the differences between the integrated and fractionated models may be exaggerated by the present lack of specification of the place of processing in the fractionated model. If the phonological loop and visuo-spatial sketchpad rehearse and manipulate the representations they store, then they should show (modality-specific) storage-processing trade-offs comparable to those claimed by proponents of integrated models. Alternatively, if the central executive contributes to rehearsal of representations in the slave systems, and if that contribution is greater for material that is harder to store, then the fractionated system as a whole should show storage-processing trade-offs akin to those predicted by integrated models.

Competing models from a theoretical perspective

Contributors to the Theoretical Perspectives part discussed two types of competing model: more detailed, *quantitative models* of verbal serial recall and competing *qualitative models* of memory and executive function.

Page and Henson, and Lovatt and Avons, discuss quantitative, computational models of immediate serial verbal recall. Correct serial recall requires maintenance of both item information and order information. Most models tackle the task in two stages, one which encodes an item's relative position in the list (e.g., as differing item activation levels or positional codes) and a second which encodes detailed phonological information (e.g., item nodes). Typically, the phonological similarity effect is modelled as a consequence of the second stage, ie. item node activation, being a noisier process for similar items. Thus, in contrast to the original WM model, quantitative models tend to assume that the phonological similarity effect reflects output processes, such as response selection, rather than storage mechanisms. Otherwise, these models tend not to compete directly with the WM model but offer a more detailed specification of the mechanisms of short-term memory, lack of which was frequently cited as a problem with the WM model. Page and Henson compared quantitative models of serial recall with respect to two findings, the rapid decay of the phonological similarity effect over short retention intervals and the tendency for items to intrude from the same position in the previous list. These two findings present an interesting problem if one assumes that the phonological similarity effect and correctly ordered immediate recall both reflect the functioning of phonological loop. The rapid decay of the phonological similarity effects suggests that the phonological loop is labile whereas the between-list retention of position information suggests that it is relatively long lasting. Page and Norris (1998), basing their primacy model fairly directly on the qualitative phonological loop model, deal with this situation by assuming that the between-trial effects reflect the operation of an episodic system that is used as a back-up when task conditions render the phonological loop inadequate. Of the five models discussed, only Henson's (1998) start–end model explains both findings, doing so by proposing relatively long-lasting positional codes which activate labile phonological representations of items in a separate short-term store.

Lovatt and Avons discuss the adequacy of a similar set of quantitative models for explaining the word-length effect. Although these models are better specified than the original phonological loop model, they tend to incorporate time-based decay and therefore offer no explanation of why some words with long spoken duration are recalled as well as words with shorter duration. For example, Page and Norris (1998) and Burgess and Hitch (1999) assume that rehearsal offsets decay, arguing respectively that longer words take longer to rehearse or that they suffer more from decay. Brown and Hulme (1995) invoke decay without rehearsal, proposing that long words are more prone to decay and interference because they occupy more time-segments. Neath and Nairne (1995) also assume that long words occupy more time-segments but argue that this makes them harder to reassemble at output. Although they model word length without invoking decay or rehearsal, the fact that they define word length in terms of time-segments means their model cannot explain why some words appear to occupy more time when pronounced yet are remembered as well as shorter words. The failure of competing models to explain the lack of a reliable effect of spoken word duration on recall helps to protect the WM model from these contradictory data. Kuhn (1962) argued that theories tend not to be abandoned until there are copious conflicting data and better theories to supplant them. Until a new theory is proposed that is compatible with the unreliability of the word-length effect and explains the other data encompassed by the WM model, researchers have time to try and identify the circumstances under which the word-length effect does and does not occur.

Ward offers a competing qualitative account of immediate serial recall performance, albeit one which has also helped make quantitative predictions about performance on free recall tasks (Tan & Ward, 2000). He suggests that recall in both tasks is achieved through the operation of a General Episodic Memory (GEM) system comprising rehearsal processes, an episodic memory store of items associated with the context in which they were presented, and modality-specific information which supplements the item-information in episodic memory. In this model, working memory refers not to a temporary short-term store with associated limited-capacity executive processes, but rather to the set of items that are currently most accessible in episodic memory. Because it does not propose separate short-term and long-term memory stores, the GEM system can explain 'long-term' memory effects, such as serial position effects in free recall, as well as 'short-term' memory effects such as performance on immediate serial recall tasks. Although Baddeley and Hitch (1974) conceived of working memory as a gateway into long-term memory, several subsequent authors have thought of it as the set of currently activated long-term memory representations. The latter versions of working memory may be broadly compatible with the GEM model, though the details of the models may differ. For example, Ward argues that apparent capacity limitations in the GEM model are an emerging feature of the way different concurrent processes interact, rather than being due to the size of a hypothetical short-term store that is separate from episodic memory (a similar viewpoint is discussed by Towse & Houston-Price). In contrast, Logie (1996) argues that working memory serves as a separate 'workspace' for manipulating activated representations, and that the storage capacity of this workspace is limited. The nature of rehearsal remains an issue for supporters of both the GEM and WM models. Ward debates whether rehearsal might be a modality-specific process or whether common amodal processes rehearse information in all modalities. The same problem concerned other contributors to this volume, framed as whether rehearsal is a function of the slave systems of working memory or of the central executive. The GEM model is attractive in the sense that it explains recency and immediate serial recall performance in a single framework, and encourages a closer look at the timing of rehearsal processes in memory tasks, but it has yet to be applied to the broad range of data that bolster the WM model, for instance, the neuro-psychological and neuroimaging data which suggest that different brain areas support the different components of working memory.

Towse and Houston-Price criticise various conceptions of the central executive. Each aspect of putative executive function can be explained without recourse to the notion of a central executive, for example, limits on dual task co-ordination may be due to task scheduling difficulties rather than capacity limits of a central executive. However, Towse and Houston-Price are pessimistic about the prospects for any general competing theory of executive function because, when analysed closely, the concept of general cognitive control does not cohere. Rather, they see 'central executive' function as emerging from the distributed control functions of the slave systems. May also advocates a more distributed account of executive function, based on Barnard's Interacting Cognitive Subsystems framework (ICS; Barnard, 1985, 1999). He argues that the 'central engine' of ICS offers a plausible and testable (e.g., Scott et al, in press) alternative to the central executive of working memory. Whereas the central executive has been conceived as set of high-level cognitive processes superior to the short-term storage functions of the slave systems, the central engine of ICS is a set of processes which are central to a non-hierarchical system of structurally identical processing subsystems. Although ICS is a broader, more general model than the WM model, the centrality of the central engine to the model actually subjects it to greater constraints than the central executive of working memory. May argues that ICS provides a better framework for exploring complex cognitive function, particularly in noisy everyday situations where subjects differ in their knowledge, goals and understanding of the task in hand, because it is better specified than the central executive in two ways. First, it states explicitly how executive function is divided up (into processes dealing with 'propositional' and 'implicational' levels of meaning) and second, it specifies the relationship between these executive processes and the modality-specific processes of perception and action. Thus, although ICS is an unwieldy model for explaining performance on laboratory short-term memory tasks, it compares favourably with the WM model on just those aspects of cognition that contributors often cited as the Achilles' heel of working memory, i.e., executive function and its relationship with temporary storage and processing of modality-specific information.

WHAT IS THE FUTURE OF THE WM MODEL?

The future of the model from an applied perspective

The contributors to the Applied Perspectives part of the book were all fairly content with the WM model as a basic framework for guiding their research but they hoped to see the functions of the subsystems, and their mutual interactions, become better specified in the future. In particular, we need a better understanding of rehearsal mechanisms, of the relationship between visual and spatial processes, and of the extent and detailed nature of central executive processes. Lack of specification of central executive function caused particular problems for authors, making it difficult for them to design experimental tasks and to test the fractionated model against integrated models. It is clearly a topic needing (and receiving, see below) urgent attention if the WM model is to remain useful for applied psychological research. Indeed, as discussed above, better specification of the central executive may help to satisfy Phillips and Hamilton's desire for a reconciliation between the fractionated WM model and the integrated models which have predominated in adult aging research.

Better specification of the components of working memory will help predict and test the relationship between working memory and other aspects of cognition. Pearson and Andrade both recommend a clear conceptual separation between working memory and processes such as attention, consciousness and imagery that have sometimes been subsumed by the WM model. Future research may reveal that these processes are indeed functions of working memory, but that research cannot be done until specific, testable limitations to the WM model are hypothesised.

Jarrold would like to see the WM model extended to specify the course of development of the subsystems. He argues that we have a relatively clear idea of how the different subsystems function in adults, and how they may fail following brain damage, but that the model should also account for how the subsystems change with age. A better understanding of how working memory develops normally should help researchers to characterise atypical developmental pathways of different aetiologies, and to predict the effects of developmental variations in cognition for individual differences in adulthood. There has already been considerable research into children's verbal working memory and some, though less, into the development of the visuo-spatial sketchpad and central executive. The next step is to integrate these findings to produce a coherent account of how early cognitive development leads to adult working memory function.

Does the WM model have a future as a framework for applied research? I am optimistic that it does. As the Applied Perspectives part of the book demonstrates, the model has already been applied to a wide variety of topics, topics as diverse as creative design, traumatic memory, language learning, aging, learning disability, and brain imaging. Those applications of the model have been successful in several ways: they have helped to characterise better the nature of the phenomena under scrutiny, they have generated new data which can be used to test competing accounts, they have contributed to our understanding of working memory itself, and they have raised new questions which will fuel future research and potentially lead to new discoveries. There surely exist numerous other real-world problems which require a cognitive level of explanation, because they are cognitive phenomena, and to which the WM model could be successfully applied. Competing theories have yet to offer the combination of breadth, specificity and simplicity that make the WM model so useful as a tool for applied research.

The future of the model from a theoretical perspective

The future of the WM model for explaining verbal short-term memory seems bright, in the sense that progress has been made in specifying the component mechanisms of verbal working memory and clear questions remain for stimulating future research. As discussed by Page and Henson, computational modelling approaches have already identified possible mechanisms underlying immediate serial recall, shifting the emphasis somewhat from item storage in the original WM model to the response selection and output processes which are an integral component of speech production (Page & Norris, 1998). Thus the modelling enterprise has helped to specify better the processes involved in working memory and suggested ways in which working memory may be linked to at least one other cognitive function. Page and Henson highlight an important direction for future research, namely the relationship between working memory and long-term memory. They suggest that a combination of two existing models of serial recall, Page and Norris's (1998) primacy model and Henson's (1998) start–end model, would produce a model that explained not only a relatively broad range of immediate serial recall data, such as the short-lived effects of phonological similarity and irrelevant speech, but also longer lasting effects such as between-list positional intrusions. In the light of the word duration data discussed by Lovatt and Avons, future research into the mechanisms of immediate serial verbal recall also needs to tackle the problem of how forgetting occurs in the phonological loop.

Many computational models of immediate serial recall comprise temporary information about item position, encoded as relative item activation levels or positional tags for example, and long-term representations of items which can be temporarily activated or selected during the memory task. They do not propose temporary memory stores in the sense of separate structures in which incoming representations are placed until recalled. In this sense, they complement Ward's proposal of abandoning the concept of separate short-term and long-term memory stores and instead conceiving of working memory as a general term for the currently activated (and rehearsed) components of episodic memory. Proponents of different models of working memory have variously conceived of working memory as a separate temporary store for incoming information en route to long-term memory, as a separate workspace for manipulating the set of currently activated long-term memory representations (e.g., Logie, 1996), or as a set of rehearsal and manipulation processes acting directly on long-term memory representations (e.g., Cowan, 1999). The proposal of a single set of permanent representations, without a duplicate set of temporary representations, perhaps seems the more parsimonious account but the implications of this and the various competing accounts have not yet been fully explored, either with respect to their ability to explain the existing data (including neurological dissociations and brain imaging data) or to their utility for making novel predictions. 'Gateway' or 'workspace' models may fare better as explanations of how we learn new information, for example, how we acquire the vocabulary of our native language (see Adams & Willis, chapter 4, this volume; Baddeley & Logie, 1999).

Towse and Houston-Price see an executive-free future for working memory. They would like researchers to explore the extent to which maintenance and manipulation processes are the function of self-organising modality-specific systems, rather than the result of centralised control mechanisms. Additionally, they feel that many of the applied issues that have been the focus of central executive research are fascinating questions in their own right and could be better investigated if they were not framed by the ill-defined term of executive function. May argues that future development of the WM model requires a clear demonstration of executive function which cannot be attributed to the functioning of the slave systems or to other cognitive processes. To fulfil this ambition requires a better specification of the central executive. He argues that, if this specification creates extra subsystems in the WM model or subdivides the central executive, then it may prove simpler in the long run to use alternative models such as ICS to explain complex cognitive function, and restrict the working memory model to short-term memory phenomena.

CONCLUSIONS: WHERE NEXT FOR THE WM MODEL?

Since its conception in 1974, the WM model has been used very widely as a framework for guiding research. Its combined virtues of simplicity and breadth have made it applicable to a diverse range of psychological problems, and as a result it has been extremely prolific in helping generate novel explanations and predictions. Relatively few models have competed for the same territory, particularly in the applied field, and now any contender to the working memory throne must explain an enormous and diverse body of data before posing a serious threat to the WM model. However, even though the WM model may not be unduly threatened by competing theories, it may be at risk of self-destruction because researchers are interpreting the model in different and incompatible ways. Even among the contributors to this volume, there is a sense in which different users are pulling the model in different directions to suit their purposes and interests. Whereas contributors to the Applied Perspectives part want a better specified version of the basic WM model, and improved understanding of the relationship between working memory and other areas of cognition, contributors to the Theoretical Perspectives part suggest several reconceptualisations of the components of working memory and their interrelationships which are not necessarily compatible with the current WM model. This is a healthy position to be in, showing that working memory remains a dynamic research topic and promising future theoretical develop-ments to the model that will in turn enhance applied research. However, it may be more problematic that researchers have idiosyncratic interpreta-tions of the core components of the model. For example, they differ in the extent to which they attribute rehearsal and manipulation to the slave systems or central executive. If two researchers mean different things by 'central executive', their studies of central executive function are likely to generate incompatible data and make it difficult to advance our under-standing of working memory function. Critical aspects of the WM model are open to different interpretations because they are poorly specified. Although applied research has bolstered the model, it has contributed to this problem of underspecification by introducing complex 'real-world' tasks such as imagery mnemonics into the laboratory when theoretical research might have been better served by specially-designed experimental tasks. To maintain its preeminent position in cognitive psychology, the WM model of the future should achieve two aims: it should preserve the simplicity of the 'egg-and-boxes' model which has made it so successful as a tool for applied research, and it should provide a clearer, more testable specification of the functions and interrelationships of the subcomponents. This concluding section of the book outlines a vision for a future WM model and a research programme by which it might be achieved.

The phonological loop

Currently, the phonological loop comprises a decay-prone store for speech-based information and a subvocal rehearsal process which offsets decay. The future model should explain how information about serial order is maintained, and what are the respective constraints on maintenance of item and order information. It should specify the relationship between short-term verbal memory and language. Two issues are pertinent here. One is the mechanisms by which the language system supports normal adult short-term verbal memory. For example, is temporary storage of to-be-remembered items affected by temporary activation of item representations in semantic memory? Are the production processes that underpin overt speech the same as those which are harnessed for rehearsal of items in short-term memory? The other important issue, upon which interpretation of a large body of data depends (see Adams & Willis, chapter 4, this volume), is how temporary storage of novel speech sounds facilitates per-manent encoding of those sounds in long-term memory.

The computational modelling enterprise has made good progress towards achieving this aim (see Page & Henson, chapter 8, this volume). Competing models have been generated, as have new data aimed at testing those models. Many of the models remain in the spirit of the original WM model, allowing researchers to continue using the qualitative description of the phonological loop as a convenient short-hand for the set of item activations and positional codes (for instance) that underpin verbal serial recall. Importantly, the quantitative models collectively suggest ways in which short-term memory may relate to speech and to long-term memory. For example, they suggest that representations in short-term memory may be quite abstract, yet the rememberer must select or reconstruct more specific, more detailed representations for output. The question of how people do this forms a potential focus for addressing the issues of how working memory relates to long-term memory (how are the relevant long-term memory representations activated?) and the mechanisms of rehearsal. If rehearsal is conceived of as a repeated, subvocal output process, then it should be subject to the same constraints as any other sort of speech production. The next step is to broaden the remit of these models, comparing how well they explain the full range of existing laboratory data on 'phonological loop' phenomena (irrelevant speech, phonological similarity effects etc.) and how well they make novel predictions that can guide research into the interfaces between working memory and language, and working memory and long-term memory.

The visuo-spatial sketchpad

The visuo-spatial sketchpad of the future should specify how pictorial information is retained, rehearsed, and manipulated, and how those processes relate to the processes which retain information about sequential spatial locations. These seem to be tractable questions, providing researchers move away from the complex imagery tasks which have often been used in the past, and which are open to multiple interpretations, and design tasks to tap specific components of visuo-spatial working memory. Progress has already been made here, in the sense that different models of visuo-spatial working memory have been suggested (see Pearson, this volume), but these models have yet to be directly tested. Perhaps most urgently, the various conceptions of the visuo-spatial sketchpad should be applied to the neuro-psychological (Levine, Warach & Farah, 1985; Owen, Sahakian, Semple, Polkey & Robbins, 1995), experimental (Logie & Marchetti, 1991; Tresch, Sinnamon & Seamon, 1993; Vuontela, Rama , Raninen, Aronen & Carlson, 1999), and correlational (Logie & Pearson, 1997) data which suggest anatomically, functionally and developmentally separate visual and spatial processes. Are visual and spatial processes separate modules of visuo-spatial working memory? Are visual representations rehearsed by spatial processes (e.g., Logie, 1995)? Or do representations in the visuo-spatial sketchpad contain both visual and spatial information?

Page and Henson's chapter illustrates the extent to which computational modelling has helped specify the processes involved in verbal serial recall. We are optimistic that future modelling endeavours could help our understanding of the visuo-spatial sketchpad and central executive. However, as Page and Henson explain, there were two important precursors to the recent burst of interest in modelling the phonological loop. One was the reasonably comprehensive description of verbal serial recall provided by the WM model and the other was the extensive body of data regarding performance of serial recall tasks. Thus modellers began their enterprise with some clear hints about the processes which might underlie serial recall and with a pool of empirical evidence against which to test their models. This sort of provision is not yet available for modellers interested in visuo-spatial working memory or the central executive. At a theoretical level, we need to make bolder, more detailed claims about the nature of these sub-systems. At an empirical level, we need to develop better tasks for assessing the functioning of the different components of working memory (see Phillips & Hamilton for examples of new tasks for assessing visual and spatial short-term memory independently of central executive function). These aims are related — theoretical development will help design better tasks, and better tasks will help test and improve new hypotheses.

Questions for the longer term include the relationships between visuo-spatial working memory and visual perception, visual attention and con-scious visual imagery. As described in chapter 2, Kosslyn (1994) provides a coherent and detailed account of the relationship between visual imagery and perception. One way forward is for researchers to explore whether his model can be extended to explain visuo-spatial short-term memory and the data which have been generated under the auspices of visuo-spatial sketchpad research. If it can, it offers potential solutions to the question of how visuo-spatial working memory relates to visual perception. Kosslyn tends to avoid using the term 'conscious' in relation to imagery but Pearson suggests that the distinction between conscious visual imagery and visual short-term memory may be an important one, reflecting different underlying components of working memory. A challenge for future research is to explain the processes by which a non-conscious representation in visual short-term memory becomes a conscious visual image, and how con-sciousness of an image facilitates performance of the task in hand. A recent study by Andrade, Kemps, Wernier, May and Szmalec (submitted) showed that a dynamic visual noise technique which interferes with visual imagery has no effect on visual short-term memory performance, supporting Pearson's conclusion that visual imagery and visual short-term memory reflect the operation of different components of working memory. Exploring the interface between working memory and attention, Luck and Vogl (1997) used rapid presentations of visual arrays to show that the storage capacity of visual working memory is four objects, where each object may comprise several features that have already been conjoined by attentional processes. This finding has yet to be integrated into the visuo-spatial sketchpad literature or to be reconciled with existing span data from matrix recall tasks (e.g., Phillips, 1983). Nonetheless it is interesting because it measures passive storage capacity relatively uncontaminated by active rehearsal, and because it tells us something about what happens to the products of visual attention processes. Attentional blink and change blindness paradigms offer further ways of investigating the relationship between visuo-spatial working memory and visual attention (e.g., Wilken & Mattingley, 2000).

The central executive

The concept of the central executive proved problematic for most of the contributors to this volume because it has been open to many different interpretations. As with visuo-spatial working memory, introduction of tasks from applied domains (e.g., tests of frontal lobe function such as the Wisconsin card sorting task) has exacerbated the problem of defining its function. However, although central executive research got off to a slow start because researchers were concentrating on more tractable problems of verbal and visual storage, there has recently been burgeoning interest in the central executive and increased dialogue between researchers proposing different models of executive function (e.g., Miyake & Shah, 1999; Rabbitt, 1997). Three approaches to the problem will be discussed here.

Individual differences studies often show rather weak correlations between different measures of executive function (e.g., Lehto, 1996). Miyake et al. (2000) argued that this does not necessarily imply that the different measures tap dissociable functions. Rather, the weak correlations could be due to differences in the lower level processes on which the executive control is imposed. They used a latent variable analysis to explore the extent to which executive processes are shared or dissociable across different so-called executive tasks. The latent variables approach statistically combines performance on several measures of the same underlying function, allowing one to extract the 'essence' of that function and discard variance due to more superficial differences between the measures. Miyake et al. tested performance on three different measures of each of three putative executive functions: information updating, inhibition of prepotent responses, and shifting of mental set. Their analysis suggested that these are separable functions and make different contributions to performance on tasks such as the Wisconsin card sorting task, tower of Hanoi, and random number generation. None of the three functions was related to dual task performance.

A key issue for contributors to this book was the remit of the central executive: should it encompass all the processes involved in the coordination and control of cognition, or are some control processes attributable to the slave systems of working memory, or to cognitive systems outside of working memory? In a sense, Miyake et al.'s study does not address this issue because its starting point was what they perceived as general agreement on important control functions, rather than a theoretical position on the central executive of a specific model of working memory. Baddeley (1996) also examined various putative central executive functions, including strategy switching, selective attention and inhibition, and activation of long-term memory. However, he began his analysis of the central executive by exploring the key function of the executive in the WM model, that of coordinating the slave systems. He described several studies of dual task performance in people with Alzheimer's disease, showing that they were impaired at coordinating verbal and visuo-spatial tasks compared with elderly controls, even when matched for single task performance. The dual task deficit increased as the disease progressed. Dual task deficits also distinguished patients with frontal lobe damage and typically disordered, 'dysexecutive' behaviour from patients with frontal damage but undis-turbed behaviour. Baddeley concluded that 'the capacity to carry out two tasks simultaneously appears to be a candidate for one separable feature of executive function' (p. 14). Given Baddeley's findings, the lack of rela-tionship between dual task performance and other control functions in Miyake et al.'s study presents an interesting starting point for future research into the issue of whether there is a coherent cluster of 'central executive' functions or whether executive functions are too diverse to be usefully encapsulated by a modified WM model.

Another approach is to define the central executive more restrictively, as only those amodal processes, if any, which are required to maintain or manipulate representations in the slave systems and to utilise those rep-resentations during complex cognitive tasks. This definition of the executive is in the spirit of the original conception of working memory as a short-term memory which was an integral part of cognition, but it deviates from the common current usage of the term central executive to cover almost all the rest of high-level cognition (goal-directed behaviour, task switching, attention, etc.). A first step, as advocated by Towse and Houston-Price, is to investigate the extent to which working memory processes are the function of the slave systems, that is, that they are modality-specific and do not compete with similar processes acting on information in other modalities. For example, can we rehearse or manipulate visual and verbal representations concurrently, or do the two maintenance or manipulation processes compete for general resources? When two processes mutually interfere, can this interference be explained in terms of the difficulty of scheduling similar tasks rather than as competition for a limited-capacity resource? In addressing this question, care must be taken to select comparable verbal and visuo-spatial tasks, bearing in mind Jones' criticism that many apparent modality-specific effects in the working memory literature are artifacts attributable to the use of verbal tasks which require retention of serial order and visuo-spatial tasks which do not (e.g., Jones, Farrand, Stuart & Morris, 1995).

Neuroimaging studies may provide converging evidence for the relation-ship between the slave systems and the central executive by demonstrating, at a neural level, how the brain regions subserving storage, maintenance and manipulation interact. Do they seem to form functional units, akin to the newly empowered slave systems envisaged by Towse and Houston-Price, or are they structured in a way that suggests modality-specific slave systems operated on by higher-level amodal control processes? Also, by revealing the relationship between perceptual systems, long-term memory, and temporary visual and verbal storage regions, neuroimaging may help shed light on the issue of whether working memory serves as a gateway for incoming perceptual information or whether it is more closely related to long-term memory, possibly acting as a workspace for activated long-term memory representations.

The episodic buffer

Baddeley very recently proposed a new component to the WM model (Baddeley, 2000; see Baddeley & Hitch, in the Foreword to this volume). This 'episodic buffer' is a limited-capacity system for temporarily storing multi-modal information. It maintains bound (integrated) information from the visuo-spatial sketchpad, phonological loop, and long-term memory as a unitary representation, serving as an interface between working memory and long-term memory. The episodic buffer hypothesis presents an interesting way forward for the WM model, particularly with respect to defining more clearly the role of working memory in complex cognition requiring concurrent processing of information in different codes. However, it is still very much in its infancy, with details such as the rehearsal mechanism and its precise relationship to the other working memory systems yet to be specified. Experimental manipulations of the episodic buffer have not yet been developed. It would therefore be premature to offer a detailed critique of the hypothesis at this stage. Nonetheless, as the addition of a new component represents a major change to the WM model, we conclude this volume by presenting some initial thoughts on the episodic buffer hypothesis.

The episodic buffer potentially helps explain several problems raised by contributors, for example between-list positional intrusions in immediate serial recall (see Page & Henson's discussion of an episodic 'back-up store'), mutual influences between verbal and visuo-spatial working memory processes, and unified conscious experience (e.g., of complex mental images). The hypothesis relates to some key issues addressed in this book: how does long-term memory influence working memory?; how does working memory influence long-term memory?; and how are separate modality-specific representations in working memory used in conjunction? Baddeley (2000) argues that the central executive cannot be the locus of these mutual influences because it cannot store the resulting representations. Rather, the executive binds the representations which are then temporarily stored in the episodic buffer, the buffer thus serving as a workspace for maintaining and manipulating integrated representations. The buffer facilitates input to and retrieval from long-term memory, and representations stored in it form a subset of the contents of consciousness.

I asked the contributors for their initial responses to the episodic buffer hypothesis. Most have mixed feelings about the benefits of adding another component to the WM model, generally welcoming the move to address data which have been problematic for the model, yet doubting whether the increase in explanatory power really outweighs the loss of parsimony. Several contributors feel that the addition of the episodic buffer brings the WM model closer to other models of memory and cognition, and welcome this; others feel that a more radical overhaul of the model is needed.

May and Jarrold both applaud the attempt to specify better the relationship between multi-modal storage and processing. May argues that adding a fourth box to the model increases its nominal complexity by a third and that this increase in complexity is justified if it increases explanatory power or specificity. He feels that Baddeley (2000) has made a good case for the episodic buffer increasing the explanatory power of the WM model, by listing a range of phenomena that the episodic buffer allows the model to incorporate (e.g., chunking, visual effects in verbal recall). May also acknowledges that the new WM model is in some respects better specified than earlier incarnations, because an aspect of short-term storage has been removed from the 'ragbag' of tasks previously assigned to the central executive (by Baddeley & Hitch, 1974, and by North American authors, see Miyake & Shah, 1999, for examples). Note, however, that the relationship between the central executive and the episodic buffer remains sketchy, thus Baddeley (2000) suggests that the episodic buffer could be 'conceived as a new component, or as a fractionation of the older version of the central executive' (p. 422). Both May and Jarrold feel that the new version of the WM model is more comparable with other explanations of the phenomena. Jarrold suggests that it now has the potential to be reconciled with the North American conceptualisation of working memory as a system in which there is a trade-off between domain-general storage and processing demands. May argues that the new emphasis on multi-dimensional processing brings the WM model closer to both Barnard's (1985, 1999) Interacting Cognitive Subsystems framework (since the episodic buffer performs some of the functions ascribed by Barnard to the propositional subsystem, which blends information derived from sound and visual structures, and builds higher-order semantic 'chunks'), and to Jones' O-OER model (1993), with its single, multi-modal storage space. He welcomes this change, because the models can now be compared on similar ground.

Like May, Towse and Houston-Price feel that the hypothesis of a system which inherently handles multiple types of representations is particularly interesting for interpreting data on memory for stimuli containing multiple codes. Adams and Willis view the episodic buffer as a potential device for explaining how previous encounters with language structures, including their social context and pragmatic function, are combined with memory for the required phonological form of the language. They suggest that the episodic buffer could help to solve the problem of how information in long-term memory is combined with working memory to reduce the processing capacity needed to comprehend or produce a sentence. They also suggest that such an account could offer a means of combining information-processing models with social interaction theories of language development. Perhaps the strongest endorsement of the episodic buffer hypothesis comes from Page, who considers the back-up store of Page and Norris's (1998) primacy model and the episodic-record in Henson's (1998) start–end model to be manifestations of the episodic buffer. Thus, at least as far as verbal short-term memory is concerned, the episodic buffer seems amenable to quantitative modelling.

Perhaps not surprisingly, several contributors feel that the proposed episodic buffer is insufficient to rectify the shortcomings of the WM model that they discussed in their chapters. Thus May claims that the problems of what exactly is being communicated between the different components, the conflation of processing and storage within the slave subsystems, and the relationship between working memory and long-term memory remain unsolved. Ward views the addition of the episodic buffer as a welcome acknowledgement of the difficulty of explaining general episodic memory phenomena in terms of an active phonological loop and a passive long-term store. However, he argues that the problems highlighted by Baddeley (2000) could be better overcome by viewing episodic memory as a continuum and concentrating on the contributions of different processing codes over different time periods. As argued in his chapter, he suggests that any given stimulus activates representations in many different modality-specific and modality-general codes. Interference effects may occur at different rates for different processing codes. Therefore, phenomena formerly considered to be 'capacity-limitations' may be reformulated as the difficulties in perfectly discriminating between representations from a continuum of episodic memory, due to (a) recency-based mechanisms for retrieving order information, and (b) interference between items or, more strictly, processing codes. Proposed phonological loop and visuo-spatial sketchpad deficits may be explicable as deficits of particular phonological and visuo-spatial processing codes operating across the whole continuum of episodic memory. Avons concurs that what is needed is not a separate short-term store for episodic information, but rather a closer look at the properties of a general episodic memory which functions over a continuous timescale and range of processing codes. He too suspects that modality-specific lesions could be explained as loss of particular coding systems or of their access to the general episodic memory system.

Specific criticisms of the episodic buffer hypothesis took up four themes: rehearsal, testability, re-interpretation of the existing data, and binding. Pearson takes issue with Baddeley's (2000) argument that, because visuo-spatial rehearsal seems unlike subvocal rehearsal, it might be better to postulate a general, attentional rehearsal mechanism for non-verbal material, presumably one that is shared by the sketchpad and the episodic buffer. Baddeley (2000) implies that current uncertainty about the nature of rehearsal in the episodic buffer is no worse than current uncertainty about visuo-spatial rehearsal, hence 'although additional assumptions will need to be made about the process of rehearsal operating within the proposed back-up store, similar assumptions are already necessitated by the question of rehearsal in the sketchpad' (p. 420). Pearson feels this is an unfair characterisation of current understanding of visuo-spatial working memory where, although there is not yet agreement on the nature of visuo-spatial rehearsal, there have at least been testable hypotheses about it. For example, Pearson (see chapter 2) proposes that visual and spatial representations may be rehearsed by separate processes which are different again from the attentional processes that maintain visuo-spatial representations in conscious awareness. Jarrold makes the more general point that it seems odd to ascribe rehearsal processes to a storage system. If the episodic buffer both stores and rehearses integrated representations, then the new version of the WM model seems to be overcoming the problem of a central executive which processes and stores information by adding another system which processes and stores information.

The episodic buffer hypothesis is still in an embryonic form so it would be inappropriate to criticise it for lack of specificity. Baddeley (2000) outlines several issues needing further conceptual and empirical work, namely the relationship between the episodic buffer and the modality-specific slave systems, the relationship between the episodic buffer and long-term episodic memory, and the role of executive processes in chunking and binding of information. He suggests that neuropsychological case studies and neuroimaging studies will help test future specifications of these relationships and processes. Nevertheless, several contributors doubt whether the episodic buffer could really be formulated in such a way that the WM model as a whole would remain testable. For example, Avons is concerned that, as the episodic buffer can store information in any modality, it can mimic the activity of the other slave systems. He is sceptical that neuropsychological data could help resolve this issue. If a patient with a deficient phonological loop and an intact episodic buffer should still perform reasonably well at any span task, then selective lesions of the phonological loop will be difficult to detect, and may go unreported. Towse and Houston-Price argue that it will be difficult to manipulate the component responsible for integrating information across modalities without also affecting the components which are modality-specific. Even if we can develop techniques for selectively loading the episodic buffer, May suggests that the complexities of experimental design using the four component model will reduce its intuitive appeal, removing what he sees as one of the WM model's strongest points.

In chapter 12, May writes 'Every addition to a model requires all previous research findings to be reassessed, to check that the addition does not contradict earlier conclusions.' (p. 275). With respect to the postulated episodic buffer, he asks whether sketchpad capacity measured by performance on

Corsi block tasks has been overestimated, because performance is boosted by the contribution of the episodic buffer. If performance on tasks such as non-word repetition is similarly supplemented by the new buffer, does this undermine the established link between the phonological loop and language learning? Ward likewise argues that reassessing existing data in the light of the new hypothesis reveals that the original storage systems are not really responsible for much storage at all. Baddeley (2000) suggests that the episodic buffer hypothesis may help explain why the effects of articulatory suppression on immediate serial recall of visually presented word lists are not catastrophic (reducing performance from around seven items to around five items) and why patients with apparent phonological loop deficits perform relatively well with visual presentation of verbal stimuli (recalling around four items rather than one item with auditory presentation). Ward infers that the episodic buffer must therefore store five of the seven words recalled by healthy participants in immediate serial recall tasks, and three of the four words recalled by short-term memory patients in memory span tasks with visual presentation. Thus the addition of the episodic buffer to the WM model considerably reduces the role of the original slave systems in explaining short-term memory phenomena. May suggests that this may lessen the appeal of the model for applied research, because detecting working memory involvement in complex cognition will no longer be a relatively simple matter of looking for modality-specific effects of concurrent tasks on the phenomenon of interest. Null results may reflect involvement of the episodic buffer, or the central executive, or no working memory involvement at all.

From my viewpoint, the most exciting aspect of the episodic buffer hypothesis is that it offers a new way of conceptualising problems of consciousness within the framework of working memory. Baddeley (2000) postulates the episodic buffer in part to explain our ability to maintain and manipulate multi-modal information. He cites data from some research we carried out into the role of working memory in vivid imagery (Baddeley & Andrade, 2000). Using dual task methods, we found modality-specific interference effects (concurrent verbal processing reducing the vividness of auditory imagery more than visual imagery, and vice versa), suggesting a role for the slave systems in vivid imagery. We also found general interference effects and influences of long-term memory, which Baddeley (2000) interprets as support for a system which can store integrated representations containing information from the slave systems and long-term memory. I am not convinced that the concept of a dedicated store for integrated representations is necessary to explain such data. An alternative explanation is that binding of auditory, visual, and long-term memory representations into unified multi-modal representations requires constant attentional (central executive) input, and that is why we observed general secondary task effects on image vividness, as well as the modality-specific effects. This is akin to Pearson's suggestion (chapter 2) that information stored in the slave systems is not conscious unless acted on by the central executive. A neurobiological solution to the binding problem is to suggest coherent, time-locked activation of the representations to be bound (e.g., Crick & Koch, 1990). In those terms, maybe one role of the central executive is to activate representations in the slave systems in synchrony. Thus a multi-modal representation is functionally available to other cognitive processes, and gives rise to the subjective experience of a unified mental object, for as long as its constituent parts continue to be activated simultaneously. Although the episodic buffer is one possible way of conceptualising binding, I am not sure it is the simplest explanation because it begs the question of whether representations are conscious by virtue of being stored in the buffer or whether they are conscious only when acted upon by the central executive.

To conclude, contributors offered a cautious welcome to the episodic buffer. Although they were not all convinced that empirical support could be gained for the revised WM model, they welcomed the attempt at better specifying the role of working memory in cognitive tasks requiring multi-modal processing. As the preceding discussion illustrates, the new hypothesis is already stimulating debate and will ensure that working memory research continues to generate new and exciting data.

FINALLY . . .

As the variety of chapters in this book illustrates, working memory research has moved in many different directions since the conception of the WM model. Despite this, contributors agreed in many ways in their assessment of the strengths and weaknesses of the WM model. There was consensus that the strengths of the model as a framework for guiding applied research were considerable and promised a bright future for the model, particularly for exploring cognition in situations where people tend to combine verbal and visual processes to boost their performance, and for comparing the development of different cognitive processes. There was also consensus that underspecification of the nature and interrelationships of the subcomponents of working memory made the model hard to use and hard to test. This weakness has not yet been satisfactorily addressed, perhaps in part because unsuitable, multi-componential tasks have been imported into the laboratory from applied research, meaning that much of the existing empirical data does not directly test the assumptions of the WM model. More precise experimental tools are needed for strengthening the WM model as a theory of short-term memory and its role in cognition. Progress has been made in this respect in verbal short-term memory research, where detailed error analyses have informed quantitative models of serial recall, and tasks have recently been developed to selectively tap other putatative components of working memory (e.g. Phillips & Hamilton, this volume).

The preceding discussion suggests a research programme by which such tasks could be used to investigate the central executive and its relationship with the slave systems. For the recommended programme to succeed, researchers need to keep abreast of developments in other areas to avoid everyone using the term 'working memory' to refer to different sets of functions and processes. We hope that this book helps to make the task a little easier for them.

ACKNOWLEDGEMENTS

I would like to thank the other book contributors, particularly Anne-Marie Adams, Steve Avons, Alan Baddeley, Rik Henson, Graham Hitch, Chris Jarrold, Jon May, Mike Page and John Towse, for their constructive suggestions for this chapter.

REFERENCES

Andrade, J., Kemps, E., Wernier, Y., May, J. & Szmalec, A. (in press) Insensitivity of visual short-term memory to irrelevant visual information. *Quarterly Journal of Experimental Psychology*.

Baddeley, A. D. (1986) *Working memory*. Oxford: Oxford University Press.

Baddeley, A. D. (1996) Exploring the central executive. *Quarterly Journal of Experimental Psychology, 49A*, 5–28.

Baddeley, A. (2000) The episodic buffer: a new component of working memory? *Trends in Cognitive Science, 4*(11), 417–423.

Baddeley, A. D. & Andrade, J. (2000) Working memory and the vividness of imagery. *Journal of Experimental Psychology: General, 129*(1), 126–145.

Baddeley A., Della Sala, S., Papagno, C. & Spinnler, H. (1997) Dual-task perform-ance in dysexecutive and nondysexecutive patients with a frontal lesion, *Neuropsychology, 11*(2), 187–194.

Baddeley, A. D. & Hitch, G. J. (1974) Working memory. In G. Bower (Ed.), *The psychology of learning and motivation* (pp. 47–89). New York: Academic Press.

Baddeley, A. D. & Logie, R. H. (1999) Working memory: The multiple-component model. In A. Miyake & P. Shah (Eds.) *Models of working memory: Mechanisms of active maintenance and executive control* (pp. 28–61). Cambridge, UK: Cambridge University Press.

Baddeley, A. D., Thomson, N. & Buchanan, M. (1975) Word length and the structure of short-term memory. *Journal of Verbal Learning and Verbal Behavior, 14*, 575–589.

Barnard, P. J. (1985) Interacting cognitive subsystems: A psycholinguistic approach to short-term memory. In A. Ellis (Ed.), *Progress in the Psychology of Language* (Vol. 2, pp. 197–258). London: Lawrence Erlbaum Associates Inc.

Barnard, P. (1999) Interacting cognitive subsystems: Modeling working memory phenomena within a multiprocessor architecture. In A. Miyake & P. Shah (Eds.), *Models of working memory: Mechanisms of active maintenance and executive control* (pp. 299–339). Cambridge, UK: Cambridge University Press.

Bishop, D. V. M., North, T. & Donlan, C. (1996) Nonword repetition as a behavioural marker for inherited language impairment: evidence from a twin study. *Journal of Child Psychology and Psychiatry, 37,* 391–403.

Brown, G. D. A. & Hulme, C. (1995) Modelling item length effects in memory span: no rehearsal needed? *Journal of Memory and Language, 34,* 594–621.

Burgess, N. & Hitch, G. J. (1999) Memory for serial order: a network model of the phonological loop and its timing. *Psychological Review, 106,* 551–581.

Cowan, N. (1999) An embedded-processes model of working memory. In A. Miyake & P. Shah (Eds.) *Models of working memory: Mechanisms of active maintenance and executive control* (pp. 62–101). Cambridge, UK: Cambridge University Press.

Crick, F. & Koch, C. (1990) Towards a neurological theory of consciousness. *Seminars in the Neurosciences, 2,* 263–275.

Dosher, B. A. & Ma, J.-J. (1998) Output loss or rehearsal loop? Output-time versus pronunciation-time limits in immediate recall for forgetting-matched materials. *Journal of Experimental Psychology: Learning, Memory and Cognition, 24,* 316–335.

Gathercole, S. E. & Baddeley, A. D. (1989) Evaluation of the role of phonological STM in the development of vocabulary in children: a longitudinal study. *Journal of Memory and Language, 28,* 200–215.

Henson, R. N. A. (1998) Short-term memory for serial order: the start–end model. *Cognitive Psychology, 36,* 73–137.

Jones, D. M. (1993) Objects, streams and threads of auditory attention. In A. D. Baddeley & L. Weiskrantz (Eds.) *Attention, selection, awareness and control* (pp. 87–104). Oxford: Oxford University Press.

Jones, D., Farrand, P., Stuart, G. & Morris, N. (1995) Functional equivalence of verbal and spatial information in serial short-term-memory. *Journal of Experimental Psychology: Learning, Memory and Cognition, 21,* 1008–1018.

Kosslyn, S. M. (1983) *Ghosts in the mind's machine.* New York: Norton.

Kosslyn, S. M. (1994) *Image and brain: The resolution of the imagery debate.* Cambridge, MA: MIT Press.

Kuhn, T. S. (1962) *The structure of scientific revolutions.* Chicago: University of Chicago Press.

Lehto, J. H. (1996) Are executive function tests dependent on working memory capacity? *Quarterly Journal of Experimental Psychology, 49A,* 29–50.

Levine, D. N., Warach, J. & Farah, M. J. (1985) Two visual systems in mental imagery: dissociation of 'what' and 'where' in imagery disorders due to bilateral posterior cerebral lesions. *Neurology, 35,* 1010–1018.

Logie, R. H. (1995) *Visuo-spatial working memory.* Hove, UK: Lawrence Erlbaum Associates Ltd.

Logie, R. H. (1996) The seven ages of working memory. In J. T. E. Richardson, R. W. Engle, L. Hasher, R. H. Logie, E. R. Stoltzfus & R. T. Zacks *Working memory and human cognition* (pp. 31–65). New York: Oxford University Press.

Logie, R. H. & Marchetti, C. (1991) Visuo-spatial working memory: Visual, spatial or central executive? In R. H. Logie & M. Denis (Eds.) *Mental images in human cognition* (pp. 105–115). Amsterdam: Elsevier.

Logie, R. H. & Pearson, D.G. (1997) The inner eye and the inner scribe of visuo-spatial working memory: evidence from developmental fractionation. *European Journal of Cognitive Psychology, 9*(3), 241–257.

Lovatt, P. J., Avons, S. E. & Masterson, J. (2000) The word-length effect and disyllabic words. *Quarterly Journal of Experimental Psychology, 53A*, 1–22.

Luck, S. J. & Vogl, E. K. (1997) The capacity of visual working memory for features and conjunctions. *Nature, 390*, 279–281.

Miyake, A., Friedman, N. P., Emerson, M. J., Witzki, A. H., Howerter, A. & Wager, T. D. (2000) The unity and diversity of executive functions and their contribution to complex 'frontal lobe' tasks: a latent variable analysis. *Cognitive Psychology, 41*, 49–100.

Miyake, A. & Shah, P. (1999) *Models of working memory: Mechanisms of active maintenance and executive control.* Cambridge, UK: Cambridge University Press.

Neath, I. & Nairne, J. S. (1995) Word-length effects in immediate memory: overwriting trace decay theory. *Psychonomic Bulletin and Review, 2*, 429–441.

Owen, A. M., Sahakian, B. J., Semple, J., Polkey, C. E. & Robbins, T. W. (1995) Visuo-spatial short-term recognition memory and learning after temporal lobe excisions, frontal lobe excisions or amygdalo-hippocampectomy in man. *Neuropsychologia, 33*(1), 1–24.

Page, M. P. A. & Norris, D. (1998) The primacy model: a new model of immediate serial recall. *Psychological Review, 105*, 761–781.

Phillips, W. A. (1983) Short-term visual memory. *Philosophical Transactions of the Royal Society of London, series B, 302*(1110), 295–309.

Rabbitt, P. M. A. (1997) *Methodology of frontal and executive function.* Hove, UK: Psychology Press.

Salway, A. F. S. & Logie, R. H. (1995) Visuo-spatial working memory, movement control and executive demands. *British Journal of Psychology, 86*, 253–269.

Scott, S., Barnard, P. J. & May, J. (in press) Specifying executive function in random generation tasks. *Quarterly Journal of Experimental Psychology.*

Tan, L. & Ward, G. (2000) A recency-based account of primacy in free recall. *Journal of Experimental Psychology: Learning, Memory, and Cognition, 26*, 1589–1625.

Tresch, M. C., Sinnamon, H. M. & Seamon, J. G. (1993) Double dissociation of spatial and object visual memory: evidence from selective interference in intact human subjects. *Neuropsychologia, 31*, 211–219.

Vuontela, V., Rama, P., Raninen, A., Aronen, H. J. & Carlson, S. (1999) Selective interference reveals dissociation between memory for location and colour. *Neuroreport, 10*(11), 2235–2240.

Wilken, P. & Mattingley, J. B. (2000) Capacity limitations in the detection and identification of change in visual arrays. *Consciousness and Cognition, 9*(2), S46.

Author index

Subject index